Discovering Music

A COURSE IN MUSIC APPRECIATION

HOWARD D. McKINNEY
Professor of Music, Rutgers University

and

W. R. ANDERSON
Lecturer, Morley College, London
Critic of *The Gramophone*

SECOND EDITION

New York   Cincinnati
AMERICAN BOOK COMPANY
Chicago · Boston · Atlanta · Dallas · San Francisco

E. P. 4
MANUFACTURED IN THE UNITED STATES OF AMERICA

Prelude

THIS book has been written with a double purpose: (1) to guide the uninitiated traveler who would embark upon a journey into the complex land of music; and (2) to be a Good Companion to those who, having already set sail, have made some discoveries for themselves and are eager to shape their course towards wider worlds.

The ability to " listen " to music rather than merely to " hear " it is not, as such, a natural capacity, but one that has to be acquired and developed by active, continual, and highly pleasurable observation. The power to cultivate this listening skill varies as does any other human accomplishment, but no cultivation is possible without guidance.

The principles used in the preparation of this guidebook have been shaped out of extended experience rather than fashioned out of theories. We believe that the greatest incentive for embarking upon voyages of artistic discovery should be the pleasure that one can derive from them. Housman has said that the nature of such arts as poetry and music is more physical than intellectual; it is the sense of delight that can be obtained from reading a poem, or looking at a picture, or listening to good music that attracts and holds us. It is this yielding of delight that will lead us on in a search for other wonders. Art educates in the proportion that it gives pleasure. We have shaped our treatment along sound pedagogical lines, and have proceeded from the known to the unknown; it will be found that we have placed the points of departure in familiar and interesting territory.

Some books of this nature are based upon the traditional educational process of starting at the earliest times and working up to the present. Others begin at the present and work as faithfully backwards. In the course of the treatment, they too often give historical and technical information as to how music has been put together and how it can best be listened to so as to recognize its formal structure, but pay insufficient attention to the actual cultivation of the reader's enjoyment and enthusiasm. Our method is to begin with the everyday musical experiences that are both real and satisfying, and use these as stimuli and points of departure for further artistic development. That is why we have not kept to strict chronological order. This arrangement of material has been found useful in giving students, in a year's work, a realization of their own capacity for participating in the world's heritage of musical experience. The authors believe it will prove equally useful in the hands of the general reader who has had no formal musical training.

We have felt that a book planned along these lines must be more than just a history of music or a dictionary, although it should contain much historical material and include a glossary of musical terms in common use. Impressed by the cultural value of music, still insufficiently recognized, we have constantly associated musical ideas with those of other arts. Though it is impossible, in a book of reasonable size, fully to develop these comprehensive ideas, enough has been given, it is hoped, to show how music can take its proper place in civilized life. As part of the life of its period, music, like everything that has contributed to growth, can be analyzed and reasoned about and its existence justified. Through such processes its nature and influence can be understood. To help in the realization of all this, we have prepared a time chart showing what was going on in music and the other arts through the ages.

We think that most books try to do too much, and especially to tell too much. Telling does not go far in music — doing and discovering are so much more important. Talking about music is of very little value unless one hears it, too, so we have discussed musical works that are constantly to be listened to, these progressing from the easily understood compositions to the more abstract — a logical outcome of the emphasis on enjoyment as the chief end of listening. We have taken most of the illustrations from the repertoire of phonographically recorded music. Thus laymen, teachers, and students will have in their hands lists of the finest material upon which to build a good library of records.

In our discussions, we have used ordinary technical terms, as far as they were necessary; surprisingly few of them are needed. When they are necessary, however, it seems foolish to go out of the way to avoid them. If anyone is interested enough in a subject to study a book of this sort, he will learn its vocabulary quickly enough, and be pleased to call a thing by its right name. We have not tried to make this a critical book, though we hope that its readers will get out of it a great deal that will broaden and strengthen their critical judgment. If all of the music mentioned herein is not immediately liked, the student will find out why this is so, and thus gain valuable knowledge.

The subject matter has been arranged in a manner suitable for presentation in class form, and appropriate topics for further discussion along similar lines have been furnished at the end of each chapter. Suggestions for further reading have likewise been made, and the reader who follows these will find himself possessed of a great fund of information which will be of inestimable value in the development of his listening powers.

Acknowledgment must be made of the help that has been received from various sources, especially the members of the " music-appreciation " courses who have proved the value of this material in actual use over a period of years. F. Austin Walter has helped in preparing and copying different sections; C. C. Stover has drawn the valuable chart to be found at the end of the work; Dr. Edwin J. Stringham of Teachers College, Columbia University, has given valued criticism and suggestions; Wilbert B. Hitchner and his staff of music teachers in the Wilmington, Delaware, schools have proved the effectiveness of this method of treatment for high-school pupils. A word of appreciation is also due those authors and publishers who have given permission to quote from their works.

Prelude to the Second Edition

The use of this book over a period of some years and in widely varying circumstances has suggested the changes and additions made in this new edition. A number of new chapters containing additional information and musical examples have been added; but the fundamental method of approach to the subject, a method that has proved itself time and time again in practice, has not been altered.

Owing to the exigencies of war, the cordial co-operation and constant consultation that made the first edition of *Discovering Music* so successful have not been possible in preparing this second edition. While I must be held responsible for most of the changes and additions that have been made, this new volume goes forth on its mission with the fond hopes of both authors for its continued usefulness in its important field.

HOWARD D. McKINNEY

Acknowledgments

The authors and publishers herewith offer thanks to the following, who have kindly given permission to reproduce copyrighted material:

The American Mercury for permission to quote from Winthrop Sargent's article of September, 1941.

D. Appleton-Century Co. for a passage from Sacheverell Sitwell's *Mozart*.

Percy Buck, author, and Ernest Benn, Ltd., for the passages from *History of Music*.

William Henry Chamberlin and the *New York Times* for permission to reprint the article on Russia from the *Times Magazine* of July 6, 1941.

The John Day Co. for quotations from *What Is American?* by Ernest Hill.

Alban Dobson and the Oxford University Press for the poem, " Love Comes Back to His Vacant Dwelling," by Austin Dobson.

J. Fischer & Bro. for the poem by George Ashdowne Audsley.

Glenn Frank for the extract from his address, " Liberal Education and the Liberalizing Arts."

Lawrence Gilman for several quotations.

Dr. Grace, editor of the London *Musical Times*, for the passage by him from the *Musical Times*.

W. J. Henderson for the passage from one of his articles in the *New York Sun*.

Hubbard Hutchinson for the passage from one of his articles in the *New York Times*.

John Lane The Bodley Head Ltd. for the quotation from Philip Heseltine's *Frederick Delius*.

John Lomax for permission to quote the passage from *Cowboy Songs*.

Longmans, Green & Co. for the quotation from Dean Inge's *Personal Idealism and Mysticism*.

Lincoln MacVeagh, The Dial Press, Inc., for the sentences from Olin Downes's *Symphonic Broadcasts*.

Edward B. Marks Music Co. for twelve measures from their score of *L'après-midi d'un faune* by Debussy.

A. Z. Mathot, Paris, for the two measures from Milhaud's *Sonata*.

Modern Music for permission to quote from Roger Sessions and Grigori Schneerson.

New York Times for permission to reprint an excerpt from " Reaching the Man in the Street," *New York Times*, July 27, 1941; and William Henry Chamberlin's article on Russia from the *Times Magazine* of July 6, 1941.

Ernest Newman and the London *Sunday Times* for permission to quote from Newman's critical articles.

Oxford University Press for the passage from Mowat's *History of Europe*, selections from Cobbett's *Cyclopedic Survey of Chamber Music* (articles by Cobbett and Hadow), selection from Hannam's *On Church Cantatas of J. S. Bach*, and the poem by Austin Dobson.

George Sampson for the quotation from his works.

The *Saturday Review* (London) for the poem by " F. E."

G. Schirmer, Inc., for the passages from Rimsky-Korsakoff's *Scheherazade* Suite, Dvořák's *New World Symphony*, and Tchaikovsky's *Andante cantabile*. These passages as used in this book were taken from the Schirmer editions. To G. Schirmer, Inc., also, for permission to quote from Stanford's article " Some Thoughts Concerning Folk Song and Nationality " in the *Musical Quarterly*, April, 1915.

Karl Schlageter for permission to reproduce his painting, *Crossing*.

Charles Scribner's Sons for the passages from Edward Dickinson's *Spirit of Music*, and from Augustine Birrell's *Collected Essays and Addresses;* for Gosse's paraphrase of Mallarmé's *Eclogue*, and the selection from the poem, *Arabian Nights Entertainments*, by William Ernest Henley.

Basil de Sélincourt for an extract from his notes written for concert programs.

George Bernard Shaw and Constable and Co. for the passage from Mr. Shaw's *Music in London, 1890–1894.*

Simon and Schuster for the quotations from Durant's *Story*

of Philosophy, Dimnet's *Art of Thinking,* and *The Victor Book of the Opera* by Charles O'Connell.

H. Royer Smith Co. for permission to quote parts of the article " Has the Organ a Place in Our Present-day Musical Sun? " from *Disques.*

The eight measures from Křenek's *Toccata und Chaconne* are used by permission of the Universal Edition of Vienna, Copyright, 1923.

Contents

Illustrations

Discovering Music

CHAPTER I

The Co-operating Beginner

BEAUTY IN THE LIFE OF TODAY

IN an article which appeared on the feature page of a pragmatic American newspaper, a thoughtful reporter who has spent considerable time wandering about the Old World, enjoying and admiring the beauty left behind by the genius of the past, asked the practical question: " Of what use is beauty in the world? " In a period which has been inclined to see beauty in the machinery that performs its daily work, in factories that provide its money, or in skyscrapers that house thousands of its workers, of what use is an understanding and appreciation of the beauty of paintings, statues, mosaics, churches, palaces, or of the literature and the music of the past? A number of years ago John Ruskin made the statement that the most beautiful things in the world are the most useless, a statement which stands the test of time better than do some of his other pronouncements. The modern reaction to this would probably be the ingenuous question asked by the modern factory manager: " Well, if beautiful things haven't any use, what good are they? "

Our newspaper writer answers this question by saying that the only use that he can see for beauty in this world is for developing taste. The more one learns to appreciate the beautiful, the more he will avoid and despise the ugly. A man cannot learn really to like Shelley and Keats, Goethe and Shakespeare, and at the same time continue to enjoy reading pulp-paper confession magazines. If a man becomes enthusiastic about the music of Beethoven or Brahms, he loses his taste for the products of the Tin Pan Alley fabricators. An understanding of and liking for the works of Michelangelo and Rembrandt, Da Vinci, or El Greco is the best possible antidote for the cheapness and vulgarity of so many of the present-day movies and modern paintings.

All right, you may say. Granted all this, what then? Is the

I

person who spends his time cultivating his taste any better off than the one who is concerned only with the useful things in life? Does the man who can see the beauty in a field of daffodils or in an Alpine sunrise or in that " loveliest of trees, the cherry hung with bloom along the bough," get more out of life than he who derives his pleasures from reading the favorable reports received from the management of the company in which he has been shrewd enough to invest his money, or from scanning the financial pages of his newspaper during a rising market? The hard-headed newspaper writer says that he does, for the observing reporter has noticed that the people who have taken the trouble to develop their taste derive more happiness from life than those who have not. He wonders whether the modern concern with usefulness is not thoroughly idiotic and suicidal, and if the world would not be much better off by cultivating a sense of abstract beauty and giving *usefulness* a good rest. If the admiration — he goes so far as to say the adoration — of beauty can develop our taste to the point where we can learn to appreciate it to the full, he is sure that the avenues of life's enjoyment will become wider and more spacious; that we will find more joy in life, and with no additional expense.

The vivid and forceful appraisal of the place which beauty should occupy in our present-day life, made by the late Glenn Frank of the University of Wisconsin, shows the drift of contemporary educational thought. He said that an understanding of the beautiful is one of the most vital needs in the sort of education we must have if in the years ahead we are to master, instead of being mastered by, the vast, complex, and swiftly moving technical civilization that has been born of science and the machine. " The education of the future must educate the whole man, not just his reasoning powers; it must educate his physical, emotional, and social reactions as well as his reasoning powers. . . . We once thought our job done when we had trained a man to think straight. This belief rested on assumption that men thought their way into their living. We now know that men live their way into their thinking. . . . Because this is true, education for the future must, in addition to the more obvious diets for the mind, include those stimulations and disciplines that sensitize and enrich men's capacity for worthy emotional and aesthetic response to the . . . needs of modern life. . . .

" A nation that forgets beauty will in time find even the foundations of its technical and economic achievements crumbling. A people dares not allow beauty to become the exclusive possession of antique dealers and millionaire collectors unless it wants to face a social reckoning sooner or later. . . .

" Social unrest finds its readiest recruits among men who have never been able to find beauty and joy in their jobs and in their environments. It is an old observation that hungry men turn radical, but what we are likely to forget is that men with full stomachs may still be hungry with a gnawing hunger for the things that make life free and adventurous and abundant. . . . A community, state, and national life that stimulate and satisfy men's hunger for beauty — these are the things that turn the ruin of revolt into the radiance of creative living. . . ."

The cultivation of beauty not only gives the individual a more enjoyable life but is absolutely necessary for his protection against the ravages and depredations of the machine. Men who are as widely divergent in their ideals as newspaper writers and university presidents have felt this keenly, and their advice in this respect is worth our most serious consideration. There are, of course, many other things which might be said as to why our taste for the beautiful should be cultivated — as, for instance, the usefulness of beauty in giving gracefulness and a marvelous sense of proportion to life. In the light of our present-day conditions it would hardly be too presumptuous to change Ruskin's dictum to read, " The most beautiful things in the world, although they may seem its most useless, in reality may be the most essential."

BEAUTY IN MUSIC

When the creative artist produces beauty for us he undergoes an exceptionally intense experience which he realizes is of universal concern, or he apprehends the truth of some ideal which he feels to be of general interest to mankind. With his heaven-sent powers he is able to report these experiences and to express these ideals so as to make them readily comprehensible to the average man. By means of brush and pen, sculptor's tool or architect's square, the transcendent truths and emotional strength of the creators are communicated to us. There are many forms which this created beauty may take — forms which we rather snobbishly call the " fine arts "; of these the one that is most universally appealing and most readily apprehended is music. For it speaks to us in a language that is entirely its own — a universal language that does not need to be translated into the medium of any of the other arts and which can hint to us of concepts that are quite beyond the range of painting, literature, sculpture, and architecture. Not needing to deal exactly with thoughts and ideas, music can speak to us with a force and a power that are readily felt by all who have learned to listen. Concerning itself so very largely with emotion, it is the ideal means for transmitting the experiences of a sensitive artist directly to a responsive listener.

MUSIC FOR ITS OWN SAKE

These resources for communicating beauty we are too apt to take for granted. We have become so accustomed to presuming that music is an essential part of our everyday lives that only in moments of reflection and introspection do we become fully conscious of its tremendous power. The average person seems to think of music always as a means to something else — to reading, to relaxation, perhaps to nothing more important than passing away the time. Music is generally considered as an amenity rather than as something that is satisfying in its own right, something that can dominate our whole lives, possess our whole beings. There is nothing in listening to music, according to popular conception, other than placing ourselves under its sway — sitting quietly and letting it flow through our consciousness. We may receive some vague sort of emotional thrill from it, or we may be interested in the mannerisms of the orchestral conductor as he interprets the music for us or of the pianist as he forges his way through some intricately difficult passage. We may be entertained by this bit of music because it reminds us of an army on the march, or that because it suggests a May morning in the country, a rippling brook, a crowded square in an Oriental city, or whatever our imagination may be able to suggest. But we are not greatly concerned if we do not like what we have heard, for there is plenty of music with pleasing tunes and vigorous rhythms, without bothering about this difficult music of the classics.

There seems to be little need for considering music otherwise than as something to be enjoyed — and by "enjoyed" the average person means something to be whistled, hummed, or danced to. It may be used as a means for putting in the time when there is nothing better to do, or as a background for some other activity. What could be better than some music on the radio as an accompaniment for luncheon, a bridge game, or for the few quiet moments available to the businessman as he peruses his evening paper? Perhaps our average hearer may be inveigled into going to a concert because some internationally known star is to sing or play, or (if he is honest enough to admit it) for no more serious reason than that it has become the fashionable thing to do. But he rarely thinks of music as a thing to be listened to seriously and enjoyed for its own sake.

Granted that there is a type of music so light and "recreational" that we need have no compunction in talking or playing bridge through it, and that concert-going may have certain pleasures other than purely musical ones; nevertheless, it hardly seems possible to some people that there are others to whom music is life's chief interest and joy, people to whom the hearing of a great piece of music means as much as does the reading of Shakespeare, Goethe, or Dante to a lover of literature. Lawrence Gilman tells of a philosopher who, during the time he was occupied in reading his favorite subject, became white as a sheet. Are there listeners who feel as intensely about music? We often make the statement that a person is "passionately fond of music." Is he really? As Gilman pointedly asks, what does such an individual do with his music, or for it? "Will he forgo leisure, forget his meals, face poverty? Will the blood leave his face after he has spent an hour with Beethoven's *Appassionata*?"

How Listeners Develop

The reader of this book, because of the very fact that he has enough interest in music to want to know how to get more out of it than he does at present, knows that there are people, plenty of them, who realize the tremendous potential powers of music. In the lives of these people music is an important factor far above that of mere social amenity, even though perhaps an hour with

Beethoven does not make any great disturbance in their vaso-
motor system. These fortunate ones seem to have acquired a technic by means of which they are able to get something from music
that is not perceptible to the average person. They seem to have
found some sort of touchstone that brings them closer to the
infinite. What is this technic that enables the individual to train
himself so that he can hear things which otherwise would be
missed entirely? Is there really a means by which the initiate into
the mysterious art of listening gets more out of music than does
the man in the street, who knows nothing about it except " what
he likes "?

   If there is any doubt in the reader's mind as to the answers to
such questions, let him talk to someone to whom the art of music
has become indispensable, overpowering, imperative — some person who has learned to enjoy intelligently such music as the Bach
Passacaglia, or the *First Symphony* of Brahms, or Debussy's *Pelléas et Mélisande.* Such a music lover will tell the inquiring listener
that his appreciation of such music is a treasure which he values
the more because he has not always possessed it; that he has come
through the gradual, cumulative process of learning to understand what the composer has put into such music, a process of
acquiring ears to hear. In cases where the man who possesses these
great treasures of music is honest, he will admit that the music of
Bach and Brahms and Debussy has not always meant to him what
it means to him now; that at one time in his listening career he
preferred the romantic harmonies and colorful suggestiveness of
Tchaikovsky's *1812 Overture* or Grieg's *Peer Gynt Suite.*

THE ADVENTURER'S CONQUESTS

   Then he will go on to tell how, when this more obvious kind
of music had yielded him everything it possessed, when he had
learned to recognize the reasons for its popular appeal and to
realize its special weaknesses, he of necessity passed on to works
of greater scope and more general significance. New composers
were taken up, men whose music was somewhat more reticent in
revealing the secrets of its beauty but which possessed greater
universality of content and emotion and was more skillfully constructed. This music was in turn enjoyed, its particular excel-

lencies recognized, its unique shortcomings noted. The process was again repeated and the conquest extended to type after type of music until the music lover came into the realm of the immortal composers. Here, no matter how much he may hear of their music or how eagerly he may try to solve the riddle of their beauty of utterance, no matter how often he reacts to the intellectual and emotional stimuli of their music or how great is the satisfaction he obtains from it, there is always something in reserve. There is something beyond the reaches of his searching, an inexhaustible supply of beauty ready to satisfy any demands which may be made upon it. He has at last arrived and is ready to understand and love the finest things in the art of music, fully equipped to share the spiritual contributions of its greatest composers.

All this is not to say that a process such as this has necessarily been consciously directed. Hearing a great deal of music, the student has subconsciously chosen what happened to be best suited to his particular stage of development at the time, letting the rest go by. The process has of necessity been a slow one, and there have been many " blind spots " — things which have not been clear to him as he progressed. Some of these may always remain, for nobody can appreciate everything; it is not often worth while to try, though we can always enlarge our range of sympathy and understanding if we want to. Any man can improve his taste; and that, as we have said, is the important thing — the thing that will bring joy into our lives. We should lay ourselves open to *quality* in general and give all reputable composers a good trial. Frank Roscoe has a good saying: " Education is more a matter of infection than injection "; and if we expose ourselves to the infection of great music, we are bound to catch it. Some may start with an enthusiasm for music of the jazz type, but they cannot go far there, for jazz is peculiarly of an inbred, feeble-stock race, incapable of development. In any case, the people for whom it is meant could not understand it if it did develop. Jazz is sterile. It is all right for fun, or as a mild anodyne, like tobacco. But its lack of rhythmical variety (necessitated by its special purpose), its brevity, its repetitiveness and lack of sustained development, together with the fact that commercial reasons prevent its being, as a rule, very well written, all mark it as a side issue, having next to nothing to do with serious music; and consequently it has proved itself entirely useless as a basis for developing the taste of the amateur.

The ambitious listener might better start from the level of Chopin's melodious piano music, or Grieg's northern elegiacs, or Tchaikovsky's gorgeous colorfulness. Given certain native ability and a willingness to keep his ears open and his mind free, the problems of his musical evolution will quickly solve themselves. All that is necessary is the opportunity of hearing a great many good performances of fine music, together with some hints as to how he can co-operate in the process of listening to them.

LIST OF SUGGESTED MUSIC

If you would see how easy it is to begin the adventure, listen to the following works:

Fantasie impromptu, Op. 66   Frederic Chopin
Berceuse in D flat major, Op. 57

Peer Gynt Suite No. 1   Edvard Grieg
                    Morning   Anitra's Dance
                    Death of Ase   In the Hall of the Mountain King

Elegiac Melodies (String Orchestra)   Edvard Grieg

These different selections show the great Norwegian composer in various moods: the *Peer Gynt* music (written for Ibsen's play of the same name) is full of the spirit of the north; the lovely lyrics for strings contain some of his most concentrated sentiment.

The Nutcracker Suite   Peter I. Tchaikovsky

The last number of this popular and delightful ballet suite gives the enterprising listener an excellent chance of realizing how a simple piece of music is put together.

Symphony in B Minor (Unfinished)   Franz Schubert
                    First Movement

Waltz — *Tales from the Vienna Woods*   Johann Strauss

To obtain the full flavor of this, one of the most colorful and melodious pieces of popular music ever written, it should be heard as played by those thoroughly familiar with the Viennese waltz style, not in one of the streamlined versions which are current today.

Overture to *The Magic Flute*   Wolfgang Mozart

This is deservedly one of the most popular short pieces of great music available for the listener.

First Symphony   Johannes Brahms

Last Movement

Listen to this, just to hear what the biggest music sounds like. An ardent admirer of this composer characterizes him as follows: " Brahms does not dazzle, but is true and lasting; he stands like a rock in the welter of strife, of problems and experiments, and holds out his hands to all those who strive towards what is great and noble, regardless of sensation."

TOPICS FOR FURTHER DISCUSSION

What place should music hold in a scheme for a liberal education?

Is it your experience that familiarity breeds contempt in the case of music? of any grade of music — *classical* as well as *jazz*?

Is there any circumstance in which it may be legitimate to have music going on without attending to it?

Discuss the dictum of Arnot Robertson, the novelist, who speaks of " Thinbrows " as " the pests of the literary world, who have not the courage to be either highbrows or lowbrows, according to their own tastes, but who keep always on the safe side by admiring only what it is fashionable to admire." Do these exist in music?

Comment on the statement made by a music critic to the effect that " consistently with all the inescapable tasks and sacrifices, there will be no truer deed than that which propagates the art of music, that we may not forget, in the midst of evil, the truth for which men die."

SUGGESTIONS FOR READING

The Spirit of Music, Dickinson. (New York: Scribner)
    Introduction
The Scope of Music, Buck. (New York and London: Oxford)
    Chapter III: The Nature of Beauty

Music, Health, and Character, Savill. (New York: Stokes; London:
    John Lane)
    Part I: The Autobiography of a Musical Conversion
The Principles of Aesthetics, Parker. (New York: Silver Burdett)
    Chapter II: Definition of Art
    Chapter III: The Intrinsic Value of Art
A Musical Pilgrim's Progress, Rorke. (New York and London: Oxford)
Art as Experience, Dewey. (New York: Minton, Balch; London: Allen)

Why We Like Music

THE best reason in the world for undertaking the study of a subject is the natural liking and aptitude that we may have for it. And, although we may not be able to explain why, most of us are conscious of the fact that we do have a liking and a certain amount of aptitude for music. Someone has well called it the most universal avocation, meaning that it is the thing we most naturally turn to for a hobby, when we would have our attention diverted from our usual pursuits. Most people think of music in this way and are quite indifferent to the great role which it might play in their lives; even so, they react instinctively and naturally to this art in ways that are different from their ordinary experiences. Why?

In an attempt to account for this affection, a well-known psychologist [1] who has spent the most fruitful years of his long professional career in the study of music and its action upon the human consciousness has recently written a little book which he calls *Why We Love Music*. In it he gives a sort of natural history of the psychological origin and development of our love of music in terms of its objects and motives. We can profitably study what Seashore says in this respect, for he probably knows as much about the subject as anyone today. Put into simple terms, the reasons for our liking music are these:

MORALE: PHYSICAL AND SPIRITUAL

1. We like music because it instills in us a sense of well-being; it sets us up, so to speak, both physically and emotionally. We seem to be endowed with some sort of mechanism that reacts and responds to *sounds* without any conscious effort on our part. This mechanism involves not only the central nervous system

[1] Carl E. Seashore, Professor of Psychology at the University of Iowa.

which controls the actions of our muscles and the functions of our internal organs, but also the so-called autonomic nervous system, with its regulation of the internal secretions which are thought to be the physical bases of all our emotional reactions. Experiments have shown that sound can directly affect such physical functions as the circulation of the blood, digestion, hunger, and thirst, as well as the psychological backgrounds of pleasure and pain.

Thus do the scientists explain our instinctive physical and emotional response to such sounds as the blare of trumpets or the sweetness of violins. Other considerations quite aside, the purely physical effect of the hundred members of an orchestra playing in full accord and the stirring strains of a good military band as it leads a regiment in parade are important factors in our lives. We may be aroused and enlivened by some sound combinations, quieted and dispirited by others. This natural reaction of our organism to sound underlies all our musical experience; we are not capable of controlling these responses, but without them music would lose a great deal of its natural appeal.

FROM ANOTHER WORLD

2. Another, and a very important, reason for our liking music is the fact that its domain is so largely outside our ordinary world, its field of operation so entirely beyond these sensory impressions and physical reactions. We may not be able to help reacting to music physically, but our greatest enjoyment of it comes from the fact that its world is so largely one of memory, imagination, and feeling. In the midst of a humdrum, practical, pressing world, one which badgers and confuses, music takes us outside ourselves, transports us, as nothing else can, into another existence. In listening to such intricate and refined manipulation of tonal resources as we find in Delius's *Over the Hills and Far Away,* we do respond, certainly, to physical sensuousness and tonal allure; but what haunts our minds and captures our spirits is this music's imaginative, other-worldly atmosphere, its peculiar blend of a reminder of things that exist best in the memory, and its suggestion of things that have never really existed at all.

In this way, music possesses us as does a dream; it lives within us, something entirely apart from our material and tangible experiences, its appeal heightened by the fortunate necessity of this art's indefiniteness. All the arts are conditioned by the physical means they employ: the writer is naturally limited by the meaning of the words he must use, the painter by certain exterior associations connected with the objects he represents on his canvas; music, based as it is on sound, has no need for any exact connotation or literal significance outside itself. And so it exists as the ideal means for communicating inward and subjective concepts.

Music as Play

3. We like music also because it is an ideal form of play. Seashore reminds us that we are all really of the same age — born millions of years ago, and that, in spite of inhibitions and restraints developed through the centuries, we delight in play. For it is in play that we get a definite and liberating sense of freedom, a feeling of creative power, of doing things purely for the joy of achievement, without ulterior motive or designed effect. Moreover, play is a positive force, and one whose success, in strong contradistinction to the world about us, depends upon our accepting its fictitious nature: " It rests upon make-believe; liberated from realities, it accepts the ideal and lives it as real."

All art is play, of course; but none of the other arts lend themselves so ideally to fulfilling these psychological needs as does music. The man singing lustily in his bath, somehow stimulated by the sound of running water to do his noisy best; a group of listeners under the sway of a great interpretation of a forceful piece of music; the dancer, stirred by the rhythmical excitement of the music, or perhaps lulled by its dreamy flow into an ecstasy of pleasure — all these are playing in the ideal sense. Music furnishes them with a medium for expressing themselves, for exhibiting their joy in living, their aspirations for the future, their nostalgia for the past, their desire for freedom, their love of action. This is one of the simplest and most direct of the charms which music possesses, and one of the reasons people turn instinctively to it for recreation.

THE ATTRACTION OF RHYTHM

4. We are also strongly attracted to music because of its rhythm. By " rhythm " in music most of us mean but one thing — that regular pulse which we all feel in the flow of the music, the pulse that is marked by a regular recurrence of what we call a " beat." Unless this is present we cannot sense music at all. All of us, even though we are hardly able to distinguish one tune from another, seem to be able to learn to " hear with our feet " — to beat out the underlying rhythmic impulses inherent in music.

Using the term in its wider sense, however, as meaning movement marked by a regular recurrence of certain features or elements, we find that there are plenty of other rhythmic attributes of music to which we react. The human ear seems to demand some sense of " grouping " in what it hears. So we find the composer grouping the musical ideas he uses — measures into phrases, phrases into sentences, sentences into still larger units, all being gathered together to make a unified yet varied rhythmic whole. We likewise demand certain dynamic rhythms (alternations of loud and soft) and timbre rhythms (alternations in the various tonal qualities) in the music we enjoy. All this gives us, without our being aware of it perhaps, great listening pleasure, and increases the satisfaction we derive from music.

The psychologist explains this by showing us what this rhythmic grouping does: it enables us to perceive more easily what we hear; it brings into relationship certain features that give a sense of balance and expanse to what we hear; there is an alternation of stimulating and soothing influences which enriches and objectifies our associations and tones up our whole organism. Seashore expresses it well when he says that rhythm in music is a play within a play: the composer realizes the need for it, the performer makes us aware of it; and we, the listeners, react to it.

AN EXPRESSION OF EMOTION

5. Music has often been called the language of the emotions; and certainly, while aestheticians may question the complete validity of such a statement, a great deal of our pleasure and en-

joyment in music comes from the fact that in its essence it expresses and embodies emotion.[2] In its truest sense, art is an " objectification or expression in a communicable form, of an artist's actual reaction to some stimulation or of his ' experience.' " [3] In the case of music, this stimulation or experience is likely to have been an emotional one, and thus one readily understood by us all. A great artist — Beethoven, for example — is moved by some profound personal experience; he reacts keenly to the sorrows and sufferings of humanity or to the personal awareness of a limitation of his physical powers. Through his ability, first as a sensitive human individual to feel these emotions, and then as an artist to grasp their essence and objectify it in a medium by which it can be communicated to others, he produces great works of art — the *Eroica Symphony* and the *Symphony in C Minor*.

It is a demonstrable fact that of all the sensory mediums, tone is most closely associated with the emotions: thus music becomes the ideal communicative medium for artists, and the most purely emotional of all the arts. When we add to this the fact that music, in order to be intelligible to us, must be re-created for us by an interpreter — a third person who comes between us and the composer, and this interpreter must of necessity add his own emotional significance to what he plays — we realize the secret of music's great human appeal and its power in the lives of men.

In this sense we can say that music is a language of the emotions, for it is at once both a message and a means of communication which, for the moment at least, puts creator, interpreter, and listener in the same world of experience.

MUSIC AND INTELLIGENCE

6. Intelligence also plays a strong role in music. We like music because we can learn to understand it as a thing in itself, can recognize how it is put together, how it proceeds from point to point and reaches a climactic finish. Such pride in intellectual achievement is very human and lies directly at the base of all artistic interest. The ability to understand different art forms,

---

[2] The psychologist defines an emotion as " any one of the states designated as fear, anger, disgust, joy, grief, surprise, yearning, etc."

[3] From F. R. O'Neill's definition of art in *The Relation of Art to Life*. London: Routledge.

to analyze the ways by which the artist achieves his effects, to
see the relationships between the different elements that go to
make up the whole, to sense the affinity between the different arts
— all these deepen our insight and increase our understanding of
music, or painting, or architecture. Then, too, there is the joy
of acquiring interpretative skill in music, of learning to read
those symbols left behind by the composers (the notes), of securing sufficient physical and mental agility to be able to play an
instrument or to sing. These " glimpses into the vistas of unex-
plored resources " cannot but intensify our love of music, our
awe and admiration for it as an art that, no matter how ardently
we may try, can never be fully mastered.

THE POWERS OF SUGGESTION

7. A final reason, and one of the most potent of all reasons
why we love music, is that it tends to give some form of realization to our inmost dreams and longings, because it stands as a sort
of symbolic suggestion of everything we desire, or believe in, or
hope for. The listener tends, as Seashore says, " to live himself
concretely into the feeling " suggested by the music. Most of us,
as we listen, live realistically within the music, in so far as the
realm of our interests allows us. Such associations and suggestions
may be enjoyed for their own sake; the listener often tends to
forget the music entirely in the imaginative associations it stirs
in his mind. But the truest enjoyment comes when these symbolic suggestions are somehow fused in their general meaning with
the music which calls them to mind.

To make this clear, let us take a concrete example, one of
the most significant pieces of music ever written, a work that
stands up magnificently through the years because of its quality
as *music*, and yet which probably has as powerful, direct, and
human an appeal as any other music in existence: Beethoven's
Fifth Symphony. Anyone who is at all sensitive to music will
come under the spell of this work; for there is evident in it a
titanic struggle, a wrestling with some of life's greatest problems,
together with a decision as to some of its deepest meanings. At
once, without being aware of the mechanics of the process, we are
apt to be diverted, when listening to this music, by all sorts of

symbolic suggestions — the harshness and ruthlessness of life, the necessity for human struggle, the consolation that beauty brings, the ominous precariousness of our existence, the exalted happiness that comes from surmounting difficulties. All these, and many more like suggestions, may come to our minds as the music progresses. We realize that all the diverse forces of our lives are present in this music, for it shows us as well as anything ever created by the mind of man that " we ourselves are our own Heaven and Hell." We can, and probably do, enjoy these associations for what they are themselves, as a sort of work of art deserving of separate consideration. But not until they have become blended and fused in their general meaning with Beethoven's music do we realize their full impact. Not until we are conscious of how inextricably they are woven into the warp and woof of Beethoven's glowing fabric (a realization which comes only after study: see Chapter XXIX) do we really " enjoy " this symphony.

So it is with all other types of music, whether they sound the note of joyous exaltation, religious fervor, or consuming passion. Sacred oratorios, dramatic operas, moving symphonies, even the small piano pieces, all make use of this fundamental power of music to " seize the individual for some form of dreamlike realization of the subjects of his longing." The professional musician tends to frown upon this enjoyment of associations and images; to him music exists for its own meaning and beauty, and he hears it as a combination of note patterns, colors, rhythms, and so on. He consciously tends to suppress any of his own feelings, associations, and characterizations that the music might evoke, and assumes a critical, analytical viewpoint, from which he surveys the materials of which it is composed and the way it is put together. In so doing he may easily miss the real significance of the music, just as does the untrained listener, for whom music's only appeal is through the associations it arouses.

The wise music lover avoids both extremes. But he must never forget, as Henri Bergson puts it, that " beneath the thousand rudimentary actions which are the outward and visible signs of an emotion, behind the commonplace conventional expression that both reveals and conceals our individual mental state," it is the emotion, the original mood, that composers attain and wish to communicate to us. " Beneath their joys and sorrows . . . they grasp something that has nothing in common with language, certain rhythms of life and breath that are closer to man than his inmost feelings, being the living law — varying with each individual — of his enthusiasm and despair, his hopes and regrets." To miss these aspects of the reality of human experience as revealed to us by a composer is to miss the greatest significance of his music.

We will soon show that the fullest understanding of music depends on something more than natural tastes and aptitudes. One must always remember that there are many degrees and levels of musical understanding, and that we are not all capable of liking music to the same extent and in the same way. The individual's attainments in music depend not only upon his natural, innate capacity (which, of course, differs greatly with different people) but also upon his musical experience and training. This accounts for the wide divergences of opinion that we hear expressed on every hand. Not many people are so honest as Mark Twain about this:

Huge crowd out tonight to hear the band play the *Fremersberg!* I suppose it is very low-grade music — I know it must be low-grade — because it so delighted me, moved me, stirred me, uplifted me, enraptured me, that at times I could have cried, and at others split my throat with shouting. The great crowd was another evidence that it was low-grade music, for only the few are educated up to a point where high-class music gives pleasure. I have never heard enough classic music to be able to enjoy it, and the simple truth is I detest it. Not mildly, but with all my heart.

What a poor lot we human beings are anyway! If base music gives me wings, why should I want any other? But I do. I want to like the higher music because the higher and better like it. But you see I want to like it without taking the necessary trouble, and giving the thing the necessary amount of time and attention. The natural suggestion is to get into that upper tier, that dress circle, by a lie — we will *pretend* we like it.

LIST OF SUGGESTED MUSIC

Here is a short list of recordings of well-known musical compositions. Listen to each one carefully, and then, referring to the reasons given in this chapter for our liking music, try to decide why *you* like the music.

Gaité Parisienne	Offenbach
España Rapsodie	Chabrier
Sixth Symphony, Last Movement	Tchaikovsky
The Water Music	Handel
The Washington Post	Sousa
Fugue in G Minor ("Little")	Bach
Concerto in E Flat for piano and orchestra K482 First Movement	Mozart
Valse triste	Sibelius

TOPICS FOR FURTHER DISCUSSION

Imagine yourself at a gala concert of a world-famous orchestra. In looking over the festive and well-dressed audience, try to determine the percentage of those present who came (*a*) because it was the thing to do; (*b*) so as to be included in the social and intellectual elite; (*c*) to satisfy their curiosity; (*d*) so as to be able to say they had heard the orchestra under its famous conductor; (*e*) to learn something about music; (*f*) really to enjoy the music.

Which inherited traits do you consider most helpful in the development of a love of good music? Which would make such development difficult?

SUGGESTIONS FOR READING

Why We Love Music, Seashore. (Philadelphia: Ditson)
    Chapter I especially
The Psychology of Music, Schoen. (New York: Ronald)
The Psychology of Beauty, Puffer. (Boston: Houghton Mifflin)

CHAPTER III

How We Like Music

IT has been shown that it is natural enough for us to like music; practical experience has proved, on the other hand, that there are plenty of people who do not like it. In general we may say that this is due to some deficiency in training. We have just made the statement that a full response to music is the result of native capacity plus experience and training; it is this experience and training that are so often wanting, and any device (such, for example, as this book) that will increase our musical experience and train our musical reactions cannot but add to our enjoyment.

There are some individuals, of course, who are completely incapable of ever liking music: evidently Charles Lamb was one. You may remember his experiences as related in his *Essays of Elia:*

It is hard to stand alone in an age like this (constituted to the quick and critical perception of all harmonious combinations, I verily believe, beyond all preceding ages, since Jubal stumbled upon the gamut), to remain, as it were, singly unimpressible to the magic influences of an art which is said to have such an especial stroke at soothing, elevating, and refining the passions. Yet, rather than break the candid current of my confessions, I must avow to you that I have received a great deal more pain than pleasure from this so cried-up faculty.

I am constitutionally susceptible to noises. A carpenter's hammer, in a warm summer noon, will fret me into more than midsummer madness. But those unconnected, unset sounds are nothing to the measured malice of music. The ear is passive to those single strokes; willingly enduring stripes while it hath no task to con. To music it cannot be passive. It will strive — mine at least will — 'spite of its inaptitude, to thread the maze; like an unskilled eye painfully poring upon hieroglyphics. I have sat through an Italian opera, till, for sheer pain, and inexplicable anguish, I have rushed into the noisiest places of the crowded streets, to solace myself with sounds which I was not obliged to follow, and get rid of the distracting torment of endless, fruitless, barren attention! I take refuge in the unpretending assemblance of honest common-life sounds; and the purgatory of the Enraged Musician becomes my paradise.

I have sat at an oratorio (that profanation of the purposes of the cheerful playhouse) watching the faces of the auditory in the pit (what a contrast to Hogarth's Laughing Audience!) immovable, or affecting some faint emotion, until (as some have said, that our occupations in the next world will be but a shadow of what delighted us in this) I have imagined myself in some cold Theatre in Hades where some of the *forms* of the earthly one should be kept up, with none of the *enjoyment;* or like that

> — Party in a parlor
> All silent, and all DAMNED.

Above all, those insufferable concertos, and pieces of music, as they are called, do plague and embitter my apprehension. Words are something; but to be exposed to an endless battery of mere sounds; to be long a-dying; to lie stretched upon a rack of roses; to keep up languor by unintermitted effort; to pile honey upon sugar, and sugar upon honey, to an interminable tedious sweetness; to fill up sound with feeling, and strain ideas to keep pace with it; to gaze on empty frames, and to be forced to make the pictures for yourself; to read a book, *all stops*, and be obliged to supply the verbal matter; to invent extempore tragedies to answer to the vague gestures of an inexplicable rambling mime — these are faint shadows of what I have undergone from a series of the ablest-executed pieces of this empty *instrumental music*."

Fortunately, there are comparatively few of these people. Most of those who do not like music simply beg the entire question and protest: " It is all away beyond me: music is too full of technicalities that I cannot understand. I know what I like, so why should I bother with trying to learn any more about it? "

To which the reasonable answer is, as Edwin Alden Jewell has said in an article on " Reaching the Man in the Street " [1]:

Art is beyond nobody who cares. Technicalities are but means employed by the artist in expressing what he has to say, and it is the expression that counts. Besides, once you have really *heard* what the artist has expressed, it is simple — and fascinating — to work back, step by step, through the technique. Thus may one share in the task of creation. And no one who has learned really to share in that can be thenceforth indifferent. Learning to share and learning critically to discriminate may well end in learning to love.

[1] In *The New York Times*, Sunday, July 27, 1941.

Here is the crux of the whole matter. This is what we mean by learning to appreciate music. This expression has been criticized for its ambiguity, for the fact that it can mean so many different things to so many different people. But until a better one is invented, we must continue to use it; *appreciate* means, Webster says, " to set a just value on; to esteem to the full the worth of; to approve of; to be grateful for; to be sensitive to the aesthetic value of." These are exactly the meanings we give to this phrase in connection with music.

How Can We Learn to Appreciate Music?

We see immediately, when we come to consider this topic, what an enormous difference there is between appreciating an art and enjoying it. We all enjoy hearing a tune or whistling a theme or tapping out rhythms with our feet; we love to call up all kinds of images and imaginings in connection with music. We have seen how natural these pleasures are: they are available even to those people who have had no musical training whatever. But not until we are conscious of music as one of life's full and rich experiences can we be said to appreciate its value. A consciousness of music as one of the most significant expressions of the human mind, a vital element in the world's culture, as something that lifts us into an atmosphere above time, place, and circumstance and all the realities of life — this is something far deeper than mere enjoyment. The acquirement of such a consciousness may well be the task of a lifetime, but it is one that will give a lifetime of pleasure.

One of the first things that we must do in an attempt to increase our appreciation of music is to develop the physical capacities by which we receive musical stimuli. We must learn to hear acutely, and to differentiate between, the various pitch levels, to recognize various rhythmic patterns, melodic ideas, and so on. Music is physically a matter of *sound,* and until we can learn to recognize clearly its physical attributes, we are certain to be more or less in the place of the man who is blind and to whom any appreciation of painting is impossible.

We should also try to develop habits that will enable us to retain these stimuli as meaningful musical ideas. That is, once having developed the powers of pitch discrimination, rhythmic recognition, and so forth, we must learn to relate them to the musical apparatus used by composers. We must be able to realize how they combine various pitches — how " out of three sounds they frame a star," to use Browning's rather high-flown phrase; how they weave complex musical fabrics out of a number of separate themes; how they relate the various parts of their compositions to the whole; in short, we should learn the simple rules of musical grammar, structure, and form.

Then, too, we must learn to recognize and apperceive the different emotional and mood reactions engendered by music and to evaluate these in comparison to their other elements. This is a matter of nice discrimination and avoids the extremes of being completely swept away in a state of emotional hysteria on the one hand, and of entirely abjuring the emotional significance of music on the other. What the music does to us is one of its important powers and should be neither overemphasized nor neglected.

The listener should try to make the composer's experience his own, crystallizing it as definitely as possible so that he can seize it, reflect upon it, and even, perhaps, use it as the basis for an imaginative creativeness of his own. We have said that all art is communicative; we should prepare ourselves so that we stand ready on the receiving end, qualified to make part of our own experience whatever the music can give. The development of a certain ability to describe such experiences in words may help in this respect. When Charles O'Connell writes in this vein of the first movement of Beethoven's *Fifth Symphony,* we know that he has made the music's experience his own:

The bitterness and violence of this movement have no parallel in music. The sheer power that moves it, the utter logic and inevitableness and finality of this music almost remove it from the manipulations of the conductor; given instruments and knowing hands, it plays itself. Many a conductor has found that there is but one interpretation — Beethoven's — and *that* one speaks, rudely and clamorously and sufficiently, for itself. This is an utterance of the supreme and ruthless ego, momentarily frustrated but unconquered, and it does not brook interference.[2]

[2] From *The Victor Book of the Symphony* by Charles O'Connell. New York: Simon & Schuster.

In music, sounds often have other-than-ordinary significance; we should try to realize these special meanings, in other words, learn to relate music to other experiences. This involves the understanding of such things as national idioms in music, certain qualities of musical " atmosphere " (the aesthetic tone or mood of, or harmony of effects in, a work of art), and the like. When we argue whether Tchaikovsky's symphonies are or are not Russian in character; when we demonstrate, to our own satisfaction at least, that Dvořák's *New World Symphony* has more of a Bohemian than an American [3] flavor; or when we speak of Debussy's music as being impressionistic, we are relating music to experiences and ideas outside itself. As we progress we shall see how really important is this single phase of musical understanding.

And finally we must relate music to other values of life. We should realize how it has developed historically, how it parallels other phases of man's development, what it stands for now, and what are its possibilities for the future. This historical aspect of music's development is a lengthy study in itself and involves plenty of careful reading and patient listening. But it is absolutely necessary if we are to obtain anything like a proper perspective in listening. To know why and how Palestrina's *Missa Brevis* differs from Beethoven's *Missa Solemnis* is an essential factor and fundamental necessity in our appreciation of the qualities of these two different works. If we are to take any reasonable view of present-day developments in music, we must know how these have grown out of the past and how they point towards the future. Otherwise we may become confused and lose our way altogether.

Goals

These then should be our goals. The process of Discovering Music, we will find, is nothing more or less than the process of becoming aware of these various aspects of music's rich and complex structure. The more we can make them a part of our intellectual and artistic experience, the deeper will be our understanding and the fuller our enjoyment of the music we hear.

[3] See Chapter XX.

LIST OF SUGGESTED MUSIC

Arrange the following numbers in the order of their difficulty of appreciation, starting with the work which seems to you easiest to " discover " and ending with the one which seems most difficult to enjoy:

Country Gardens	Grainger
Orpheus in Hades Overture	Offenbach
Prelude to *Die Meistersinger*	Wagner
Variations on " Pop Goes the Weasel "	Caillet
Quartet No. 3, First Movement	Hindemith
Romeo and Juliet Overture	Tchaikovsky
Air, " When I Am Laid in Earth," from *Dido and Aeneas*	Purcell

TOPICS FOR FURTHER DISCUSSION

Which aspect of musical appreciation mentioned in this chapter seems most difficult to you? Which is most attractive? Why?

SUGGESTIONS FOR READING

The Relation of Art to Life, O'Neill. (London: Routledge)
The Influence of Music on Behavior, Diserens. (Princeton: Princeton University Press)

CHAPTER IV

Music as an Art

IN what we have said about music so far, we have referred to it as an individual experience, a matter of personal enjoyment.

Its significance reaches far beyond this, however. Because of its peculiar nature, the art of music is a factor of tremendous importance in our modern social and educational development. Let us see why.

We have said that music's appeal must always be primarily to the senses; we have to realize that it need not tarry within such bounds. Cutting through them, it addresses itself directly to man's spiritual nature, acquainting him with those great realities that are too far-reaching to be expressed in mere words. Someone has put this poetically by saying that while " speech is but broken light on the depths of the unspoken, music is a mystical illumination of these depths, which the rays of language are too feeble to reach." We feel this time and time again when listening to great music.

Poets and essayists, novelists and playwrights, painters and sculptors have left us clearly formulated and carefully articulated thoughts and ideas cast into permanent and tangible form. These constitute one of our great cultural heritages as well as one of the most important factors in our educative process. For it is this enhancement of the qualities which make ordinary experiences appealing, appropriable (capable of full assimilation), and enjoyable that makes art an important factor in education, as John Dewey tells us. Since the great artists have been men possessed of special, what might be called *intuitional*, powers, the experiences which they have revealed and communicated cannot but deepen our understanding of human life in relation to the universe in which it is lived. No better definition of real education could be formulated: the study of art is thus not the educational luxury that so many would have us believe; it gives emphatic expression to that which makes all life worth while.

Music as a Humanity

Music is of special importance in such an educational development. For its mission is to give expression to such passions and inspirations, such imageries and realities as are too mighty or subtle, too suggestive or spiritual, to be imprisoned within the meanings of words or the bounds of canvas or stone. Of necessity less precise than literature, less definite than painting or sculpture, music's very vagueness gives it a vastness of meaning that thereby becomes more powerful and significant. With the other arts we somehow have a feeling of a crystallization of emotions from which the vital essence has escaped; by defining, they necessarily limit. It is only music which can reveal to us the " illimitable which lies behind the barriers of time." If properly understood, music can tell us more of life than living itself.

To be more exact: the material of which music is made is tone, just as the material out of which poetry is fashioned is words, or the material of painting is spatial shape and color. Words, however, are associated with things, for they are ordinarily used to symbolize and communicate ideas. So, too, shapes and colors are associated with such external objects as houses, rocks, trees, sky, and so on, and have comparatively little to do with spiritual qualities. The elements of which a building is composed — the pillars, pediments, openings, and so on — are so closely associated in our minds with their functional purposes that we cannot see them separately without immediately associating them with building.

All of which is decidedly limiting to the artist who would work with general ideas and convey universal concepts — who would deal in what the artists call abstractions.[1] Such a generic word as " house " suggests to us a definite material concept, even though it has different associations for different people living in different lands: in even such a poetic phrase as " house of many mansions," it is difficult for us to remove the ordinary connotations of the term. This makes the language of words a difficult one for the transference of ideas that go beyond ordinary experience. The painters are similarly limited. The representations of flowers, landscapes, human figures, and the like which they put

[1] *Abstract:* " considered apart from any application to a particular object."

into their pictures are so closely associated with things in the natural world that it is difficult to make them " mean " anything but what they represent externally. And when a painter tries to get away from this idea of natural association and convey his thoughts and feelings by using what to the ordinary person are meaningless shapes and patterns, he is likely to be thought unintelligible.

PARTICULAR POSSIBILITIES

With the musician it is different. The tonal material which he uses has, with the exception of a direct imitation of a few sounds which occur in nature, no association with anything outside itself. Moreover, these tones can reach directly any hearer who has ears to hear; they do not have to be translated into any other language, and they constitute what is, in every real sense, the only universal language in the world, one supremely capable of conveying emotions and feelings. This makes music the ideal means for the communication of those abstract ideals and imaginative concepts that so exalt the mind and lift the spirit. The musician is envied by all other creative artists; he does not have to mean anything and therefore can mean everything. And so his medium is capable of giving expression to that which has no counterpart in the external world and which belongs only to the inner world of the spirit and imagination.

A concrete example will make this clear. From time immemorial artists of all kinds have been concerned with the fundamental problem of man's existence — from whence he came, why he is here in the midst of so great tribulation, and whence he is going. The struggles of man against his manifest fate, his feeble attempts to live nobly in the midst of a tempestuous and unfriendly world, the question of his perishing so that he might continue existence in another life — these have been some of the universal themes of art. Such questionings have concerned man from the earliest days of his history. The great sacred writings — the Bible, the Veda, the Koran — are full of them. The great national epics — *The Iliad* and *The Odyssey*, the *Eddas*, the *Nibelungenlied*, the *Kalevala* — deal with little else. Dramatists from Euripides to O'Neill have tried valiantly to answer them. Painters as widely different in time and spirit as the fifteenth-century

PAUL GAUGUIN: I GREET YOU, MARIA   PIERO DELLA FRANCESCA: RESURRECTION

Adolph Lewisohn Collection

A MAGNIFICENT EXAMPLE OF RHYTHM IN ARCHITECTURE

Rhythm is a characteristic common to all the fine arts. It may be defined as the regular recurrence of like features in an artistic composition, producing a harmonious whole through the correlation and interdependence of parts.

This is the twelfth-century doorway of Kilpeck Church, England.

Piero della Francesca (in his *Resurrection*) and the nineteenth-century Paul Gauguin (in his *Ia Orana Maria*) have tried to express, with poignant and impressive means, their understanding of this inner need of man for quieting such challenges of his spirit.

A comparison of these art works, great as they may be, with such pieces of music as Beethoven's *Fifth Symphony*, Brahms's *First Symphony*, or even Tchaikovsky's *Fifth Symphony* will show the peculiar properties of music in this respect. For all attempts on the part of writers and painters to solve this problem of man's eternal struggle between life and death, between hope and despair, have had to deal with particularities. Figurative some of them are, of course; but our imagination, even in such great works as *The Iliad*, or Shakespeare's *King Lear*, is limited because of the necessity of using meaningful words and interpretable symbols. The treatment of special ideas and concepts makes anything like a universal application of them difficult. Whereas the significance of Beethoven's *Fifth Symphony*, *The " Fate " Symphony*, to take one of many possible examples, may be said to lie in the fact that it is an expression of his own personal defiance of fate and struggle against despair; or in that it is the " utterance of a tormented and puzzled and cynical and hopeful — and finally triumphant humanity "; or in that it embodies, as those engaged in the second great World War have interpreted it, the spirit of man's triumphant victory over the forces of evil and despair. Any of these interpretations fit this comprehensible and human music; many others might be read into it. Being absolute art in the real sense of that term, Beethoven's music is not bound to anything outside itself; so it does not need to mean anything and can mean many things to different people. To realize something of this particular potentiality of music is to sense its peculiar significance as an art and its importance as a factor in our everyday life.

LIST OF SUGGESTED MUSIC

First Symphony, First Movement	Brahms
Fifth Symphony	Tchaikovsky

Listen to these works, mentioned in the chapter, along with Beethoven's *Fifth Symphony*. What does the music mean to you? Look up some of the interpretations given to this music by more experienced listeners and see how yours agrees or differs. O'Connell's *Victor Book of the Symphony* and Philip Hale's *Boston Symphony Programme Notes* are excellent books to use for such references.

SUGGESTIONS FOR READING

Music and Its Lovers, Vernon Lee. (New York: Dutton; London: Allen
    & Unwin)

CHAPTER V

Getting Behind the Music

ENJOYMENT, EMOTIONAL AND INTELLECTUAL

I F one were rash enough to begin a catechetical inquiry into the subject of aesthetics, his first question might well be, " What is the chief end of art? " and the answer, " To be enjoyed — in the literal sense of the term, to give pleasure, to be delighted in." A painter plans his canvas or distributes the elements of his mural decoration so as to produce a design, appealing in its proportion, balance, rhythm, use of color. The writer produces his prose or poetry so as to give pleasure to the reader, either an intellectual satisfaction in the ideas conveyed, or an aesthetic one through the beauty of their expression. Even the most practical of the fine arts, architecture, if it is true to its principles, must formulate its designs so that they are structurally proportioned, and thus pleasing to the eye, as well as practically useful.

So it is with music; unless it provides us with a sense of enjoyment it will be of very little value to the listener. There are, of course, various ways of enjoying music, just as there are of enjoying life. We may approach it through the senses, in the manner of those who seem to feel that sensual enjoyment is the great end of all existence. Music possesses tremendous powers of sensual appeal through its rhythms, its melodies, its charm of sound. Even the most unmusical person feels the essential appeal of repeated rhythms — witness the appeal of the nervous drumbeats of the African savage, or their more sophisticated modern counterparts, the American jazz rhythms, to people today. We all react to the appeal of a sentimentally turned tune, as well as to the trumpet's wild blare or the seductive strains of muted strings. On the other hand, we may enjoy our music primarily from the intellectual standpoint through realizing how it is constructed, how logically it develops through various stages to a final climax, how well it succeeds in varying its constituent parts so as to provide variety and achieve unity. This sort of enjoyment is like that of the intellectual who derives his greatest pleasure in life through the processes of his mind and who distrusts the pleasures of his senses.

Both these ways of enjoying music are legitimate and need to be cultivated. But after all they are but the means through which we come in the end to the fullest sort of enjoyment, that which comes through sharing the feelings that impelled the creation of the music in the first place. Our greatest art productions are obviously the result of their creator's overwhelming enjoyment of an idea, a formal design or color pattern, a state of mind or a feeling. Something takes possession of the creator which he cannot resist, and we feel that the music or the painting or the poem which he produces forms itself without conscious effort, the creative artist being a mere instrument in the hands of some power outside himself. Every great work of art is born in such a glow of creative enthusiasm, whether the result happens to have been an immediate one, as in the case of a Schubert song or a Mozart symphony, or whether the creative effort was spread over a long period of time, as in the *First Symphony* of Brahms, or in Goethe's *Faust*. Perhaps even centuries may have elapsed between the beginning and the finishing of a work of art, as was the case of the medieval cathedrals. But the delight in each case is the same, a delight so keenly felt that the artist is driven to share it with posterity through the mysterious powers of creation. Through his abilities as a craftsman he has been able to communicate his delight to others; and the greatest enjoyment that can come to us as listeners or readers or beholders of the work he has created is in sharing this delight, in experiencing a glow similar to that of the creator, even if necessarily a much feebler one. Aldous Huxley has reminded us that of all the arts, music is that which has the least connection with what we call reality, and that, like mathematics, it is an almost unadulterated product of man's inner world. And it is this inner world that will best understand it and derive the greatest pleasure from it. We should be able to experience such a sense of pleasure in hearing music that we go out from it with " joy in our hearts and like the poor cripple in the story, walking the streets like a god," as Mr. Edward Dickinson tells us in his fine book, *The Spirit of Music*.

Our study of the technic of musical construction, necessary

as it is to the full comprehension of what we hear, must be used
as a means to help this spiritual understanding. The full meaning
of music and the pleasure to be derived from it are gained only
when to analytic dissection of its structure we add the evaluation
of it as an expression of human experience. To paraphrase William Blake, we must learn to hear *through,* not *with* our ears.
Lewis Mumford has observed that painting is an organization of
human experience in terms of the image, as literature is in terms
of the word; and we might justly add, as music is in terms of
sound. And music, because of its essential characteristics, is able
to communicate this experience even more significantly than do
its sister arts.

THE ADVANTAGES OF THE MODERN LISTENER

One of the chief reasons why music has been so long in reaching the height of its development, as compared with the other
arts, has been the peculiar necessity for the interpolation of a
third person — the performer — in order to establish contact
between the minds of the composer and the hearer, while a poem
or a painting or a building is in itself the contact between its creator and ourselves. The fact that music has to be re-created each
time it is to be enjoyed has given the re-creator a prestige out of
all proportion to his real importance in the scheme of musical
things. To make matters still more complicated, a poor interpretation can, of course, change the whole complexion of the music
and completely distort the composer's intentions. So a great deal
of the effect which music has upon the listener is due to the manner of its interpretation. Things have changed for the better in
this respect, however. Much of the dominance of the interpreter
has gone with the advent of present-day conditions in the reproduction of music through means such as the phonograph. Music
has now really a better chance to speak for itself.

Any study of music that has any other purpose than that of
leading the student directly to the music itself is, of course, value-
less. As someone has put it: to talk of music without hearing it is
about as fruitful as to sit in an Eveless desert discussing the beauty
of women. Until recently, however, unless one were a Maecenas
and able to possess his own musical establishment, the only way

of approach to music was through the means of an occasional concert, or through one's own efforts or one's friends' efforts at reproduction. Now what have been called the miracles of science
have changed such conditions. The phonograph and the radio
give us invaluable means for providing repeated hearings of
music whenever we desire them. Even in the present stage of their
development, admittedly far from perfection, these products of
the machine age are able to give us a repertoire of the greatest
music, interpreted by the world's greatest artists, with rather
startling fidelity of reproduction. And the experts tell us that
within a few years the recorded reproductions of music will be
even finer. Thus, in so far as the listener is concerned, the performer in a personal sense is no longer the necessity he once was.

The Listener's Pitfalls

All of the foregoing is true enough, and we should be ready
to take every advantage of these marvelous opportunities offered
to our generation for the study of music and for increasing our
appreciation of it. But there are very obvious dangers to be
avoided in the process. Even in the case of such an art as music,
an art which is above all things to be enjoyed, as we have already
insisted, its full glories are revealed only to those who have shown
some proof of their worthiness to comprehend it. And by worthiness to comprehend we mean a willingness to exert some active
desire. The idea of " mere hearing " suggests a superficial and
passive process, rather than the necessary personal effort in learning to hear what is in the music. The old idea of " appreciation "
of an art was largely that of exposing oneself to it, of perhaps
putting oneself in the same room with it, and then daring it to
exert some influence upon us. And, of course, in the great majority of cases, nothing happened. Music, especially, because of its
blessed ability to dispense with the aids of reality and fact, specially tempts us to enjoy it in passive and sensual ways. As a
recent writer in the London *Musical Times* says, " We love to sit
dozing in a symphony just as we sit dozing and bathing in the
warmth of the sun. And when an art that is both too difficult (because of its spiritual qualities) and too easy is made suddenly accessible to everybody by the pressing of a switch, it is likely to

lose at least as much as it gains. That is the danger of music today; there is so much of it and it is so promiscuous that it is being heard rather than listened to. And there are ninety passive listeners to ten live (participative) ones, because listening calls for knowledge as well as effort, and only ten (or even less) have been given the knowledge. Since taste is largely dependent upon knowledge, it follows that the ninety either prefer bad music, or don't know the difference between good and bad."

If you are inclined to doubt the truth of such a statement, consider the parallel case of the art of literature. Never before in the history of the world have there been so many books published; they are spread far and wide by the activities of both author and publisher. And yet there is probably less reading today — that is, reading with real understanding — than in the times when books and magazines were less easily available. The mere presence of such a bulk of literature and music may act as a deterrent from putting forth personal effort in trying to understand them. Probably the very extent of the flood does some good, but the proportion of value, of virtue absorbed into the reader, is apparently small in most cases. Things these days seem to be just turned on like a tap — reading, seeing, hearing — and the senses become completely dazed. In art appreciation, as in all phases of human activity, the truth holds that we get just as much out of our efforts as we put into them.

Another danger that we must guard against as we take advantage of these mechanical devices in the reproduction of music is that such processes are liable to short-circuit our experiences. When we seem to be transported at once where we desire to be, we are likely to forget that we may not be really there, that we can really get there only by the slower process of going around. Basil de Sélincourt puts it well: " Our first impression when music is delivered over to us in these mechanical fetters is that this most difficult of arts has been made easy at last. What a dangerous illusion! Within a few years we find our opportunities for hearing it multiplied a thousandfold. Everybody now can have all he wants; but curiously enough, this does not mean that it is easier to be musical. It is in the nature of music to provide experiences of an exceptional and critical kind, and if the critical comes too often, it ceases to be critical.

" The danger of these mechanical facilities is that they make

music customary, they produce a bad habit and spoil our freshness of attention before we know what they would be at. This
we can correct only by allowing for it, and being for that reason
more careful. Wireless and gramophone can train us for direct,
personal contact with music, for which there is no substitute.
Just as most people read stupid books and only a few find out
the good ones, so in a little while when music is everywhere, avoiding bad music will be as difficult as crossing a crowded traffic in-
tersection, and the good will be available only if we care to climb
for it and accustom ourselves to high altitudes and the vigor and
splendor in which it lives."

TYPES OF LISTENERS

Psychologists who have made careful study of the subject
tell us that there are in general four different ways in which
music affects listeners:

I. To many people music appeals largely as a sensory, emotional,
or conative experience;[1] in listening to such a work as Tchaikovsky's
Symphonie pathétique, these listeners are apt to follow the differing
aspects of the composer's inner experience, to suffer and rejoice with him,
to be moved first to hope and finally to despair, the while they are
thrilled with the colorful sonorities and the appealing charm of his
melodies.

II. For others music arouses all sorts of associations, many of
them having little or nothing to do with the music itself. A certain
phrase or rhythm may remind such listeners of a day in the country or
a trip to the mountains, and awaken some very intimate, personal associations connected with such events. One thing leads to another, and
often the listener reflectively connects these personal associations and
experiences with universal moods and feelings, thus giving the music
a larger, more human significance.

III. There is likewise an objective method of enjoying music, by considering its value *per se*, without reference to anything else. Those who
enjoy music in this fashion refrain from an individual response to music;
to them matters of form and technic are of paramount importance, and
they criticize music largely, if not entirely, from this viewpoint.

---

[1] The psychologists are careful to distinguish here: *conation* means " the power
or act of striving with or without a conscious goal." *Joy* and *sorrow* are " emotional
states "; *hope* and *despair* are " conative attitudes."

IV. Perhaps the simplest response to music — in this case the listener does not " get behind the music " at all — is through personifying its character — thinking of it as morbid, joyful, light, heavy, and so forth. Very little discrimination is needed for this kind of listening, and comparatively little satisfaction results from it.

One listener may, and often does, react in all these different ways to music, according to his mood and to the type of music he is hearing. Generally speaking, however, listeners fall naturally into such classifications as are mentioned above.

LIST OF SUGGESTED MUSIC

In order to ascertain the ways in which you listen to music, hear the following pieces, trying to determine whether your reactions are those of type I, II, III, or IV mentioned above.

L'après-midi d'un faune   Claude Debussy

Here is a fine illustration of the possibility of " getting behind " music and sensing it as poetic experience in terms of sound. Before listening to this, read Chapter XXIII of this book and also Aldous Huxley's translation of Mallarmé's poem upon which the selection is based, in *An Anthology of World Poetry*, edited by Mark Van Doren.

Russia   Mily Balakirev

This is a brief orchestral piece depicting some of the most stirring events in the colorful history of Russia and using themes of Russian folk character.

Theme and Variations
from *Quartet* in D minor, No. 14   Franz Schubert

This is the second movement from the *Death and the Maiden Quartet*, one of Schubert's finest chamber-music works.

Romeo and Juliet Overture   Peter I. Tchaikovsky

Listen to this magnificent tonal narration of one of the greatest love stories of all time.

Suite in B Minor   J. S. Bach

Here is a delightful set of eighteenth-century dance tunes.

TOPICS FOR FURTHER DISCUSSION

Do you think that any amount of technical knowledge, however great, can spoil enjoyment? Compare music, in this respect, with sport as seen by an onlooker.

Can too much talk about music harm a work of art or weaken the hearer's appreciation of it?

Is it possible for a listener's appreciative faculty to outstrip his technical facility — in other words, can a person learn to appreciate music that it would be impossible for him to produce? And is the reverse possible, or likely — a performer becoming highly skilled, and not understanding what he performs?

Discuss the belief that " the great composers always held their art as an open one, without mystery-mongering." Is mystery-mongering a modern development? How does art fare in the present-day craze for publicity and stunting?

SUGGESTIONS FOR READING

The Spirit of Music, Dickinson. (New York: Scribner)
Chapter II: How to Find the Spirit of Music
This should be read and reread by teachers and students of music appreciation.

CHAPTER VI

Equipment for the Listener

Doing versus Listening

ONE of the most commonly suggested means for acquiring a transforming taste in music is through learning to do something in it — to play an instrument or to sing. No one in his proper senses would wish to deny the importance of the performing musical amateur. Active participation in music gives a kind of interest that can come in no other way; it fosters an admiration for and an understanding of the skill of a composer that can hardly be gained through hearing alone. It is one of the most pleasant and beneficial means of occupying leisure time, this amateur playing and singing, and it often leads, of course, to a real knowledge and understanding of music. But there are obvious dangers which have to be considered; anyone who has observed at all carefully will have noticed that sometimes the process of acquiring mental and physical dexterity and powers of co-ordination sufficient to perform music with any degree of facility weakens the very thing which should above all else be developed — a love for the music itself. What is more, this faculty of performing, once acquired, often occupies the interest and attention of the player or singer to the exclusion of attention to what he is playing or singing. Too few singers, for instance, after they have spent years in acquiring a technic, know or care about the finest things in vocal literature — the songs of Schubert, Franz, or Wolf. Too few pianists pay much attention to the supreme things in piano literature unless these happen to provide an abundant opportunity for exhibiting technical prowess. There have been many movements for stimulating active participation in music in recent years — massed singing movements, choral and instrumental contests, and such. But the net results of all these activities, in so far as concrete gains in musical knowledge and consequent improvement in taste are concerned, are often

39

dubious. A stimulation of activity does not always mean an attainment of worth-while results; it is not unknown for localities which have shown the greatest activity to exhibit the poorest taste in the music they have chosen to perform.

No, the ability to perform music does not provide an open sesame to an awareness of its beauty or understanding of its message. If cultivated properly, performance is assuredly a stimulating and fructifying influence; but we must not confuse our issues here. The ability to perform music and a knowledge of and love for the best music are individual attainments, the second by no means always the consequent of the first.

SELF-ACTIVITY

The idea of doing something, of producing practical and concrete results in every process we undertake, no matter whether we should be aiming for intangible and spiritual ends, is a peculiar characteristic of our times. But because educators in other fields are struggling to be practical and to gauge the results of what should be a purely intellectual process in the terms of the market place, that is no reason why those of us who deal with music, the unadulterated product of the inner world, should attempt to follow suit. We are not going to foster much love for music or develop an understanding of its place in life by using methods similar to those of a worthy cathedral organist who, in his zeal for improving the love for music among the children of his town, invited them into the cathedral and played a Bach fugue for them; coming provided with pencil and paper, they were asked to mark down each entrance of the theme they heard in the course of the doctor's playing, and their appreciation of the music was judged by the correctness of the papers they turned in.

Especially in America there is at present a great wave of enthusiasm for all sorts of musical activities. Recognition contests, singing and playing contests, even " discriminating listening contests "; movements for class instruction in everything imaginable, from harmonicas to saxophones; the institution of civic and school concerts and the fostering of group activities in vocal and instrumental music — all these may be looked upon as hearty manifestations of interest in music. But that does not necessarily mean that they are entirely healthy ones. Unless those responsible for these undertakings understand that they must be but the means toward the end of more intelligent, discriminating appreciation and the development of a love for the finer things in music, all this activity will prove to be but another manifestation of what one writer calls " bluff culture," a tangible, marketable, " successful " imitation of the real thing. There is no short cut nor royal road to musical or any other kind of culture, the advertising writers of this utilitarian age to the contrary notwithstanding. These ingenious gentlemen may try to tell us that health is largely a matter of keeping fit with some type of apparatus; they may try to assure us that education is a matter of spending an hour a day with a book chosen from their carefully selected lists; but they would never be able to convince us that real culture can be gained by any means other than the slow, tortuous route of constant application, of making steady progress toward a fixed goal.

Sport in Music

All this should not lead us to infer, however, that activity is not a necessary part of listening; learning to appreciate music is not a task for a lazy man. The power to listen has to be won; it does not come without being earned, any more than does any other wage. There is no truer saying than that we get, in the long run, exactly what we earn.

There is a grace in listening to music; a technic also, and, if pursued with real keenness, a fairly complex one. There are many parallels between music and sport, and one might say that we need to lay ourselves out for some good cross-country work if we are to get results. But only those who have thrown themselves into music as into a favorite sport can know the delight of its pursuit; and it need not be like some of those school subjects the study of which is pursued but never overtaken. As in everything else, we need to develop by easy stages.

In the word " musician " we make no distinction between amateur and professional; there ought to be no antipathy between them. Perhaps the most needful things for the amateur to remember are that music, although it gives up great beauty on demand, holds some of its deepest delights in complexity; that of all the arts it is the longest, while life, admittedly, is short — but patience must not be! The professional musician might well recollect, on his part, that he did not acquire all his profound knowledge of music in one day; that he cannot expect everybody else to be, all in a moment, as great a devotee as he is; that everybody has to work out his own salvation; and that music, like religion, has many mansions.

Therein lies the peculiar freedom and fineness of music; and therein, too, consists a great deal of its appearance as a sealed mystery to the person who is not yet a freeman of music. There are splendid works of musical art which depend on a story; but they depend also on their convincing power of form, the beauty of their logical structure. So that, whilst program music is reckoned the easiest to grasp — and in very simple, short forms, it certainly is — such music when brought to the pitch of perfection of a Richard Strauss in his work *The Merry Pranks of Till Eulenspiegel* presents a double responsibility to the keen listener — the problem of its story (which may be readily solved, perhaps) and that much more subtle problem of the relation of the story to the *form* of the music.   ·

We shall see as we go on that the appreciation of the more complex forms is a responsible part of the listener's happy task. This, we admit, will take time and pains; but, as in all other pursuits, everyone is free to decide whether the game is worth the candle. It is perhaps not putting it too strongly to say that if one is really fit for music, if music is to be the fulfillment of some of the deepest aspirations, as thousands from their experience declare it to be, then no amount of cheerful work at its admitted complexities can be too great, no time better spent than in self-activity among its masterpieces.

THE NECESSITY OF MEMORY

Music lovers often ask if there are any special qualities, apart from the natural faculties of keenness and the power of attention which nature may have given them, that they should cultivate. Apart from the actual ability to read music, the greatest technical need of the music lover is to develop his powers of memory. Music is unlike any other art in that it goes past us like a flash, and every particular piece may not be immediately available again. (Here, obviously, is the advantage of the phonograph.) One may stand before a piece of sculpture, before the Parthenon or a painting, and take one's time in enjoying its details. Even if a piece of music be played over many times, one may not remember all its fine detail; and from one hearing the less experienced listener, however eagerly he may desire to take it in, may well come away baffled. Patience and time are needed, and the cultivation of the memory — not only for tunes, but for what the composer does with them — for the structural logic of a musical work. A symphonic movement may last a quarter of an hour or more; symphonies oftentimes go on for fifty minutes, some of them for an even longer time. It is obvious that only the impatient and thoughtless listener would expect to understand all that such a work had to tell him even after two or three hearings. The best resource of all, undoubtedly, is the power to read the printed score; but that power we shall not presume to exist in our readers, while congratulating those who have cultivated it or are cultivating it, and offering them every encouragement to persevere in this valuable exercise, in which the beginner can soon begin to make headway if he starts with simple enough scores. One of the best mottoes that a group of musical amateurs could adopt would be: *Poco a poco*. Little by little is the right way to tackle any study; and if music is worth our attention at all, it is worth being taken seriously, like any other study in which we seek to educate ourselves and by which we wish to make of ourselves whole and balanced citizens of the world.

Yet music is not, and should not be made, a forbiddingly difficult subject. Any such statement would be no friendly act upon the part of authors of such a book as this, whose greatest desire is to make the enjoyment of music possible. We do not pretend that it is necessary to know all the big works; our object is rather to select some of the most characteristic examples of the art, examples in which can be studied the beauties of form and feature, of tune and rhythm, of program and pageantry, and to show how an understanding of all these increases the listener's enjoyment.

"Knowing What We Like"

Into all appreciation some degree of criticism must come. We shall not attempt to make a specialty of that; but the real meaning of appreciation is to sum up, to strike a balance. There is a world of amusement and much profit not yet gained, in the study of bad music; but, mercifully, we shall not pursue that — we are already overtaken by too much bad music every day, willy-nilly. We suggest that stern criticism may well be left to mature with time and experience. As to " knowing what we like," we do our readers the courtesy of presuming that they are too wide-awake to mistake that for criticism. In the right man, it may be; but for Everyman it is usually no more a manifestation of artistic appreciation than is his preference for mustard over ketchup, or his enjoyment or dislike of olives or tomatoes.

It is a commonplace among music lovers that, in distinguishing among qualities — in even the most mild form of criticism — it is essential that we do not decry a work for failing to do what its composer did not set out to do. We do not blame the lightweight boxer for failing to stand up to the heavyweight champion, or the butterfly for being apparently less industrious than the bee. Each works according to his nature and his build. But an essential question must not be omitted here: Is what the composer is striving to do worth doing?

George Sampson, a discerning critic of literature, has a wise word on this: The good student is " not to be taken in by novelties, or to be put off with accidentals. Confronted by the mass of Walt Whitman's work, with all its disconcerting irregularities and inequalities, he does not waste time by asking painfully and fruitlessly, Is this poetry? Is this prose? Is it both, or neither? He asks what is, after all, the real question for critics: Does this succeed artistically? In days when religion was decisively a part of life, there came suddenly to certain men rare moments when they felt strangely uplifted in spirit and moved beyond themselves. Such moments of ecstasy come also from the great creative arts of poetry and music. The moments that make you catch your breath, the moments in which you are carried beyond space and time, and feel as if the powers from afar had touched you with their wings — these supreme moments of beauty are, in plain terms, the moments of artistic success. To create such moments is the prerogative of the artist; to share them is a privilege of the humble receiver." Could we have a better ideal than that in our search for significance in the beauty of music?

LIST OF SUGGESTED MUSIC

Slow Movement of the *Surprise Symphony* Haydn

Here is an idea first presented in its simplest form and then differently shaped in a series of variations without losing its essential meaning. In following the different presentations of this idea, we learn to look with concentration to details and to develop the power of memory as we constantly compare the new form to the old.

Last Movement from *Suite*, Op. 19 Dohnányi

There is good practice here in following the reappearance of one main theme and in appreciating a first-class craftsman's use of the orchestra.

Prelude to *Lohengrin* Wagner

Notice how the whole of this music grows from the single theme heard high on the strings near its beginning. Wagner is one of the greatest masters of musical construction.

TOPICS FOR FURTHER DISCUSSION

Is it possible to insist too strongly on the necessity of " doing "? It has been said that there are " three graces: a grace of composing, a grace of performing, and a grace of listening." Discuss their respective and combined values.

In your experience, why are so many people uninterested in serious music? Is this due to defects in temperament, or in training?

Why is the criticism of music, taken in bulk, generally poorer than the criticism of literature?

As an aid to remembering music heard, prepare a small card index or loose-leaf notebook, and alphabetically record therein each composition that you hear, either on phonograph, radio, or in actual concert. A few comments on the characteristics of the music and on the composer may well be added. Information regarding the latter will be found in Grove's *Dictionary of Music and Musicians*, or in any standard history of music, such as Pratt's or Dickinson's.

SUGGESTIONS FOR READING

The Scope of Music, Buck. (New York and London: Oxford)
Chapter IV: What Is Musical Criticism?
Chapter V: The Meaning of Appreciation
The Oxford Companion to Music, Scholes. (New York and London: Oxford) Article on " Appreciation of Music "

CHAPTER VII

The Composer's Materials

BUILDING A BACKGROUND

A N accurate taste in poetry, as in all the other arts, is an acquired talent, which can only be produced by severe thought and a long continued intercourse with the best models of composition."

We have already indicated our belief in this opinion of Wordsworth and suggested that it is as true of music as he says it is of poetry; there are no short cuts to culture. Augustine Birrell puts this truth in lighter phrase when he says that " you may as well expect to be born with a silk hat on your head as with good taste. To go wrong is natural. To go right is discipline. . . ." It is well to keep this in mind when we hear people question the sincerity of those who would improve their taste by asking whether such subjects as the appreciation of music, or of poetry or of painting, can actually be taught. Some advice may be acceptable as to where lie the most desirable destinations, and some suggestions for help in reaching them. The listener's early concern should be the acquiring of enough musical background to make his listening as intelligent as possible from the very beginning. This does not imply the superficial sort of knowledge that is so often evidenced in the persons who *know* practically nothing about music, yet who *talk* about it with an authority quite astonishing to the professional musician. Rather does it mean that the listener should so direct his musical education that he may know what music actually is, how to distinguish the materials of which it is composed, how these are used, and what aims they seek to accomplish. If we stop for a moment to consider the relationship of music to the other arts, of how it is like them in some respects and how utterly unlike in many others, we will find a starting point from which this approach can be made.

47

The Raw Materials of Music

All the arts, of course, make use of materials of one sort or another, materials which the artist selects, organizes, and interprets for his particular purpose. The heaven-soaring ideals of the medieval architect were carried out through the organization of such simple materials as wood and stone, materials that were shaped into forms relating mass to mass through the genius of the builders. Our masterpieces of literature were formed from words used in ordinary speech, shaped through the power of poet or novelist. The raw materials of sculpture consist of certain three-dimensional blocks of various materials — stone, wood, clay, and so on — capable of assuming, under the skilled hand of the artist, the shapes he desires. The world's greatest paintings, in so far as their materials are concerned, are simply colored pigments applied to canvas, wood, or plaster.

But there is something beyond these purely physical substances which we must consider when we think of materials with which artists work, something that is all the more important because it cannot be seen, something upon which the real quality of any work of art depends. For example, we cannot truthfully say that the materials of architecture are merely the wood and stone, the bricks or concrete that have gone into the building we know. Beyond these and the physical laws which enable man to use them as he wishes are all those necessities and inducements that have led him to plan and erect buildings — such necessities as those of providing shelter from the elements, or depositories for his goods, or temples for the worship and glorification of his gods. Without these spiritual and social necessities the art of architecture as we know it could never have come into being.

Similarly we realize that what we call " literature " would never have been created if man had not been impelled to use words in a manner that far transcends their ordinary purpose of communicating simple ideas. We can say that the desire of man to acquaint his fellows with his reactions to the world about him or his reflections on his own inner and personal experiences constitutes as important a material of literature as the significance and symbolism of the words he uses.

So it is with music. The physicist tells us that the raw material of music is auditory sound [1] having variations of pitch, intensity, timbre, and duration. And to a certain extent they are right. These musical materials can be studied as laboratory phenomena; that is, the structure of sound can be analyzed and stated in terms of scientific and mathematical formulas. And it is important that the listener, if he aspires to anything like a real understanding of music, be familiar with them in a general way. But he must always remember that in themselves these physical materials do not necessarily constitute music; that there are certain spiritual concepts and ideas without which music is merely an interesting physical phenomenon, a dead series of tonal relationships and mathematical ratios, with no power to stir the imagination or move the hearts of men. It is necessary that we consider both these aspects of music's materials; let us take the physical ones first.

THE PHYSICAL CHARACTERISTICS OF TONE

The physical material of which music is composed is, as we have just said, sound [2] — tones, vocables, and noises — together with an occasional use of silence, what the musicians speak of as a " rest." For systematic purposes, and in order to account fully for certain of their characteristics, the physicists are careful to describe these variations of auditory sound — pitch, intensity, timbre, and duration — as being both physical phenomena (pulsations in the ear) and psychological effects (sensations) perceived by the listener. This need not concern us too much as practical musicians, for we naturally assume that the one implies and causes the other.

Long and detailed experimentation has shown that the vibratory motion producing sound has four important characteristics:

1. *Frequency;* that is, it occurs a certain number of times a second. The term *cycle* is used to designate one of these complete vibrations.

---

[1] They mean sound that is produced by some sort of vibrating medium, transferred through alternate compressions and rarefactions of the atmosphere and registered in the auditory centers of the brain through the human ear mechanism.

[2] As one writer puts it, " Sound is the auditory experience, the stimulus for which is the vibratory motions of some elastic body." (Schoen: *The Psychology of Music*)

2. *Amplitude;* that is, it has a certain extent or range.

3. *Form.* The series of pulsations which transmits sound through the air is called a " train " of sound waves and consists of longitudinal vibrations of the air molecules. The physicists have devised machines which graphically represent these linear motions of the sound waves, and these graphs show that the vibratory motion has definite form that is sometimes simple and sometimes complex.

4. *Duration;* that is, the vibratory motion lasts a certain definite length of time.

The sound waves produced by any single tone possess all four of these characteristics; and, since any two waves may differ in one or more of them, we can readily see how complex is the matter of producing even a single tone on any one of the musical instruments.

Now each of these physical properties produces a certain psychological effect upon us, and it is these psychological concepts with which we as listeners are concerned. What we have come to know as the *pitch* of a tone depends largely upon the frequency of the sound wave it generates.[3] That quality in a tone that we recognize as *loudness* depends upon its amplitude.[3] *Timbre* or *tone quality* depends upon the form or overtone structure of the sound wave.[3] And the existence of a tone in time, its persistence as an auditory experience, depends upon the objective factor of duration.[3]

A change in any of the physical characteristics of a tone thus produces a reciprocal change in that which we hear; which is simply another way of saying that the experience of listening to music is an exceedingly complex one, made up of a number of experiences that unite to form a single impression.

These properties of tone are not merely of theoretical interest: they underlie the most fundamental concepts of music. For, as we shall see, the scales which are at the base of our present-day musical structures are simply expressions of certain intrinsic arrangements of pitch relationships. The dynamic quality in music, upon which so much of its beauty depends, is a matter of degrees of loudness and softness. The specific tone qualities of

---

[3] Also, to a much less degree, upon other physical characteristics. Certain changes in the form of a sound wave produce definite changes in pitch; the intensity of a tone likewise affects its pitch to some extent. Experiments have shown that the loudness of a tone depends upon the frequency and form of its sound wave as well as upon its intensity. But in general the statements given above are true.

the various instruments, qualities that color and condition all
the music we hear, are a matter of overtone arrangement. And
rhythm, that " life force of music," depends greatly upon the
relationships of tonal durations. All these factors are basic to
musical organization of even the simplest sort.

PITCH

By *pitch* we mean the relative highness or lowness of a tone; [4]
it is easy enough for all of us to distinguish between the high-
pitched voice of a boy and the low voice of a man, or between the
high pitch of a piccolo and the low voice of the bassoon. One
of the earliest series of physical experiments in the field of music
(made by the Greek Pythagoras, about 550 B.C.) showed that
the pitch of any tone depends on the number of vibrations per
unit of time set up by the vibrating body which produces the
tone. Every body capable of being set in vibration — be it string,
reed, elastic membrane, or air column such as an organ pipe
or a tin whistle — has its own frequency of vibration (number of
vibrations per second), depending on the materials of which it
is made, its size, its density or the degree of its tension, and its
shape. Experiments have shown that the normal ear is capable
of distinguishing frequencies of vibration ranging from about
16 to approximately 18,000 cycles per second; but only a section
of this frequency range — from about 50 to 10,000 cycles —
serves any practical musical purpose. The chart on page 52 shows
the vibration frequencies of the principal musical instruments
and the human voice.

One of the greatest triumphs of man's co-operative effort
(a triumph not, alas, duplicated in all the fields of his endeavor)
has been the adoption, by most of the countries using the Western
system of music, of a uniform standard of pitch for their music-
producing instruments. According to this standard, the note A
when sounded in a temperature of 68 degrees Fahrenheit has

---

[4] Technically, tone is sound that is produced by regular periodic vibrations
and having fixed pitch; it is thus distinguished from " noise," which is produced by
vibrations that are scattered and irregular. " Vocables " are the sounds we use in
speech, and they occupy, according to the theorists, a sort of intermediate position
between tones and noises.

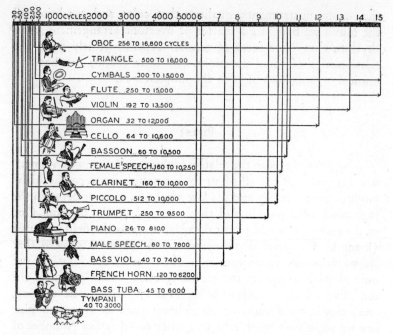

Chart Showing the Complete Frequency Range (Fundamentals and Overtones) of the Principal Musical Instruments and the Human Voice

440 vibrations per second; [5] this is an interesting fact that may perhaps serve the music lover on some music quiz, but it has little practical bearing on his problem of learning to listen to music. It is important for him, however, to inquire what happens when an instrumentalist plays a scale from any note such as A, going up a tone at a time. He will find that as the pitches of the instrument become higher and higher, their wave lengths become shorter and shorter, and the number of waves which

[5] The Department of Commerce says that the present standard pitch was first adopted in Germany in 1834 but was rejected by the rest of the world in favor of A–435, which the French favored and which was established there as official pitch in 1859. The fact that the Allies of the first World War captured so many good German instruments having an A–440 pitch is credited by the Department of Commerce with having started a movement which has since resulted in the establishment of A–440 as standard. For those interested it will be important to know that the Bureau of Standards in Washington broadcasts this note continuously, 24 hours a day, over Station WWV. According to the Department's claims, this broadcasting is accurate "to better than one part in ten million." This A–440 is middle A, the one represented on the second space on the treble clef.

reach his ear per second becomes greater and greater. Finally he
will recognize a tone which bears a strong resemblance to the
original tone from which the player started; this relative of the
first tone, the physicist will show him, has a wave length that is
exactly half that of the original and whose frequency is exactly
twice that of the starting note. This second tone we call the
" octave " of the first. To make this more concrete, if the length
of the sound wave set up by an oboe sounding A is 31.02 inches,
measured from the crest of one wave to that of the next, the wave
length of the A above will measure exactly 15.51 inches; if the
frequency of vibration of the first is 440 cycles per second, that
of the second will be 880.

This relationship between a tone and its octave, discovered
by Pythagoras, is one of the most important phenomena in all
music. For it is easy to see that there would be absolute chaos
in a world in which such a great number of vibrations is capable
of being recognized by the ear, were it not for this happy relationship of the octave. The fact that doubling or halving
the number of vibrations set up by any tone produces another
tone so like the first that we can immediately recognize it as its
twin brother reduces the vast range of sound waves at our disposal (from about 16 to 18,000, remember) to a workable unit
that is repeated over and over again at various pitch levels. The
88 different tones represented on the modern piano keyboard,
giving vibrations from 27½ to 4186 and covering only a part
of the entire range of audibility, is thus conveniently divided into
a seven-octave system (with a few notes over).[6] How much more
difficult would the recognition of pitch relationships be, were
there no such inter-relationships in which a cycle is completed
and then started all over again, and we had to learn to relate each
tone directly to all the others!

It is possible, even within the octave, to obtain an indeter-
minate number of pitch variations, and we should be little
better off in our attempts to avoid confusion had not musicians
agreed upon the necessity for using only a certain few of these
pitches for their musical systems. The number and character
of these within-the-octave pitch relationships have varied in different parts of the world and at different times in history. Our

[6] This can readily be realized by playing through this piano range, taking note
of the number of times the same tone is repeated in octave relationships.

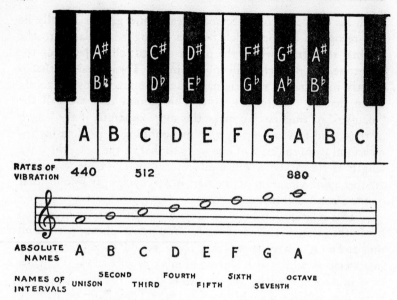

Chart to Show Notation of Pitch and Names of Tones

present-day usage employs twelve pitches within each octave — count them on your piano keyboard. Out of these pitches we form certain basic tonal relationships called scales (see page 75); and in speaking of them we use two kinds of names:

(*a*) Absolute, based on the number of vibrations per second — A, B, C, D, E, F, G

(*b*) Relative, based on the relationship of one tone to another, such as that of octave, second, third, fourth, fifth, sixth, seventh (These terms refer to the interval or ratio of vibration frequencies between the tones.)

These relationships, common to all Western music, may be expressed in mathematical-physical ratios. For reference, here is a complete table of the frequency ratios corresponding to the most commonly used intervals:

Octave, for example from c to c[1]	2:1
Fifth, for example from c to g	3:2
Fourth, for example from c to f	4:3
Third (major), for example from c to e	5:4
Third (minor), for example from c to e flat	6:5

Sixth (major), for example from c to a	5:3
Second, for example from c to d	9:8
Seventh (major), for example from c to b	15:8

LOUDNESS

As the arc of the swing of a vibrating body increases (that is, the extent to which it moves away from its normal state of rest), the energy of a tone increases and it becomes louder to our ears. If we pluck a violin string or strike a piano string lightly, a certain number (say, 256) of slight vibrations per second will be set in motion; if we strike harder, the same number of vibrations per second will result, but their amplitude will be wider, and thus the tone will be louder.

The relationship between physical cause and psychological effect here is a peculiar one; for it has been shown by experiment that the sensation of loudness does not vary directly as the intensity of the vibrations but as the logarithm of the intensity. For example, if we increase the intensity of a vibrating sound-producing body from ten to a hundred times, the resulting loudness which we hear is increased only from one to two times.[7] In nonmathematical terms, doubling the intensity of a sound does not double its loudness. The practical results of this scientific formula are important: two flutes playing together are not twice as loud as one flute; ten pianos played at the same time are not ten times as loud as one. It has been estimated that twenty players would have to be added to an eighty-piece orchestra to produce a difference in loudness that would be appreciably noticeable.

These facts suggest the reason why comparatively few degrees of dynamic intensity are needed by musicians: it has been argued [8] that seven different degrees of dynamic intensity are all that are necessary to cover the extremes of *fortissimo* and *pianissimo* used by a pianist in interpreting ordinary music written for his instrument. Other theorists would insist that there are more; but in any event, compare this with the eighty-eight different degrees of pitch relationships that are at the disposal of the pianist.

---

[7] Since the logarithm of 10 to the base 10 is 1, and that of 100 is 2.
[8] By Guy Montrose in *The Journal of Applied Psychology*, April, 1928.

TIMBRE

The scientist can take us into his laboratory and show us that it is entirely a matter of vibrations that determines the characteristic quality of a tone, or its *timbre*. By means of his specially constructed instruments he obtains graphs which tell us strange things. A tuning fork, which gives the simplest of all musical tones, forms this sort of graph:

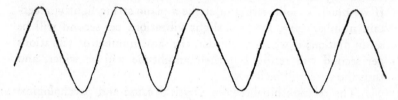

Most elastic bodies (including all the musical instruments) produce, on the other hand, complex sound waves, resulting in graphs like this one, representing clarinet tone pulsations:

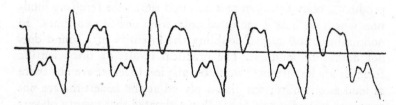

Being properly interpreted, this means that a body which produces this sort of wave vibrates not only as a whole but also in parts or segments; and that it therefore produces not only a fundamental tone but also a number of supplementary or " partial " tones. The vibration of the body as a whole is the strongest and loudest of the compound tones we hear when a note is produced; this is what we call its *fundamental,* and when we speak of the pitch of a tone we refer to the number of vibrations of this fundamental. The tones produced by the fractional vibrations of the body are called *overtones* or *harmonics.* These stand in simple ratio to the vibration of the whole (producing the fundamental) — namely, 1:2:3:4:5:6, and so on — and vary in intensity and number according to the composition of the vibrating body, the manner in which it is sounded, and so forth. It is the number and relative intensities of the overtones which determine the quality of any musical tone. When we hear such a tone as is produced by a piano or an orchestral instrument, we may think that we are hearing only one tone — the fundamental; in reality, we are hearing also many other tones of lower intensity, and it is the presence or absence of these in combination with the fundamental which determines the *timbre* of the instrument.

Taking any note, G for example, as the fundamental produced by a vibrating string of an open-air column, we find that the overtones produced in conjunction with it would be,[9] according to the most commonly accepted theory, as follows:

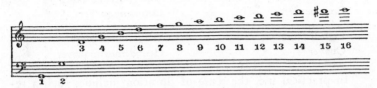

The pure qualities of the upper tones of the flute are caused by the fact that practically no overtones are heard except the second (that is, the octave above the fundamental); and the characteristic quality of the tone of the clarinet is due to the presence of the odd-numbered harmonics — the third, fifth, seventh, and so forth; and we find that the orchestral horn gives out a strong fundamental tone, with more than twenty overtones. Since the first investigations of Helmholtz (1821–1894) regarding these physical bases of tone quality, a great deal of research has been done, and we know that there are other factors that help to determine timbre. But in the main, his theories are still considered correct.

Duration

The duration of a musical tone is obviously the time which elapses between the commencement and the cessation of vibrations. It has been estimated that the shortest possible lasting pe-

[9] The overtones present in any tone depend partly upon the instrument producing the tone and partly on the manner in which the tone is produced.

riod, if it is to give rise to any consciousness of existence, is about 1/20 of a second. It is not customary to measure the duration of tones by any absolute units, but by making relationships between the relative time value of different tones or groups of tones. We say, for example, that the duration of a whole note (o) is twice that of a half (♩) and four times that of a quarter note (♪). Here are the relationships in general use now:

Whole Note Semibreve [10]	o		
Half Note Minim [10]	♩	Sixteenth Note Semiquaver [10]	♪
Quarter Note Crotchet [10]	♪	Thirty-second Note Demisemiquaver [10]	♪
Eighth Note Quaver [10]	♪	Sixty-fourth Note Hemidemisemiquaver [10]	♪

In practical use, the sense of duration includes such a related capacity as *tempo*, the rate of speed at which a piece of music moves. Its indication may be made either by means of some Italian adjective like *adagio, andante*, or *presto* affixed to the music, or by means of a definite reference to the metronome, an instrument devised for marking exact speeds.

THE SPIRITUAL FACTOR IN MUSIC

It was Beethoven who defined music as the " link which connects the spiritual with the sensuous life "; what he meant was that in addition to its existence as sound, music is a means of communication by which something of the processes of a man's inner life is revealed to his fellow men. The composer expresses not what lies outside him but what goes on inside him: through the external physical means which we have just outlined he communicates his inner feelings and spiritual concepts in such a way that they can be perceived through the senses of those who listen. As someone has said, " The musical composition which a composer makes is the expression in musical tones of his inner life."

[10] These are the names given to these notes by the English.

On the afternoon of the day before this was written, the authors met with an experience which should furnish sufficient proof, if such be needed, of the validity of the statements just made. In a large metropolitan concert hall an audience that taxed the capacity of the auditorium had gathered to hear one of the world's great orchestras interpret the music of one of its greatest composers. As the program progressed, it was evident that the audience came more and more under the spell of the music; forgotten were the immediate surroundings, the discomfort of the crowded hall, the technical perfection of the playing, even the sympathetic interpretation of the orchestra, in the emotional significance of the music. Here was a great man speaking simply, out of the depths of his spirit, with a direct vigor and forcefulness of utterance that could not be denied, of things that matter today just as they mattered in the time they were first put on paper and as they always will throughout the history of the human race. There was a great deal more to this music than " auditory sound organized with variations of pitch, timbre, intensity, and duration." Something was being communicated from composer to listener so forcefully, so directly that, to quote a poetic observer of the occasion, when the finale of the last symphony came and the " portals of the skies swung asunder and the great chant of victory and defiance was heard," the audience crashed into applause and wild cheers.

This is what we mean when we say that there are spiritual as well as physical materials to be reckoned with in music. An audience listening to Koussevitzky and the Boston Symphony Orchestra playing a program of Sibelius's music would never have received the impressions it did at the concert described above had it not been for the physical means used to convey the ideas of the composer — the superb timbre of orchestral tone, the carefully adjusted matters of pitch relationship, intensity of tone, correct relations of tempo, and so on. Had there been nothing else, however, the music would have been but sounding brass and tinkling cymbal; what made it memorable was the fact that the conductor and the orchestra were able to convey, through these physical means, what the composer had so evidently put into the music — " the full expression of his inner life." To paraphrase St. Paul: music is an art not only of the letter, but also of the spirit; and he said, " The letter killeth, but the spirit giveth life."

TOPICS FOR FURTHER DISCUSSION

Discuss the true significance and limitations of the phrase " the man behind the music." Can music conceal as well as reveal a composer's nature? Can you think of any instances of this?

Liszt is said to have had a duality of nature — to have been partly a religious aspirant and partly a Barnum. How does this come out in his music? (See Chapter XIV.)

SUGGESTIONS FOR READING

Introduction to Musicology, Haydon. (New York: Prentice-Hall)
Music: A Science and an Art, Redfield. (New York: Tudor)

CHAPTER VIII

Means by Which Materials Are Made into Music

AS we listen to a piece of music, there are certain factors which organize the raw materials of physical sound in ways that heighten our understanding and increase our enjoyment. Although we may not realize it, our interest in a composition is dependent upon one or more, perhaps all, of these factors: we may not be conscious of the presence of a single one of them, but, nevertheless, it is their combined effect that makes music capable of being apprehended. So one of the first needs in learning to listen to music is that of training our ears to recognize these fundamental factors by means of which its raw materials are organized: *rhythm, melody,* and *harmony.* These might well be called the elements of the language of music, and a complete understanding of them demands much study and belongs to the highest intricacies of the art. But even if the music lover is enabled to hear how their use helps to shape the composition to which he is listening, his appreciation of it will be tremendously advanced. These factors are present in all music; and the importance of great masterworks results partly from the significant ways in which a composer employs them.

RHYTHM

Rhythm is the most easily perceived of these fundamental factors of music. There is good reason for this, for rhythm is one of the most fundamental elements in nature. A famous musician is quoted as saying that "in the beginning there was rhythm," and if we stop to consider the universe in general we will see that this is true in many other things besides music. Our life is being

61

sustained constantly by the rhythmic beating of our heart, the beats occurring in pairs, one accented and the other unaccented. Our breathing is likewise rhythmical, the inhalations corresponding to unaccented beats, the exhalations to accented ones. Our walking and running are rhythmical, as is, indeed, the natural pace of all animals. The larger operations of nature occur in rhythmical sequence — the succession of the seasons, the movements of the stars and planets, the ebb and flow of the tides, the beating of the waves on the shore, and so on.

So an art is merely conforming to a universal truth in insisting that the elements of which it is composed be arranged in some sort of harmonious correlation. The rhythmic schemes of the space arts — architecture, sculpture, and painting — are rather easily discernible to the eye, just as those of the time arts — music and literature — are to the ear. Every work of art worthy of the name is arranged according to some succession of weak and strong units that gives it interest and makes it intelligible to the mind of the beholder or listener. The façade of a building, the arrangement of details in a painting, the distribution of the elements of a piece of sculpture, all these give grace and serve to stimulate the interest; they are among the most important means which serve to make the art work intelligible to the beholder. In music and poetry there is need for even more careful organization of rhythmic elements if we are to have a sense of order and balance. We do not have to listen to a piece of poetry or music long before we realize that its constant flow is marked by a succession of beats or pulses, arranged into definite groups by means of heavier stress coming every so often. For instance, in the nursery rhyme that begins:

> Bobby Shafto's gone to sea
> Silver buckles on his knee.

there are four periods of stress or accent in each line. In the first line they fall at the first syllable of " Bobby " and of " Shafto," and on " gone " and " sea." This point of stress we call an accented (strong) beat, as opposed to the others, which are unaccented (weak). We can diagram the above lines thus, letting ↓ represent a strong beat, and ∪ a weak beat:

$$\downarrow \cup \downarrow \cup \downarrow \cup \downarrow (\cup)$$
$$\downarrow \cup \downarrow \cup \downarrow \cup \downarrow (\cup)$$

Such a tune as this one has exactly the same general rhythmic scheme, one which we may call duple, since the meter consists of two beats or pulses, a heavy and a light, with the first one in each group accented:

On the other hand, such lines as these will be found to have quite a different scheme:

> Spotted and veinèd with various hues
> Through the clear realms of azure drift

and a tune like this famous one represents the same pattern:

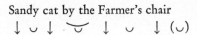

This is what we call triple time, for the meter consists of three beats or pulses, with the first one in each group accented.

Practically, it will be found that most of the more complicated regular rhythmic schemes may be resolved into these two elemental ones, duple and triple. For example, such a line as this:

> Sandy cat by the Farmer's chair

where the heavy accent really comes on the first beat of each group of four, with something of a secondary accent halfway between, is obviously an elaboration of duple rhythm. In music we have this well illustrated by such a tune as the old round "Frère Jacques":

Such a scheme as the following is clearly a modified triple rhythm, with the main accent coming on the first beat of each group of six and a secondary accent midway between:

> Often I think of the beautiful town

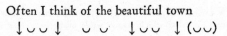

The old French folk tune illustrates this well:

The fundamental time units which occur in music are called *measures;* they are assumed, in ordinary music, to be of equal length and to be made up of a certain number of beats, organized and bound together by the principal accent with which they begin. Thus, in duple time we speak of two beats in a measure; in triple, of three; in quadruple, of four. The vertical lines which are placed on the music score to designate its division are called *bar lines,* while the divisions themselves bear the name *measure.* When writing or printing music, the general rhythmic scheme is indicated at the very beginning by means of a fraction placed before the first note, the numerator of which indicates the number of beats that there are to be in each measure, and the denominator, the kind of note which represents each beat. Thus, 2/4 has two quarter beats to a measure; 4/4, four quarter beats to a measure; 6/8, six eighth beats to a measure; 9/8, nine eighth beats to a measure, and so on.

MUSIC'S METER

This aspect of music's rhythmic structure may be called its *meter* [1] (or measure), since it is concerned with its division into units, called *measures,* each of which consists of a certain number of beats or pulses. The principal meters used in present-day music are:

2/4 meter: two beats to a measure, each a quarter note

2/2 meter: two beats to a measure, each a half note

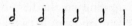

---

[1] This is often erroneously spoken of as *time;* the latter is not a musical term at all, but refers to " that which elapses while music is being played."

4/4 meter: four beats to a measure, each a quarter note, the accent com-
    ing on the first and third beats, with the third-beat accent slightly
    weaker than the first

3/4 meter: three beats to a measure, each a quarter note

3/2 meter: three beats to a measure, each a half note

3/8 meter: three beats to a measure, each an eighth note

6/8 meter: six beats to a measure, each an eighth note, the accent com-
    ing on the first and fourth beats, the fourth being slightly less ac-
    cented than the first

9/8 meter: nine beats to a measure, each an eighth note, dividing itself
    into three groups of three eighth notes each

12/8 meter: twelve beats to a measure, each an eighth note, dividing it-
    self into four groups of three eighth notes each

It is possible, of course, to have 2, 3, or 4 beats in a measure
with *any* length of note as the unit; this note length may be
simple (divided into halves) or compound (divided into thirds).
As can readily be seen, the 6/8, 9/8, and 12/8 meters are illustrations of this — multiples of simple meters with 2, 3, and 4
units in measures that have internal divisions of thirds.

Such regular patterns of meter, when used with invariable
regularity, lay the music open to the charge of being monotonous.
So composers are apt to use various means for avoiding this
monotony incurred by an overdose of regularly recurring down-

beats. One of the most popular of these is syncopation — the shifting of an accent in a measure, so that it does not come where we expect it naturally. For example, instead of having the accents in a measure occur according to the usual scheme, ↓⌣↓⌣ | ↓⌣↓⌣ |, we may have ⌣↓⌣↓ | ⌣↓⌣↓ |; or instead of ↓⌣⌣ | ↓⌣⌣ | we often have ⌣↓⌣ | ⌣↓⌣ |, or even ⌣⌣↓ | ⌣⌣↓ |.

This device seems either to dull our rhythmic sense by confusing us as to where the strong pulse actually should come and thus gives a ʻcertain flagging or rhythmically dulled character to what we hear; or, by strongly stimulating our curiosity as to where the beat will fall, it heightens effect and makes the music that much more interesting. (*Vide* the feet of those listening to popular music, which contains so many interesting syncopated effects.) In passing it should be noted that, despite the belief generally held that syncopation is peculiar to contemporary popular music, it has been in wide use by composers since the time of the Renaissance. For a good illustration of this listen to the last movement of Handel's *Concerto grosso in B Flat,* Op. 6, No. 7.

Another device employed by composers, especially the more modern ones, to avoid monotony is that of inserting a measure or two of different metrical pattern into the regular flow of pulsation — of putting, for instance, a three-beat pattern into music that is regularly in two-beat measure. Tchaikovsky does this most effectively in the principal tune in his *Andante cantabile* from the *String Quartet,* Op. 11. (See page 195.) Composers from Debussy on have not hesitated to mix more or less indiscriminately the metrical pattern of their measures; in Debussy's *Afternoon of a Faun,* as we shall see, the meter fluctuates between 9/8, 6/8, 12/8, 3/4, and 4/4, and in Stravinsky's *Sacre du printemps* one page may contain as many as four metric patterns.

A new rhythm is sometimes superimposed over the regular one, a device often used by Brahms, in this fashion: 1 2 3 | 1 2 3

1 2 | 1 2

Sometimes in these superimposed rhythms the first beats of the succeeding measures do not coincide; then we have an even more striking polyrhythmic effect, thus:

| 1 2 3   1 2 3 |
| 1 2 | 1 2 | 1 2 |

This can be heard in good jazz music: over a fundamental, unchanging bass rhythm, the popular composer places freer rhythms, which often seem to play havoc with the underlying pulse of the piece. Again this is nothing new, for the same device was used, and very cleverly, too, by the scores of madrigal composers who flourished all over Europe before the time of Shakespeare; some of these madrigals contain most ingenious conflicts of meter between the various parts of which they are made up.

PRACTICE IN METER

The metrical pattern of a piece of music is comparatively easy to recognize, since this sort of rhythmic pulse is so largely physical and our response to it is almost a reflex action. Everyone can be taught to " keep time " to a metrical beat, even if some of the other fundamentals of music persist in escaping him. Here are some suggested examples for practice in determining the difference between duple, triple, quadruple, and sextuple meters. Hum or whistle the tunes, tapping out the heavy beats with a pencil, or with your foot on the floor:

" Old Black Joe "
" America " (" God Save the King ")
Humoresque
" Long, Long Ago "
" Abide with Me "
" Onward, Christian Soldiers "
Sur le pont d'Avignon (" On the Bridge at Avignon ")
" The Last Rose of Summer "
" Annie Laurie "
O Tannenbaum (" Maryland, My Maryland ")
Ach! du lieber Augustin
" Minuet in G "

OTHER ASPECTS OF RHYTHM

It should not take much listening practice to make one realize that there are rhythmic schemes in music other than purely metrical ones. In other words, the recurrence of some readily recognized metrical pattern is not the only way by which the features of a musical conception may be organized so as to " produce a harmonious whole through the correlation and interdependence of its parts." (See the definition of *rhythm* at the bottom of the picture facing page 29.) There is, for example, the rhythm of note duration, which music imposes upon the underlying metrical scheme of a composition. We do not necessarily have a note for each beat of the meter; some notes are held for one or two beats, while often a beat is divided among several notes.

In the familiar tune " Old Folks at Home," we can easily establish the underlying metrical pattern as being 4/4; but if we tap this out rhythmically while singing the melody, we shall find that the note values of the melody are in the following proportions:

The nature of these note values contributes another rhythmic scheme to the whole effect which we gain from listening to music and has a great deal to do with the impressions we receive.

Then there are other rhythmical designs in music, many of them intricate and difficult to hear, for they are made up of melodic and chordal features; these we may leave to the carefully trained expert to recognize and enjoy. The idea that several kinds of rhythmic schemes exist side by side in an art work may be difficult for the listener to grasp at first; but if we compare music with literature, which likewise has various types of rhythmic organization,[3] the realization may be made easier.

[2] Silence regarded as the mere absence of sound is an important factor in music; its length of duration is indicated by rests, which have values corresponding to the notes.

[3] In order to avoid confusion we should apply the term *rhythm* in general to the organizational schemes by which the various features of a piece of music or poetry are formed into an integral whole — the organization of tones of differing lengths, the subtleties of placing measure against measure, phrase against phrase, sentence against sentence. Meter should be used to describe that type of rhythm which is measured by dividing the flow of music or poetry into units made up of definite arrangements of pulses or beats.

If we recite Housman's lines from "A Shropshire Lad," stressing the regular beats of the metrical scheme, we get the following:

˘ ↓ ˘ ↓ ˘↓˘↓
With rue my heart is laden

˘ ↓ ˘ ↓ ˘ ↓
For golden friends I had,

˘ ↓˘⌒ ↓ ˘ ↓˘ ↓
For many a rose-lipt maiden

˘   ↓˘⌒ ↓   ˘ ↓
And many a light-foot lad.

Notice (1) that there is a certain rhythm in the line lengths — lines 1 and 3 have four metrical units in them, but lines 2 and 4 only three; (2) that in order to get the real sense of this verse we must continue without pause (we must " phrase," as the technical term has it) from line 1 into line 2 and from line 3 into line 4. Full comprehension of these lovely lines comes only when we combine, when reading them, all the rhythmic elements they possess.

So, too, with music; it is made up of many subtle interactions of the various rhythmic elements. This is easy enough to prove; listen to these examples of 2/2 meter, all of them chosen from Beethoven's scores. Notice how all the elements which go to make up the rhythmic impression are responsible for the total effect you receive from the music:

(1) *Eroica Symphony*, Second Movement (at the beginning). Here the slow tempo (pace of the music) and the way the notes are grouped in the measure give a solemn-heavy, funeral-march effect.

(2) *Seventh Symphony*, Second Movement. Here a quicker tempo and a broad arrangement of the notes give an effect that is not so over-powering and oppressive.

(3) *Fifth Symphony*, Fourth Movement. The dignified tempo and the exultant melody combine to give a joyous, buoyant effect.

It is the same with 3/4 measure:

(1) Johann Strauss's waltz, " Tales from the Vienna Woods," or any other good waltz, such as Tchaikovsky's from *The Nutcracker Suite*. The lively tempo and the enticing melodic patterns make us want to dance.

(2) *Largo* by Handel. Here the slow tempo and the dignified arrangement of the notes give a sort of religious effect. If you look at the melody carefully, you will find that only two measures of those which contain more than one sound have the same rhythmic pattern. This theme *grows*. In the hands of an ordinary patterner, measures 5–8 would probably have reproduced the lengths of measures 1–4. But Handel was after real rhythm, and so he subtly varied his scheme. This subtlety is an essential part of musical form.

If further time allows, you will be interested in determining the metrical schemes of such examples as these:

March from *Tannhäuser*	Wagner
Mazurka in C Sharp Minor, Op. 63, No. 3	Chopin
Polonaise in B Flat Major, Op. 40, No. 1	Chopin
Minuet from *G Minor Symphony*	Mozart
Bolero	Ravel
Pavane pour une infante défunte (*Pavan for a Dead Princess*)	Ravel
Tango in A Minor	Albeniz
Twilight in Turkey	Scott

Enough suggestions have been given here to enable the hearer to realize how some recognition of the rhythmic structure of a piece of music will help his enjoyment. The important thing to remember is that in learning to listen, everything cannot be grasped at once; a general conception of the rhythmic flow is all that is necessary for the amateur. If you want more detailed accounts of the possible intricacies of rhythm, you will find them in the books listed at the end of this chapter.

TOPICS FOR FURTHER DISCUSSION

Lovers of modern dance music often speak of it as " rhythmic music " as if to distinguish it from " classical " or " serious " music. But the first complaint of musicians against jazz is that it lacks rhythmic life. What do the musicians mean?

Is rhythm an end, or a means?

What is meant by " cross rhythms "? Find and discuss the use of cross rhythms in such composers as Brahms and Beethoven.

SUGGESTIONS FOR READING

What to Listen for in Music, Copland. (New York: McGraw-Hill)

The Art of Enjoying Music, Spaeth. (New York: McGraw-Hill)

Chapters II, III, and IV deal with rhythm in an extended way which may interest you if you are familiar with popular songs.

CHAPTER IX

Means by Which Materials Are Made into Music (Continued)

MELODY

IF, as we have said, " in the beginning of music there was rhythm," the element of melody could not have been far behind; it is impossible to discuss one of these primary factors of present-day music without considering the other. Melody, which can be defined as a successive sounding of tones that are related to each other in such a way as to make musical sense and coherent expression, has an emotional significance in music, just as rhythm has a physical significance. Neither can be thought of as separate, disembodied entities; except in the most primitive music (such as the exciting examples brought to us from Africa by the recording companies), whenever we think of rhythm we think also of the shadow of the melody associated with it. You can easily prove this for your own satisfaction: try to think of the rhythm of even such a simple piece as " Old Folks at Home " or " Tales from the Vienna Woods," and you will find yourself humming the melody in order to do so. These two elements may be called the inseparable Siamese twins of music.

All compositions are made up of some sort of melodic and rhythmic patterns, repeated and varied in different ways throughout the course of the music. And so if we are to gain an adequate knowledge of the music we hear, it will be necessary for us to train ears and minds so that we become conscious of these musical *themes* and remember them. Such simple tunes as we have mentioned above are recognizable to us readily enough because we have heard them from our earliest days. But what about those others with which we are not familiar — those hundreds of themes or motives, sometimes only a few notes in length, some-

times several measures long, which occur in the compositions that
are unknown to us — how are we to learn and remember these?

Here are some hints for assisting your memory in this
respect:

(1) Notice the peculiarities of the melodic flow, whether,
for instance, it is limited, as is the case of this theme from the
slow movement of Beethoven's *Seventh Symphony* (the interest
here is almost entirely rhythmic):

Or whether it skips about more or less adroitly, as in these
two examples from Mozart's *G Minor Symphony*, first movement:

(2) See whether the quality of the melody is essentially vocal or instrumental — whether it was meant to be sung or played.

Such a theme as this, from Beethoven's *Ninth Symphony*,
first movement, is obviously instrumental in style, its wide range
and great leaps making it almost impossible to be sung:

The following theme, from Verdi's *Rigoletto*, was, on the
other hand, meant for singing:

Such themes as that from Handel's opera *Xerxes,* quoted on page 70, or from Schubert's *Unfinished Symphony,* first movement (page 77), or Dvořák's *New World Symphony,* second movement (page 186) are suitable for either playing or singing. They are naturals in this respect, a fact which accounts for their unusual popularity.

(3) Observe the characteristic rhythmic patterns of the themes.

The theme from Beethoven's *Seventh Symphony,* quoted just above, has a rather monotonous rhythm — probably Beethoven intended this in order to emphasize its quality. But notice the rhythmic vitality of this melody from Mozart's *G Minor Symphony:*

Here is one of the most carefully organized melodies in all music, so far as its rhythmic patterns are concerned. But even a first hearing of it will tell you that Beethoven begins with a complicated, " dotted " rhythm and then follows with a broad, simple one:

(4) Take notice of the scale or scales used by the composer in forming his melody. Technically speaking, all melodies exist within the limits of some scale (a term which Webster defines as " a graduated series of tones, ascending or descending in order of pitch according to a specified scheme of their intervals "). Such scale arrangements have varied at different times and in dif-

ferent countries; in general they may be said to have been arbi-
trarily chosen, although they have a certain justification in
physical laws.

At the present time we use three of these scale patterns in
our ordinary music. Others exist, but they are variants of these
three — either obsolete scales, such as were used in medieval
church music, or foreign variants, found in other musical systems.

A. The simplest of these " alphabets of music " is the major
scale. If you look at the keyboard of a piano, you will notice that
the black keys are placed in a certain definite position amongst
the white. Each represents a tonal difference of one half tone (the
smallest interval in common use in music) from its neighboring
white key. The white keys are a tone's distance away from each
other, with the exception of E and F, and B and C, which (since
there are no black keys between them) are only a half tone away
from each other.

Now if you start from C and play all the white keys in succession until you reach the next C (easily recognizable because
of its tonal similarity to the note from which you started), you
will have traversed a certain recognizable series of tones and half
tones in a definite order:

C to D; D to E; E to F; F to G; G to A; A to B; B to C
tone ; tone ; ½ tone; tone ;   tone ; tone ; ½ tone

This series — tone, tone, half tone, tone, tone, tone, half
tone — is known as the pattern of the major scale. Starting from
any tone on the piano, the same order of sequence may be used,
thus forming the major scale of the starting tone. Try it and see,
starting on D or E, and using the black notes where necessary to
keep the proper sequence of tones and half tones. A great deal of
the music that we know well is written in one of these major
scales; the use of this pattern gives the music a bright, rather full
and cheerful character which is all the more noticeable when
compared with most music written in the minor scale.

B. There are several types of minor scales. One, which we
may call the " natural " minor, is just one of the ancient ecclesiastical modes, lying between A and A on the piano (white keys
only). Its succession of spaces runs: tone, half tone, tone, tone,
half tone, tone, tone. (From C it is C, D, E flat, F, G, A flat,
B flat, C.)

In the "harmonic" minor, only one of these tones is changed — the seventh, which is raised. The order is thus: tone, half tone, tone, tone, half tone, tone and a half, half tone. Taking it from C, it produces these tones:

C to D; D to E flat; E flat to F; F to G; G to A flat; A flat to B; B to C
tone ;   ½ tone ;   tone ;   tone ;   ½ tone   ; tone and ½; ½ tone

The extra-large space (tone and a half) making this inconvenient for singing melodies, we use the "melodic" minor scale, in which a different arrangement ascending and descending gives a smoother progression. Thus:

ASCENDING:
C to D; D to E flat; E flat to F; F to G; G to A; A to B; B to C
tone ;   ½ tone ;   tone ;   tone ;   tone ;   tone ;   ½ tone

DESCENDING:
C to B flat; B flat to A flat; A flat to G; G to F; F to E flat; E flat to D; D to C
tone ;   tone   ;   ½ tone ;   tone ;   tone   ;   ½ tone   ; tone

C. The chromatic scale comprises all the notes that lie within the space of an octave on the piano; it thus uses both the black and the white keys, producing a scale of twelve tones (or thirteen, if we include the octave duplication of the starting note):

C, C sharp, D, D sharp, E, F, F sharp, G, G sharp, A, A sharp, B, C

It is these various scale tones that, arranged according to the composer's desires, form our melodies. When these conform generally to the major scale, we call them "melodies in the major mode"; when they lie mostly in the minor scales, we speak of them as being "minor melodies." Both major and minor melodies often make excursions into the chromatic scale without losing their distinctive major or minor flavor.

To our ears music in a minor mode has a more somber or melancholy sound than that in the major, though this distinction is by no means universal, for there are lively dances written in the minor in some countries. Listen to the same melody when played in the major and the minor and you will quickly recognize the difference:

In Major   In Minor (Harmonic form)

Here are some fine melodies on which to practice. Get them firmly fixed in your mind and then notice the way they are used by the composer in building up a larger organized piece; you will realize the necessity of holding fast to melodic units when listening to music:

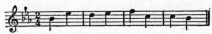

Although consisting of but two different notes, this motive can be easily remembered because of its strong rhythmic pattern; it is the first theme (or melody) of the opening part of Beethoven's *Fifth Symphony* and might be in either major or minor mode, according to the harmonies that are used with it. Beethoven uses it here as a minor melody.

This beautiful, longer melody in the major mode is the second theme of the same movement of the *Fifth Symphony*:

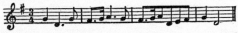

Listen to the whole movement and you will hear how it is built up largely of manipulations of these two germ themes.

Here is a still longer melody, but one that is easily remembered, nevertheless. It is a theme from the first movement of Schubert's *Unfinished Symphony*, and is in the minor; notice that the first two measures are exactly the same:

The next theme of the same movement is one of the best-known melodies in existence:

Listen to the movement as a whole, and you will hear these two tunes used constantly throughout.

Sing this melody; it is built simply and sturdily and therefore is not hard to read and remember:

It is from the second movement of Haydn's *Surprise Symphony*. Hear the whole movement and you will notice that here, even more than in the other examples cited, the composer makes use of it throughout the movement.

In this famous tune from the first section of Grieg's first *Peer Gynt Suite* there is so much repetition that it stays easily in the mind:

The whole piece will give you a fine idea of how music can logically grow out of a short, simple melody.

If a melody stays for most of its existence in the chromatic scale, we call it a *chromatic* melody; on the other hand, if it does not stray from its major or minor outlines, we speak of it as being *diatonic*. There is almost as much difference between music that is based largely on chromatic melodies and that which is diatonic in character as there is between major and minor melodies. Chromatic tunes are bland and lush; in comparison, diatonic ones seem severe and plain. Compare, for example, Rimsky-Korsakoff's well-known " Song of India " with the melody quoted above from Haydn's *Surprise Symphony* and you will quickly hear this difference. Or notice the difference in effect (carefully calculated by the composer) between such diatonic themes of Wagner's as that of " The Sword " from *The Ring of the Nibelung*

and his famous chromatic theme from *Tristan and Isolde*, portraying with relentless intensity the burning anguish and longing of the two famous lovers:

Here is one of the most famous short themes in all music, and no better or more appealing example of how melodies are wrought into larger wholes could be found. This gives us a definite illustration of the fact that one of the best means for getting an " ear-hold " upon music is through learning to recognize good melodies, and then listening how the composer builds his musical fabric out of them. This little germ is at the basis of nearly all the Prelude to Wagner's opera *Tristan and Isolde*.

(5) Finally, listen carefully to the characteristic tone quality of the instrument or instruments producing the melody.

Try to memorize themes *in their instrumental timbres;* an oboe theme, for example, stays in the memory longer if we can remember it as being played on the oboe and not just as a succession of notes.

We have already discussed this matter of *timbre* in another chapter; here it simply remains to be said that the ability to distinguish " tone color " (we use this phrase because no better one is available) or quality of the various instruments and voices singly and in combination is one of the most obvious pleasures we can derive from listening. It will be treated at greater length later on in this book.

HARMONY

It is common practice to use the word *harmony* to mean a pleasing concord or a musical consonance; so it will be necessary at the beginning of our discussion of this, the most sophisticated of the elements of music, to say that the musician uses the word in a different way. We may define *harmony* as the simultaneous sounding of tones as opposed to their successive sounding in melody. Both melody and harmony use the same materials: melody gives contour and color to the structure, and harmony provides it with body and substance. Although we must here treat these factors individually, melody, harmony, and rhythm are interdependent in actual practice. The detailed consideration of harmony is hardly a matter for the amateur listener, although he can readily enough realize that most of the music he hears is dependent upon harmony for its effect. Harmonic support is given melody through the forming and connecting of simultaneous clusters of tone that we call *chords,* and the science of harmony consists of a study of the ways in which these chords are built and related to one another. There are many tonal combinations that can be formed by putting together clusters of three, four, five, sometimes even as many as six and seven notes; these progress and come to rest according to certain grammatical laws common to the language of music.

If you listen to the overture to Wagner's *Tannhäuser,* you will quickly realize that the effect of the opening strains is due as much to the chords that Wagner uses as to the suitable rhythm and the impressive melody. When the change of mood comes in the middle of the overture, you will notice that the type of harmony changes as well. How much of the broad effect that we receive from Handel's *Largo* is due to the fine, straightforward, majestic chords employed! A review of the excerpts already quoted as illustrations of melodies and rhythms will show how much the chords employed in each example contribute to our interest in the music. Perhaps the most striking example of this is the Schubert melody, quoted on page 77. Hearing it alone gives us a great deal of pleasure, but when we put chords beneath it, it seems almost like another thing in the fullness of its beauty.

In general when the chords used in a composition conform to the major or the minor scale, we say that the piece is " in the major " or " in the minor." When the chords used are built out of the tones of the chromatic scale, the harmonization is said to be *chromatic;* or if the notes used keep in the diatonic scale, we speak of the chords as being *diatonic.* In the *Tannhäuser* overture the opening measures are in diatonic harmony; the middle section is decidedly chromatic in its harmonization.

Certain harmonic units, such as the chord usually found at the very end of a composition, are static and reposeful; we call these chords *consonances.* Others, used to provide impetus and zest to music, are not static, but restless and unfinished, and require some other chord to follow them and complete them. These we call *dissonances;* and the process of finishing a dissonant chord by a consonant one is called *resolution.* As music has advanced through the centuries, composers have turned more and more to the dissonant type of harmony. The music of a composer of as late a period as the eighteenth century consists largely of consonant harmonies, with occasional dissonances used to spice it up and heighten its interest. The process is almost exactly reversed in the music of almost all of the twentieth-century composers.

TONALITY

Even the briefest consideration of music from the viewpoint of its harmonic context must include a mention of *tonality*, one of the most subtle and yet powerful assets of the art. Practically all the music we hear (except that of some contemporary composers) is in one " key " or another; by this we mean that the notes which comprise our tonal system are grouped in specific sets of relationships to a tone which serves them as a sort of axis — a tone from which the movement within each of these sets of relationships (called *keys*) starts and to which it returns as a final resting place. This tone is the keynote or tonic. Since any one of the twelve tones within the octave can serve as a tonic, the composer has at his disposal twelve different tonal planes in which to write his music. Suppose he chooses one — that of the key of C, for example; he may decide to write music composed of melodies and chords that use the major scale which begins on that tonic, as Beethoven did in his *First Symphony,* or he may write music using the minor scale starting on that tonic, as Beethoven did in his *Fifth Symphony.*[1]

And so with all the other tones within the octave — C♯, D, D♯, and the rest: each can serve as a tonic for either a major or a minor scale and, since each of these scales has its own set of tonal relationships and its own groups of chords, composers have twenty-four tonal levels on which to erect their music — twenty-four keys, twelve major and twelve minor. When we speak of the tonality or the key of a piece, then, we describe (1) its specific tonal level; that is, the tonic around which its tonal structure is centered; and (2) the set of tonal relationships (the scale or the mode) which generally prevails. The title of Bach's *Suite No. 1 in C Major* means simply that its prevailing tonality centers around C as a tonic and that the scales, chords, melodies, and so on which go to make up its fabric are in the major mode. His second suite, on the other hand, centers about B as a tonic (its pitch level is thus half a tone lower than that of the first suite), and it is written in the minor mode. When Bach wrote the two great collections of clavier music which comprise his *Well-tempered Clavichord,* he deliberately used each of the twelve major and twelve minor keys as tonics for the pieces, thus making a total of twenty-four in each collection.

[1] In the case of large works such as symphonies, sonatas, and quartets, the tonality is determined by the prevailing key of the first movement — thus we have Beethoven's symphonies in C major and C minor, in E flat major, in B flat major, and so on.

This may seem intricate enough to the amateur listener, but it is not all that he should learn about the subject of tonality. For pieces have tonality not only as wholes but also in parts; in other words, a composer does not keep to the same tonality (or, putting it into other words, does not keep in the same key) throughout the course of a piece. He purposely uses changes of key (called *modulations*) to hold and increase the interest as the music progresses; a simple song usually contains several of these key changes, and a great work, such as a Beethoven or a Brahms symphony, contains scores of them. The constant shifting of tonal levels, now lower, now higher, intrigues our interest as we listen to a long work much the same way that a hiker's progress up and down a mountain affects his appreciation of the view that greets his eye as he walks. In each case the general impression received is not altered, but the continual change of points of view gives renewed interest and freshened enthusiasm.

In the case of the composer, these modulations must be skillfully and effectively wrought; any violent or awkward change from one key to another is liable to destroy rather than create interest. And it is a tribute to the technical skill of the great composers that most of us, in listening to their music, are quite unaware that such changes are taking place until they are pointed out to us. We have been affected by them unconsciously; they have increased our enjoyment of the music and heightened our imaginative realization of its content; and yet they have been so unobtrusively accomplished that we probably never knew they existed. Any attempt which the listener may make to realize the manner in which a composer takes him on these tonal adventures cannot but increase his enjoyment of the music he hears. It may be difficult to follow all the devious paths and windings; that is hardly necessary. Just to realize what is happening adds zest to listening.

TOPICS FOR FURTHER DISCUSSION

It is charged against some modern works that they lack melody. Their defenders reply that melody formerly meant simply a familiar succession of sounds and that, as modern music presents unfamiliar successions, the old definition will not do. Is there a better one?

How did our present-day conceptions of harmony originate? Do you think that these are final, or will they eventually change?

What are some of the values in the ability to follow changes of tonality in a piece of music? Name any particular instances of changing tonality which give you special pleasure.

SUGGESTIONS FOR READING

The Scope of Music, Buck. (New York and London: Oxford)
Music: An Art and a Language, Spalding. (Boston: Schmidt)

CHAPTER X

How Does the Composer Work?

EVERYONE who has come under the spell of a great picture, a powerful novel, or a moving piece of music has wondered at some time or other what it was that impelled the painter or the writer or the composer to create — what there was about an artist that made him so different from his fellow men that he could paint as El Greco did, or compose as did Bach and Beethoven. Granting that such creative artists are endowed by nature with certain abilities which, when trained, enable them to excel their fellows in the technical procedures of putting ideas into paint or onto music paper, does this fact in any real way explain the qualities of such a picture as *The Penitent St. Peter*, painted by El Greco, or the glories of Bach's *B Minor Mass* and Beethoven's *Eroica Symphony*? What constrained the artist to bring such things into being; how was he able to give his work the meaning it has for us; what were the processes of his creation? These are the sort of questions the amateur is likely to ask as he becomes more and more familiar with art.

THE CREATOR A UNIQUE FIGURE

Such questions are not easy to answer. The first thing we must realize, in trying to arrive at some explanation of the way in which a creative artist " out of nothing brings a world into being," is how far apart such an individual is from those about him. He is no ordinary man, merely interested in the world as it appears to his senses; rather is he one who searches for significance in the scheme of life. He gathers the subject matter for his painting or his music partly from his own experience as a sensitive member of human society, partly through his sympathetic observation of the actions and reactions of such a society. His great-

EL GRECO: THE PENITENT ST. PETER

The penitence of the Apostle who denied his Lord was a favorite subject of the great Greek painter. This picture shows St. Peter awakening, as from a dream of despair. Hope for his forgiveness fills him with ecstasy, and reaches him, in the form of spiritual light, even after he had denied his Master, who had presented him with the keys of Heaven.

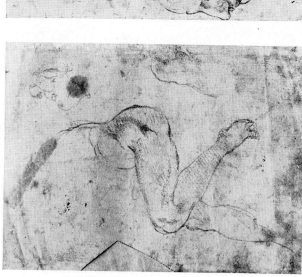

THE WAY FROM THE IMAGINATION OF THE PAINTER TO THE IMAGE

These sketches are excellent examples of the manner in which Michelangelo evolved the various sections of his great mural painting on the ceiling of the Sistine Chapel in Rome. Compare these sketches for the figure of the Libyan Sibyl with the finished painting. Then contrast this method of painting with that of Winslow Homer, the American artist, who, in painting his water color of a West Indian scene (facing page 88), obviously did so without any hesitation, putting his idea on paper as quickly as possible.

est endowment — outside that of technical aptitude — is his imaginational ability to extend and develop his own experiences, which necessarily are limited and fragmentary. Such a power, in itself, gives the creator an insight into human experience that is far superior to any participation he may have had at first hand. It explains El Greco's ability to project so vividly St. Peter's suppliant hope of forgiveness, or Beethoven's powerful concept of man the hero, bestriding the narrow world like a colossus.

Most of us are too closely concerned with life and its difficulties and joys to see things in perspective: we lack imagination to link what we experience today with what we have experienced in the past or what will follow after. Such specialists as the scientist and the historian are too far removed from realities to sense, or even comprehend, the quality and purport of life. The artist is the only one who seems able to see life steadily and as a whole, who is able to look at it as a " human being and yet not merely as a single individual, with passionate intensity, yet with dispassionate lucidity." This is what we mean when we say that men such as El Greco and Beethoven were inspired when they painted or composed; there is something in their best work — something put there by their very attributes as artists — that far transcends technical achievements or artistic proficiencies. And it is this that distinguished them from their less fortunately endowed fellows.

Most professional artists would probably deny that they have any such spiritual bases for creation. A contemporary American musician [1] has put himself on record as saying that to a composer composing is like fulfilling any other natural function such as eating or sleeping: he composes because he feels that he has been born for the job — because he can't help it. Of course, he adds, after the thing is done, everyone, especially the composer, hopes that it will turn out to have been " inspired." But that is really an idea that is tacked on at the end.

This is true enough, so far as generalities go, as everyone who has had any experience with creative workers must acknowledge. As a rule, artists do not sit around waiting for the divine afflatus; they turn to their creative tasks, whatever they may be, day after day, simply doing the best job of which they are capable. The dif-

[1] Aaron Copland in his book *What to Listen for in Music* (New York: McGraw-Hill).

ference between the great and the minor painter or composer is that the great artist, once the creative process is started, is likely to produce something of real significance to the world because of his greater sympathy with its experiences and his keener imaginative ability to extend and develop these sympathies — in a word, because of his ability to " apprehend the man in men." In so far as the actual physical processes of creation are concerned, the great men do not differ from those who merely produce competent work. A casual examination of such physical processes can give the listener a great deal of information that will be of value to him in criticizing the music he hears.

Various Composer Types

We have to face the fact, at the beginning of such an examination, that there can be no such being as a typical composer and no such thing as a regularly followed method of composing. There have been some composers — only a few — who have written music as if they had been possessed of some Apollonic daemon. Music simply welled out of their consciousness as water from a spring; their greatest difficulty seems to have been that of finding time enough to put it on paper. For them there were few problems of choice or arrangement of materials; whole works seem to have been spontaneously created in their minds with little or no conscious effort on their part. We have evidence of such prolific spontaneity on the part of two of the greatest of all composers, Mozart and Schubert, who must always remain as the outstanding examples of the inspired composer, writing music because nothing else in life seemed important or necessary.

Then there are those who have labored carefully and long over their works, starting with a few germinal ideas and painstakingly weaving them into an imposing and closely designed musical fabric. Beethoven may be cited as the characteristic example of this type; most of the oustanding men since his time — such composers as Brahms, Wagner, Strauss, for instance — have followed his example in this respect. The record shows that Beethoven was busy with his *C Minor Symphony* for a period of over five years, and that it took Brahms over twenty to write his great symphony in the same key [2]; naturally both men were busy with other things at the same time.

Some composers have given very little thought to any sort of constructive process: they simply took traditional patterns which had become well established by the time they arrived on the musical scene and used them to suit their own purpose. The composers of the Renaissance — such men as Byrd, Di Lasso, and Palestrina — used only the patterns and formal molds of their time, the motet, mass, madrigal. And Bach, when he started on the tremendous project of writing the forty-eight preludes and fugues in his *Well-tempered Clavichord,* or the Brandenburg concertos, did not depart from the accepted models of his time.

However, there have been other pioneering spirits who, dissatisfied with things as they found them and with the musical styles in which they had been reared, revolted, often at the expense of the quality of their music. In different centuries, Monteverdi, Berlioz, Debussy, and Schönberg are examples of this type of composer who has opposed conventional ways of doing things and who has sought, through experimenting with new resources, to develop a different, nonconformist type of writing. Naturally such a man's method of working would differ greatly from that of the traditionalists.

FIRST, THE IDEA

But there are certain fundamental practices common to all composers; the first of these is getting started. How is the creative process actually begun? A famous old recipe for rabbit pie, written in the days when meat was not so plentiful as it is today, starts with the admonition: first, you must catch your rabbit. Similar advice must be followed by every composer who would set about concocting tonal delicacies. All compositions, whether they are short or long, whether they are traditional or experimental, start with a musical idea [3]; perhaps it first occurs to the

---

[2] An early draft of Brahms's *C Minor Symphony* dates from 1850; the work was finished in 1876.

[3] Sometimes these ideas come to the composer in the most incongruous circumstances. It was the Austrian composer, Bruckner, who, pointing out the theme of a movement in one of his symphonies, is said to have remarked that it had come to him on a picnic, just as he was unwrapping the sandwiches.

composer in the shape of a melody that he can hum to himself, or a rhythmic pattern, sometimes merely as a suggestion for an accompaniment. Whatever it is, or however it may come, this theme (the name we give to such a musical idea) is the real *germ* out of which the composer later fashions his whole piece. It is, as Copland rightly says, a " gift from Heaven which comes almost like automatic writing "; the composer has no control over it except to write it down as quickly and as accurately as he can, adding it to his collection of similar items.

Obviously an important part of the composer's creation of such a musical theme is his evaluation of it in what might be called both its emotional and its musical terms. He is aware of its emotional value instinctively, realizing whether or not it provides the starting point for, or helps to develop, the type of human expression with which he is concerned at the moment. He examines it as music, noting its outline, its possibility for later " development," perhaps altering it here and there so that it may better fulfill his musical requirements. It may be that he is quite unconscious of the process, but the composer, once his thematic material has been revealed to him, immediately sets out to determine its nature and then to see what can be done with it.

It may be that a theme carries with it some emotional suggestion which the composer feels called upon to develop; it may well be the other way about, that some sort of emotional background was realized first, and that out of it there came the musical idea; or it may be that the whole creative process took place on a largely formal plane, the composer thinking of his music as music, without paying much attention to its expressive values. There are examples of all three of these different processes of composing. The sketches left by Beethoven may be interpreted to show that many of his themes came to him in a purely musical form, and that such expressive ideas as those dealing with the " awful powers of Fate and ending with a triumph song of the human will " were evolved afterwards, during his long struggle with his material. We know, on the other hand, that in such works as Richard Strauss's *Don Juan* and *Don Quixote* the whole of the extramusical program was achieved first, and that out of it came the musical material. And it is difficult to believe that Bach had anything in mind other than the formal manipulation of his material when composing some of his great works.

"Tornado" — Water Color by Winslow Homer

A MODERN PHOTOGRAPH OF THE RUINED PARTHENON ON THE
ACROPOLIS IN ATHENS

It is impossible to know whether the composer decides as to the medium that he will employ — whether he will write a string quartet, a symphony, an opera, or a piano sonata — before or after the time he catches his musical rabbit; that is, conceives his thematic material. Here again we have conflicting evidence. Instead of pondering as to whether his theme belongs in a symphony or in a string quartet, many a composer has evolved his themes directly for some work he had in mind. No other medium than the opera could ever have been intended for the delineative themes that Wagner created; he evolved them for particular dramatic purposes. Schubert's lyric melodies were, for the most part, conceived as songs, with no thought of their being used in any other medium. On the other hand, we have Brahms hesitating whether to use the thematic materials which finally went into his first piano concerto, in a sonata for two pianos, a symphony, or a concerto. Some of the most effective thematic material in Bach's great choral work, the *B Minor Mass,* had been used by him in earlier works, sometimes in quite a different medium [4]; his contemporary, Handel, did not hesitate to lift themes from his own works — and sometimes from those of another composer — whenever they seemed to fill some particular need of the moment.

Generally speaking, however, the composer has little trouble in satisfying himself as to either the inherent value or the essential quality of the ideas he has conceived. Once he has decided what he is going to write, his immediate problem is what to do with his thematic material, for, significant and suggestive as it may seem, it is far from being a piece of music. How is he going to spin it out into a composition that will last anywhere from several minutes (in the case of a song) to an hour (in the case of a symphony) or to several hours (in the case of an opera)?

PRINCIPLES OF DESIGN

In following the conventional ways of accomplishing this, the composer instinctively uses certain principles of design which are the foundation of all good art. If we examine any outstand-

---

[4] The theme of the *Osanna,* for instance, was originally used in a composition written as a welcome song to Bach's monarch, the King of Saxony.

ing art work — a finely designed building, a beautifully executed painting, a good piece of sculpture, a poem or a drama that has survived through the centuries — we shall find certain general principles of design that control the use of its structural elements. The creator may have followed these principles of design consciously or intuitively: the one thing for us to realize is that he did follow them. The most important of these principles are:

1. *Repetition,* usually according to some rhythmic scheme
2. The dominance of some particular feature of design and the subordination of others, so as to secure *Unity in Variety*
3. *Balance* or *Symmetry,* by means of which the various elements are held together and yet synthesized and organized into a harmonious whole

No definite rule or formula can be given for the use of these, or any other, artistic principles. But there exists within us a certain innate sense for good design, which, if we cultivate it, will grow into a power of discrimination of which we can be strongly conscious. We all react, for example, to these structural principles as they have been exemplified in the Parthenon, a religious temple built on the Acropolis at Athens, after plans by Ictinus and Callicrates: we instinctively know that this must have been a *good* building. Even today, some twenty-four hundred years after it was built, this magnificent structure still holds our attention and arouses our enthusiasm.

Notice the rhythm of the repeated vertical columns; the builders definitely established this sense of verticality as the dominant feature of their building; but see how carefully they used it in contrast to the horizontal lines above and below the repeated upright columns. The manner in which the various structural details are balanced and symmetrized, each having its part in the harmony of the whole, shows how keenly sensitive to beauty the Greeks were, and how highly developed were their tastes.

The composer, if he wishes to create a musical work of lasting value, pays careful attention to the same schemes of design. The principle of repetition is essential to any real intelligibility in music: in such a transitory art, the listeners must have certain features that can be grasped easily and recognized pleasurably. If you are inclined to doubt this, listen to some easily followed popular song, or to such a composition as Gershwin's *Rhapsody in Blue,* and see how many times certain themes and phrases [5] are repeated. This device of repetition is not confined to simple or popular music, however; composers of all sorts and in all periods have woven their musical fabrics out of a repetition and diversification of some melodic, harmonic, or rhythmic pattern.[6] While not many of them have gone to the lengths of Bruckner, who, in the scherzo of his *Eighth Symphony,* repeats the same pattern dozens of times, this device of repetition must always remain one of the composer's most useful assets. In the case of music, as has been well said, variety may be the spice of its life, but repetition is its bread and butter.

Every intelligent listener to good music has realized that there are certain dominant elements that stand out clearly in the musical fabric, that certain themes are emphasized and others added to complement or supplement them. These secondary themes may contrast strongly with the original ideas, or they may carry them along to final completion. Since the composer cannot jump abruptly from one theme to another, he has learned to make use of certain subordinate passages which he calls " bridge passages " — carefully designed links which carry the listener almost imperceptibly from one main idea to another. The beautifully constructed bridge material linking the first and second themes in the first movement of Beethoven's *Fifth Symphony* is a case in point.

Still another device at the disposal of the composer for this purpose is what we call *development,* something that is difficult to describe in words, although it can be recognized readily enough when heard. Listen to the middle section (that immediately following the double bar) of the Beethoven first movement just mentioned, and you will find that the composer views his original theme in a number of different aspects and puts it through a number of metamorphoses; this is the development, a logical and almost inevitable process that, when well used, adds greatly

[5] By *phrase* in music we mean certain melodic " sentences " which belong together and which come to a natural pause at their end; they are usually discernible by such exterior means as the number of measures they contain and the symmetry of their harmonic background.

[6] Here are some striking and easily recognized instances of musical repetition of one kind or another:

"Drink to Me Only with Thine Eyes"

Preludes in A major, C minor, and E minor, Op. 28, by Chopin

Opening movement, *Appassionata Sonata,* by Beethoven

to our listening enjoyment. We shall have more to say about this later on.

There are a number of different ways by which the composer may obtain balance and symmetry of design in his music. In fact, the musical *forms* — such as the fugue, the sonata form, the theme and variations — about which we have so much to tell later, are simply convenient and well-tried devices for achieving this end. They have changed throughout the centuries and are still in process of evolution; they have been variously used by different composers, but they all help to solve the same problem, that of attaining good balance and effective symmetry.

All these devices must be used by the composer in such a way as to secure an intelligent and pleasurable whole. This is where the skill of the composer comes in, in this welding together of disparate elements according to the structural principles of good design. He does not necessarily follow any rules, but he must so order his music that the listener can find his way around in it, can realize at any given moment what is going on. The piece, no matter how long it may be, should proceed logically from its beginning to its end; there should be a sense of relation of parts that leaves no room for confusion in the hearer's mind; and the music should be so cunningly put together as to show none of the seams by which its parts are joined, to use Tchaikovsky's picturesque phrase. Above all else there must be, in Mahler's words, " abundance and continuous *flow* if the music is to be any good." This all sounds easy enough in the telling; as a matter of fact, it is tremendously difficult of achievement, and upon it depends to a large degree the real quality and staying powers of a composer's output.

TOPICS FOR FURTHER DISCUSSION

Novelists have described their various methods of composition; for example, some think first of a plot, some of the idiosyncrasies of character in their figures; others build around a dramatic situation or a single scene. Are these processes paralleled in music?

Discuss the possible influence of *place* on composition.

Find elements of unity and variety in any simple compositions you may study.

Compare development in a symphonic movement with that in a novel or a play, either generally or with specific instances in mind.

Compare unity-plus-variety in a musical work with the same elements in a familiar picture or piece of sculpture.

SUGGESTIONS FOR READING

What to Listen for in Music, Copland. (New York: McGraw-Hill)
The State of Music, Thomson. (New York: Morrow)

CHAPTER XI

Beauty

THE RECOGNITION OF FORM

THE materials of which we have just spoken must be combined and used in such a manner as to convey a definite impression to our minds. Melodies cannot be introduced indiscriminately, without relationship to one another; there must be some definite rhythmic scheme underlying the music and some consistent plan of using harmonies. In other words, what the music is doing at any one moment depends upon and grows out of what it has done before and must point the way to what it is going to do next. Otherwise there is no sense in what we hear, no order — nothing but disjointed babblings of sound incapable of being apprehended by our minds, even though they may seem somewhat intriguing to our ears. This is the reason why so much of the recent music sounds bewildering. Although it may have a sense of order and form, we cannot grasp it because of the newness to us of this formal order, its difference from anything that we have known before. A first hearing of such a work as Stravinsky's *Le sacre du printemps* (*The Rite of Spring*) may give the impression that there is little or no evidence of formal order, although such order actually does exist.

WHAT IS BEAUTY?

Of course the newness of the formal " layout " is not the only reason why so much of the more modern music sounds strange; the conceptions of melody, harmony, and rhythm have changed throughout the course of the development of the art, and those used by the more recent writers — men like Stravinsky, Schönberg, and their followers — are entirely different from those with which we are generally familiar. We do not have to listen very long to a work like *Le sacre du printemps* to realize how true this is. There may be formal order and reason here, but it is of a sort difficult for us to find. There is certainly harmony, but how different it is from that to which we are used; there is melody of an unusual kind, and a peculiar, explosive, complicated set of rhythms. It seems somehow difficult to feel sure that these combine to make music that is worthy of our attention. Is this music anything more than an intellectual exercise done for the gratification of some esoteric individual's sense of pride in his skill? Has it, after everything is said and done, real beauty?

This question, like that famous one propounded by Pilate nineteen hundred years ago as to the nature of truth, is one that has troubled man ever since he has been aware that " beauty " exists. " What is truth? " and " What is beauty? " are questions that have held a strange fascination for men throughout the centuries. From Aristotle, who died in 322 B.C., to Croce, the present-day Italian philosopher, these perplexing questions have intrigued the minds of men, perhaps the more so since no real answer is possible. Only the Italians have been wise enough to realize that " truth is a mirage, while beauty, however subjective, is a possession and a reality." Schiller said that truth exists for the wise and beauty for the feeling heart, and Oliver Wendell Holmes said that " beauty is an index of a larger fact than wisdom."

How may we recognize beauty when we experience it in art? How can it be measured, since it is difficult to find anything which some persons will not declare beautiful, and some — now more, now fewer — ugly? How can there be any hope in trying to ascertain whether or not there is beauty in the music we hear, when one of the greatest artists who ever lived, Anatole France, admits in his book, *On Life and Letters:* " I believe that we shall never know exactly why a thing is beautiful "? Such questions the bewildered amateur listener has every right to ask. As sensitive and thoroughly equipped a critic as Lawrence Gilman told us that there is no touchstone that will enable us to detect the presence or absence of beauty in a piece of music. No wonder, then, that it is difficult for less experienced individuals to know what attitude to take towards music that they are disinclined to like! A short résumé of the general conception of the philosophers on the whole subject may help to clarify this problem.

TWO INTERPRETATIONS: DESIGN OR ETHICS?

Roughly speaking, there have been two general schools of thought throughout the years as to the nature of beauty: First, that which holds that the intangible quality of beauty in an object lies in the skillful arrangement of its parts in terms of order and symmetry, in repetition of design — in a word, in its form. Kant (1724–1804) in his *Critique of Judgment* correlates design and beauty; the beautiful, he says, is that which shows symmetry and unity of structure " as if it had been designed by intelligence." Beethoven's *Fifth Symphony* to such a thinker would be a work of beauty because of its strongly knit design, its progressive and continuous development from its beginning to its inevitable conclusion, its manifest signs of having been wrought by a great " intelligence." The other great school of thought upon the subject maintains that the beauty of a thing resides in the reactions which it arouses in the mind of the beholder. Beauty is not intrinsic in the object itself, but has rather an aesthetic existence in the observer's perception. Spinoza (1632–1677) considers " ugly " and " beautiful " to be two subjective terms: " Only in relation to our imagination can things be called beautiful or ugly, well-ordered or confused." And Professor E. F. Carritt of University College, Oxford, whose book *What Is Beauty?* contains a good summary of thought upon this whole subject, holds as his own belief that beauty is to be found in what is " expressive of feeling . . . when an arrangement of sound, shape, or color seems the natural and not artificial embodiment of an experience." To thinkers of this school, Beethoven's *Fifth Symphony* would be beautiful because of its ability to suggest naturally to the hearer concepts of an experience which he can recognize in it — Fate challenging Man to come out and do battle with his destiny, or whatever else it may be.

There have been other teachings as to the nature of beauty. The Greeks identified it with what was good and often with what was useful. Some of the more poetic thinkers have asserted that beauty and truth are synonymous. Ruskin thought beauty to be a reflection or emanation of divine perfection and so insisted that it is correlated with goodness, a point of view hardly tenable today! Anatole France says that our feeling for the beautiful is our

only guide in trying to determine what is or is not beautiful; but
this is not very helpful, unfortunately, since there are not many
men so sensitively equipped as he was. Professor Langfeld in his
The Aesthetic Attitude tells us that beauty is a relationship between two variables: the human organism and the object. And
this is the conception which Gilman advises us to hold regarding
beauty in music; he thinks that we should not try to speak of it
as if it were an absolute, detectable quality, " as positively present or absent as the property of roundness in a ball or sharpness
in a needle." It can be neither subjective nor objective, neither
the result of intellectual and emotional activity nor a value inherent in the object, neither dependent entirely upon the person
who experiences it, nor upon the thing experienced.

WHAT IS THE MUSICIAN'S SOLUTION?

Although it negates the validity of the contentions of both
great groups of thought, this practical way seems to be the only
one for the music lover to follow. We do not have to hear a great
deal of music in order to realize that our ideas of beauty can
never coincide with those of others, nor should we expect that
they would. To some, Schubert's music is supremely satisfying
in its natural beauty; others are not so enthusiastic about it.
There is beauty in Tchaikovsky for some, in Stravinsky for
others. There can be no real reason why we should affirm or
deny any of these " beauties "; only by adopting the point of
view that whatever beauty there is in music is a relationship between us as human individuals and the music which the composer has left us can we proceed to discuss what we hear intelligently and reasonably. Such a viewpoint clears up the seemingly
inexplicable differences of opinion that are constantly arising
among music lovers and critics. A person may be sincerely convinced, for instance, that Debussy's *L'après-midi d'un faune*
(*The Afternoon of a Faun*) is one of the world's great masterpieces, full of a strange beauty, belonging to a world entirely
outside our ordinary existence. Another person may strongly
deny this and feel that the texture of the music is thin, vapid,
that its peculiar method of construction does not lead us anywhere, even that its elusiveness and vagueness are pretenses for

hiding its essential poverty of ideas. At first we are inclined to
say, of course, that either the first man is right and that the other
is so obtuse that he cannot recognize beauty when it does not
conform to the usual models of Brahms, Beethoven, and Company; or that the second is right and that the first cannot recognize poor music when he hears it. It is, of course, difficult to put
aside these absolute ideas of music's being either beautiful or not
beautiful, for there are so many times when we feel sure, as in
the case of the music of Bach and Wagner. Yet the wise listener
knows that it must be done; he has learned from experience that
often beauty for him fades out of music which he once thought
would hold it to the end of his days, and that it can come into
music which he was sure could never possess it. The more experienced the music lover, the less dogmatic are his opinions as to
whether or not music is beautiful.

Yet there are guides which will help a musical pilgrim
through the confusing thought of conflicting opinions, pillars of
cloud and fire that he can trustingly follow in his long journey.
For it would be ridiculous to suppose that a person's opinions on
the beauty of music are merely a matter of taste, like that in
soups, dress, or other matters of individual opinion. There is,
however, one test that we may well apply to the music we hear:
is it alive — does it communicate to us a vividness of life, does
it seem as if the creator had been " alive with it at the moment
of creation "? As we become more and more familiar with music,
we realize the value of such a test: for all the works that have
survived the period that produced them certainly do possess this
sense of freshness, vividness of life, feeling of creative vigor.
This creative breath exists, of course, in varying degrees; it must
have blown with tremendous force when Bach wrote his *B Minor
Mass,* or Beethoven his *Eroica Symphony,* or Wagner his *Tristan
und Isolde.* It came more slowly and calmly to Brahms as he
set down for us the majestic measures of his *First Symphony,* or
to César Franck, lovable mystic in his organ loft, as he composed
his mighty *Chorals.* We may think it to have become almost
somnolent in Debussy as he depicts the pagan pleasures of *L'après-
midi d'un faune,* or tells us the sad story of those shadowy, symbolic figures, Pelléas and Mélisande, in one of the loveliest operas
ever written. But it breathes through all these works, as it does
through all the other great masterpieces of music.

Music in Its Own Terms

There is another reasonable test the listener might make: Does it keep within the limits of its own element, tone? Does it degenerate into noise, or, on the other hand, appeal largely through the intellect? In either case, it is not great music. Applying this to *Le sacre du printemps:* Does the composer descend to the level of mere noisemaking in his attempts to describe musically the rites of primitive man, or has he overstepped the natural boundaries of tonal possibilities and written music that is largely an intellectual *tour de force?* In either case, he would exceed the natural limitations of his material, and the result could not reasonably be called great art.

LIST OF SUGGESTED MUSIC

Le sacre du printemps   Stravinsky

A good problem in musical aesthetics is presented: Is it, or is it not, beautiful? If so, or if not, why?

Prelude and Love Death, *Tristan und Isolde*   Wagner

This is music that possesses the " sense of freshness, vividness of life, feeling of creative vigor."

TOPICS FOR FURTHER DISCUSSION

Where do you conceive beauty to exist in the mind and intentions of the type of serious composer or artist broadly described as " extremist "?

Is there any parallel between the qualities of extremist music and those of modern sculpture or painting?

How is it that lovers of classical or romantic music can definitely describe and account for the beauty they find in that music, while lovers of extremist music seem unable to do so? Is this ability a legitimate standard of beauty?

Can there be a type of beauty which only the producer of the work can see or hear?

SUGGESTIONS FOR READING

What Is Beauty? Carritt. (New York and London: Oxford)
The Aesthetic Attitude, Langfeld. (New York: Harcourt, Brace)
Discords Mingled, Engel. (New York: Knopf)
    Chapter on *De Gustibus*

CHAPTER XII

Our Way of Approach

ART AND LANGUAGE

A POETIC critic, Romain Rolland, has said that music can be all things to all men: tonal architecture in certain centuries and among certain peoples; design, line, and plastic beauty to such nations as have cultivated a sense of form — to painters and sculptors like the Italians; an intimate poetry, a lyric efflux, a philosophical meditation to a poetic and philosophical nation such as the Germans; an *art de coeur,* gallant and graceful to Francis I or Charles IX; a weapon of faith and combat to reformers such as Martin Luther; a matter of princely pride and royal pomp to kings such as Louis XIV; an art of the salon during the eighteenth century; a lyric expression of tremendous personalities during the nineteenth. It is obviously not only an art but a language, capable of expressing widely divergent ideas and conceptions, including those generally regarded as belonging to the spheres of the other arts.

MUSIC'S WORLD OF THE SPIRIT

A moment's reflection, however, will show us that music has its own distinct province and that while it perhaps can go as far as embodying moral ideas, it expresses some things much better than others. Its great strength lies in depicting emotions rather than thoughts, in realizing intangible moods rather than concrete forms, in depicting ideality rather than reality, and most of all, in appealing to the spirit rather than to the senses.

We readily follow a great man like Beethoven when his music stirs our emotions as it does in the *Fifth Symphony*. But we are not so sure of him, or of ourselves, when he places mottoes

like *Tantôt libre, tantôt recherché,* or *Muss es sein? — es muss
sein* at the beginning of certain movements in his last quartets
as if he would convey some metaphysical concept in his music.
We quickly respond to the melancholy brooding of Tchaikovsky
in his *Symphonie pathétique,* or to the alluring Eastern colors of
Rimsky-Korsakoff's *Scheherazade,* or to the healthy vigor of
Brahms's *First Symphony;* but it is more difficult for us to realize
the comparatively simple structural design of these compositions,
and thus to appreciate their architectural proportions. We seem
ready to follow Brahms in such a song as his *Feldeinsamkeit,* when
he muses so beautifully upon the fields and the sky, but we are
more reluctant to trail Honegger's locomotive, *Pacific 231,* as
it snorts and groans in its attempts at realism. Wagner, who wrote
that great series of operas, *The Ring of the Nibelung,* and Debussy in his tone poem, *L'après-midi d'un faune,* appeal mightily
to our spirits, but it will seem difficult for many of us to get
" sense " from these works.

Furthermore, music possesses a distinction from its associated
arts in that it is so largely independent of exterior associations,
this very fact constituting one of its chief glories, or its most
confusing difficulties, according to our point of view. By comparison the static arts are easier of comprehension. No matter
how imaginative the treatment, in order to convey his meaning
the painter, architect, or sculptor commonly uses means that are
closely associated with the consciously experienced world. Even
literature, which comes closest to music as a means for emotional
and imaginative suggestiveness, must use a medium closely associated with everyday life — that of language.

Everyone knows the familiar story of Turner, the English
artist, and the woman who told him that she had never seen such
sunsets as he painted. " No, but don't you wish you could? "
was certainly the right answer to such a statement. Music does
not even need to try to explain the lack of such relationships.
Although it works with two familiar yet intangible factors,
rhythm and sound, it uses them for the most part in ways entirely different from those in which they occur in nature. The
combination of these elements in music affects our senses in ways
different from those of the other arts, ways which we hardly
understand and which have no counterparts in our other emotional experiences. And they make of music a peculiarly dynamic

art; instead of allowing it to be examined at any length, they cause it to rush precipitately at us, sometimes with the passionate eloquence of a great orator, sometimes with almost intangible persuasiveness. But in any case it is gone beyond recall almost before we are conscious of its having existed, and must be re-created before we can again be aware of its qualities.

PROGRAM MUSIC

Various types of music differ in their extra-musical associations. All of us can remember music which definitely imitates sounds such as bird-calls, storms, and so on, for who has not at some time in his listening career suffered under the " storms " of the sensational organ player's making? That such definite imitations of nature are not necessarily the resort of cheap musicians only is shown by the fact that no less a composer than Beethoven makes use of these very devices; in his *Pastoral Symphony* we find the mood of the music heightened by a musical suggestion of a peaceful brook rippling over the stones, the calls of various birds, the growling of the thunderstorm. We all know that certain sounds definitely suggest certain states of mind to us; in fact, these sounds may induce these states of mind. The hunt is suggested, for example, by the sound of the horn as it is heard at the beginning of the second act of Wagner's *Tristan und Isolde*. In the last section of Liszt's rather oversensational *Les Préludes*, the blare of brass, delivered in all the enthusiasm of this composer's style, excites us to martial ardor. The plaintive longing of the English horn, wonderfully expressed in the shepherd's tune at the beginning of the last act of *Tristan und Isolde*, awakens our consciousness to an answering mood of brooding melancholy. Many other similar examples could easily be cited. And so a composer, using these means and coupling them with the various devices of composition, may easily give music an extraneous implication, may make it set forth a sequence of pictures, tell a story, or what you will. This kind of music having connection with something outside itself we know as program music.

Here comes in again the consideration as to the composer's working within the natural limitations of his material, a matter discussed in the previous chapter; for program music does require an intellectual approach. Since tone, the natural sensuous element of music, does have duration in time, it would seem aesthetically justifiable to relate, by means of a " program," what is happening at any particular moment in the music to what has already happened and to that which is going to happen in the future. Provided — and this is the crux of the whole matter — the composer can convey the objective quality demanded by the program of the music itself. In other words, in works inspired by a literary association, if the music as music (and not because of its intellectual program) communicates to us a conception of inherent beauty and organic unity, our enjoyment of it cannot be questioned, even on the strictest aesthetic grounds. For this reason, Beethoven's *Eroica Symphony* in memory of a great man is an outstanding musical triumph, for the music is essentially heroic in itself; Strauss's *Till Eulenspiegel* and *Don Juan*, Wagner's " Siegfried's Funeral March " or " Isolde's Love Death," all of them frankly programmatic to the utmost degree, can nevertheless be ranked as among our greatest masterpieces. In all of them one can sense the spirit of their program *in the music itself*, and one does not have to depend upon an intellectual reading to give them meaning.

ABSOLUTE MUSIC

In direct contrast to this is the pure or absolute type of music. This music is based upon definite laws of structure and development rather than depending upon an appeal through associations with literary or illustrative ideas. In this music the tone must be good, the proportions well-balanced, the harmonies clear and understandable. But it is difficult to draw a line of demarcation between these types and say that on one side is program music, on the other absolute. Such a thing as a Bach fugue (the organ *Fugue in G Minor* is a good example), in which the structure of the music is a matter of paramount importance, the whole thing growing to a tremendous climax under the structural genius of its composer; or a Haydn quartet (the one in F major, Op. 3, No. 5, for instance) with its detached, impersonal attitude to everything except the weaving together of tonal patterns — these are as near to absolute music as we can get. The materials in these compositions are arranged in certain sequences, and their significance is of aesthetic beauty rather than of emotional content. But music which seems to have been written with the idea of pure tonal concepts may contain dramatic and impressionistic material, and vice versa, so that definite boundaries between these types are not easy to establish.

The subject of program *vs.* absolute music has given rise to many vigorous debates. One of the best discussions of it will be found in Ernest Newman's *Musical Studies.* We need not even attempt to summarize further the arguments here; the topic would make an excellent one for debate among music lovers. It will suffice to suggest that, as program music has always existed (there are naïve examples in the earliest art music) it evidently springs from a deep natural desire to relate music to life. Obviously, such music is likely to appeal in its own terms. If we are really musical, we work through the more simple forms of program music pretty quickly, but he would surely be a sadly pedantic person who would refuse to open his heart to *Till Eulenspiegel* because of cast-iron convictions about the inferiority of program to absolute music! The main thing is to consider all music on its merits. A good program should not allow poor music to scrape through; on the other hand, we must not expect a program piece either to declare its program without the use of words or to be as impressive without its program as with it. In the best program music, the composition so richly interprets or suggests the verbal ideas that the two are inseparable. There are many examples of this: for instance, Vincent d'Indy's *Istar,* wherein the music suggests by its essential structure the story of the goddess, who, to free her lover, must pass through seven doors, at each of which a demon robs her of adornment.

It is well to remember that the novelty of an exciting program may attract for a while, and then become stale with familiarity. Hence, we should give program pieces a good many hearings before deciding whether they wear as well as non-program favorites.

In listening to program music we have a double task, because we have to take in the program plus the music, and be deciding all along how the music carries out the literary idea. There must be *form* in both, and the comparison of the two provides an enjoyable task.

HERE WE TAKE THE ROMANTIC ROAD

We have now arrived at a point from which it is possible to see the best road to use in approaching this difficult problem of learning how to listen. It lies naturally through that kind of music which recognizably maintains a connection with things outside itself, with things which can be definitely recognized and easily understood. Most of the works known and loved by the intelligent amateur in music belong in this category. This is a realm of beauty and interest, " a land bounded on one side by the austere peaks of the classics and on the other by the broad plains of conscientious mediocrity. It is an irresistibly lovely tract, its valleys and mountains perpetually varied by the wandering clouds of romanticism, its streams darkened by winds blowing from the other world of mysticism; a land where sensuous beauty, the immediate delight of the ear is of primary importance and logic a reluctant necessity." (Hubbard Hutchinson in *The New York Times*.) Using this kind of music first of all to establish a delight in listening and then as a means for acquiring familiarity with the problems of technical structure, details of melody, harmony, rhythm, orchestration, and so on, the would-be listener can soon journey into the more abstract difficulties as well as the greater beauties of absolute music. Using his days in the delectable land of romantic beauty as a preparation, he should gradually gird his loins and quicken his spirit for the journey to the rarer heights and wider visions of the " austere peaks of the classics."

Throughout his whole journey the musical wayfarer must keep in mind his ultimate goal — the acquiring of the ability to listen to music in its own terms, without the outside props that have helped him to get started. Thus only can he do full justice to its glories by giving it a fair opportunity of working in its own particular field. It is in its very being-itself-ness that music becomes most difficult — so that when it is most necessary to understand it (that is, when it is " purest "), it is most difficult to grasp. This applies, of course, to the more complex works; but we must point out, at the same time, that there is ample music that is only slightly complex and at the same time as absolute as can be; and that the complexity of the music is a real necessity, not a thing put in by the composer " to make it more difficult," like a mis-lead in a cross-word puzzle. A student starting to learn to listen to a piece of absolute music that is fairly complex is apt to think that the composer has made it as difficult as possible, whereas all good composers strive to make their utterances as clear to the hearer as they can, consistent with the magnitude of the ideas they are expressing. Complexity in music is more obvious than in the other arts, and more difficult to grasp, because of music's fleeting character and its appeal to the least trained of our senses.

But we have already warned the student that he has not set forth on an easy journey, even though it is a very delightful one, and that too rapid progress cannot be expected at first. The listener can gradually learn to get from the music the sense that the composer would convey, once his attitude towards the art is an active rather than a passive one. By developing an ability to remember musical phrases and patterns, by trying to train his powers of discrimination, and by keeping an open mind and a sympathetic attitude towards all kinds of music, he will greatly forward his own progress. By confining the music he hears to that which, because of its content, can justify its existence as a means of " enriching and sanctifying life," he will educate himself in the real sense of the term. In a valuable essay on *Music and the Cultivated Man*, Gilman quotes William Orton's definition of education as an initiation of the mind to ever new and finer types of experiences. And it is these new and finer types of experience which music will give us if we learn to choose it carefully and to listen to it properly.

LIST OF SUGGESTED MUSIC

Symphonie pathétique   Tchaikovsky

The last movement especially should be heard, since it is illustrative of " melancholy brooding."

Scheherazade Suite   Rimsky-Korsakoff

The third movement has " alluring Eastern colors."

First Symphony   Brahms

The last movement is full of " healthy vigor."

Feldeinsamkeit   Brahms

Here is a good translation of this beautiful song:

Ich ruhe still im hohen grünen Gras und
Quietly I lie midst the tall green grass and

sende lange meinen Blick nach oben;
watch the changing heavens above me;

Von Grillen rings umschwirrt ohn' Unterlass, von
All around me the unceasing whirr of crickets, above me the

Himmels Blaue wundersam umwoben,
ceaseless glory of the heavens,

Die schönen weissen Wolken zieh'n dahin durch's
The fair white clouds against the heaven's blue

tiefe Blau wie schöne stille Träume;
seem like sweet, quiet dreams;

mir ist, als ob ich längst gestorben bin, und
It seems as though I long were dead, and

ziehe selig mit durch ew'ge Räume.
with the blest were borne along to heaven.

Pacific 231   Honegger

Does the train get anywhere?

" Siegfried's Funeral March "
   from *Götterdämmerung*
" Isolde's Love Death " from *Tristan und Isolde*
Introduction to the second act of   Wagner
   Tristan und Isolde
Introduction and Shepherd's Song, third act of
   Tristan und Isolde

Sixth (*Pastoral*) *Symphony*   Beethoven
                Second Movement — By the Brook

Fugue in G Minor (Lesser)   Bach
                (Starts G, D, B flat, etc.)

Quartet in F Major, Op. 3, No. 5   Haydn

TOPICS FOR FURTHER DISCUSSION

Has music any emotions of its own which have no connection with any other kind of emotion? Or are the feelings that music arouses all derived from our experience of life and literature?

Do you think that program music is in itself a lower type than absolute music?

Is Honegger's *Pacific 231* (a railway engine) a legitimate subject for a tone poem, or not? And why?

Discuss Charles Morgan's dictum that " Art is news of reality not to be expressed in other terms." And this artist's recipe, from Bourget:

Sois belle, et tais-toi!

SUGGESTIONS FOR READING

Musical Studies, Newman. (London: John Lane)
The Scope of Music, Buck. (New York and London: Oxford)
The Principles of Aesthetics, Parker. (New York: Silver Burdett)
Music and the Cultivated Man, Gilman. (New York: W. E. Rudge)

CHAPTER XIII

"Till Eulenspiegel's Merry Pranks"

A Gay Beginning for Our Journey

OUR musical journey may well begin with one of the most significant pieces of program music ever written, *Till Eulenspiegel's Merry Pranks* by Richard Strauss. Upon hearing this, even for the first time, we can hardly fail to be impressed with its greatness. It is very evident that the orchestra is telling us a story in which something is happening every minute. What is perhaps not so immediately evident is that the composer's ability in construction is on a par with his imaginative facility. Here is music inspired by the liveliest of imaginations and created by the most consummate skill imaginable.

Strauss, who wrote this music in 1895, tells us that his original intention was to let the music speak for itself, giving the hearer the title, and letting him guess the details and enjoy the music for its own sake. But this was said with his tongue in cheek, for no one knew better than did Strauss that if the hearers are to share a composer's enjoyment in the treatment of a programmatic subject, it is necessary that they know something of the story unfolding in his mind as he writes the music. So he later gave us his program. " Till Owlglass," to use an English translation of the fanciful name, is a character not very well known in this country; in Germany every schoolboy could tell the adventures of this medieval character who is the hero of a fifteenth-century book which relates his journeys through life and tells of how he managed to live by his wits. He is supposed to have lived in Brunswick, and to have died in 1350 at Mölln, near Lübeck in the north of Germany. He came to be recognized during the Middle Ages as a sort of personification of the triumph of nimble wit over bourgeois dullness and vanity. He was an amusing rogue, as amoral as Punch, jack-of-all-trades, a universal swindler, yet ingratiating himself with everybody by his hail-fellow-well-met gusto; something of a poet, with a streak of childish heedlessness; ramshackle, a danger to the community, yet with a likable turn to his folly; likable, perhaps, mostly in the retrospect; not so much when his insolent pranks drove nearly frantic the honest dullards on whom he delighted to exercise his wits. " When he was grabbed by the collar and hauled along to the gallows, he went as a matter of course, without knowing why. He took life after the manner of a poet, just as he took the goods of others " (Eugene Bacha).

AN IDEAL PROGRAM

What a program for a creative musician of Strauss's imaginative power and technical resource! And in working it out, the composer makes his music not only an apotheosis of this medieval folk character, but, as we have said, a running commentary on life in general and the individual who dares to stand out against generally accepted opinions. Coming as he did after Liszt and Wagner, Strauss was able to base his developments upon the foundations laid by these great giants. Possessed of a most unusual talent in writing for the orchestra, he was able to make this huge instrument subject to every dictate of his thought. Even a casual hearing of this music will prove that its pictures are very clearly drawn, the instruments saying exactly what the composer wants them to say. There is a strong sense of folk-feeling pervading this work; in the first bars we hear two themes which seem to suggest to us that " once upon a time there lived a wag named Till Eulenspiegel." And Strauss carries these themes throughout his whole work, weaving them in the most manifold guises, moods, and situations, right up to the catastrophe where Till, after he has been condemned to death, is strung up to the gibbet. We can learn a great deal as we enjoy this vivid, vigorous score. The chief thing to observe is how the composer builds his music out of the manipulations of the two main themes, following, in as much detail as possible, the various phases in the process.

The two themes are strikingly characteristic; they are both heard at the very beginning of the composition.

The first four notes from the orchestra (measures 1–2) vividly suggest the rogue-hero, the quirk of the notes describing him as exactly as music can describe anybody or anything. Almost immediately after the first little theme, we hear a rising, quickly repeated, humorous theme played on the horns (5–12). The ability to recognize such tone color in the orchestra will give added pleasure to our listening! *Keep these two Till themes in mind*, for out of them is fashioned the fabric of the whole piece.[1]

TILL IN THE MARKET PLACE

As the music gets under way, notice how the second theme (the rising, repeated horn theme) gradually becomes more lively

---

[1] BY WAY OF PRACTICAL SUGGESTION: There is much to be said in favor of the listener following this and other music which will be suggested later in this book with the printed score before him — provided that he is able to read musical notation. Picking a detailed structure apart is as good a way to find out how it is put together as can be found, if the observer has technical knowledge to appreciate his analysis. The logical build-up and " feel " of the music can be obtained better in this way than in any other. If the hearer can even find the places in the score where the principal themes occur, he will gradually learn to read the printed page more eloquently. In order to help him in this process, figures are inserted in the text in this and following chapters, these figures referring to the numbers of the measures in which the feature under discussion occurs. The piano score is best for the amateur reader, for it is a condensed version of what the whole orchestra is doing; later on he may learn to use the orchestral score, where all the parts for the various instruments are laid out before him. In each chapter reference will be made to the publishers of both orchestral and piano scores. Reference will not always be given to the various phonograph recordings, but no music is used for illustration that is not immediately available in one or more recordings and which is not likely to remain permanently in the lists.

If the listener does not read music, he need pay no attention to the figures. In numbering the measures, passages that are repeated have not been counted twice.

The piano score of *Till Eulenspiegel* is available in the following: Universal Edition No. 1106; Breitkopf Edition No. 2752.

The orchestral score (miniature size) is available in the Kalmus Edition, an American reprint, excellent and reasonable in price.

(25–35); it is taken up by the various instruments in turn and finally proclaimed in a *fortissimo* passage by the whole orchestra (35–40). " The *milieu* is thus given by which we are enabled to recognize the pranks and droll tricks which the crafty schemer is about to bring before our ears." (This and following quotations are from the analysis of the score by Klatte, approved by the composer.) A clearly marked drop of an octave (44) suggests that the rogue is really off on his adventures. Till is suddenly before us; the clarinets sound his theme and there follow a few sharp chords for the wind instruments (49–50). It is not difficult to recognize the outlines of the story which Strauss tells us were in his mind; Till, his clothes tattered and torn, puts on his best manners, slyly passes through the gate of a city and enters the market place. " It is market day; the women sit at their stalls and prattle. Hop! Eulenspiegel springs on his horse, gives a smack of the whip, and rides into the midst of the crowd. Clink, clash, clatter! A confused sound of broken pots and pans and the market women are put to flight. In haste the rascal rides away, an incident suggested by the trombones in a loud phrase, and secures a safe retreat." The jogging market tune (51–54) heard in this incident is obviously a variant of the second theme, using many of its very notes. As Strauss works up this scene to a climax, notice how he plays with the first theme, making it serve in different ways, breaking it up into little two-note groups (110–120), and expanding it to fit the situation exactly (135–150).

TILL THE PRIEST

The first prank is followed immediately by a second. A straightforward tune is suddenly heard in the midst of the whirling music (179–182), strongly resembling a German folk tune. Thus it is that the scene changes for us. It shows Till disguised as a priest, dripping with unction and morals, Strauss tells us. Note the sudden interpolation of the quirky Till theme on the clarinet (191) in the midst of the bourgeois folk tune; it is as if the preacher's mask has slipped and suddenly Till's mocking, grinning face is revealed beneath. But he begins to get qualms at having mocked religion, and fears for the success of his scheme. A veiled proclamation of the horn theme suggests that perhaps he does not feel any too comfortable in his borrowed glory. He makes up his mind — away with all scruples, he is himself again.

TILL IN LOVE

A sort of shuddering phrase for a solo violin (207) marks the beginning of a new adventure, and the music which immediately follows shows its character. The principal theme is brought forward in lively time, but subtly metamorphosed and chivalrously colored (209). There is no doubt about it — Till is in love. " He has become a Don Juan and one pretty girl has made quite an impression." Hear how now, glowing with zest, the violins, clarinets, and flutes sing! (229) But all this ardor is in vain; Till's advances are received with derision and he goes away in a rage, swearing vengeance on all mankind. A tremendously loud passage on the brass (267) developed out of the first short theme, with change of rhythm, and several times repeated, leaves us in little doubt about this.

TILL AND THE PHILISTINES

Then after a short pause another adventure starts. The violoncellos announce, with a peculiar hopping insistence (293), the arrival of some strange personages, who turn out to be honest, worthy doctors and professors. In an instant Till's anger is forgotten in his joy at the opportunity offered of making fun of these solemn old self-important dry-as-dusts. The second theme suits itself to the new rhythm (303–305), as if to suggest how easily Till falls in with the ways of living and thinking of his new companions. He begins to propound a few amazing theses to them, as is apparent from the way fragments of the theme come from various parts of the orchestra. There follows a rhythmic phrase (344) representing the dull stodginess of the Philistines and the rapid quirks of the Till motive, as if he were propounding one amazing idea after another in such quick succession as to leave his hearers open-mouthed in astonishment. He works himself up into a perfect frenzy of excitement, but after he has had his joke, he loses interest in the whole thing and drops

it, leaving the professors and doctors behind in amazed stupe-
faction.

To Be or Not to Be Himself

Now comes material more suited to the real domain of music than these pictorial elements with which we have been concerned up to now. A happy *gassenhauer* (a street song) is heard
(375), its short staccato phrases emphasizing Till's essential
naïveté. Then follows a sort of psychological struggle in the
hero's mind, between the various elements in his character. The
different themes are taken up and bandied about in various
rhythms as if Till thought sometimes he ought to reform his
ways and settle down, and then again he decided against it. But
the arch villain " gets the upper hand and the merry jester, the
born liar goes wherever he can succeed with a hoax. His inso-
lence knows no bounds; the Till themes fairly dance in unholy
glee (555). Finally the coarse street tune is heard again, sung
by the whole orchestra as if in jubilation at the hero's final determination to be himself again."

Till's Sad End

Suddenly comes the denouement. " The drum rolls a hollow roll (575); the jailer drags the rascally prisoner into the
court room." This is one of Strauss's happiest characterizations,
this Court of Justice theme — heavy, pedantic, threatening
chords on the wood winds and lower strings (577–580). The im-
pudent Till theme (582) replies brazenly to these somber thun-
derings of the court; it sounds as if the prisoner were thumbing
his nose at the solemn-faced jury. Finally he realizes that the jig
is up and his pranks are over. Fear seizes him as he is marched
to the gallows. There he swings as the trap is sprung, this rather
gruesome incident being marked by a peculiar drop in the pitch
of the entire orchestra. A last, piteous struggle suggested principally by the clarinet and the flute (615), and his soul takes
flight. The mortal Till is no more.

After a sad *pizzicato* passage for the strings (625), the composer adds a delightful epilogue, a sort of improvisation on the opening measures. It is as if he would say, " Till thus becomes a legendary character; after all, there was a lovable side to his ramshackleness, and the people will always tell tales about him — ' Once upon a time,' etc." But in all the retrospective affection with which Strauss clothes Till, he does not let us forget the fact that he was a devil and an immortal rogue. To this the final measures, sounded by the full orchestra, testify most eloquently.

FEELING BEFORE ANALYSIS

No matter whether he can read the score or not, the listener should always keep clearly before him the necessity of cultivating an eloquence of heart if he is to come to a real understanding of this magnificent music. He must realize the necessity of getting back of the music, of sensing its spiritual communication, of letting himself be " reminded by the instruments," as Walt Whitman has put it. This does not mean that he should give himself over merely to the summoning of vague, shifting, sentimental images when he listens to the music. This sort of thing is ridiculed by the purists in art, and with good reason. But the more one hears, sees, and reads, the more one must be convinced of the necessary and salutary relationship between art and life. All art must spring from nature; art for art's sake is nonexistent, nor can it be produced. If art is to maintain itself and is to assure its own existence, some kind of moral and spiritual stimulus must be given to the people. It is the sharpening of his faculties of apperception so that he can realize this relationship, that is necessary for the listener as he hears this music. He must learn to respond to the emotion in such music as this, to feel its beauty, before he attempts to explain it. He should sense its connection with life in general, its " ulterior and philosophic meaning "; in this particular case he must realize, as we have said, that this music is jubilantly conscious of that which " soars high above and beyond prison bars or scaffolds, or even the excellent rulings of worthy people." [2] Then can he proceed to analysis and appraisement, a mental process which will no longer hinder his

[2] Olin Downes, *Symphonic Broadcasts*. New York: Dial Press.

progress by assuming undue importance. Rather will it increase his enjoyment by rendering his possession of the music more sure. This process of developing from a purely sensual and subjective state of hearing into a more objective and analytical type of listening is a glorious experience.

Till Eulenspiegel should awaken within us a new understanding of life and the universe; in realizing the humor as well as the tenderness, the eloquence as well as the joy of life that is in this music, in signalizing its triumph of the spirit over material obstacles, we open our hearts to new powers of feeling and understanding. And, having cultivated this power of understanding, we can learn to appreciate the effective arrangement of idea and event within this music, its masterful descriptive ability, and its outstanding scheme of construction. Only then can we really say that we have made it our own.

ADDITIONAL EXAMPLES OF PROGRAM MUSIC

L'apprenti sorcier	Dukas
Danse macabre	Saint-Saëns

The first is a humorous translation into music of a ballad by Goethe about a magician's lazy apprentice who, while his master is away, uses the incantations he has learned for bringing to life brooms and buckets. These he succeeds in making work for him, but they get out of control, for the apprentice forgets the spell which will make them stop. Frightened, he chops the broom in two; but then the halves begin sweeping. The floor is deluged with water from the buckets. Finally his master returns and solemnly utters the spell which puts things right.

Saint-Saëns's symphonic poem (written in 1874) was based upon a French poem describing how at midnight Death summons the skeletons in the graveyards to revels. We hear him tuning his fiddle; then midnight strikes and the specters arise. They dance to waltz themes, and on the xylophone we hear the clanking of their bones. When the cock crows at break of dawn, they speed back to the shades.

TOPICS FOR FURTHER DISCUSSION

What in your mind makes *Till* so perfect a work of art? What else has Strauss done in the field of program music? Do these works equal

Till in vividness, truth, and the balancing of description and imagination?

Do any of the episodes seem to you less completely successful than others? If so, which, and why?

SUGGESTIONS FOR READING

Master Tyll Owlglass, His Marvellous Adventures and Rare Conceits, translated by Mackenzie. (New York: Dutton)

Till Eulenspiegel, Abenteuer, Streiche, Gaukeleien, Gesichte, und Träume, Hauptmann. (Berlin: S. Fischer Verlag)

This is an interesting re-creation of Till's life by a modern writer.

Richard Strauss, Newman. (London: John Lane)

The book is not at all complete but is a good study as far as it goes.

Richard Strauss, Finck. (Boston: Little, Brown)

A prejudiced but interesting account, the story is complete to 1917. (Now out of print)

CHAPTER XIV

Romanticism: Liszt's "Les Préludes"

A New Spirit Develops in Music

HAVING enjoyed an objective piece of program music such as *Till Eulenspiegel,* in which the composer carefully elaborates a detailed program, the listener may well turn to music which extends into a wider imaginative realm and does not of necessity follow an exterior programistic outline. Liszt's *Les Préludes* will do well for an example, although it can hardly be ranked with the Strauss work as a musical masterpiece. Play through a good interpretation of this music of Liszt's. You will find it introspective and contemplative as well as external and pictorial; the composer is dealing with emotional states as well as with objective events — more so, in fact. In this sense this music belongs to the real realm of art, since it presents us with images rather than ideas, and these images produce in us definite states of feeling. It was written at a time when men were not ashamed to feel deeply and express themselves luxuriantly. Full of color, possessing dramatic force, with melodies of frank and robust sentiment, *Les Préludes* is characteristic of the Romantic Movement which gave it birth, and in which its composer played so prominent a role.

A revolt against the more formal and severe elements of the classic ideals of the seventeenth and early eighteenth centuries, the Romantic Movement in art came into existence during the late eighteenth and early nineteenth centuries. Its tendencies were marked by such writers as E. T. A. Hoffmann and Jean Paul Richter in Germany, Lamartine in France, and Wordsworth, Byron, Coleridge, and Shelley in England. Through the aspirations which developed from experience in the new political ideals of the time, aspirations which insisted upon more freedom for the individual, the Romantics came to look upon the world not so much as it affected the past, but in the light of its effect upon

the individual. " I am different from all men I have seen; if I
am not better, I at least am different," said Rousseau, one of the
leaders of the movement in France. And it was this self-conscious
attempt to give expression to the qualities which determine the
characteristics of personality that typifies the art of the time and
gives this music its peculiar quality.

AN ART OF REVOLT

It will be worth our while to turn briefly aside and try to
realize the true character of this Romantic spirit, the better to
sense it when we come across it in music. Artists of the time were
so preoccupied with self, so lacking in surety of proportion and
balance, that they plunged wildly into a passionate, surging
conflict with life, to come out of the struggle, not with balance
regained, but with a sense of dissatisfaction, a resolve to flee the
world and retreat into the solitude of self. A quotation from
Shelley's " Ode to the West Wind " will give us as good an example of Romantic characteristics as could be found:

> If I were a dead leaf thou mightest bear;
> If I were a swift cloud to fly with thee;
> A wave to pant beneath thy power, and share
>
> The impulse of thy strength, only less free
> Than thou, O uncontrollable! If even
> I were as in my boyhood, and could be
>
> The comrade of thy wanderings over heaven,
> As then, when to outstrip thy skiey speed
> Scarce seemed a vision; I would ne'er have striven
>
> As thus with thee in prayer in my sore need.
> O! lift me as a wave, a leaf, a cloud!
> I fall upon the thorns of life! I bleed!
>
> A heavy weight of hours has chained and bowed
> One too like thee — tameless, and swift, and proud.

It is all here: the apotheosis of self, the pessimism, the sense
of passionate struggle, the poignant dissatisfaction with life,
the nostalgic longing for the past, the struggle against destiny
and the final resignation. We could well choose a motto for Ro-

mantic art from the above lines: " I fall upon the thorns of life! I bleed! " It is this exaggeration, this insistence upon the picturesque and extravagant, that has brought the whole Romantic Movement into disrepute in more recent years; our present-day attitude of realism rather mercilessly exposes these very evident weaknesses.

And yet Romanticism has been one of the most stimulating influences in the whole development of music. Before the Romanticists, the basis of music's life was a sort of disciplined intellectualism, with its beauty largely of the abstract, impersonal sort. There was a classic reticence, a carefully maintained balance in this earlier music that subordinated, while of course by no means rejecting, personal feeling. Beethoven marked a transition; after him came the Romantic deluge. Schubert, Schumann, Liszt, Chopin, Wagner, Strauss, Brahms, even men of our own time like Delius and Schönberg (at least in the latter's earlier works), all have been possessed of the Romantic spirit and have written music which is not content only to shine, but which must also sparkle. These qualities, because of their very nature, were destined to make music a more human goddess, and one much more immediately appealing.

"LES PRÉLUDES," TYPICAL ROMANTIC ART [1]

Liszt's music is characteristic; it suggests both the strength and the weakness of this type of art. Its very program is somewhat extravagant, its melodies overluxuriant and nostalgic to a generation so thoroughly removed from the vapors of Romanticism as to incline to the other extreme, that of demanding art without expression. But Liszt was no precious *poseur;* he knew how to make his music telling, and he had a thorough command of the technic of musical construction. He may have been exotic and picturesque, but he was never disorderly or flabby. We may well examine this tone poem, not so much as an example of great music as of consistent, well-ordered construction in the Romantic vein. A realization of its fervor and exuberances should not deter us from gaining a helpful insight into the processes of its musical composition.

[1] The piano score of *Les Préludes* is available in the Breitkopf Edition No. 2443. The orchestral score (miniature size) is available in the Kalmus Edition No. 29.

Liszt chose a quotation from Lamartine as his program: " Is our life anything but a series of Preludes to that unknown song of which death sounds the first and solemn note? Love is the glowing dawn of all existence, but in whose destiny are not the first delights of happiness interrupted by some storm whose blast dissipates its fine illusions? And where is the cruelly wounded soul, which on issuing from one of these tempests, does not endeavor to find solace in the calm serenity of country life? Nevertheless man can hardly give himself up for long to the simple beneficence which he at first finds in nature, and he hastens to the dangerous post wherever war calls him to its ranks, in order to recover at last in the combat full consciousness and entire possession of his energy."

This obvious program gives us life as material for the composer to work upon, viewed first from the aspect of Love, its greatest fulfillment; second, as a struggle for an Ideal, and the inevitable disillusionment that follows; third, as an opportunity for regaining spiritual equilibrium in the solitude of Nature; and finally, as a glorious re-entry into Conflict. Liszt made his tone poem conform to these four varying moods of the program, and to give unity to his work, he used only two short themes (47–50 and 70–73)

as a basis for the whole structure, changing and coloring these to suit the needs of the various parts of the orchestral poem. Thus the hearer is given the necessary contrast without which any music becomes unbearably tiresome (witness the modern jazz piece), as well as coherence, without which it would be meaningless. Notice that the first four notes of the first theme constitute a germinal unit out of which Liszt makes a great deal, particularly in the long introduction which precedes the sounding of the first theme, and the effective concluding measures which give a sort of post-oration effect. The little three-note germ is sounded by the whole orchestra at the very beginning (1–3):

The music that follows is obviously developed out of this idea and is self-propellent, moving towards a definite goal. This goal we

"Der Erlkönig" ("The Erlking")

Johann Wolfgang von Goethe (1749–1832)

Wer reitet so spät durch Nacht und Wind? Es ist der Vater mit seinem Kind;
Who rides there so late, through night and wind? It is a father with his small son;
Er hat den Knaben wohl in dem Arm, Er fasst ihn sicher, er hält ihn warm.
He has the boy safe in his arm, He holds him tightly, he holds him warm.
Mein Sohn, was birgst du so bang dein Gesicht? Siehst, Vater, du den Erlkönig nicht?
My boy, why in terror do you hide your face? Father, can't you see the Erlking?
Den Erlenkönig mit Kron und Schweif? Mein Sohn, es ist ein Nebelstreif.
The Erlking with crown and robe? My son, it is only a streak of mist.

Painting by Moritz von Schwind (1804–1871)

"Du liebes Kind, komm', geh' mit mir! Gar schöne Spiele spiel' ich mit dir;
"Pretty boy, won't you come with me? Such merry games I'll play with you;
Manch' bunte Blumen sind an dem Strand, Meine Mutter hat manch' gülden Gewand."
Many gay flowers are blooming there, And my mother has golden robes for you."
Mein Vater, mein Vater, und hörest du nicht, Was Erlenkönig mir leise verspricht?
Oh, Father, my father, cannot you hear what the Erlking is saying to me?
Sei ruhig, bleibe ruhig, mein Kind, In dürren Blättern säuselt der Wind.
Don't talk so, my boy. It's only the wind in the dry leaves.
"Willst, feiner Knabe, du mit mir gehn? Meine Töchter sollen dich warten schön;
"Come, pretty one, and fairy princesses shall wait upon you,
Meine Töchter führen den nächtlichen Reihn Und wiegen und tanzen und singen dich ein."
They'll play with you, dance with you, sing to you."
Mein Vater, mein Vater, und siehst du nicht dort Erlkönigs Töchter am düster'n Ort?
Father, Father, don't you see the Erlking's daughters there?
Mein Sohn, mein Sohn, ich seh' es genau, Es scheinen die alten Weiden so grau.
My boy, there is nothing there but the old gray willows.
"Ich liebe dich, mich reizt deine schöne Gestalt, Und bist du nicht willig, so brauch ich Gewalt."
"I want you, pretty one; if you're not willing, I shall use force."
Mein Vater, mein Vater, jetzt fasst er mich an! Erlkönig hat mir ein Leids gethan!
Father, Father, he is seizing me! Save me, save me!
Dem Vater grauset's, er reitet geschwind, Er hält in den Armen das ächzende Kind,
The father shudders. He rides like the wind, the pale, sobbing child close in his arms.
Er reicht den Hof mit Müh' und Noth; In seinen Armen das Kind war todt.
Gasping and sweating, he pulls up at the gate of home. But the child in his arms is dead.

FRANZ LISZT

find to be the expressive first theme, broadly sung by all the
strings; as though to make sure we shall not forget it, the composer repeats it almost immediately, this time with some of the
brass instruments added. Then comes the second theme, a quiet
but intense tune, softly intoned by the brass and then repeated
on the wood winds (oboe, clarinet, and bassoon). There is no
doubt that Liszt, *l'homme d'amour*, as Pourtalès calls him, is here
discoursing at some length upon a subject dear to his heart!

The cellos and clarinets (110) unite to give us the first ink-
lings of the coming storm which occupies the second section of
the musical form. A series of chromatic rumblings, based again
upon our little three-note theme, presages the storm. When it
finally arrives, the keen observer will note that the material from
which these storm passages is built (131–160) is a shortened,
intensified version of the principal theme:

This works up to a climax in which the second theme is brilliantly
used (161). But unfortunately this Lisztian storm is more objective than subjective; we are reminded of the rushing roar and
muttering outbursts of a storm in nature, rather than of the tempestuous, spiritual struggle that is suggested by the program.
And it does not help the general effect that these chord progressions used some seventy years ago by Liszt have come into the
current repertoire of the movie-mongers, so that the whole episode today has a melodramatic, cheapened aspect undreamed of
when it was written.

The next section (201–344) contains some of the most colorful music in the whole tone poem; here the oboe gives out the
first theme in languorous, pastoral eloquence:

Here is really

> Beauty clear and fair
> Where the air
> Rather like a perfume dwells.

Liszt sings his charming *bergerette* with great skill and colors his
themes with unfailing good taste.

Once again the mood changes, and we hear the two themes (346 and 370) in a quick martial rhythm,

and delivered with so much pompous grandeur as to make them sound like different tunes from those heard in the first episode. All is bustle and stir; the struggle and glory are, however, again purely objective. It is in the pomp and circumstance of war that Liszt's hero recovers his individuality and regains possession of his energy. A vigorous coda (405 to end), already mentioned as suggestive of the introductory measures, brings the work to a close; in it notice how the reference to the thematic material with which the piece began rounds out the whole, and gives the effect of unity.

A DOUBLE PERSONALITY

Liszt once jokingly referred to himself as a musician-philosopher, born on Parnassus, coming from the Land of Doubt, and journeying towards the Land of Truth — a description of himself that is more accurate than this sometimes rather tawdry music would lead us to believe. Ernest Newman in one of his articles in the London *Sunday Times* wonders " how there came to be so much originality, so much distinction, so much downright commonness united in Liszt. . . . Somewhere or other in the course of even his best and most sincere thinking the old *cabotin* will rise up in him again and he becomes, once more, the flashy, flowery, too-effusive Liszt of the Paris salon. Here in *Les Préludes,* for instance, we can see, again and again, the self-conscious and self-approving air with which, in the days of his handsome and seductive youth, he was wont to throw back his mane, put his whole romantic soul into his fingers and his eyes, and slay a gushing countess with a glance."

ADDITIONAL EXAMPLES ILLUSTRATING THIS CHAPTER

Vltava (The Moldau)   Smetana

Smetana, the Czech composer (1824–1884), who was the most notable
Nationalistic musician in that country before Dvořák, told in his score
how in the deep Bohemian forest two streams arise, one warm and swift,
the other cold and quiet. Rushing down from the rocks, they unite and
flow happily in the rays of the morning sun. In time the swift brook becomes a river, the Vltava. It flows through dark, mighty forests, where
the huntsman's horn is heard; it streams through rich pastures in the
plains, and hears the songs of peasants at a village wedding. By moonlight water nymphs play in its waters. Upon its bosom are mirrored the
towers of castles that in past days resounded with the clash of arms and
the great deeds of warriors. In the gorge of St. John rocks seek to op-
pose it, but it bursts through in foaming torrents. Then, broadening
out into full majesty, it sweeps nobly past Prague, greeted by the ancient
fortress of Vysehrad, and then in all its power and splendor it is lost to
the poet's vision.

The Fountains of Rome   Respighi

Though Italy has not so far, like some of the Middle European nations,
new and old, developed a strongly self-conscious school of composition
based upon folk music, those of its writers who have turned rather to
orchestral than to operatic expression have upheld the country's reputation for brilliant, colorful, dynamic depiction. Among them one of the
most notable is Ottorino Respighi, born in 1879. Though he has written for the theater, much of his best-known work is in the form of tone
poems, a series of which is devoted to the glories of Rome. Typical
of a certain pictorial luxuriousness which is widely enjoyed, and may
well be compared with Liszt's, is his *Fountains of Rome*. It may be suggested that there is some special consonance between this type of program music, with its flowery, literal, prose style (as distinguished from
Liszt's poetical searchings) and some aspects of modern life and thought.

In his clever depictions, which date from 1916, the composer has
(in his own words) " endeavored to give effect to the sentiment and
vision suggested by four of Rome's fountains, contemplated at the hour
at which their character is most in harmony with the surrounding landscape, and in which their beauty appears most impressive to the observer."

1. The Fountain at Valle Giulia, at Dawn. " A pastoral landscape.
Droves of cattle pass and disappear in the mists of a Roman dawn."
Muted violins suggest the fountain, wood winds the pastoral scene.

2. The Fountain of the Tritons, in the Morning. "A sudden loud and insistent blast of horns . . . is like a joyous call, summoning troops of Tritons and Naiads, who . . . pursue each other and mingle in the dance between the jets of water."

3. The Fountain of Trevi, at Noon. "A solemn theme from the wood and brass assumes a triumphal character. Trumpets peal across the radiant surface of the water. Neptune's chariot passes, drawn by sea-horses and followed by Sirens and Tritons. The procession vanishes. . . ." The magnificence of the fountain, with its waterfall, its statues of Neptune and those illustrating the legend of the discovery of the Virgin's Spring, gives the composer fine scope for elaborate, gorgeous writing.

4. The Fountain of the Villa Medici, at Dusk. "A sad theme rises above a subdued warbling. The air is full of tolling bells and birds twittering; then all dies peacefully in the silence of the night." The music suggests the chaste dignity of the fountain in its oak-guarded seclusion — a scene meet for half-sweet, half-melancholy meditations as the day is dying.

Carnival of the Animals   Saint-Saëns

A bulwark of conservatism and a believer in the value of absolute music, Saint-Saëns (who died in 1921 at the age of 86) did not allow this "grand zoological fantasy" to be published or performed during his lifetime. One hearing will show why; for it is a most unconventional piece (it was originally written as a sort of musical joke), and its realism has become famous. In the various sketches the composer not only reproduces the sounds made by the various animals but he also delights in satirizing the music of his own day. The orchestration includes a two-piano part and a well-known solo for cello. The sections are labeled:

> Introduction and Royal March of the Lion
> Hens and Cocks
> Wild Asses
> Tortoises (The composer here mocks an Offenbach cancan by playing it very slowly.)
> The Elephant (The tune to which the elephant lumbers is Berlioz's *Waltz of the Sylphs!*)
> Kangaroos
> Aquarium
> Personages with Long Ears
> Cuckoo in the Woods
> Birds

Fossils (Saint-Saëns does not hesitate to ridicule himself, for he
includes a theme here from his *Danse macabre*.)

The Swan (This is the most famous of all the sketches, and includes the famous cello solo, " The Swan.")

Pianists (Concert players, with their phenomenal runs and crash-
ing chords, are here put in their place. Without interruption,
the music goes into a brilliant Finale, in which all the animals
are passed in review.)

The whole thing is not much more than a well-done pre-Disney
" Silly Symphony "; but it is clever and witty music and has found a
place on concert programs.

TOPICS FOR FURTHER DISCUSSION

Is *Les Préludes* as fine a work as *Till?* If not, where is it weaker?
What do you like most, and least, in *Les Préludes?* Do you find any of
its qualities prominent in any other music by Liszt that you have heard?

Could you summarize, in a single phrase, Liszt's besetting sin? In
so far as music history is concerned, what is his outstanding contribution to the development of the art? What do you know of his qualities
as a man, not as an artist?

Do you think any revival of the *Les Préludes* type of Romanticism
is possible in the near future? Would such a revival attract you personally?

Discuss the theory that history moves in cycles, and that the same
" movements " return at intervals (this with reference to Romanticism).

What is the present tendency in art, and what seems likely to
follow it?

SUGGESTIONS FOR READING

Rousseau and Romanticism, Babbitt. (Boston: Houghton Mifflin)
The Romantic Quest, Fairchild. (New York: Columbia; London: Ox-
ford)
A History of French Literature, Nitze and Dargan. (New York: Holt)
Romanticism and the Romantic School in Germany, Wernaer. (New
York: Appleton-Century)
These books give a fine idea of the literary aspects of the Romantic
Movement in the different literatures.

Apollo, Reinach. (New York: Scribner)
    Chapter XXV: Art in the Nineteenth Century
How to Study Pictures, Caffin. (New York: Appleton-Century)
    Chapter XX: David and Delacroix
Men of Art, Craven. (New York: Simon & Schuster)
    Chapter XVI: Delacroix.
    Romanticism in painting is well described.

Studies in Modern Music, Hadow. (New York: Macmillan; London: Seeley)
    Hector Berlioz and the French Romantic movement
    Robert Schumann and the Romantic Movement in Germany

Beethoven: Impressions of Contemporaries. (New York: Schirmer)
    In this book a great musical Romanticist is described as seen by his fellows.

Franz Liszt, Pourtalès. (New York: Holt)
Franz Liszt, Huneker. (New York: Scribner)

CHAPTER XV

The Question of Form

FORM in art means exactly what it means in life in general — the successful co-ordination of elements so as to produce the most effective results possible. When we speak of the form of an athlete, we have reference to the intangible something that has enabled him to bring all his powers into proper relationship and co-ordination so as to attain the greatest possible effectiveness. Form in art means the organizing process — in plain terms, the plan — by which all the fundamental elements which go to make up that art are arranged so as to secure the maximum impression upon the consciousness of him who perceives. A piece of music, for example, may have good melody, with well-arranged rhythmic patterns, may be well harmonized, with effective combinations of timbre; but unless it has, in addition, a good plan of organization by which its materials are significantly ordered, it fails of full effect. This ability effectively to organize his materials is the most intellectual part of a composer's equipment; it may to a certain degree be acquired, but it must be present if a man is to write good music. The greatest composers have been those who have had consummate skill in creating great ideas and an organizing ability to present them well.

We have already suggested the need for design and form in all art; that need is even more necessary in the immaterial and transient art of music, which goes as quickly as it comes, than it is in the material arts of painting, sculpture, and architecture. A composer must know how to present his ideas so as to arrest our attention and so as to hold it. The various elements that make up his whole composition must be contrasted in a way that will give effective balance, without being so diffuse as to make them difficult to remember. A composer must have some design or formal scheme in his mind when he writes, else his music will be simply a hodgepodge of ideas, unintelligible to other minds.

FORM IN PROGRAM MUSIC

We have just studied some representative examples of program music; the composers of these works were not greatly concerned with the problem of " how to make their music last." They simply took a suitable story or a philosophical concept and, using a few themes as generative material, let the music they wrote follow the necessities of the program. We can be sure, however, that when composers such as Liszt and Strauss chose programs, they kept a weather eye out for genetic possibilities: they made sure that the program in itself was constructed so as to provide elements of contrast, balance, and unity (review briefly the programs of *Till Eulenspiegel* and *Les Préludes* and see how true this is), that it made an effective start, and that it led through a number of contrasting episodes to a convincing finish. Hence the music with which they clothed the program possesses the quality of good formal design.

FORM IN ABSOLUTE MUSIC

An even greater concern with the principles of good construction is necessary in writing absolute music, for in it there is nothing in the way of an underlying poetic program to carry us along. The best way to sense this is to listen carefully to a well-constructed piece of absolute music where the formal patterns are comparatively easy to follow — again the first movement of Beethoven's *Fifth Symphony* is an ideal example. Upon hearing music such as this, even for the first time, you will observe that there are several well-defined themes, such as were found in the program pieces, that occur and recur frequently. But in the absolute music these themes are presented in a logically and carefully ordered manner so that they may be readily grasped; they have, of course, no connection with any story. It is not difficult to see, then, that some understanding of this controlled imaginative thinking, as form has been defined, is necessary if we are to increase our enjoyment of music through comprehending it.

Before we try to explain the rather intricate details of musical design, it will be well to clear up one prevalent misunderstanding as to the general nature of form. In discussing the problems of the composer (page 92) we have said that he has at his disposal a number of structural plans or molds, evolved by his predecessors through the centuries, which aid in the coherent organization of his material. We are apt to think that a composer chooses one of these formal molds that seems best suited to his purpose and then designs the substance of his music to fit its requirements. It is customary to suggest in this respect that in art there is *form* and *substance* — the vessel and that which the vessel contains. This is not true; an examination of any great masterpiece of music, painting, or architecture will show that it seldom fits neatly into a prearranged scheme of formal design such as is laid down by textbooks. In art, form and substance are one, inseparable, born together in the mind of the creator and growing together as do the veins and arteries in our bodies and the blood they contain. Rightly considered, any study of the formal element in music or in any other art is made in order better to understand the living thing, a process similar to that undertaken by the medical student in order that he may thoroughly understand the living organisms with which he must deal. We must realize that a composer can, at the same time, work within a formal mold and yet be independent of it. Almost every great symphony written is a good example of this: while keeping to the general formal outlines laid down by his predecessors, Beethoven did not hesitate to depart from them whenever he felt that such a procedure would make his music more effective. It may truly be said that the " form of any genuine piece of art is unique."

It would seem foolish for any composer to discard the well-tried and proved forms that had been developed through the combined effort of generations preceding him. These predetermined forms are in the back of his mind as he writes, acting as guides and incentives. But it would be even more foolish for him to attempt anything in the way of absolute fidelity to such forms; this could only result in what the Germans realistically call *Kapellmeistermusik* — music that is correctly written but which possesses no spark of life. The character of the composer's thought, the exigencies that develop as he proceeds in his work, make it necessary that he use any formal scheme that he may choose only as a prop, discarding it whenever it does not seem to suit his particular and personal need. In this sense we can see that each masterpiece makes its own rules.

All this does not mean, however, that the listener cannot profit greatly from an understanding of these design patterns that have been used by the composers. There are a number of ways in which we may classify these forms, the better to realize their full significance. Perhaps the most useful of these distinctions is that between

(1) forms used in vocal music,
(2) forms that may be either vocal or instrumental, and
(3) forms peculiar to instrumental music.

There are a number of these various types of forms, and they are discussed in some detail in various sections of this book. We are giving here a complete table of them, arranged so that you may see their relationships and significance:

VOCAL FORMS

In Secular Music:
    1. The song
    2. The opera
    3. The madrigal
    4. The cantata

In Sacred Music:
    1. The song
    2. The chant
    3. The hymn (chorale)
    4. The motet (anthem)
    5. The mass (communion service)
    6. The oratorio (passion — cantata)

FORMS THAT ARE BOTH VOCAL AND INSTRUMENTAL

    1. Contrapuntal forms based on a *cantus firmus*
    2. The fugue

INSTRUMENTAL FORMS

Sectional Forms (Form in relation to separate, short divisions of a work)
    1. Unitary form (One-part form)
    2. Variation form
    3. Rondo form
    4. Binary form (Two-part form)

    5. Ternary form (Three-part form)
      a. In songs
      b. In short instrumental pieces — the minuet, and so on
      c. In small piano pieces — nocturne, waltz, impromptu, and so forth
      d. In slow movements of sonatas and symphonies
      e. In first movements of sonatas and symphonies (sonata form)
    6. Free forms: overture, fantasia, prelude
Conjoint Forms (Form in relation to the piece as a whole)
    1. The march
    2. The waltz
    3. Small instrumental pieces (nocturne, étude, and so on)
    4. The suite
    5. The sonata
    6. The symphony
    7. The concerto
    8. Chamber music: trio, quartet, quintet, and so forth
    9. The symphonic poem (program-music form)

VOCAL FORMS

It is difficult for most listeners to realize that vocal music reached a height of perfection long before instrumental music did, for our attention is largely centered on the latter type, almost to the exclusion of interest in the former. Naturally form in vocal music follows the words; the composer of vocal music takes a series of words — a poem, a liturgical text, or a dramatic libretto — and " sets " them to music. The result depends so largely upon the character of the text that the first requisite in following the vocal forms is a complete understanding of the words used. We come here upon a difficult and vexatious problem, one that is of great importance for the English-speaking listener who would familiarize himself with vocal music: the outstanding examples of the various types of vocal form — song, oratorio, opera, mass — have foreign texts. And, strange as it may seem, fashion and usage have decreed that nations such as the United States and England, where the people generally have little experience with any language other than their own, must listen to their songs, operas, and oratorios in Italian, German, French, and Latin, but have difficulty in hearing them in English. Little wonder that opera in both these English-speaking countries is almost a dead issue, precariously supported by all sorts of social snobberies and extra-musical resuscitators; or that the song litera-ture, one of the finest in all music, is so little known!

There is no need to attempt a definition of a *song;* every individual, whether or not he is really musical, has experienced the satisfaction of expressing his feelings through bursting into song: it is the most immediate and intimate musical manifestation that man knows. We shall have a great deal to say later about the various types of songs (see page 359). Here we can distinguish between the simple *folk song* and the consciously composed *art song;* both have their own form, and there can be no prescribed patterns. We should also mention here the difference between the semi-spoken portions of opera, called *recitative,* and the songlike *arias,* so often used apart from their context (see Chapter XXXVIII); and the *madrigal,* a song for several voices, set to secular words, with or without instrumental accompaniment, so popular in the sixteenth and seventeenth centuries.

There are a number of forms in sacred music. The simplest of these is the *hymn,* a stanzaic religious song composed in a style that is effective for massed singing. Hymns have been used by all civilizations and have become an integral part of the Christian liturgy; the type introduced by Luther into the Protestant Church at the time of the Reformation — the *chorale* — avoids the unfortunate sentimentality found in so many English hymns and constitutes one of music's greatest treasures, especially as elaborated and harmonized by J. S. Bach.

A *motet* may be defined as the sacred counterpart of the madrigal; a sacred song for a number of voices, it has no definitely fixed place in the liturgy of the Church. Its English counterpart is the *anthem.*

The *Mass,* speaking musically, is the setting given to those fixed portions of the Eucharistic rite of the Roman and Greek churches that are appointed to be sung by the choir. Some of the world's finest music has gone into these settings, most of them unheard today because of their specific ritualistic character. Be-ginning with those unknown composers who wrote Gregorian chant settings of the Mass away back in the early centuries of the Church's existence, almost every composer up through the seventeenth century has given attention to this form. Even such outstanding men as Bach and Beethoven wrote Masses, compositions which, considered as music, rank high among the works of these composers, although they are not suitable for liturgical use in church. The *Requiem Mass* is a special type sung for the repose of the souls of the dead. The *Communion Service* consists of the translated parts of the Catholic Mass that have been retained in the ritual of the Anglican churches.

An *oratorio* can be described as a sort of non-acting version of opera, having a dramatic text or libretto (which may be either sacred or secular in character), recitative, arias, and choruses, with orchestral accompaniment, but no stage action, scenery, or costumes. The *Passion* is a special form of oratorio developed in the German Lutheran Church, with the text, drawn from the gospel narratives, descriptive of the sufferings of Christ between the night of the Last Supper and his death. Literally a *cantata* refers to any composition that is to be sung; specifically it means a small dimensioned oratorio; historically it may be either sacred or secular in character, for either a solo voice or the usual performing apparatus of the oratorio — solos, chorus, and so on.

Forms that Are Both Vocal and Instrumental

It does not take a great deal of musical experience to realize that most of the forms employed by composers through the ages have been either vocal or instrumental; but there have been a few forms, developed at the time when vocal music, which, as we have said, reached a high point of development long before the appearance of a distinctive instrumental style, was gradually being supplanted by instrumental. Early instrumental music was merely the playing on instruments of that which had been written originally for voices; through a method of trial-and-error experimentation, there gradually developed a style that was characteristically suited to instruments. At first this imitated vocal music, and so the earliest instrumental forms that we find in the developing history of music were those that could be used for either singing or playing. An examination of these identical forms will show that they were all *contrapuntal* in character.

TEXTURES IN MUSIC

The term *contrapuntal* is one which needs special description; this seems as appropriate a place to attempt it as any other, even though such a description risks a diversion from the main points at issue. In general, the texture of music (its peculiar structural quality resulting from the blend of its elements) may be said to be of three different kinds: *monophonic, homophonic,* and *polyphonic.* Derivatively, the first two of these words mean the same thing: sounding alike, of the same pitch; technically, they have two quite different meanings. The third word means, literally, " many voiced."

Monophonic music is the simplest we know — a one-voiced, unaccompanied line such as is found in Chinese, ancient Greek, or Hindu music; or, in our Western system, in the Gregorian chant of the early Church.

Homophonic texture in music can easily be recognized in such selections as Handel's *Ombra mai fu* (Largo) from *Xerxes,* the second movement of Dvořák's *Symphony No. 5,* or, in fact, in most of the music written from the end of the sixteenth century to the present day. Its distinguishing characteristic is that it consists of a principal melodic line supported by a *chordal* accompaniment, the sort of thing we discussed in our earlier remarks about harmony. This accompaniment may consist of simple successions of blocks of chords, as in the Handel excerpt, or these chords may be broken up, their tones sounded not simultaneously but one after the other, in some sort of *arpeggio* formation, like this:

There is a third kind of texture, one that is much more difficult to recognize and hear than the two we have just described, largely because it is not used in the music making of today as it was in earlier times, and therefore our ears have to become accustomed to its peculiar characteristics. This kind of musical texture was employed by composers before they adopted the general ideals of the homophonic style somewhere around the beginning of the seventeenth century. We call it *polyphonic* because it is made up of a number of separate and independent melodic strands, each with its own rhythmic values, which, taken together, form harmonies. This is the way all part music before 1600, and a considerable amount of it for some time afterwards, was written; and it is necessary to learn to listen to this type of music in a different way from that which is used for the works of later composers. In polyphonic music we should try to hear separately the various strands that are sung or played by the different parts, instead of being content to hear the customary main melody, supported from moment to moment by chords in vertical fashion.

Even for those who do not read music, the following selections will help to clarify the differences between these three textures: the very look of the notes on the paper shows the essential characteristics of the music.

(A) Monophonic Music

(B) Homophonic Music

Symphony No. 5, in E Minor
Second Movement

Dvořák

(C) Polyphonic Music

Mass, "Assumpta Est Maria"
Christe Eleison

Palestrina

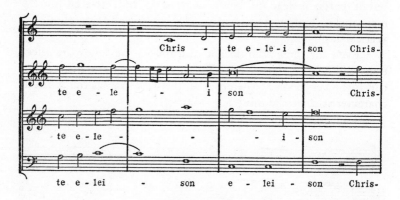

A piece of music does not necessarily keep strictly to any one of these textures. Generally speaking, the earlier it comes in the line of historical development, the greater the probability that it will be written with only one kind of textual fabric. We have already said that the earliest European music we know consists of a single unaccompanied melodic line, and that up to the beginning of the seventeenth century music was almost entirely polyphonic. After that there was a graceful blending of the homophonic and the polyphonic manners of writing until the nineteenth century, when composers began to emphasize the basic homophonic style. Of late, because of a neoclassic reaction against the romantic excesses of the nineteenth century, there has been a revival of interest in counterpoint (a term synonymous with polyphony).

A good example of distinction between homophonic and polyphonic styles is in the chorus " Glory to God " from Handel's *Messiah;* this is written at first in harmonic blocks, and then, at the words " good will towards men," it changes to polyphony. This is easy both to hear with the ear and to see with the eye, in the score. Another outstanding example of the practical use of these various textural styles is the slow movement of Beethoven's *Seventh Symphony:* the earlier part is almost entirely homophonic — all chords, with hardly a suggestion of melody. Then comes a middle part that is partly contrapuntal, partly homophonic, because of a new, fully expressed melody that is woven against the chordal background. Later on, there are several short, purely contrapuntal sections where the violins weave a distinctive counterpoint against the melody that was heard in the opening measures.

This distinction between the polyphonic and homophonic styles of writing is a vital one, and it is necessary to understand it thoroughly if we are to realize the fundamental qualities of music written in different historical periods. The polyphonic style, with its intricate weavings of parts, was a natural one for composers to use in writing for voices. When the instrumentalists began to develop an independent style that would realize the possibilities of their instruments, they started with some of these vocal contrapuntal forms, and so it came about that certain forms were used both vocally and instrumentally.

These were all based on some clearly defined theme that

could easily be recognized and followed throughout the course of the music; they consisted of ingenious contrapuntal manipulations of this fundamental generative idea, which was called the *cantus firmus* (literally, " fixed song "). Composers of the great polyphonic period (the fifteenth, sixteenth, and seventeenth centuries) did not consider themselves so much inventors as builders; sometimes they did not even use their own themes for the foundations of the imposing tonal structures they reared. Many of the countless Masses and other church compositions written during this time were based on themes taken from Gregorian chants or from the works of other composers, or, strange as it may seem to us today, on the often incongruous tune of a popular song of the day. Later, in the Lutheran Church, the same practice was followed, except that the *cantus firmus* was usually a chorale tune well known to the congregation for which the music was written. Many of Bach's church cantatas contain elaborate contrapuntal numbers for voices and orchestra consisting entirely of the treatment of some chorale *cantus firmus*. Likewise Bach and his predecessors and followers wrote a large number of *chorale preludes,* service pieces for the organ with a chorale as *cantus firmus;* and these little works, many of them programatic in character, since they often depict some idea suggested by the words of the hymn, show Bach's genius at its zenith.

The *fugue* was one of the most popular of these overlapping vocal-instrumental forms; it may be said to have been the outstanding form for both vocal and instrumental music during the seventeenth century. Technically it consists of a certain type of treatment of a germinal theme, a treatment that is described in detail later on in this book. (See Chapter XXXIV.) It is mentioned here as one of the great musical forms, which, in spite of its rather austere quality, was widely used in certain formal periods of music's development, and which has appeared, more as a style perhaps than as a real form, occasionally since.

LIST OF SUGGESTED MUSIC

Folk Songs: Early American Ballads

These comprise a number of American mountaineer ballads which can be traced to English, Scottish, Irish, and Welsh sources, sung in traditional manner by John Niles: *The Gypsy Laddie; My Little Mohee; I Wonder as I Wander Out Under the Sky; Lulle Lullay; The Seven Joys of Mary; Barberry Ellen.*

Art Songs: *Der Erlkönig*	Schubert

For a translation of the German text, see facing page 122.

Feldeinsamkeit	Brahms

For a translation of the German text, see page 108.

Aria: *Cielo e mar!* from the opera *La Gioconda*	Ponchielli
Madrigal: " Sweet Honey Sucking Bees "	Wilbye
Hymn: " Onward Christian Soldiers "	Sullivan
Chorale: *Ein feste Burg*	Luther
Motet: *O Bone Jesu*	Palestrina
Anthem: " The Bell Anthem "	Purcell
Mass: *Assumpta est Maria*	Palestrina
The Requiem Mass (K. 626)	Mozart
Oratorio: *The Messiah*	Handel
St. Matthew Passion	Bach
Cantata: (Sacred) *Christ lag in Todesbanden*	Bach
(Secular) *Nell dolce dell' oblio*	Handel

Monophonic Music: Any part of the Gregorian setting to the Mass *Lux et origo*

Homophonic Music: *Ombra mai fu* from the opera *Xerxes*	Handel
Polyphonic Music: Any part of the setting of the Mass *Assumpta est Maria*	Palestrina

Mixed Styles (both homophonic and polyphonic):

Seventh Symphony, Second Movement	Beethoven

Instrumental Treatment of a *Cantus Firmus:*
    Chorale Prelude: *Das alte Jahr vergangen ist*   Bach
    Chorale Prelude: *Liebster Jesu*   Bach

Fugue in G Minor (Lesser)   Bach

TOPICS FOR FURTHER DISCUSSION

Can Form and Substance ever be separated in a work of art?

Discuss the peculiar suitability of early forms to the use of either voices or instruments.

Consider the importance of Key in form, taking as an example any simple two-part or three-part form and noting how key changes afford variety.

Is Polyphony as valid for our pleasure and for the creation of masterpieces today as it was three hundred years ago? If not, account for its decline.

Can you think of any new musical form that the future is likely to produce, or any return to an old one?

CHAPTER XVI

Instrumental Forms

WHEN we listen to music that has no association with words, it is often difficult to recognize the various units which go to make up its formal architecture, for we do not have the structural outline of the poetry to help us. Just as in writing this book words are put together to form phrases, phrases are joined into sentences, sentences grouped so as to make paragraphs, paragraphs are molded into chapters, and chapters added together to form the whole work, composers deal with similar structural units in building their music. The smallest is a little melodic or rhythmic group, sometimes containing only a few notes, such as the famous so-called Fate *motive* in the first movement of Beethoven's *Fifth Symphony*. These motives are usually combined into larger units, forming a more complete melody of several measures, called a *theme*. These themes can, in turn, be extended and enlarged with congruous material into *sections*. And sections can be gathered together to form what is called a *movement*, the very meaning of which suggests that it is a structural division of an even more extended composition such as a *symphony*.

A description such as this cannot be exact, and you will find in reading about musical form that there is by no means any uniform agreement about these terms. In studying form as a help in listening we should be content with finding out generalities and approximations, and " look for exactness only so far as the nature of the subject permits," to borrow an Aristotelian phrase. General methods of procedure can be deduced from observing individual works of art; but no genuine art work can be formulated according to exact prescription. If it were, it would certainly cease to be art. Although there are general formal principles that underlie the construction of all instrumental music, each composition, large or small, elaborate or simple, must in reality make its own rules.

VARIOUS TYPES

The easiest musical forms for listeners to recognize are those which are put together sectionally, each section being made up of material that hangs together naturally.

I. The simplest of these sectional forms is that which consists of a single division — a short composition that was conceived all of a piece, without break from beginning to end. This type of form is not very usual and when employed is limited to small pieces in which there is no need for contrast. The first prelude in Bach's *Well-tempered Clavichord* and Chopin's Prelude Number One in his Opus 28 can be cited as effective examples of this " unitary " form.

II. It would be perfectly possible to make an extended piece of music out of an indefinite repetition of one of these single-division forms; but the result would hardly be interesting. Basically, as the early composers of instrumental music quickly found out, either one of two things can be done to a tune to stretch it into an extended composition: repeat it or vary it. And, since literal repetition is dull, they soon found out how to repeat it with diversity. So we find the *theme and variations* (which may be represented to the literal-minded by the formula: $A — A^1 — A^2 — A^3$, and so forth) used by many of the earliest instrumental composers. Some of the first examples of this form are not very exciting to modern ears: such things as Byrd's " The Bells " and Morley's " Goe from My Window " are variations done according to formula and tend to become tiresome. The seventeenth-century and eighteenth-century *air with doubles* (so-called because each successive variation was written with faster notes), although not profound, contains some interesting technical devices. The most famous example of this type of variation is the one that has been dubbed " The Harmonious Blacksmith," from Handel's *Suite in E Major*. Other early variation forms were the two varieties of the *basso ostinato* (literally, obstinate bass, since a short phrase is repeated over and over in the bass), the *chaconne* and the *passacaglia*, forms which consist of a series of variations built around the reiteration of a melody or a set of chords. All these were widely used by the " pre-classic " composers: Monteverdi and Purcell wrote some of the best we know.

With the advent of the classic composers, Haydn, Mozart, and Beethoven, the theme and variations became a more interesting form. The theme was usually straightforward, and the variations followed it closely as to melodic outline, dimensions, and structural relationships. Haydn's well-known set in the second movement of his *Surprise Symphony*, the first movement of Mozart's *A Major Piano Sonata*, the slow movement of Beethoven's *Kreutzer Sonata*, Op. 47, should be listened to carefully as excellent examples. Even the nineteenth-century composers found this form exceedingly useful although they did not follow it closely: their compositions might better be called " meditations " or " divagations " than " variations." Schumann's *Études Symphoniques*, Brahms's *Variations on a Theme by Haydn*, César Franck's *Symphonic Variations*, and, above all others, Elgar's *Enigma Variations* are works of considerable length and great interest. Such modern writers as Stravinsky (in his *Octet for Wind Instruments*), Roy Harris (in a string quartet), and Hindemith (in his *Schwanendreher*) have used this oldest of all instrumental forms for shaping their contemporary musical thoughts.

III. The *rondo* form is another way of organizing an extended piece out of a single-sectioned form. Here we have a scheme in which a section is literally repeated a number of times, with extraneous material in well-varied keys (which play a considerable part in the interest of the work) inserted between each repetition, thus: A–B–A–C–A, and so on. There are different kinds of rondos, but they are all symmetrical in construction; their derivation was probably from the literary *rondel*, invented in the fourteenth century and largely used by medieval French poets. There was a certain rhyme scheme in its fourteen lines; here is a nineteenth-century example, by Dobson:

A
Love comes back to his vacant dwelling
The old, old Love that we knew of yore!

B
We see him stand by the open door,
With his great eyes sad, and his bosom swelling
He makes as though in our arms repelling
He fain would be as he lay before:

A
Love comes back to his vacant dwelling
The old, old Love that we knew of yore!

C
> Ah, who shall keep us from over-spelling
> That sweet, forgotten, forbidden Love?
> E'en as we doubt, in our hearts once more,
> With a rush of tears to our eyelids welling

A
> Love comes back to his vacant dwelling
> The old, old Love that we knew of yore!

It is not difficult to see how the composers adapted this repetitive scheme for their purposes; and so we have the rondo, with its sections contrasted in key and character.

IV. A sectional form that has been widely employed, especially by composers of an earlier time, is the *binary* or *two-part* form (represented symbolically by the formula A–B), consisting of two consecutive divisions[1]; sometimes the second is entirely different from the first, sometimes it is simply a new aspect or rearrangement of it. The A section usually ends in the key of the dominant; B leads back to the tonic. The tune " America " is an illustration of simple binary form; the musical phrases to which the first three lines of the text are sung comprise the first section; those set to the last three lines make up the second division. Many of the Schubert and Brahms piano waltzes are written in this form.

Binary form was extremely popular in the seventeenth and eighteenth centuries and was often used by such composers as François Couperin and Domenico Scarlatti in the pieces they wrote for the harpsichord. Listen to some of Couperin's fancifully titled clavecin pieces or to one of Scarlatti's brilliant sonatas, and you will have heard this form in its best estate.

V. Still another easily recognized scheme is that of *three-part* or *ternary* form (A–B–A), perhaps the most universally used of them all. Listen to this French folk song:

The two sections marked A are exactly alike, excepting at their end; the second has a more final air about it than had the first at this point. This is likewise true of this German folk tune:

---

[1] Either or both of these divisions may be repeated, but it is customary in analyzing forms not to take these literal repetitions into account.

But if you follow these tunes through, you will find that their composers were not satisfied with just this simple repetition of ideas. In the French song, a new contrasting idea is inserted, consisting of two short phrases, the second an exact duplicate of the first; and after this the first section, A, returns again:

So with the German song:

This gives us a basic picture of the pattern which is used continuously throughout music, in all kinds of simple and complex ways:

1. The statement of an idea or a section
2. The placing in contrast of a new idea or section
3. The restatement of the first idea so as to give unity and finality

We find examples of this form in music of many styles and periods:

1. It has been employed by the composers of many simple songs. Hum or whistle through the following tunes, and you will find that they are all built according to this three-part form:

" Ye Banks and Braes," Scots folk tune
" The Flight of the Earls," Irish folk tune
" All Through the Night," Welsh folk tune
" Drink to Me Only with Thine Eyes," English folk tune
" Turkey in the Straw," American folk tune
O Tannenbaum, German folk tune
Humoresque, Dvořák

2. It was used by composers of the classic period for certain of their short instrumental pieces, particularly the minuet. Of all the dances developed during the course of European history, this seems to have had the greatest effect upon music; starting as a French peasant dance, it was adopted by the aristocratic court circles and then taken over by the writers of instrumental music. Almost from its earliest existence it has been written in ternary

form — a first stanza, followed by a second, and then the first again. In Bach's time the two contrasting sections of a minuet were thought of as separate pieces and so labeled: Minuets I and II. These were played successively, after which Minuet I was repeated (see Bach's *B Minor Orchestral Suite*). In order to provide better contrast, the second minuet was written for three instruments or in three-part harmony, and so came to be known as the *trio*. This name stuck, even after the reasons for it had been lost. So the plan came to be:

(*a*) Minuet
(*b*) Another minuet called a *trio*
(*c*) The original minuet repeated intact

When Beethoven supplanted the minuet with the *scherzo* in his piano and orchestral pieces, he kept the same general form, merely changing its mood and speed; some of this composer's most characteristic contributions to symphonic literature took the form of *scherzo* and *trio*: for example, the third movement of the *Eroica* and the *Seventh Symphony*. Many composers since his time have followed his example in using the scherzo in their symphonies.

3. The three-part form, with slight adaptations, was used for many of the small pieces which were popular with the nineteenth-century piano composers, such things as the nocturne, the waltz, the prelude, the impromptu, and so on. It makes an ideal form for this purpose, for in a limited scope it offers plenty of opportunity for ingenious architecture and strong emotional contrasts. Here are some characteristic examples from Chopin:

Nocturne in F Major, Op. 15, No. 1.

A beautiful slow melody (marked *adagio cantabile*) is the feature of the opening section (1–24); the middle section (25–48) is marked by a fiery series of broken chords and brilliant runs for the left hand; and then the quiet, peaceful melody returns in its original mood.

Nocturne in F Sharp Major, Op. 15, No. 2.

Here again the A section (1–24) is marked by one of those slow, rather melancholy melodies that Chopin knew so well how to write. The middle section (25–48) has in contrast a series of interlocking chords supporting a melody that moves twice as fast as did the original one. Then the first section is again heard almost exactly as before.

Prelude in D Flat Major, Op. 28, No. 15.

Here the contrasting section (28–75) is carried over logically from the first (1–27) by a clever device: the almost maddening repetition of a note that has been very prominent in the melody and harmony of the first section. Upon its return A is somewhat shortened.

Étude in F Major, Op. 10, No. 8.

The different sections are not always clearly defined. Here the middle section (41–60) is marked out, not by the introduction of new material, but by the reshaping of the ideas of the first part. A (1–40) is distinguished by a running figure in quick time in which the accent is heavily marked out at the beginning of every second measure. In B we seem to sink to a new tone level, and the rhythmic pattern is obscured by the bright chromatic harmonies, making a blaze of color which quickly subsides when A (61–86) is reintroduced. There is a distinct coda (87), a prolongation of the section, due to the natural tendency of an artist to end whatever he attempts in as impressive and complete a way as possible.

4. An extended ternary form is sometimes used for the slow movements of sonatas and symphonies; when this is the case, the result is simply a lengthened song form such as that employed by the unknown composers of *Sur le pont d'Avignon* and *Ach! du lieber Augustin*. Grieg has used this extended three-part song form most effectively in the second movement of his *Sonata in C Minor* for violin and piano, Op. 45. In this the first division of 44 measures is played by the piano alone, and then repeated by the piano and the violin together; the B section offers new material in decided contrast to the A; and then A returns, this time with the violin part an octave higher than before.[2]

5. The most complex and, at the same time, most widely used of the tripartite forms is the *sonata-form*, generally used in

[2] Wagner, the great opera composer, had a peculiar name for this form: he called it a *bogen*, and used it frequently during the course of the musical development of his great works. A slightly different three-part form was also used frequently by him, a form consisting of two identical or similar parts (each of which he called a *stollen*), completed by a third part, known as the *abgesang* — A–A–B instead of A–B–A. This unit Wagner called a *bar*, taking the name from the old nomenclature of the medieval guild of the Mastersingers. Indeed, his whole opera *Die Meistersinger* is filled with *bars*, varying in length from phrases a few measures in length to others occupying many pages of score. Notable among these is the music which fills the Prize Song section in the last act and which accompanies Walther's *Am stillen Herd* in the first act.

the first movements of sonatas, symphonies, and quartets. Musical nomenclature is here sadly at fault, for it gives plenty of opportunity for confusion in the use of this term. Sonata-form is unfortunately used for two different things: we use it when we speak of the form of the sonata as an entire work, consisting of three or four movements; we use it also when referring specifically to the structural plan that is generally used in the first (and sometimes in the last) of these movements. So the listener must keep this distinction clearly in mind between (a) the sonata as a whole, and (b) sonata-form, better termed *first-movement form,* as an entity in itself. It was first generally adopted by Haydn in the latter part of the eighteenth century, this composer basing his work upon the experiments of earlier German composers. It became from that time the usual form for the first movements of sonatas, symphonies, string quartets, and other instrumental music. Its cardinal principle is that of the varied manipulation of two contrasting main themes, one vigorous, active, masculine in character, the other quieter, more lyric, and feminine. The years have proved this scheme to be sound in its structural details, and it has satisfied the needs of composers as widely different as Haydn and Brahms. Some of our greatest music has been written according to this plan, and it has stimulated some of the leading writers to do their best work.

For handy reference, the basic construction of this form may be diagrammed in this fashion:

AN INTRODUCTION (Not an essential part of the scheme, and not found in many instances after Haydn)

A: THE STATEMENT OF THE THEMES (Sometimes called " The Exposition ")

Tonic key	(1) First theme, usually repeated and then connected by means of a bridge passage to
Dominant key (*Relative major, if first theme is in minor*)	(2) Second theme (or group of themes), complementary in character, often repeated and sometimes (as in the developed Beethoven style) closely connected with
	(3) Closing passage. This may consist of a new theme (which would then be called the third theme) or of a modification of the other themes, or perhaps of both. This part brings the whole section to a definite close.

B: THE DEVELOPMENT OF THE THEMES

Many keys	Here the composer re-creates his themes in new ways, often pulling them apart and re-combining them in new patterns, letting his skill and imagination deal with them in various ways. This section is marked by many changes of key, thus providing constant new interest.

A: THE RESTATEMENT OF THE THEMES (Recapitulation)

Tonic key	(1) Restated as before, and connected with
	(2) Restated, and in turn often connected with
	(3) Restated, after which the movement is brought to a close.

The *coda*, or post-oration, often follows, thus providing a final climax.

This, it must always be remembered, is a simplified, skeletonized plan of sonata-form, and many deviations from it are possible and have been made by various composers. Actual listening practice [3] will show that the sonata-form is not so simple as the above outline might lead us to believe. For instance, what we have called the first and second *themes* are often not so much clear-cut themes as series of compacted fragments of themes. The important thing to realize is that this section which we have labeled " The Statement of the Themes " contains one group of themes that are similar in character in juxtaposition with another group of themes that are like in character; the strong contrast between these two groups provides dramatic interest and the material for this section of the movement. The first group is usually powerful and aggressive, vital — masculine, if you will; and it stands in strong key contrast to the second group, which is exactly opposite in mood — relaxed, lyric, feminine. The last theme or themes may be of almost any nature, so long as the material is sufficiently conclusive to indicate the end of this whole " statement " section, and suggest that the " development " is about to begin. In passing, we may note that this A or " Exposition " section is sometimes repeated (as was the custom in earlier times), or the interpreter may go on directly to the development. The bridge

[3] No better example of this form can be found than the first movement of Beethoven's *Fifth Symphony*: here everything is as clear and forthright as it possibly can be. See Chapter XXIX.

passages may be short or long, but they should always be consistent, really leading out of one set of thematic ideas into another. The tendency with some composers has been to use rather meaningless musical figuration in such passages — what Wagner (in speaking of Haydn's symphonies) rather pointedly described as " the clatter of the dishes between the courses at a royal feast." Most of Beethoven's bridge passages are striking examples of what can be accomplished.

The great second or B section of the sonata-form, instead of consisting of new material such as we found to be the case in the other tripartite forms, features the development of materials already presented. This feature of evolving new musical substance out of old ones challenges the skill of every composer, for it requires not only technical resource but outstanding imagination. All sorts of expedients are available: fragments of the themes with which the listener has become familiar are tossed about, pulled apart, recombined in different ways, put into new key relationships. Sometimes all the themes are treated, sometimes only one or two. There are no fixed rules nor set patterns other than the fact that the section usually opens with at least a suggestion of the first theme in order to orient the listener, and, after modulating through a varied series of keys, finally arrives at the end back in the original key level of the first theme, so as to be ready to start the recapitulation. Almost anything may happen in between; even new themes are sometimes introduced. In the hands of a skilled composer such as Beethoven, whose architectural sense was matched by his imaginative phantasy, this development section can be the source of the greatest possible pleasure and excitement for the listener.

The restatement or recapitulation follows the development section without pause; in the classic sonata-form it is almost exactly like the statement, except for the fact that all the themes are now in the same key, in order to give a sense of unified finality. The bridge passages have to be altered somewhat, since it is no longer necessary to lead from one key level to another, and the tendency of modern composers has been to shorten this section. Even those who do so, however, take care that the recapitulation ends with a definite culminative impact, sometimes in the shape of a forceful coda, sometimes without it. Beethoven, especially, wrote mighty codas, containing sometimes almost a new development. A well-constructed first movement should leave us with a satisfied sense of arrival home after a series of colorful and exciting adventures.

Composers, ever seeking freer forms, devised the so-called *sonata-rondo*, a combination that is much more fluid than the rather square, older, simple rondo type; it likewise allowed for more development than did the rondo, which rarely had much. The usual plan was to introduce the development section thus: A–B–A–Development–A–B; thus the sonata-rondo has, in general, something of the continuous building power of the first movement. It was this type of rondo (with slight variants) that was most often used by Beethoven; examples may be found in his *Piano Sonata in B Flat,* Op. 22; the piano *Rondo in G,* Op. 51, No. 2; and the *Piano and Violin Sonata,* Op. 12, No. 2.

FREE FORMS

Strictly speaking, there is no such thing as " free " form, for no matter how free a piece of music is, it must always have form; that is, it must have some basic structural plan if it is to make any sense for the listener. But there are certain kinds of musical writing that do not fall naturally into the basic formal types that we have just been considering. These, for lack of a better term, we call *free forms.*

One of the most important of these is the *overture,* literally an opening piece. In its essence it is closely connected with the theater: it may be the opening selection before a play, provided to heighten emotional mood; more likely it is the introduction to an opera, with themes taken from the score. Sometimes it merely sets the mood — suggests whether the work to follow is a light comedy (*vide* Mozart's inimitable overture to *The Marriage of Figaro,* which is in modified first-movement form, without development [4]), or a deep tragedy (such as the music provided by Wagner for playing before his *Tristan and Isolde*). Or it may

---

[4] Mention should be made here (this is as good a place as any to introduce such an irregularity) of this sort of first movement that has no real inner structure, the sort of thing that is used in many *sonatinas* (sonatas of less serious, or less developed, character) and opera overtures. Other examples may be found in Mozart's *Piano Sonata* in F (K. 280) and Schubert's *Rosamunde Overture.*

foreshadow the events to come, as Beethoven did in the overtures which he wrote for his one opera, *Fidelio*,[5] thereby, as someone has sagely remarked, making the opera itself unnecessary. Composers have also applied this term to independent concert pieces composed in the style of an operatic overture, as Brahms did in his " Academic Festival " and " Tragic " overtures.

Originally overtures were written without any great concern for form: they just " grew." In the seventeenth century they crystallized into two general types, the Italian and the French overtures; both were in more than one movement. The Italian type (popularized by A. Scarlatti, 1659–1725) was made up of

> A quick movement
> A slower movement
> A quick movement

The French overture (most effectively used by the composer Lully, 1632–1687), on the other hand, had

A slow movement (played twice)
A quick movement
A slow movement, usually part of the first, sometimes a new, slow
   dance form

These types, especially the latter, were in use for a long time (the overture to Handel's *Messiah* is a good example) but were gradually pushed aside by the development of the sonata-form, which became the accepted type of overture form during the nineteenth century. Later composers freed themselves again from formal considerations in writing overtures, as, for example, Wagner did in the overtures to his operas *Lohengrin* and *Parsifal*.

As a matter of fact, Wagner called the overtures we have just mentioned " Preludes " — the word in this sense meaning the same thing — an introductory piece played before an opera. The term is likewise applied to small, independent orchestral or piano pieces and to introductory pieces placed before a fugue; in both cases the free form of the prelude is a distinguishing feature.[6]

A *fantasia* may be defined as a composition in which the

---

[5] The composer made four attempts at writing an overture for this work.
[6] Some preludes, as we have seen, are in strict three-part form.

formal demands are subordinated to those of imagination or perhaps pure willfullness; one dictionary definition goes so far as to say that a composer uses the term *fantasia* when no other name happens to occur to him. But there is always a suggestion of the imagination in this term. Rousseau, in the great dictionary of music he published in the eighteenth century, defines *fantasia* as " a piece of instrumental music that one performs as one composes it " and adds that a *fantaisie* can " never be written, because as soon as it is written or repeated it ceases to be a *fantaisie* and becomes an ordinary piece." This is not strictly true, because Beethoven, Chopin, Brahms, all left us fantasias, some of them quite informal in character, others rather strict as to form. Classic examples of the fantasia are two which Bach wrote as introductory movements to organ fugues, one in G minor, the other in C minor. (The complete titles are *Fantasia and Fugue in G Minor; Fantasia and Fugue in C Minor*.) Mozart wrote three fine piano fantasias, two in C minor (K. 396 and 475), and one in D Minor (K. 397); the first of these is strangely prophetic of Beethoven's style. Unfortunately, the term has had rather too many meanings, good and bad, over a long period of years; in its tawdry sense, this form can descend to a very low level, for example, when applied to strings of tunes from an opera or a musical comedy, hashed together and served up in unappetizing fashion. Notice the *Fantasia on William Tell*.

If he has followed this chapter thus far, the musical neophyte is probably thoroughly confused by this time in his attempt to grasp the underlying principles of so many different kinds of form. He is, in fact, probably tempted to turn his back on the whole matter and ask, " After all, what is the use? Can I honestly expect to enjoy music any more by trying to follow these architectural plans and understand all these technical terms, many of them so confused and inexact in meaning? "

The only answer that we can give is that even a slight acquaintanceship with the way music is put together will help to remove this sense of bewilderment and futility from which so many suffer when listening to great music. In its place there will come — gradually, to be sure, but none the less surely — the pleasure of observing a composer's designs and of realizing how they are (or are not) being fulfilled. This sense of the design and plan back of the music becomes an almost intuitive part of the listener's equipment, and, when added to the sensuous pleasure he gets from what he hears, helps his experience and cultivates his taste. Form is by no manner of means all there is to music; it is not even the most important aspect of it. But the more one understands it, the surer he is of his musical judgment.

LIST OF SUGGESTED MUSIC

One-Part Instrumental Form

Prelude in C Major, Op. 28, No. 1	Chopin

Theme with Variations

" The Bells "	Byrd
Suite for Harpsichord, No. 5 in E major	Handel
Passacaglia: Last Movement, *Fourth Symphony*	Brahms
Chaconne in D minor from Partita No. 2 for violin, unaccompanied	Bach
Surprise Symphony, Second Movement	Haydn
Kreutzer Sonata, Op. 47, Second Movement	Beethoven
Variations on a Theme by Haydn	Brahms
Symphonic Variations	César Franck
The Enigma Variations	Elgar
Octet for Wind Instruments	Stravinsky
Der Schwanendreher	Hindemith
Under the Spreading Chestnut Tree "	Weinberger

Rondo

Rondeau	Chambonnières
Surprise Symphony, Last Movement	Haydn
Piano Concerto in D Minor, Last Movement	Mozart
Suite for Orchestra, Op. 19, Last Movement	Dohnányi

Two-Part Instrumental Form

Twelve Ländler, Op. 171	Schubert
Waltzes, Op. 39	Brahms
Sonatina in D Major (Longo No. 262)	D. Scarlatti

Three-Part Instrumental Form

Humoresque	Dvořák
Nocturne in F Major, Op. 15, No. 1	Chopin
Nocturne in F Sharp Major, Op. 15, No. 2	Chopin
Étude in F Major, Op. 10, No. 8	Chopin
Sonata in C Minor for violin and piano, Op. 45, Second Movement	Grieg

Minuet

From *Suite in B Minor* for orchestra	Bach
Symphony in G Minor, Third Movement	Mozart

Scherzo

Symphony No. 7 in A major, Third Movement	Beethoven
Symphony No. 4 in F minor, Third Movement	Tchaikovsky

Sonata-form

Symphony No. 5 in C minor, First Movement	Beethoven
Symphony in G Minor, First Movement	Mozart

Sonata-Rondo Form

Rondo in G Major, Op. 51	Beethoven
Piano Sonata in B Flat, Op. 22, Last Movement	Beethoven

Free Forms

Overture

Overture to *The Marriage of Figaro*	Mozart
Overture to *Fidelio*	Beethoven

" Academic Festival Overture "	Brahms
Overture to *Semiramide*	Rossini
Sonata for Flute and Strings, First Movement	A. Scarlatti
Overture to *Thésée*	Lully
Overture to *The Messiah*	Handel
Prelude to *Tristan and Isolde*	Wagner
" When Johnny Comes Marching Home " (An American Overture)	Harris

Fantasia

Fantasia in G Minor for organ	Bach
Fantasia in C Minor for organ	Bach
Fantasia in C Minor, K. 396, for piano	Mozart

TOPICS FOR FURTHER DISCUSSION

Find and briefly analyze other good examples of simple binary and ternary forms.

Compare the older (for example, up to the time of Mozart) variations with the more modern ones (those of Franck and Elgar). What seem to be the chief differences?

If you can, hear some of the late Beethoven works in the variation form (for example, Op. 109 and the string quartets, Op. 127 and 131) and consider whither Beethoven's variations were tending, and what spiritual qualities they seem to express.

Why did composers of operas prefer an overture that had no real development?

To your mind, has the sonata-rondo form any great advantage over the simple rondo form?

CHAPTER XVII

Instrumental Forms (Continued)

CONJOINT FORMS

HAVING obtained an idea of the sectional forms that have been used through the centuries by composers, the listener should investigate some of the larger aspects of form — how it shapes the constitution of a piece as a whole. For he will find that a great deal of the instrumental music he hears at concerts and over the radio consists of compositions of extended length — sometimes lasting well over an hour — that are made up of a number of separate elements or " movements," as the musician calls them. When these are grouped together under a single title, they may be called one of several names, depending on the general character of the composition and the instrument for which the music was written.

Among the simplest of these conjoint forms is the *march*, a piece of strongly rhythmical music designed or fitted to accompany marching and used from early times to " enliven the spirits and minimize fatigue." As used today, it consists of a sort of rondo, with a principal, strongly melodic section that comes round again and again, separated by intervening tunes, some of which are called, with as little reason as in the minuet, *trios.*

Another simple conjoint form is the *waltz*, which, while designed for dancing, is often played in concerts. It consists of a string of seven or eight different short waltz themes, the whole being prefaced with a suitable *introduction* and often followed by a *coda* recapitulating some of the tunes used in the body of the work. See Johann Strauss's *Wiener Blut* and *Geschichten aus dem Wiener Wald,* two of the finest waltzes ever written.

Still another of these simple conjoint forms is the *suite;* the literal meaning of this word gives us its musical definition: a series or group of things belonging together and forming a unit. Just as we have suites of rooms or of furniture in everyday life, so in music we have suites of compositions, each of them complete in itself. These separate units may be written in any form — binary, ternary, rondo, theme with variations, sonata-form — that the composer may choose, and can be played and enjoyed as entities, without relationship to any other music. But they were intended by the composer to be played in sequence, and they give their full effect only when so used.

In the early days of instrumental music, suites were invariably made up of dance tunes which were all in the same key. The usual convention was that there should be four of these — the allemande, the courante, the saraband, and the gigue; between these, the composer was at liberty to insert as many other types of dances as suited his fancy — gavottes, minuets, polonaises, rigadoons, bourrées, and so on. Usually a prelude or an overture was added and the whole work was arranged so as to secure the maximum effects of contrast in tempo and style. The form was thus quite free, and may best be studied in the suites of Purcell, Bach, Handel, and Corelli. Other names were often given to the suite by some older composers: serenade, *partita, divertimento*, and cassation. All these have the same general structure and were written for a wide variety of instruments, singly and in combination.

Suites are, of course, often written today on the same free lines as in the eighteenth century, although the classic dance forms are no longer used. Sometimes composers try to evoke the spirit of former times, as in Ravel's lovely suite, *Le tombeau de Couperin;* sometimes they simply string together materials from theatrical or ballet music, as Grieg did in his much-played *Peer Gynt Suites,* or Tchaikovsky in his *Nutcracker Suite;* sometimes they simply try to provide a series of entertaining and contrasting movements such as there are in Dohnányi's fine *Suite for Orchestra*, Op. 19.

A whole group of compositions, numbering among them some of the greatest things ever written, may be classified under one generic category. These works are of an extended type and are made up of a number of separate divisions or movements (usually four, quite frequently three), each of which, while maintaining its individual identity, is an inherent part of the whole. These compositions have been given different names, according to the usage for which they were designed:

1. A *sonata* (literally a composition that is sounded or played, in contradistinction to one that is sung) is a work of the type described above, written for one or two solo instruments.
2. A *trio* is a sonata for three instruments.
3. *Quartet* means a sonata for four instruments, usually first and second violins, viola, and cello.
4. *Quintet* means a sonata for five instruments.
5. *Sextet* means a sonata for six instruments.
6. A *symphony* is a sonata for orchestra.
7. A *concerto* is a sonata for solo instrument (or instruments) with orchestra.

Here again, although there are no fixed rules, tradition has dictated that each movement of these works should be written according to a different form. The usual procedure has been as follows:

The First Movement (of a vigorous, quick, *allegro* character) is written in sonata-form (perhaps better termed "first-movement form").

The Second Movement (usually *andante* or *adagio*) is, in contrast, slow and lyric in character. It may be in sonata-form, a theme with variations, or in ternary (song) form.

The Third Movement is strongly rhythmic in character and provides relaxation for the listener. In reality it is a dance movement: with the composers Haydn and Mozart it took the form of a minuet and trio; Beethoven substituted a scherzo, in which the tempo of the minuet was speeded up and the general mood of the movement lightened. Later composers have in general followed Beethoven's example.

The Fourth Movement is again rapid and complex, something like the first but with more of an air of finality, leading to either a triumphant or an irresistible close. It is usually in rondo or sonata-form.

What a common-sense procedure this is! The first movement is designed to arrest our attention; the second to set us dreaming, or at least contemplating; the third gives us a chance to relax; and the fourth puts us in a cheerful or exalted frame of mind. All composers, from Haydn to Shostakovich, have realized the effectiveness of this traditional scheme and have followed it more or less closely, for to date it has been impossible to think up a better one. The greatest composers have excelled in maintaining the essential character of each of these movements, at the same time weaving them into a congruous and climactic whole. They have been, as Lawrence Abbott has said, master architects and dramatists in the opening movement; imaginative poets and tender lyricists in the second; rhythmic dance musicians in the third, with plenty of boisterous rhythms up their sleeve; and eloquent prophets and effective spellbinders in the fourth. Study such works as Beethoven's *Fifth Symphony* or Sibelius's *Second Symphony*, and you will hear how effectively these plans have been used by the great men.

There are some changes from this general procedure that have become familiar with certain composers: the order of the second and third movements is sometimes reversed, the scherzo coming second and the slow movement third (as in Beethoven's *Ninth Symphony*); there is often, especially in sonatas, only one middle movement; usually it is the scherzo that is omitted, or the slow movement and the scherzo may be telescoped into one whole.

In the concerto [1] the listener must realize that there are two masterly forces in action throughout, the solo instrument, or instruments, and the full orchestra; care must be taken by the composer that he does not slight the one or the other, and that there are plenty of opportunities for drama in the interaction of the dominant powers. Since the same opportunities for dramatic contrast exist between the two themes of the concerto, this form may be said to be a sort of heightened and intensified symphony, with two important dramatic interactions being developed. So, too, in a sonata for violin and piano: the two instruments are on an equal footing and are supposed to share the honors equally. Throughout the trio or the quartet there must be a constant interchange of ideas between the various instruments; if one is exalted too greatly at the expense of the others, the essential quality of the composition is sure to be lost. The best way to familiarize oneself with the characteristics of these compositions is to listen to a number of representative examples of each and compare them carefully. A list of good ones to choose from will be found at the end of this chapter.

For completeness of record, there remains a word to be said regarding the form which program music usually takes — that

---

[1] We refer here to the three-or-four movement concerto; *concerti grossi,* an earlier type, are really suites for solo instruments and orchestra.

of the *symphonic poem*. We have already studied several representative examples of these works, and the listener should be able to recognize the fact that in them the form follows the program, rather than there being any strict structural outline — rondo, theme and variations, and the like. A work of this kind having several movements, such as Rimsky-Korsakoff's *Scheherazade* Suite (to be studied soon) is called a *symphonic suite*. There is usually little thematic development in these works, its place being taken by alterations and paraphrases of the themes to fit the necessities of the program.

LIST OF SUGGESTED MUSIC

March

| *Semper Fidelis;* " The Stars and Stripes Forever " | Sousa |
| " The Washington Post "; *El Capitán* | Sousa |

Waltz

| *Wiener Blut* | Johann Strauss |
| *Tales from the Vienna Woods* | Johann Strauss |

Be sure to obtain authentic Viennese interpretations of these, not modern, streamline versions; there is all the difference in the world.

Suite

Pre-classic

Suite No. 1 in G major	Purcell
Sonata for Flute and Strings	A. Scarlatti
Suite No. 2 in B minor	Bach
Suite for Strings	Corelli

Post-classic

Holberg Suite, Op. 40	Grieg
Le tombeau de Couperin	Ravel
Suite, Op. 19	Dohnányi

Caucasian Sketches	Ippolitov-Ivanov

The first three of these attempt to catch the spirit of the old suites, but employ more modern idioms; the last is a descriptive program suite.

Peer Gynt Suite No. 1	Grieg
L'Arlésienne (Suite) No. 1	Bizet
Nutcracker Suite	Tchaikovsky
Daphne and Chloe Suite No. 1	Ravel
Pulcinella (Ballet Suite)	Stravinsky
Lieut. Kiji Suite, Op. 60	Prokofiev
Things to Come Suite	Bliss
The Incredible Flutist (Ballet Suite)	Piston

These are all based on concert treatment of theater music.

Sonata

Sonata pathétique (for piano), Op. 13	Beethoven
Sonata in A Major, Op. 47 (for violin and piano)	Beethoven

Trio

Trio for Piano and Strings, Op. 99	Schubert
Trio for French Horn, Violin, and Piano, Op. 40	Brahms

Quartet

Quartet in F Major, Op. 18, No. 1	Beethoven
Quartet No. 2 in D major	Borodin

Quintet

Quintet in A Major (Trout)	Schubert

Sextet

Sextet in B Flat Major for Strings, Op. 18	Brahms

Septet

Septet in E Flat Major, Op. 20	Beethoven

Octet

> *Octet in F Major,* Op. 166   Schubert

Symphony

> *Symphony No. 5 in C Minor,* Op. 67   Beethoven

Concerto

> *Concerto in D Minor* (piano and orchestra)   Mozart
>
> *Concerto No. 4 in G Major,* Op. 58
> (piano and orchestra)   Beethoven
>
> *Concerto in D Major,* Op. 35
> (violin and orchestra)   Tchaikovsky

TOPICS FOR FURTHER DISCUSSION

What is the function of the cadenza in a concerto? Discuss its value.

What advantages has the symphonic poem over the symphony as regards (*a*) freedom of form, and (*b*) interpretative power? Are there any drawbacks or dangers to be considered along with the advantages?

Have any composers been equally remarkable in writing both symphonic poems and symphonies?

Do you think that ability in writing one of these forms tends to cramp it in another?

Do you know of any symphonies that have more than four movements? If so, where are the extra movements added?

CHAPTER XVIII

Rimsky-Korsakoff's "Scheherazade" — Nationalism

A New Path in Music

WE have seen how Romanticism meant a revolt against the accepted traditions of the past and an intensification of the qualities that determine the characteristics of the individual. In order to secure material for their struggle against the heritages and conventions of the Classicists, the Romantic artists went to the half-forgotten folk tales and colorful legends of the various countries. This was the beginning of an intellectual movement towards national freedom, a movement that was aided by the series of European wars caused by the Napoleonic ambitions. These nineteenth-century wars aroused feelings of national consciousness and stirred hopes of revolt in all countries, hopes and feelings which were, after all, but the magnifications of the consciousness of the individual. And this Romantic ideal, once aroused and abetted by the political situation of the times, developed into an artistic chauvinism, the effects of which we are still feeling.

In the latter part of the nineteenth century we thus find the people of the various countries turning their attention more and more inwards, striving in practical as well as spiritual ways to foster their own resources in every possible way. It was but natural for the artists of each country to fall in with the movement, and we find them struggling to free themselves from the bondage of the foreigner, using every means to stimulate their own national expression. The unique environment of each land, its physical and climatic conditions, its historic vicissitudes, its future possibilities — all of these were excellent grist for the nationalistic mill. In so far as the production of music was concerned, Italy, France, and Germany had had the field pretty much to themselves up to the beginning of the nineteenth century; but in 1843 Schumann, the outstanding musical *littérateur* of the time, had the perspicacity to realize that the nations bordering on Germany were strongly desirous of freeing themselves from the influences of German composers, and he advised the musicians in these countries to develop the qualities to be found within their native music in every possible way. The middle years of the nineteenth century saw a number of important men arise in these countries: Smetana and Dvořák in Bohemia, Grieg in Norway, Glinka, Borodin, Balakirev, Moussorgsky, and Rimsky-Korsakoff in Russia. Thus a new and important phase of Romanticism developed, a phase that we call *Nationalism*.

This does not seem to hold true for Russian music, however. There is good reason for the widespread popularity of this kind of national music outside the boundaries of its native land. Not all of it genuinely Russian in that it does not always express racial ideals and emotions, this music has an unusual imaginative appeal for countries having a different racial heritage. Russia — we are speaking of the Russia before the revolution, the Russia which produced this music in large quantities — in every way, geographically, culturally, ethnographically, was partly Asiatic, and the influence of the East is a potent one in this music. There are exotic and unfamiliar rhythms, unusual and different harmonies; the hearers of this music are brought under the influences of its visions, its eternal longings. The lethargy of generations is heard in its strains, and the spell of its rhythms and harmonies transports us as upon a magic carpet to lands that are far beyond our ken; there we find welcome refuge from the commonplaces of our everyday life.

" SCHEHERAZADE " [1]

Rimsky-Korsakoff, although not the most important figure in the group of Russian nationalist composers, has produced the most popular composition of the whole movement: *Scheherazade*, a Symphonic Suite after the *Thousand and One Arabian Nights*. There is excellent reason for the popularity of this music, for

[1] The piano score of Rimsky-Korsakoff's *Scheherazade* is available in the Schirmer Edition, New York. The orchestral score (miniature size) is available in the Kalmus Edition No. 82.

aside from the appealing nature of the subject, Rimsky-Korsakoff
has written music that has hardly been surpassed in genuine poetic quality and descriptive power. Much might be said here regarding the program of this music; but we shall be wise if we
follow the composer's wishes in this respect and listen to the
music as a piece woven out of a number of themes chosen for
their musical rather than for their descriptive qualities. We have
here a kaleidoscope of fairy-tale image and design, chosen at
random from that classic folk-tale collection, the *Arabian Nights
Entertainments*. With its rich interpretative fantasy and its unusual sense of color, this score of Rimsky-Korsakoff's is a masterpiece among works of its kind.

The composer has given us the following preface to his
music, all the program that we really need: " The Sultan Schahriar, convinced of the faithlessness of women, had sworn to put
to death each of his wives after the wedding night. But the Sultana Scheherazade saved her life by diverting him with stories
which she told him during a thousand and one nights. The Sultan,
conquered by his curiosity, put off from day to day the execution of his wife and at last renounced his bloody vow. Many
wonders were narrated to Schahriar by the Sultana Scheherazade;
for her stories the Sultana borrowed the verses of poets and the
words of folk songs and fitted together tales and adventures."

The composer's additional information is helpful, however,
information that was given to the public at the time this music
was first performed. He suggested the following titles for the
four movements of his Suite:

   I. The Sea and Sinbad's Ship
  II. The Story of the Kalendar Prince
 III. The Young Prince and the Young Princess
 IV. Festival at Bagdad — The Ship goes to pieces on a Rock surmounted
     by the bronze figure of a Warrior — Conclusion

There is no logical sequence to such a program. Rather, we
have a series of incidents which stimulated the composer's imagination as he planned the various musical sections of his work.
There is no difficulty in following the poetic suggestiveness of his
music, however; its direct appeal and beautiful orchestral speech
guarantee it immediate popularity everywhere. It will be of interest for us to examine this music in detail in order that we may

observe the manner in which a composer builds his fabric out of simple materials. Rimsky-Korsakoff uses several principal themes in his composition, but they are not employed as we found them in the Liszt or the Strauss tone poems, that is, directly linked with the fixed poetic ideas of the program. Here they are " purely musical material, themes for musical development," to use the composer's own words. And we find that sometimes the same theme is used to suggest quite different incidents in the program.

First of all there are two themes

that occur throughout the whole Suite, serving to provide a sort of unifying thread to connect the different sections: (1) a harsh, threatening phrase (I, 1–4), heard at the very beginning — Rimsky-Korsakoff tells us that it is meant to suggest the stern Sultan, always ready to listen to the fair Scheherazade's stories, but just as ready to cut off her head should she fail to interest him; (2) the theme of the Sultana herself (I, 14–17), graceful, lithe, given to the violin with accompanying chords on the harp. These two themes are repeated again and again in the course of the music, as if they would keep us properly oriented. Then there are other motives which thread through the various sections, alternating and twining each with the other, appearing in different contexts and different moods. In the first section, after the introduction of the Sultan and the Scheherazade themes, we hear an undulating arpeggio figure (I, 18–23), suggestive of the roll of the sea. Listen to what the composer does with it after first bringing it to our attention: first heard low in the orchestra, it mounts steadily, growing more and more intense, to a loud climax; after this quite another development of it is heard, with a different instrumentation. The climax this time leads to a new theme (I, 70–75), a series of detached chords on the wood-wind instruments. Then follow fragments of the sea theme, to which is later added the violin figure of the Sultana motive (I, 94), and finally the Sultan motive comes thundering in the bass (I, 110). A vigorous " development " follows: the different themes are tossed about in various parts of the orchestra, they are heard in varying keys and in different orchestral combinations, sometimes loud, sometimes very soft. The whole section gives a fine idea of the manner in which a skilled composer can treat germane material. This corresponds in manner of treatment, of course, to the development section of the sonata form. Listen to this part several times, trying to fix in your mind the intricate weavings and manipulations of the melodies, and you will secure ideal practice in listening. Naturally, as we learn more of these methods of how music is put together, our admiration of the composer's craftsmanship will add another factor to our capacity for enjoyment.

The second movement, after a brief reminder that the Sultana is still busy at her life-preserving task (II, 1–4), launches into a story told by a wandering Oriental beggar. The bassoon takes the center of the orchestral stage and sings us a theme (II, 5–25) suggestive of the burlesque, sometimes of an almost pathetic mock heroism. The oboe takes up this theme (II, 26), followed in turn by the violins (II, 48), and then the brass and wood winds (II, 71); the pace quickens and there are furtive suggestions of the Sultan and Sultana themes. Suddenly a brilliant fanfare of the brass (II, 105) announces a new twist to the story; Rimsky-Korsakoff has wisely left us in the dark as to what particular incidents figure in it. The trombones give us a new theme of brilliant character (II, 108), and it is answered as if in echo by muted trumpets (109). A lively development follows, interrupted by two graceful arabesque-like reminiscences of the Sultana theme, the first of them given to the clarinets (II, 161), and the second, following soon after (II, 421), to the bassoon. The section between is given over to a rapidly moving development of the brilliant trombone theme heard shortly before. Fragments of these various tunes follow thick and fast, and the whole section ends with a solemn pronouncement of the Sultan theme.

The third movement is a romantic love idyl. Like all ardent

lovers, the Prince speaks first, his theme being a light folklike passage for the strings (III, 1–8). There is a rushing oriental-like passage for the clarinet (III, 21), and then the Prince theme is repeated with an oboe added to the strings and in a lower, darker register of the orchestra (III, 25). When the rushing theme comes again, it is given to the flutes (III, 46). These two themes are now alternated, one answering the other until, with a sudden change in color, the Princess is heard, her theme being given to the clarinet with an accompaniment of snare drum, tambourine, and triangle (III, 70–78). The two principal themes are as much alike as lovers' themes should be; their distinguishing characteristics are their rhythms. They are now heard intermingled in lovers' discourse, only to be suddenly interrupted (III, 142) by the Sultana theme, as if to remind us that, after all, this idyllic story is a product of the Sultana's lively imagination.

The motives of the Sultan (IV, 1–4) and the Sultana (IV, 8–9) are heard at the beginning of the last movement. Then we are suddenly in the midst of a colorful festival at Bagdad in the days of the mighty Caliph, when the city was at the height of its gorgeous splendor (IV, 30 ff.). The metropolis of a huge empire, Bagdad was a city of pleasure, the Paris of the ninth century, and Rimsky-Korsakoff gives us a colorful picture of its busy streets. A riot of milling crowds, shrill Oriental instruments, the music is ablaze with the color and radiance of Asiatic cities. Suddenly, as in a sort of unbelievable dream, we are no longer on the hot Bagdad streets, but aboard Sinbad's ship, headed for the fateful rock upon which it is doomed to crash (IV, 595). The undulating sea theme and the giant Sultan theme have joined forces, and we get a vivid picture of the menacing storm, the winds whistling through chromatic passages for clarinet and flute (IV, 605–610 and 615). The waves seem to have risen with increasing force, and the vivid description of the incident as given by Henley is recalled to our minds:

> Tearing their beards
> The sailors wept and prayed; but the grave ship,
> Deep laden with spiceries and pearls, went mad,
> Wrenched the long tiller out of the steersman's hand,
> And, turning broadside on,
> As the most iron would, was haled and sucked
> Nearer and nearer yet:

> And, all awash, with horrible lurching leaps
> Rushed at that Portent, casting a shadow now
> That swallowed sea and sky; and then,
> Anchors and nails and bolts
> Flew screaming out of her . . . and she lay
> A broken bundle of firewood, strown piecemeal
> About the waters.

The whistle of the wind in the storm, the shattering of the ship, the following peaceful calm, all are clearly delineated in Rimsky-Korsakoff's music. And then in the silence, Scheherazade's " appeasing fiddle " is once more heard as she comes to the end of her tale.

" And the Sultan of the Indies could not but admire the prodigious and inexhaustible memory of the Sultaness, his wife, who had entertained him for a thousand and one nights with such a variety of interesting stories.

" His temper was softened and his prejudices removed. He was not only convinced of the merit and great wisdom of the Sultaness Scheherazade, but he remembered with what courage she had suffered to be his wife, without fearing the death to which she had exposed herself, and which so many Sultanesses had suffered within her knowledge.

" These considerations, and the many other good qualities he knew her to possess, induced him at last to forgive her. And so they lived in all pleasurance and solace of life and its delights, till there took them the Destroyer of delights and the Severer of societies, the Desolator of dwelling places and the Garnerer of graveyards, and they were translated to the ruth of the Almighty Allah."

Additional Examples of Russian Nationalism

William Henry Chamberlin, a reporter who has lived many years in Russia, has this to say of the Russian mind and character:

Russia is profoundly a Eurasian country, and in judging the Russian national character and psychology it is important to remember that Russia missed the direct effect of three movements which greatly contributed to the liberation of the individual personality — namely, the Reformation, the Renaissance, and the French Revolution. Moreover, those elements which counterbalanced absolute sovereignty in other European States, such as the existence of a powerful nobility or free cities or a substantial class of yeomanry, were absent in Russia. A Russian medieval tyrant like Ivan the Terrible could kill the most powerful boyar or noble as easily as he could the humblest serf. This tradition also is preserved under Stalin.

Oriental influence is very strong in Russian literature and music, as anyone knows who is familiar with the greatest Russian lyric poets, Pushkin and Lermontov with their frequent drawing on Caucasian themes, or the opera of Rimsky-Korsakoff or the Russian ballet. Thanks to their country's enormously long Asiatic land frontier, Russians have long possessed closer physical contacts with the Turks, Persians, Chinese, and other Asiatic peoples than most Europeans have had, and Russia has minor substantial contributions to Oriental ethnology and exploration.

There are certain traits of Russian personality and mind — even of soul — which persist throughout the greatest of external shocks.

Abstract thinking always has appeared strongly in the Russian. The Russian intellectual of the nineteenth century — and Russian civilization except for ecclesiastical art scarcely existed before the nineteenth century — as depicted now kindly, now ironically by such great writers as Turgenev, Tolstoy, and Chekhov, was always dreaming of a future perfect world, while it was usually a foreigner and not seldom a German who was making the best of an imperfect world in some practical fashion.

During years of residence in Russia I often was impressed by the intense perfectionism of the Russian mind and by an almost complete absence of mental horizon as shown in such qualities as moderation, an instinct for compromise, and gradualness. If a Soviet Communist, for instance, could prove a few cases of injustice and oppression under some foreign system, his mind was completely closed against any argument that infinitely more people were suffering injustice and oppression under the Soviet regime.

Throughout the novels of Dostoevski one catches glimpses of this tremendous yearning for spiritual extremes, this ability to plumb the lowest depths and the greatest heights of the human spirit, this impatience with anything tepid or moderate or "middle of the road." No one was so foredoomed to bitter disillusionment and cruel physical and spiritual suffering in the revolution as the Russian intellectual, who had been softened by Western study and contacts and who hoped that a regime with respect for individual personalities and civil liberties would succeed the rule of the Czars.

The Russian possesses a striking capacity to take the ideal for the real. Often when some glowing plan for the future is explained as if it were already in operation there isn't even an element of conscious deception or propaganda. Imagination has simply bridged the gulf between thought and execution.

When this quality of imagination is directed into artistic fields it yields extraordinary fruits. The country's most distinguished cultural achievement, especially in literature and music, was attained during the nineteenth century, without the process of slower growth which characterized the development of English, French, and German national cultures. Artistically, Russians are a people with more than average gifts.

With these characteristics in mind, listen to the following examples of Russian nationalism, determining which are most characteristically Russian in spirit:

Kamarinskaya; Fantasy on Two Russian Folk Songs   Glinka

Prior to Michael Glinka (1803–1857) Russia had no symphonic music worthy of the name; this is probably his finest orchestral piece.

Russian Easter Overture, Op. 36   Rimsky-Korsakoff

This is hardly anything but a splotch of eastern color, but what a gorgeous splotch it is!

Caucasian Sketches, Op. 10   Ippolitov-Ivanov

These are based on material gathered when the composer was director of a music school in Tiflis, capital of Georgia. There are four parts: " In a Mountain Pass "; " In the Village "; " In the Mosque "; " Procession of the Sardar."

Symphony No. 6 in B minor (Pathétique),
    Op. 74   Tchaikovsky

Tchaikovsky's music is usually considered less Russian both in subject matter and in idiom than that of his contemporaries. In view of what Chamberlin has said above, how would you place this work?

Pictures at an Exhibition   Moussorgsky
Boris Godunov (A Symphonic Synthesis,
    arranged by Stokowski)

Most critics consider Moussorgsky to be the greatest genius of the Russian national school. His *Pictures at an Exhibition* was originally a piano piece, programmatic in character, descriptive of various pictures painted by his friend Hartmann. The original was arranged for orchestra by Ravel, and other composers, attracted by its powerful depictions, have also orchestrated it.

Taking various episodes from Moussorgsky's greatest work, the opera *Boris Godunov*, Stokowski has made his synthesis a " gigantic orgy of orchestral tone color "; in general he has kept to the original scoring of the composer, although some of the effects are exaggerated, and the recording is done with such tremendous power that only the best phonographs can reproduce it with justice.

Symphony No. 3 in B minor (*Ilya Mourometz*)   Glière

A gorgeous program symphony based on the life and adventures of a Russian national folk hero (who is the subject of songs still being written in Russia), this work of Glière's was written before the Soviet regime came into power. It is a combination of post-Wagnerian and Straussian elements with real Russian qualities, and, for those who like its rather lush style, makes wonderful listening.

TOPICS FOR FURTHER DISCUSSION

Discuss the advantages and drawbacks of the insistence upon nationalism in music. Did the Russian pioneers overdo it?

Which national schools of Europe do you personally find most interesting, and why?

Is folk art overpraised?

What is your opinion of present-day developments in Russian art?

SUGGESTIONS FOR READING

Studies in Russian Music, Abraham. (New York: Scribner)

Masters of Russian Music, Calvocoressi and Abraham. (London: Duckworth; New York: Knopf)

Contemporary Russian Composers, Montagu-Nathan. (London: Palmer & Hayward)

Modern Russian Composers, Sabaneev. (New York: International Publishers)

The Development of Soviet Music, Slonimsky. (New York: American Russian Institute)

My Musical Life, Rimsky-Korsakoff. (New York: Knopf)

CHAPTER XIX

Wagner's "Siegfried Idyll"

A Masterpiece of Form and Feeling

WE have already remarked that the *Scheherazade* Suite is a fine example of the type of program music in which the composer is more interested in developing his musical structure than in carefully following the details of an elaborate program. We are now to consider a piece of program music which concerns itself entirely with musical development. Those who are familiar with the great operas of Wagner — music dramas such as *Die Walküre, Siegfried, Götterdämmerung* — will perhaps be surprised to see the *Siegfried Idyll,* the piece which we have under present consideration, cited as an example of German nationalistic music. Most of Wagner's works, though imaginatively sprung from Germanic sources, have transcended the narrow borders of nationalism because of their tremendous scope and the universality of their appeal. Wagner based the stories of his operas on material gathered from the great medieval poems which were the heritage of the Scandinavian and the Germanic peoples. His treatment was such, however, that these operas appeal not alone to the Germans; or to other nations because of their peculiarly Teutonic qualities. They belong rather to the whole human race; the music of these works is understood as well in New York and London as it is in Munich or Berlin; their emotions are those of humanity in general, glorified and epitomized. Men of all kinds know this music to be of themselves, and warm to it because they can sense in it their own personal characteristics.

This little instrumental piece we are about to study, the *Siegfried Idyll,* is full of a quiet German beauty that is quite outside the general run of Wagner's other works. Built on themes associated with the greatest of the German folk heroes, it suggests to us the cool depths of the dense, dragon-haunted forests. Over-

flowing with the happiness of domestic felicity, it celebrates the
family ideals of the typical German bourgeois; the intensity of
feeling, the acute sensitiveness, the fundamental reflective character of this nation is felt throughout this music. If we stop to
inquire into the history of its writing, we shall find the reason
for its unique position among Wagner's works.

Some Wagner History

Wagner's career, overwhelmingly successful as it seems to us
today, was an intermittent series of struggles, disappointments,
triumphs. His works were written over a long period of strife,
sometimes with little hope that they would ever be actually performed. Their tremendous scope, their unusual technical requirements, the difference of their constructive principles from
those to which the public was accustomed, did not make for their
immediate popularity with a people steeped in the traditions of
the Italian opera. Wagner's personal idiosyncrasies did not help
in establishing his work in public favor. Possessing luxurious
habits and expensive personal tastes, he constantly involved himself in financial difficulties; of choleric, irascible temperament,
he needlessly made many public and private enemies, and resent-
ment against him rose on various occasions to such a pitch as to
make it necessary for him to leave his native land. His personal
affairs, even when viewed from the vantage point of distant years,
seem inexplicably confused. For years he lived a troubled existence with his first wife, Minna, whom he married in 1836, and
who died in 1866. Coming under the spell of one woman after
another, he lived with Cosima von Bülow, wife of one of his
most ardent disciples and eloquent interpreters, in a villa just
outside Lucerne, Switzerland, during the years 1866–1870. At
the end of this period, Cosima having been able to obtain a divorce, Wagner was able to establish her as his wife in the eyes of
the law, and they were married on August 25, 1870. His happiness at this time knew no bounds. He had finished five of his
great works, *Tristan und Isolde, Die Meistersinger von Nürn-
berg, Das Rheingold, Die Walküre,* and *Siegfried*, works which
he knew would go down to posterity even though he could not
secure production of them immediately in the German theaters.

No one knew better than Wagner himself that it was the loyalty, devotion, and sympathetic understanding of the amazing Cosima that enabled him to go ahead with the enormous tasks and face the terrific difficulties of his later years.

A CHRISTMAS BIRTHDAY GIFT

The birth of his son Siegfried in 1869 was a significant event for Wagner. (It is rather remarkable that both Cosima and Siegfried died within a year of each other, the one in 1929, the other in 1930, after devoting their lives to carrying on the traditions of the theater established by Wagner at Bayreuth.) Richard resolved to write a piece of music in commemoration of the birth of his son and as a graceful tribute to his wife. He prefaced it with verses which gave his reasons for writing this music:

> Thine was the loving, sacrificing thought
> That gave a habitation to my art,
> And through all the conflicts that I fought
> Gave refuge that was constant and apart.
> As we dreamed, our Teuton heroes came to us
> Out of country's past reviewed in mind and heart,
> Till in my life there rang in glad acclaim:
> " We have a son — and Siegfried is his name."
>
> This music now gives thanks for him and thee —
> What greater prize could Love have hoped or had,
> Within our souls what joy could greater be
> Than now is voiced within this music glad?
> For I within this offering hold united
> Thou and Siegfried — wife and lad.
> In all its harmonies stand revealed
> Our own sweet thoughts, till now concealed.

Could any music have a more general, and yet a more personal, program? No wonder Wagner was able to write a composition which is a wondrous outburst of joy, celebrating the termination of his bitter struggles, full of tender thankfulness for the haven of Cosima's love and understanding. Using themes that were later employed in his opera *Siegfried*, where they suggest the love of the hero of that work for Brünnhilde, the composer pro-

duced a musical work of unusual beauty and quiet loveliness.
That he was writing program music is certain; we have it on the
evidence of the music itself, as well as on testimony of Glasenapp,
one of the composer's " official " biographers. We do not know
anything of the details of the program which stimulated Wagner's imagination (a fact which one critic thinks may be the
reason why several transitions in the music seem rather abrupt),
nor do we need to know. Wagner's imagination caught fire at the
idea of picturing his great love for his wife and newborn son, and
there " was no staying it until the fire had burned itself out."

The *Idyll* was composed during the autumn of 1870, in
preparation for Christmas Day, which happened to be Cosima's
birthday. Local musicians from Lucerne were gathered together
for the first performance. The score called for a small orchestra:
two first violins, two seconds, two violas, one cello, one double
bass, one flute, one oboe, two clarinets, one bassoon, two horns,
and one trumpet (played by Hans Richter, who was later to become the outstanding Wagner interpreter of Germany). This
small band was secretly rehearsed, and early on Christmas morning its members came out to the Wagner villa, set up their music
desks on its broad stairs, and after quietly tuning their instruments in the kitchen, took their places. Wagner, standing at the
top of the stairs, conducted; then came the violins, violas, wood
winds, horns, and at the bottom, out of sight of the conductor,
the cello and bass. Everything went well, and Cosima tells us in
her diary that the performance was a complete success. She was
awakened by the music; at first she thought herself dreaming,
but as consciousness gradually returned, she realized the graceful
tribute that was being paid her. When the music died away, Richard came to her room, and offered her the score of the symphonic
poem. " I was in tears," she writes, " but so was all the rest of the
household."

PECULIARITIES OF STRUCTURE [1]

It will not take a great deal of listening to realize that the
methods of construction in this piece are different from the others

---

[1] Arrangements of the *Siegfried Idyll* for the piano are available in the following editions: Schott (arranged by Rubinstein) No. 329; Universal (arranged by
Wöss) No. 5113; Breitkopf No. 4724. An orchestral score (miniature size) is available in the Kalmus Edition No. 52.

we have heard so far. Wagner's unending melody, the peculiar
method by which he built his musical structures by means of
repetition and elaborations of the same themes, gives a cohesion
and homogeneity that is found in few other musical works. Once
started, it seems as if this music must run on to its inexorable conclusion. By means of themes that are in themselves marvels of
beauty and suggestiveness, Wagner weaves a seamless web of music, always suited to the constantly changing words of his dreams.
But though there is repetition, there is no monotony, for the
composer is constantly giving us the same material in new guises.
By shifting the harmonies that accompany his themes, by changing the keys, by alternating the rhythmic design, or by combining a theme with others so that they form a complex whole, there
is attained a marvelous variety and yet a complete unity.

One of the great joys in listening to this music of Wagner's
is that of being able to recognize not only the themes as they are
used, but also the manner in which each is treated and woven into
the fabric of his enormous tapestries. Those who are at all familiar
with the opera *Siegfried* will recognize most of the themes in the
Idyll; but, as that great Wagnerite Mr. Ernest Newman has
shown, some of them were originally conceived for a string quartet that Wagner meant to write for Cosima, and were later transferred to the opera. Mr. Newman thinks that " much of the substance of the quartet has been taken over bodily into the *Idyll* ";
this makes it a lovely example of the composer's power of symphonic structure — a type of writing which, had he lived longer,
it seems reasonable to suppose that he would have developed.

The opening of the *Idyll* is a fine little study in free counterpoint, just the thing for anyone to ponder who doubts the value
of studying this important element in composition. Notice what
Wagner makes of the theme

first heard in completeness in measures 29 and 30, how he repeats
it and what he develops out of it. Shortly after, we hear the
slumber motive (37), and then the cradle song (91),

RICHARD AND COSIMA WAGNER
At about the time of the writing of the *Siegfried Idyll*.

In Memory of Dvořák

The bronze plaque can be seen on the house in which Dvořák lived while in New York.

the only theme that is not the composer's own, at first sung by
the oboe and then quickly joined with the theme heard at the beginning. These original themes are joined later (148 ff.) by new
motives which we find in the closing scene of *Siegfried* (259 ff.).

From internal evidence Newman believes that the theme of measure 148 was also originally part of the never-completed quartet,
and adapted, rather awkwardly, to the opera. But the 259 theme
" was certainly written first for the opera." As you listen, notice
the manner in which Wagner manipulates these various motives;
they are the roots from which the music beautifully grows. Near
the end we hear added the " slumber motive " of Brünnhilde
(287),

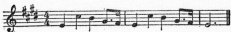

given to the oboe, and the call of Siegfried's forest bird (303 ff.).
But through all the music the love themes form a dominating
influence, weaving, in their varied forms, a background for the
whole piece.

Then, after you have heard the different sections several
times and have a knowledge of the music's imaginative and constructive background, forget this side of it entirely and put yourself into the mood for Christmas morning, 1870, and hear the
whole thing again, thinking of the intimate, affectionate meaning the music would have for Cosima — music that was not intended for publication but as a private gift in celebration of the
baby's birth. You will then appreciate to the full the clarity and
eloquence of the music, from the pastoral-like beginning to the
sighs of peace at the very end. The *Siegfried Idyll*, one of the
world's masterpieces of loveliness, is the sort of music to which we
can surrender ourselves unhesitatingly, confident that it will
never disappoint.

ADDITIONAL EXAMPLES OF WAGNER'S STYLE

A Faust Overture

Originally written in 1840, this was to be the first movement of a symphony, the rest of which was never finished. But enough is here to show that Wagner might have been as great a symphonic writer as he was an opera composer if he had so desired. It is intended to portray Faust alone — " Faust in Solitude " — Gretchen having been reserved for the intended second movement. Wagner revised the score in 1855.

> Prelude
> Isolde's Love Death   } from *Tristan and Isolde*
> Love Duet (from the Second Act)

The first two of these selections from one of Wagner's greatest operas are usually coupled together in an orchestral version; there are many good interpretations available on records, but the finest is undoubtedly that of Furtwängler. The singing of Kirsten Flagstad and Lauritz Melchior in the second-act duet will probably not be surpassed in our time.

Prelude to *Die Meistersinger*

This, one of the most healthy and energetic pieces ever written by Wagner, is a splendid example of his style of composition.

TOPICS FOR FURTHER DISCUSSION

What other great women have inspired and helped composers?

Discuss Wagner as artist and man. What was his position in the latter years of the nineteenth century? Has this changed today?

SUGGESTIONS FOR READING

Cosima Wagner, DuMoulin Eckart. (New York: Knopf)
Translated by Catherine Phillips

In the foreword to this outstanding biography, Ernest Newman summarizes the debt of gratitude which the world owes Cosima Wagner. Newman's words give us the cue for the unusual tenderness and quiet beauty to be found in the *Siegfried Idyll*. The last chapter of Volume I describes the first playing of the *Idyll* on Christmas Day, 1870.

CHAPTER XX

Dvořák's "New World Symphony"

A Symphonic Nationalist

COMPOSERS who have been interested in the various nationalistic movements have turned naturally to the writing of program music as the style best fitted to the carrying out of their ideas. So, to a small extent, did Anton Dvořák, the Bohemian nationalist, but most of his compositions, although they are full of the color, rhythm, and melody of the Czech folk music, are cast in the forms used by the composers of the earlier Classic school. He started his career in the traditions of the German Romantic school of Beethoven and Schubert, and this fact greatly influenced his choice of forms; but the first years of his artistic development coincided with a determined effort on the part of a group of older Czech composers to develop a school of nationalistic writing. The young Dvořák found this idea congenial, and from 1874 he threw himself body and soul into the new movement, filling his music with the spirit of his country.

Like Schubert, Dvořák was a man who lived only in the world of music, a fact that gives spontaneity and freshness to everything he wrote and that makes it very easy to enjoy. His genius was most at home in the writing of melodies and rhythms that have a folk flavor, and he was able to weave these into a fabric of real musical worth through his mastery of the older forms. In other words, he was at his best when writing absolute music, music that was unhindered by programs of any sort. He had a flair for striking and effective instrumentation, and his best music proceeded out of his ability to use resources in the most natural manner possible.

Without any doubt, his greatest work is his last (Fifth) symphony, the one in E minor generally called the *New World Symphony*. It was written during the composer's short stay in the city of New York as the head of the National Conservatory of Music (1892–1895), and was undertaken in an attempt to show American composers what might be done in the way of writing music in the larger forms, using folk-style themes as material. Dvořák employed melodies that are suggestive of the Indians and the Negroes, since he thought that there was no other folk music with vitality in America; but the music which he composed is Czech rather than American, and although the themes embody some of the peculiarities of the Indian and Negro music, they also seem curiously like others which he wrote before going to America. And in any case they lose any peculiarly New World characteristics they may have possessed in their development at the hands of this gifted Bohemian.

THE FIRST MOVEMENT [1]

The first movement of this *Symphony from the New World* is as strict in its form as if it had been penned by some classic writer — Haydn, or perhaps Mozart. The sonata form can again be seen here as a logical, clear-cut, and very effective means for the expression of a composer's ideas and the ordering of his material. After a rather long introduction, Dvořák plunges immediately into the leaping rhythms of his first theme, given to the horns:

There are a number of interesting things to observe about this theme: first, that it is written in the pentatonic scale, which uses only the first, second, third, fifth, and sixth tones of our usual scale; second, that it employs the folk-song " snap," a short, snappy note placed before a long one (see the second measure of this theme); third, that there are two distinct parts to the tune, the up-and-down arpeggio of the horns, and the answering bit given to the wood winds (much use is made of both these parts in the building up of the movement).

[1] The piano score of Dvořák's *New World Symphony* is available in the following editions: Simrock (arranged by Juon); Ditson (edited by Goetschius). The orchestral score (miniature size) is available: Eulenburg Edition No. 433; Kalmus Edition No. 18.

The connecting passages leading up to the second main theme are obviously drawn from the first; they are most suggestive of the lilt and gaiety of folk music. Before we reach the second theme, however, we suddenly come upon an ingratiating little subsidiary theme,

quickly repeated while the cellos thrum a bagpipe-like bass. This is simple writing with a local (Czech) flavor and personal color that are Dvořák's signature and belong to no one else. A characteristic feature of this little tune is its lowered seventh scale step (notice the accidental to the penultimate note), a peculiarity of Negro slave songs well known to Dvořák. The second theme when it arrives is somewhat like the famous spiritual *Swing Low, Sweet Chariot*:

Like most of Dvořák's themes, it is short, which makes it easy to remember and its development easy to spot.

There are just short of a hundred measures in the development section; the first and second themes are both used, although the little subsidiary theme gets no look-in, save possibly in the rhythmic pattern now and then. It may be felt that we get rather a lot of the opening measures of the first theme — that aspiring arpeggio — and that the devices are just a little overworked. Dvořák is not afraid to drive home a rhythmic pattern by repetition, a touch, perhaps, of the peasant. Compare the sometimes almost maddening repetitions of Russian composers. Color interests this writer more than debate; on the whole, the development does not lead us far down the garden, and we spend most of our time admiring the flowers.

In the recapitulation (restatement) section, Dvořák wisely makes less use of the first theme than he did in the exposition (statement); this is what we want, for we have enjoyed its company but have had enough of it for this time. The subsidiary theme comes back again, this time in a different form, which fact adds interest to our listening, even though we may not realize the reason for it. The second theme is of course again stated, and shortly after there begins a fine little coda, based largely upon the first theme.

The Second Movement

The second movement is one of the most famous in all symphonic literature, for its principal theme is known to everyone in some arrangement or other. There have been many suggestions as to its inspiration: one writer thinks that this haunting song of the English horn could have been a Negro spiritual, for it is in that vein and has a typical melancholy and pathos; another says that everybody knows that it took shape " after Dvořák had been thinking of the story of Hiawatha's betrothal to Minnehaha." Dvořák's sons are authority for the statement that this tune was suggestive of their father's homesickness for his native land, a homesickness expressed while he was in the midst of a strange and unappealing environment. It seems as if this explanation is as good as any other that might be offered, if we must have reasons for the writing of beautiful music. It is not difficult to feel the nostalgia and longing that pervade this music, and for this reason it will always appeal. The movement is of particular interest to us, however, because it is a beautiful example of the form which has so often been employed by composers for the second movements of their symphonies — what has come to be known as " song form."

An expressive movement such as this does not need very detailed analysis: if we listen carefully to it as a whole, we notice that it divides into three sections, and that the first section is repeated once the second has been finished. The first section is distinguished by the well-known tune given to the English horn (*cor anglais*):

The middle section is marked by a quicker tempo and a beautiful wood-wind and string scoring, with a plucked bass a great deal of the time:

Then after a curious and unexpected interpolation with a light-hearted, open-air flavor, the slow, expressive *largo* tune enters again, this time with some effective hesitations which have the artistic effect of making us wish that it would continue just a little longer. The section closes with the same beautiful chords that we heard at the beginning. The scoring throughout is a triumph of aptness, and the formal design is handled with masterly skill.

The Third Movement, a Typical Scherzo

It is hardly necessary to remark that the various movements of a symphony are purposely varied in character in order to provide new interest and hold the attention of the listener from the beginning to the end of the work. After a vigorous opening movement, the second (almost always called the *slow* movement), comes as a refreshing contrast. It is in this second movement that the composer usually displays his emotional powers; lyric in character (hence the name *song form*), the slow movement has a depth of feeling from which we in turn need relief. So the third movement is always brisk, more or less cheerful, and decidedly rhythmic. The older writers (Haydn and Mozart) employed a classic dance — the minuet — as a pattern for their third movements; Beethoven introduced a freer feeling and a livelier pace in his third movements and called them *scherzos* — literally " jests." Most symphony writers since his time have followed his example and have used the same form for their third movements. Dvořák is no exception; his scherzo here is a humorous, lively movement, again in three large sections with the same general idea predominant — restatement after contrast. Each of the sections has two main themes, and keen listening will show that the formal scheme is this:

A: First part, principally employing theme 1:

Second part, principally employing theme 2:

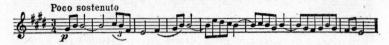

First part again

B: First part, principally employing theme 3:

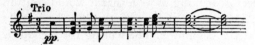

Second part, principally employing theme 4:

First part again

A: An almost literal repetition of the whole first section.

The middle, or contrasting section (B) of the scherzo (as well as of the minuet) is called the *trio*, because in early days it was usually played by three instruments. The different sections in this Dvořák scherzo are easily recognized. Just before A is re-introduced after we have heard B, there is a sudden interpolation from the first movement, as if Dvořák would bind together his whole work by such means.

THE LAST MOVEMENT

The last movement of a symphony is very often again in sonata form, although other types of construction are sometimes used — the rondo, or the variation form, for example. Here in the *New World Symphony* we have a fairly strict use of the sonata-form, with constant interpolations of themes from earlier movements; the composer seems to want us to renew our acquaintance with these older friends as the work comes to an end.

The listener may have noted that many of the themes so far used in this work have been in the minor key; but by the way he has used them, Dvořák has proved very clearly that the minor need not necessarily express a sad or doleful sentiment. The first theme of the last movement, again in minor, shows that peculiar thrusting, nervous energy and directness that is characteristic of this composer.

There are two parts, the second almost jiglike in character, giving us a hint of the rhythm that is strongly felt throughout the movement. The second theme is played by a clarinet over a delicate string tremolo:

Then follows a third theme (here is the end of it):

the last measure of which plainly says " Three Blind Mice "; just what the connection is, no one knows — perhaps just a bit of Dvořákian foolery. In the development section not only the two main themes of this movement are treated, but some from the other three are also heard. The restatement follows in due course, and the final coda brings other suggestions of earlier themes.

Perhaps the middle movements stand on their own feet best; the Largo is unequaled in its quiet beauty. Although the ideas throughout the whole work are not broadly or philosophically worked out (as we find them in the Beethoven and Brahms symphonies), and the tune material is brief, there are many ingratiating features in this symphony, and we cannot imagine that it will ever pass out of the concert repertoire. No more engaging introduction to the literature of the symphony could be found.

ADDITIONAL EXAMPLES OF DVOŘÁK'S STYLE

Slavonic Rhapsody in A major, Op. 45, No. 3

Slavonic Dances, Op. 46, Op. 72

These are enough to get a complete picture of the soul of the Czechs.

TOPICS FOR FURTHER DISCUSSION

Do you think that Dvořák's stay in America and his attempts to
show the way to American composers have had any important effect
upon American music?

Are the so-called " Negro " influences in the *New World Symphony*
(as well as in the other works Dvořák wrote while in America) really
Negro or not?

What are the qualities that endear Dvořák to us? And what are his
weaknesses? Does he share these with any other important composer?

SUGGESTIONS FOR READING

From Grieg to Brahms, Mason. (New York: Macmillan)
Studies in Modern Music (Second Series), Hadow. (New York: Mac-
         millan; London: Seeley)
Anton Dvořák, Stefan. (New York: Greystone)

CHAPTER XXI

Chamber Music, Ancient and Modern

CHAMBER MUSIC IN THE HISTORICAL SENSE

THE term " chamber music " is not always understood by the general public; witness such slips as those that have appeared in reviews in provincial newspapers when reference was made to " chamber of commerce music "; or the regret expressed by a backwoods critic that a certain piece of Beethoven's written for a string quartet — the most usual of all chamber-music organizations — had not been " played by a larger band." The expression " chamber music " (literally " room music ") originally signified the kind of music that was written to be played in the salon of a prince, in distinction to that which had been written for church or theater. Up to the time of the Renaissance the growth of music had taken place almost entirely under the protecting care of the Church; from 1600 on, it developed largely under the patronage of princes and royalty. The earlier church music was vocal in style, with little attention paid to any instrumental accompaniment. In the seventeenth century, as instrumental music came more and more into vogue, each prince gathered round him his own musical establishment for the pleasure and edification of his court, as well as for the increasing of its reputation for brilliance and splendor. Just as in recent years the great manufacturing barons often place an organ — the more expensive the better — in their show houses, so in the late seventeenth and in the eighteenth century most of the European princes and princelings had chamber-music organizations for the delectation of their guests. Some of these musical establishments were of considerable size and importance; a typical and probably average one, with the exception of its leader, was that of Prince Leopold of Anhalt-Cöthen, which Johann Sebastian Bach directed from 1717 to 1723. This organization comprised some eighteen players — violinists, violists, cellists, a bassist, an oboeist, a flautist, bassoonists, trumpeters, an organist, a drummer, and a copyist to prepare the music. The prince played the clavier himself, and Bach wrote much music for the various combinations possible within this group. This music, chamber music in the real sense of the term, was played in the great room of the castle on certain days each week after dinner, before invited guests and some of the prince's subjects who were known to be lovers of music. Frederick the Great, grim master of the art of music as well as of war, head of the more elaborate Prussian court at Potsdam, had his own chamber-music organization, with which he played the flute in the music room of his castle every evening that he was in residence.

IN THE MODERN SENSE

The modern meaning of the term has changed; princes no longer have a monopoly on music of this sort. It is now played almost entirely at public concerts, but its range is still limited to music suitable for rooms of moderate size, and it is usually played by not more than one instrument to a part. Modern chamber music may be said to date from the middle of the eighteenth century, when composers began to write for various instrumental combinations without including the clavier to hold the music together, as had been the common practice up to this time. Even though we do not know much of this earlier type of chamber music in which the harpsichord or the clavichord played an important role, we do know that its quantity was enormous. In fact there was much more of this earlier kind of chamber music written than has been produced since Haydn (1732–1809) laid the foundations for our modern style.

A further description of the part which chamber music has played in the development of our modern style will be found in a later chapter. Here we are concerned with securing an introduction to this type of music; before we take up the study of a representative work written in this medium, it will be well for us to acquaint ourselves briefly with the general characteristics of this kind of writing. In passing, a word about the development of the string family of instruments will be helpful. The medieval " fiddles," variants of the bowed-string principle, all lead to the viols,

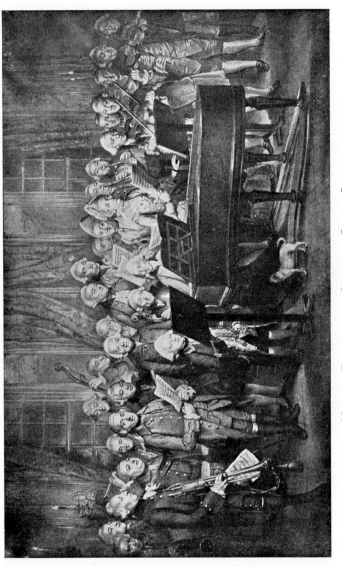

A TYPICAL EIGHTEENTH-CENTURY COURT ORCHESTRA

The Hofkapelle of Herzog Friedrichs des Frommen, Ludwigslust. Painted by Georg David Matthieu.

IMPRESSIONISM AT ITS BEST
Claude Monet's *Westminster*

which, from the fifteenth century until the coming into power of the new violin tribe in the middle sixteenth, first held the mastery, then contested it with the violins, and finally went under, as far as popular use was concerned. We can still occasionally hear the old viols at their best in the hands of such players as the Dolmetsch family, the Chaplin players, and the Société des Instruments Anciens. In Tudor and Stuart times viol-playing was popularly cultivated as part of the education of every gentleman. The violin family came from Cremona just at the right time. Amati, Stradivarius, Gasparo da Salo produced instruments of incomparable beauty, and for three hundred years the design of these instruments has remained virtually unchanged.

The most usual chamber-music combinations in use at the present time are the trio, the quartet, and the quintet, and some of the world's greatest music has been written for these combinations. In hearing such a group play, the amateur is almost always disappointed after having become familiar with one of the great orchestral works. And there is reason for his disappointment; his natural mistake is in confusing volume with quality of tone. He is disappointed perhaps that he is listening to only three or four instruments instead of a hundred; he misses the overpowering magnitude and splendid weight of the orchestral mass; there is no flashing contrast of colors, no surge of composite tone, no tremendous contrast in dynamics. The very picture before his eyes is disappointing; instead of a large group of instrumentalists, each of them blending his personality and activity with a hundred others under the kindling fire and burning enthusiasm of the conductor, he sees only three, four, or five players huddled in the middle of the stage, each of them closely engaged in reading his own music without the magnetic stimulus of a visible leader. Everything seems cool, calculated, cerebral.

But let him listen for other things! The clear sonority of the various instruments as they blend together or answer one another in dialogue or repartee; the strength of the whole, due to the equal importance of each part; the weighty matters upon which the instruments discourse — all these are worth his careful attention. We do not have to disparage the greatness of the orchestral masterpieces to realize that chamber music is like Abbé Dimnet's description of sculpture: the art of the noble or heroically minded, the passion of the severely artistic. In spite of the fact that the greatest success, and rightly so, has always gone to the writers of orchestral music, chamber music will always afford a lasting and inexhaustible delight because of its clean sparingness, its lack of anything which approaches sentimentality, its disregard for virtuosity except as a means toward a perfect expression of great thought.

SOME EXAMPLES OF STRING-QUARTET STYLE

The string quartet is the most popular of all the chamber-music groups; ever since the days of Haydn it has consisted of two violins, a viola, a cello. The music written for such a combination (this music is, by the way, called a " quartet ") is distributed almost equally among the four members. No one player is all-important and each of them must be able to subordinate his playing to the general good of the whole. The first violin naturally takes the upper part, that which is in general similar to that sung by the soprano in a vocal quartet; the second violin, while it plays the same kind of music, has more of the " filling-in " characteristics of the alto voice; the viola, with its telling tonal character, is the tenor; and the cello provides the necessary foundation tone.

Before listening to the quartet which we have selected as the first one to hear, it will be easier to study a few short movements from different quartets, that we may accustom ourselves to the general quartet style. Mendelssohn's charming *Canzonetta* from his *Quartet in E Flat,* Opus 12, is a fine number to begin with. Here there are delicate rhythms and charming melodies which admirably suit the medium; it is difficult to think of this music as being played by any other instruments. There are three general divisions (our old friend A–B–A again), the first being light, dainty, and gay, even though expressed in the minor key; the second is in major, a jolly rushing duet for the violins, while the viola and the cello supply sustaining harmonies; then back to the first section, after which comes a graceful coda to complete the whole.

Perhaps the most popular single movement in string-quartet literature is the *Andante cantabile* (literally, " leisurely singing movement ") from Tchaikovsky's *Quartet,* Opus 11. This slow movement is full of the tender wistfulness that is enhanced by the fact that it is played with muted strings. The main theme of the movement is taken bodily from an old Russian folk song; it has a peculiar alternation of measures and a most appealing melody.

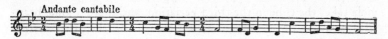

The second section is largely built over a repeated *pizzicato* figure in the cello and equals the first in beauty, while providing a fine contrast. The first section then returns, the whole movement being a good example of the three-part song form — similar to the structure of the Largo of the *New World Symphony*.

Another popular movement is the Nocturne from Borodin's *D Major Quartet*. This movement accentuates the Oriental side of the Russian temperament and is lusciously rich in its melody. It is excellently put together, again according to the scheme of the three-part form. The first theme is heard on the cello and later repeated on the first violin; the contrast section is distinguished by a long ascending theme, more vigorous in character, and ending with a little bustling figure. Later when the first section returns there is a good *canon* (see Glossary) between the first violin and the cello.

We have already remarked Haydn's importance in the development of the modern quartet style; one of his best-known quartets is the so-called *Emperor Quartet,* which in its slow movement makes use of the Austrian National Hymn, a tune which Haydn had written for the Emperor's birthday celebration of 1797 and afterwards presented to the whole nation. This movement takes the form of the *theme with variations,* a form that has been very popular with composers as a means for displaying skill and technic. We first hear the theme complete; some will recognize it as a tune to which a familiar hymn is sung.

After this we have a set of four variants of it, followed by a
short coda. In the first variation the second violin plays the tune,
while the first weaves a *staccato* embroidery above it; the other
instruments are silent. In the second variation the cello has the
melody, while the second violin plays a counter-melody, and the
first violin and viola supply an appropriate background. The
viola takes the tune in the third variation, and there is some beautiful weaving of accompanimental threads by the other instruments: notice the peculiar, veiled character of the viola here. In
the last variation the melody is restored to its usual position on
top, and is sung by the first violin while the other instruments
supply a rich background. The coda is short and quiet.

LIST OF SUGGESTED MUSIC

Canzonetta from *Quartet in E Flat*, Op. 12   Mendelssohn

(Available in the Eulenberg Edition of Miniature Scores, No. 47)

Andante cantabile from *Quartet
in D Major*, Op. 11   Tchaikovsky

(Available in the Eulenberg Edition of Miniature Scores, No. 161)

Nocturne from *Quartet in D Major*, No. 2   Borodin

(Available in the Eulenberg Edition of Miniature Scores, No. 201)

Theme and Variations from the *Emperor Quartet*,
Op. 76, No. 3   Haydn

(Available in the Philharmonia Edition of Miniature Scores, No. 344,
and in the Eulenberg Edition of Miniature Scores, No. 3)

TOPICS FOR FURTHER DISCUSSION

Discuss the benefits and drawbacks of the old system of princely
patronage of composers. By what could we best replace it today?

A newcomer to chamber music at first disliked the tone of the
string quartet, because it did not seem quite " in tune." Can you suggest the reason for his discomfort?

Name some of the outstanding chamber-music organizations of today. How many of these have you heard?

SUGGESTIONS FOR READING

Cyclopedic Survey of Chamber Music, Cobbett. (New York and London: Oxford)

This great piece of work has been done by an enthusiastic and talented amateur chamber-music player and contains fine articles by leading experts on the various phases of this type of music. Especially interesting for our present reading are the following articles:

" Chamber Music " — General survey (Vol. I, p. 244) by Donald F. Tovey

" The Chamber Music Life " — Vol. I, p. 254 — W. W. Cobbett

" Quartet: Its Origin and Development " — Vol. II, p. 253 — Adolfo Betti

" Temperament " — Vol. II, p. 501 — W. W. Cobbett

CHAPTER XXII

A Romantic Quartet — and a Classic One

SMETANA'S QUARTET "AUS MEINEM LEBEN"[1]

THE *E Minor Quartet* of Bedřich Smetana (1824–1884), the Bohemian composer who interested Dvořák in Czech nationalism, is a good beginning quartet for the amateur listener. Smetana meant this work to stand rather apart from the generally accepted quartet style, he tells us. " I have no intention of writing a quartet according to recipe and the customary forms, with which I am acquainted through the study which I made of them when as a youth I learned music theory. With me, the form of each composition is the outcome of the subject. And thus it is that this quartet has made its own form: I wanted it to paint in sounds the course of my life," he writes to a friend. And so he gave to this quartet and the one which followed it (the *Quartet in D Minor*) the title *Out of My Life*. These works show the love of the nationalist composer for program music; nevertheless, in spite of what Smetana says about " customary forms," these quartets follow the general outlines of the usual forms, although they are not so strict as the Haydn, Mozart, and Beethoven quartets are. The Smetana works, especially the first one, contain a wealth of beautiful color, many appealing melodies, and strong rhythms, and are characteristically idiomatic. Hence they serve as excellent introductions to the great riches that are to be found in string-quartet literature.

The first movement of the *E Minor Quartet* (marked *Allegro vivo appassionato*) depicts the composer's early love of art, his strongly dramatic romanticism, and youthful longings never satisfied. There are two main themes: the first

[1] The score of Smetana's *Quartet in E Minor* (miniature size) is available in the following editions: Philharmonia, No. 357; Eulenburg, No. 275.

Allegro vivo

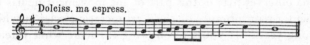

suggestive of the youthful ardor and enthusiasm and the agitated atmosphere of the fateful year 1848, when the sympathies of the twenty-four-year-old composer were enlisted in the revolutionary struggle of his country against the strong central power of the Austrian autocracy. The viola announces the theme in no uncertain terms, against the undulating accompaniment of the violins and a long-held cello bass (1–11). After a repetition of the theme by the viola at a higher pitch (20–31), and later by the violins (37–42), the music undergoes a beautiful change of key and announces the second subject,

Dolciss. ma espress.

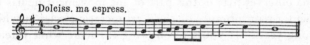

full of romantic warmth (71–77). In the development section both themes are treated, all the instruments finally working through an increasingly agitated passage to a stunning climax (163). What would correspond to the restatement in a strict application of the sonata-form here deals almost entirely with the second theme, the first being heard only furtively on the viola, almost buried under the rest of the structure. The coda, however, deals most effectively (226 to the end) with the opening theme and brings the exuberant movement to a quiet end.

Smetana gives this program for his second movement: " This section, *quasi polka*, recalls memories of my gay youth, when I used to write dance music and give it away to my friends." The polka is a Czech dance having two beats to the measure, with a tendency to stress the second, and with both beats divided to match the half steps in the dance. Smetana writes *con amore,* and the whole movement is full of gaiety and sparkle. There are three main sections (A–B–A again), the first and last of a fast, rhythmic character, and the second somewhat slower and with more feeling. In the main theme of the first section (1–4)

the cello gives the first beat of the measure alone and then all the instruments come straight in on the second, followed by a quickly rushing passage for them in octaves. The second theme (39–46)

of this section is heard at first on the viola alone, then it is imitated by the second violin, and finally, high in pitch, by the first. This is a characteristic string-quartet practice, this imitating of the same theme by various instruments in turn. The middle section (86–136) is fascinating in its rhythm, the cello introducing the pattern and the other instruments replying immediately. Smetana observes that in this part of the movement he has tried to present a remembrance of the " aristocratic circles in which I lived long years." If you are following the score while listening, you will notice that a cut is sometimes made from measures 194 to 231.

The slow movement — notice that here it is the third movement instead of the more customary second — recalls the bliss of first love for a girl who afterwards became his wife, Smetana tells us. It is the sort of movement that needs no analysis, but there are several items of interest that may well be noted. What a rhapsodist the cello is in the first few measures, speaking with the intensity and warmth of the young lover! This accomplished, he settles into a solid foundational note, while the other instruments give out the harmonies of the main theme (7–14).

The majority of the movement consists of varied treatments of this lovely theme. There is one powerful bit where the quartet plays a series of strongly repeated chords (60–63), with each instrument producing two or three tones simultaneously, thus giving an almost orchestral fullness. Towards the end the chief theme is tenderly sung by the cello, achieving a beautiful close for this charming idyl.

In the finale Smetana's writing bears out his program faithfully and gaily: " The discovery of how to treat the national material in music; joy at the feeling that this movement has achieved success." The main part of this last movement is again in sonata form, the first theme

having two distinct parts: the rushing melody that is rather suddenly halted by two longer notes (1–4), and the series of quickly repeated chords connected by a little passage given to the viola (10–16).

The second main theme

has a light deft touch and graceful melodic flow (37–44). In the development section both of these are used. The recapitulation follows according to regular plan, and we have a climactic treatment of the first theme. It seems as if the quartet is about to end in this joyous, rather triumphant vein — but no! Suddenly there occurs a complete change of mood, the interruption of the catastrophe, the beginning of the composer's deafness, a glimpse into a melancholy future. A high sustained note (which is hardly audible in some recorded versions) suggests the one which Smetana tells us whistled continuously in his ears as his deafness was coming on. "I allowed myself this little joke, such as it is, which has proved so fatal to me. There is a ray of hope, an improvement, but at the remembrance of all that was promised by my early career there comes a sense of sadness." The agitated first theme and the romantic second from the first movement are recalled as if in regretful remembrance, and the whole work ends in a quiet version of the joyous theme with which the last movement opened, here full of resignation and peace.

(Warning! In some recordings there is a cut from 163 to 207.)

This *E Minor Quartet* was written in 1876, after the composer had become stone deaf. In 1884 his health broke down completely and he was removed to an insane asylum. The comparison between the deafness of Smetana and that of Beethoven, and its consequent effect upon their lives, is inevitable. Cobbett makes it interestingly:

" The sustained E on the chanterelle (the string of highest pitch) of the violin, heard in the last section of the *Aus meinem Leben* quartet — a pathetically thin line of sound — provides one of the saddest moments in chamber music. ' It is,' wrote Smetana, ' the fatal sounding in my ear of the high-pitched tones which in 1874 announced to me my approaching deafness.'

" The Promethean strength of a Beethoven faced by the worst misfortune that can happen to a musician was not his. Whilst Beethoven, attacked by deafness, rose to greater heights than before, poor Smetana succumbed to the strain."

HAYDN'S " QUARTET " IN F MAJOR, OP. 3, NO. 5 [2]

A good contrast to the Romanticism of Smetana's work is the classic short *Quartet* of Haydn in F major, Op. 3, No. 5. As far as we can determine, Haydn wrote somewhere around eighty quartets, ranging in style from the rather tentative groping of his earliest experiments to the magnificent maturity of his later quartets. In them all there is felt very strongly his peculiar genial quality, using the word in its English sense — warm and friendly — as well as in its Latin suggestiveness of the quality of genius. And this Op. 3, No. 5 is typical, for certainly no more genial music has ever been written. The work is very short, as quartets go, but its few pages contain some great beauties.

The first movement is characteristic of Haydn's gusto and verve; it is in sonata form, with the themes easily distinguishable: the first in measures 1 to 8, and the second in measures 41 to 45. The little development section of fifty measures contains a miniature " imbroglio," produced from a subsidiary figure in the bridge material connecting the two themes; yet it sounds perfectly logical and leads beautifully back to the recapitulation.

[2] The score of Haydn's *Quartet*, Op. 3, No. 5, is available in the Eulenburg Edition No. 150.

The second movement, one of the most famous in quartet literature, is called a " serenade "; it consists of two large sections, each
of them repeated, with the melody given to the muted first violin
and the other instruments forming a *pizzicato* background.
When well played it is a particularly lovely movement, incon-
ceivable except in terms of the string quartet. The minuet and
trio run true to form, with some interesting variants of the regularity of the usual minuet rhythm. The last movement, marked
scherzando, is surely as rapidly running sonata form as was ever
written: the themes (there are three of them) are appropriately
brief and snappy, and the whole thing is over almost before we
know it. This is a perfect little example of Haydn's sympathetic
treatment of the quartet style.

LIST OF SUGGESTED MUSIC

Quartet No. 14 in D Minor (Death and the Maiden) Schubert

Quartet No. 6 in F Major (American)   Dvořák

These quartets will serve as good introductions to chamber-music style.
Schubert's great work, with its leanings toward Classicism, receives its
name from one of his songs, which is used as the main theme of its second
movement. Like everything he ever wrote, this quartet is full of lovely
melody in all the parts.

Dvořák's quartet was written while he was a resident of the United
States, and for most hearers it will seem more American in flavor than
his more famous *New World Symphony*. It is full of sprightly good
humor and strong rhythms, and so leans toward the more modern style
of chamber music.

SUGGESTIONS FOR READING

Cyclopedic Survey of Chamber Music, Cobbett. (New York and Lon-
     don: Oxford)
     " Smetana: First *Quartet* " — Vol. II, p. 427
     " Folk Idioms and National Traits in Chamber Music " — Vol. I,
     p. 412 — Leigh Henry
     " Haydn " — General characteristics of his chamber-music style.
     Vol. I, p. 515 — Donald F. Tovey

CHAPTER XXIII

Impressionism: Debussy's "L'Après-midi d'un faune"

IMPRESSIONISM IN GENERAL

THE impressionist movement in art came into being during the latter years of the nineteenth century as a protest against the exuberance and excesses of the Romantics; Claude Debussy (1862–1918) was its chief exponent in music and his masterpiece, *L'après-midi d'un faune,* one of its greatest productions. This work, although not strictly delineative in the manner of Strauss, employs definite themes suggestive of various episodes, quite in the manner of the Strauss tone poems. Instead of giving himself over to the direct evocation of emotional states in the manner of Liszt and the other Romantic composers, we find Debussy conveying his expression through the indirect power of suggestion; he tries to suggest an emotion rather than express it directly. His music studiously avoids the dramatic and narrative aspects of his predecessors, just as they in turn avoided the formal and conventional aspect of the music of their eighteenth-century predecessors. While demonstrably an off-shoot of Romanticism, *L'après-midi d'un faune* represents a strong revolt against the overpowering and almost annihilating influences which the great giants of the Romantic period bequeathed to their successors. We have already suggested that Romanticism was one of the most stimulating and virile influences ever to affect music and have said that its ideals shaped the output of one great composer after another: Weber, Schubert, Schumann, Liszt, and finally Wagner. The cry of the closing years of the century was: " After Wagner, what? " And, as it so often has done in critical periods, history provided an ideal answer in the person of the pioneer Debussy. The peculiar characteristics of his music,

those characteristics which give it " wings to send it soaring up
to heights to which it could not possibly have risen otherwise,"
were the results of an unusually effective blending of racial and
environmental influences. Nature provided Debussy with an inquiring mind, a very sensitive musical ear, and an unbounded
imagination, and in so doing formed him as the ideal leader of a
new musical movement. His music, with its aristocratic bearing,
its shunning of the exuberances which are commonplace, its essential restraint, its logic and balance, manifests typical Gallic
qualities. And circumstances provided the ideal environment for
the rapid development of Debussy's style.

Symbolism — A Parallel Movement in Literature

Early in his creative life, Debussy found himself in the midst
of movements in the other arts, especially in literature and painting, which exercised strong influences on the development of
his music. It would hardly be too much to say that just as the
German poets of the beginning of the century precipitated Romanticism in music, so the French poets and painters of the last
of the century left the very definite impress of their ideals and
methods upon the music of the next period. A group of poets —
" symbolists " they called themselves — headed by Verlaine and
Mallarmé, combined in a fight against what they considered to
be the abuses of Romanticism to be found in such writers as
Hugo and Lamartine. Delicate, tenuous poetry that stimulated
the imagination, much of it frankly sensuous and voluptuous,
expressed through extremely graceful means, was the aim of these
new writers. Words were more than words — they became symbols suggesting rather than merely expressing; they were meant
to evoke by means of their sounds certain subconscious sensations and ideas. The actual thought contained in a passage was of
less importance than what one was led to read between the lines.
Mallarmé said of these aims: " To name an object is to sacrifice
three fourths of that enjoyment which comes from the pleasure of
guessing bit by bit. To suggest, that is our dream." And he and his
followers, Rimbaud, Maeterlinck, Swinburne, and Yeats, wrote
verse that is subtly sensuous in sound and suggestive in meaning.
A translation of one of Verlaine's short poems, " Serenade,"

will give an idea of the spirit which lay behind the whole movement:

> The shepherd's star burns dim,
> Sinks in the night,
> The pilot fumbles for his light.
>
> Now is the time for him,
> Dark skies above,
> Whose hand seeks out for love.
>
> Sir Atys tunes his strings,
> His eyes to Chloris speak
> Of favors he would seek
>
> While the sad moon is up, and streams
> Down on the boat which glides and gleams
> Upon a sea of dreams.
>   — F. E. in the *London Saturday Review* [1]

No better example of the poetry written by the symbolists
could be given than the famous " Eclogue " of Mallarmé which
inspired Debussy to write this music we have at present under
consideration. This poem, with illustrations by the painter Manet, was published in 1876; it is best known to English readers
through the paraphrase of Edmund Gosse, who has translated this
" miracle of unintelligibility " as well as anyone could. Even
Gosse said that bit by bit, phrase by phrase, he did not understand the original; nevertheless, it gave him great pleasure and he
was able to obtain from it " as solid an influence as Mallarmé
desired to produce."

A faun, a simple, sensuous, passionate being, wakens in the forest
at daybreak and tries to recall his experience of the previous afternoon.
Was he the fortunate recipient of an actual visit from nymphs, white
and golden goddesses, divinely tender and indulgent? Or is the memory he seems to retain nothing but the shadows of a vision, no more
substantial than the arid rain of notes from his own flute? He cannot
tell. Yet surely there was, surely there is, an animal whiteness among
the brown reeds of the lake that shines out yonder? Were they, are they,
swans? No. But naiads plunging? Perhaps. Vaguer and vaguer grows
the impression of this delicious experience. He would resign his wood-

---

[1] By permission of the *London Saturday Review*.

land godship to retain it. A garden of lilies, golden-headed, white-stalked, behind a trellis of red roses? Ah, the effort is too great for his poor brain. Perhaps if he selects one lily from the garth of lilies, one benign and beneficent yielder of her cup to thirsty lips, the memory, the ever-receding memory, may be forced back. So when he has glutted upon a bunch of grapes he is wont to toss the empty skins into the air and blow them out in a visionary greediness. But no, the delicious hour grows vaguer; experience or dreams, he will never know which it was. The sun is warm, the grasses yielding; and he curls himself up again, after worshiping the efficacious star of wine, that he may pursue the dubious ecstasy into the more hopeful boscages of sleep.

A more recent and remarkably suggestive translation of this subtle poetry by Aldous Huxley (to be found in Van Doren's *Anthology of World Poetry*) should not be missed by anyone who would get to the heart of Mallarmé's beauty. Poetry of this kind invades the artistic realms of music, for it attempts to express emotions without ideas, and it is little wonder that the sensitive Debussy, congenitally disposed as he was towards this kind of expression, found himself in such close agreement with the ideals of the symbolists.

IMPRESSIONISM IN PAINTING

For suggestions as to technical means for his musical expression, Debussy turned to another contemporary revolt against the traditional " high art " of the middle of the century, hedged about as it was with strict rules and limiting tradition. When Édouard Manet (1832–1883) began to paint scenes from the world about him in colors as vivid as he saw them in nature, instead of using the accepted methods of painting conventional subjects in the studio, he started a revolution commensurate with that of the symbolists in literature. The followers of Manet, men like Pissarro, Sisley, Monet, and Renoir, received the name of impressionists because of their peculiar manner of painting, that of recording what a quick glance would reveal to them under varying conditions of light and atmosphere — a " realistic rendering of fleeting impression." These painters avoided drama, literary subjects of the usual order, classic proportion and balance, and all other established conventions; they tried to make out of their attempts to reproduce the quality of light on various objects a kind of " painted music." We do not get any idea of ordered structure or calculated design from these paintings — such design as we find in the Italian paintings of the Renaissance, for instance; but we do receive an impression of the scene at the moment the artist looked at it, vibrating with an effect of living light and air.

Debussy felt that this painted music could be of great service in helping him to formulate new methods of expression in his own art. Just as the impressionist painters were concerned with the constituent parts of light and were able to duplicate these on their canvases, he turned his attention to the elements which go to make up chords. He placed these in combinations different from those that had been customary, using plenty of dissonances and paying little attention to the relationship of one chord to another. Because of his unusually sensitive ear, he could single out the overtones that go to make up the timbre of the fundamental notes which we hear, mixing and blending these so as to produce entirely new effects, much in the same way that the painters mixed their colors on the canvas to produce the effects of vibrating light. Thus he arrived at the new effects which, with other devices he used — the whole-tone scale, extreme fluidity of rhythm, and indefiniteness of melody — give his music its marked individuality.

IMPRESSIONISM IN MUSIC [2]

There is little that will trouble us in understanding and liking *L'après-midi d'un faune;* here is program music that is able to make use of some of the natural limitations of the art of music in order to increase its own effectiveness. This is musical painting that conveys the emotional suggestions of a landscape rather than attempting to re-create it in musical terms. Prunières's phrase is a happy one: this is music which in order to be sensuous, poetic, and supremely effective is developed, not according to fixed formulas, but simply and logically in accordance with the poetry it seeks to express. It is a synthesis by which one is transported to

[2] The piano score of Debussy's *L'après-midi d'un faune* is available in the Fromont Edition (transcribed by Borwick), and in the Edward B. Marks Co. Edition. The orchestral score (miniature size) is available in the Kalmus Edition No. 17.

another world, one which can hardly be reached through either
the art of poetry or music alone. Olin Downes speaks of his vivid
remembrance of his first hearing of this music, the indescribable
beauty and elusiveness of its instrumentation, and the impossibil-
ity of recalling, at first, a note of the music. Probably everyone
who listens to the piece for the first time has a similar experience.
With the very first summons of the magic-flute passage at its
beginning, Debussy's score takes us completely out of the mun-
dane world of every day back to the sunlit slopes of Greece; this
is music unlike any other in the world — pagan, full of the spirit
of an ancient beauty. A dreaming faun, a child of nature in the
shape of man with the horns and feet of a beast, lies slumbering
in the noontime heat. The " arid " flute announces the principal
theme (1–4),

full of a desire in which there is a strange tenderness and melancholy; oboes, clarinets, and French horns respond, and their
chords, flooded with limpid harp tones, sustain the mood and
heighten the impression of the opening measures. The rhythm
fluctuates between 9/8, 6/8, 12/8, 3/4, and 4/4. The call becomes louder and more urgent, but dies away to let the flute
again sing its song. A clarinet solo begins a new section (32),
with a theme very much like the first in content, accompanied
by fragmentary bits from the harp. Then we hear the oboe with
a new theme (37),

again strangely like the first in outline; a lively dialogue follows
(44), the music marked *toujours en animant*, leading directly
to a third theme on the wood winds: flute, oboe, English horn,
clarinets (55) — a theme which could be said to suggest desire
satisfied.

Then the principal climax of the whole is gradually built up, and the first theme returns, more languorous than ever (79); it is flutteringly repeated by the oboe and answered by the lightest chords imaginable from the whole orchestra. New chords are heard, as harp *glissandi* suggest the fleetness of the passing vision (86). At last a solo cello joins itself with the flute (100) and then an unforgettable passage for muted horns and strings brings the whole work to a conclusion in which the music seems to vanish before our very ears. It hardly seems possible that there are only a hundred and ten measures in this score; never has such economy of means produced such wealth of beauty. Every measure is telling, with nothing wasted, the whole standing as a fitting monument to a composer who was master of a style almost too fragile and delicate for survival in this practical world.

TOPICS FOR FURTHER DISCUSSION

Discuss the close connection between nineteenth-century French arts — music, poetry, painting, sculpture.

By what means, in *L'après-midi d'un faune*, does Debussy convey or arouse emotions similar to those awakened in us by the poetry of Mallarmé?

Can you suggest why Debussy has been so little imitated with any success? Why has French music of the last decade so strikingly sought other paths than his?

SUGGESTIONS FOR READING

Men of Art, Craven. (New York: Simon & Schuster)
    Chapter XVIII
Since Cézanne, Bell. (New York: Harcourt, Brace)
Modern Painting, Wright. (New York: Dodd, Mead)
Monsieur Croche, the Dilettante Hater. (New York: Viking)
    A collection of Debussy's essays and criticisms which give an excellent summary of his ideas but which, as regards German composers, must be taken with a good spoonful of salt.
Modern French Music, Hill. (Boston: Houghton Mifflin; London: Allen & Unwin)
Theories of Claude Debussy, Vallas. (New York and London: Oxford)

CHAPTER XXIV

Debussy, Ravel, and Falla

DEBUSSY'S "NOCTURNES"

ASIDE from *L'après-midi d'un faune* and his great opera *Pelléas et Mélisande,* Debussy's best-known orchestral work is a set of three Nocturnes: *Nuages, Fêtes,* and *Sirènes.* These, upon first hearing, may seem to lack the unity and coherence which is so striking a feature of the Faun; we hear melodies unlike any with which we are familiar, and, in addition, the various sections of these Nocturnes seem to be unrelated, the instrumental combinations without apparent reason. Yet if we consider these pieces as impressionistic suggestions with a sense of beauty that is only half uttered, musical excursions into the realms of the imagination, their difficulties will quickly disappear. Of the three, the second is best known, perhaps because it is the most tangible. It is astonishingly vigorous for Debussy, for most of his music is so indefinite and intangible that it lacks force and power. But the pageants which the composer unfolds for us here are visionary ones, nevertheless; they are the imaginative and yet frightfully real spectacles such as are revealed only to the mind of the mystics. These are visions like Francis Thompson's *Hound of Heaven,* or those of which William Blake spoke: " Is it not reasonable to suppose that we can create by the working of the mind forms stronger, clearer, and more moving than anything produced by nature? If not, what is the imagination for, and what in heaven's name is the use of art? "

The composer tells us that the music of *Fêtes* is meant to evoke the " restless, rhythmic dancing of the atmosphere, with bursts of brusque light. There is also the episode of a procession — a dazzling and wholly idealistic vision — passing through and blended with the festival. But always the background of the festival remains — luminous dust participating in the rhythms of the universe." If this means anything at all, it should suggest the sort of indefinite pictures which our imagination often outlines in the dust particles that float on broad shafts of sunlight. There are strange rhythms, too, rhythms that suggest earthly rather than terrestrial forces, perhaps; but they pass, and others take their places. There is a definite climax, after which the monotonous rhythms of the opening are resumed and the " luminous particles " evidently resume their dance in the universal rhythms of all things. There is no use in attempting to explain this music — it belongs to the experiences with which all of us are familiar, experiences that border on the unconscious, hardly definite enough to be recognizable, yet strangely bewildering in their insistent appeal.

Debussy loves to envelop his music in a mysterious haze that is full of luminous color; he views the world entirely from the viewpoint of the mystic, with little desire to mingle in it. There is also a peculiar sadness, a brooding for things that might have been and never will be, in almost all of his music. But certainly all this seeming mistiness and haziness is attained by means of a technical structure that is taut and clear, a structure that would seem to assure this music of immortality. How this was attained seems to have been a secret that perished with Debussy, for none of his many imitators has been able to equal this phantasmal, chimerical, marvelously constructed music. Perhaps it is just as well; otherwise, as someone has wisely said, we might all have become lotus-eaters!

IMPRESSIONISM IN FRANCE AND SPAIN: RAVEL'S " JEUX D'EAU " AND " PAVANE "

Of all the men who have followed Debussy and who have adopted the general impressionistic qualities of his style, Maurice Ravel (1875–1937) and Manuel de Falla (1876–   ) have possessed enough individuality to raise their music above the general level. Ravel is quite as essentially French as his great predecessor and makes use of many of the same technical devices in his writing. But his music has sharper outlines and more developed contrasts; it is easier to get hold of, for he pays considerable attention to formal outline, often using the same forms that the

Photo by Paul Riefenberg, Paris

MONUMENT TO CLAUDE DEBUSSY

Sculptors, Joel and Jan Martel; architect, Jean Burkhalter

SETTING FOR " PETROUCHKA "

Classic composers have employed in their works. He has little of the Debussian sense of the mystery in life; rather is he the sharp, keen-witted, practical *homme sensuel,* viewing life as he knows it — and greatly enjoying the experience. His best-known orchestral works are *Ma mère de l'oye* (*Mother Goose* Suite), the two *Daphnis et Chloé* Suites, *La valse,* and the popular *Bolero.*

We may well approach the larger compositions of Ravel through some of his smaller works for the piano; both Ravel and Debussy, because the peculiar nature of their writing fits their music to the peculiarities of the instrument, are piano writers *par excellence. Jeux d'eau* (*The Fountain*) is as lovely a piece of program music as has ever been written for the piano. Taking a program from a quotation that is descriptive of a fountain set in the midst of an old formal French garden, its figure of an ancient god happily spouting jets of water high into the air where they are dissipated into soft rainbow clouds of vapor, Ravel has written music that carries out this poetic idea magically, and yet which carefully follows a set, formal scheme — that of the sonata form, if we dare to analyze it! The whole piece is largely an exploitation of one chord, the chord of the " ninth," as theorists call it. This chord may be found at the piano by starting with C and then playing in conjunction E, G, B flat, and finally D; out of it the composer weaves the loveliest of liquid sounds and color combinations. This is a dazzling little work, and needs consummate technic on the part of the player who attempts it.

The *Pavane pour une infante défunte* (*Pavan for a Dead Princess*) is another example of the combining of classic form and modern expression; it is one of Ravel's earliest popular works and is an elaboration of a stately Spanish dance form popular in the sixteenth and seventeenth centuries. Here again is a solidity of structure that readily allows us to understand the rather novel musical speech of the composer. The speech may be new and curiously original; but the language is the same as has served the greatest of the old masters. Ravel makes use of the rondo form here, the leading theme returning time after time like a sort of refrain.

Those who would familiarize themselves with this composer's stylistic development will find it clearly documented in his works, beginning with the *Rapsodie espagnole* (1908). This, a four-sectioned piece of program music, shows the Spanish influence which pervades so much of Ravel's writing, an influence which was natural enough, since he was born in the Basque country, the inhabitants of which show both Spanish and French characteristics. This mysterious, rapturous music is perhaps the best atmospheric musical picture we have of that strange land. The two *Daphnis et Chloé* Suites for orchestra, formed from music written in 1912 for a Paris performance of the renowned Ballet Russe, show Ravel's genius at its very best. Based on a classic story of the parting and reuniting of two lovers, these suites, especially the second, contain as atmospheric and colorful music as any ever written. Displaying the composer's consummate mastery of orchestral technic, the scores glow with color and pulse with suggestive rhythms; in nothing else that he did was Ravel quite so human and warmly appealing. *Le tombeau de Couperin* (1918) is a tender, reserved tribute to the memory of that great French musician, François Couperin; appropriately it takes the form of a classic suite. *La valse,* written in 1920, in the disillusionment of the postwar period, is likewise vivid with tonal hues and orchestral colors; but there is an inescapable feeling of bitterness and cynicism which sounds a new note in this composer's style. It is a striking comment on the spirit of futility and nihilism that seemed to seize the world after the conclusion of the first World War. *Bolero,* finished in 1928, is little else than a gigantic orchestral *tour de force;* its whole appeal rests on a mechanical rather than an imaginative basis. In his latest piano concertos, Ravel seemed to be trying to lose himself in an older classic style, a sure sign that his striking and individual inspiration was waning. His last years, marked by a terrible illness, were entirely unproductive.

A SYMPHONY IN THREE SPANISH GARDENS

Manuel de Falla's music is a happy combination of impressionism and nationalism. Making use of many of the technical devices of Debussy and his followers, this composer has infused a peculiarly Spanish idiom into all his work. To most of us the very name Spain spells romance — the land of the fabulous adventures of Don Juan; the magic stage on which Don Quixote and his faithful Sancho played out their immortal drama; the trysting place of the gypsies of Borrow's fascinating travel tales; the home of Carmen and her castanetted rhythms, of the multi-colored, cruel bullfight, of proud arrogance and fiery love. Spain arouses in our minds memories of soft music sounding through warm nights, visions of the Alhambra outlined against the radiant Andalusian sky, reminiscences of a glory that is past forever. And it is this sort of thing that we listen for in Spanish music — and with good reason. One of the most important factors which influence the popular conception of a nation's characteristics is the music it has produced. Naturally the connection between the songs (together with the verses to which they are set) and the thoughts and feelings of those who sing them is very close. It was a wise rather than a boastful historian who said: " Tell me what sort of songs a nation has produced, and I can tell you what sort of nation it will become." The music which Spain has given the world is full of a soft, undulating, poetic suggestiveness quite in line with the popular conception of the country as a land of romance. And this is meant in no derogatory sense; despite the fact that she has produced no great international figures in music, Spain is a musical country. Her genius has been for glorified dance forms, descriptive music, and charming, graceful, senti-mental songs. It is in her sense of rhythm that she stands supreme, and much of the attractiveness and appeal of Spanish music arises from this.

Luckily for us this popular music of Spain has not been ruined by academic influence, but has been preserved almost in-tact and unharmed. Before any movement for the cultivation of the music of the Classic composers of other countries could gain much headway among the Spanish, they had become aware of their own genius, and educated composers made no attempts to write after the manner of Bach and Beethoven. The music of the best modern Spaniards, men like Falla and Albeniz, although showing unmistakable influences of their neighbors the French, is peculiarly indigenous to the soil of Spain. The three numbers in Falla's suite *Nights in the Gardens of Spain* seem like a re-creation of the popular soul of the composer's native land. Based on rhythms, scraps of melody, and cadences peculiar to the folk songs of Andalusia (the southernmost part of modern Spain), this music never copies these songs exactly. If you can imagine an Andalusian trio of two mandolins and a guitar playing these

folk songs in one of the old gardens of southern Spain, flooded
with moonlight, you are in the proper mood for the enjoyment
of this music. Although, as he himself has told us, the composer
has followed a definite design as regards tonal, rhythmical,
and thematic material, this design need not trouble us just now;
it is sufficient for us to realize its presence, furnishing a unifying
skeletal background for the whole. The end for which the music
was written is that of " evoking the memory of certain places,
sensations, and sentiments " — an end much more in accordance
with the real province of the art than that of mere description.
In the orchestration, although Falla uses no unusual instruments
other than the piano, we hear many effects peculiar to the popular Andalusian mandolins and guitars.

The first number, " At Generalife," introduces us to those
romantic gardens on a hillside overlooking the Alhambra — the
most beautiful spot in Granada, if not in all Spain. When we
first hear the music, it seems as if it had already been playing
for some time, for no attempt is made at an introduction; the
music simply starts. We are set down in the midst of this picturesque setting, and memories of the ancient courts of Moorish king-
doms in Spain float before us in these melodies and rhythms.
Granada at the height of its glory has returned; under the long
dynasty of the Nascides, greatest of the Moorish rulers in Spain,
it has become the center of Spanish culture, patron of Arabic art
and learning, proud possessor of the Alhambra, its royal castle
which seems like a realized vision of *The Arabian Nights*. These
Oriental melodies with their tinkling, mandolin accompaniments
suggest the gardens all about us with gushing fountains, dreamy
patios, melancholy cypress thickets, and flowering pomegran-
ates, much the same as they were when they belonged to the summer palace of the Moorish kings above us on the hill. All about
are ghosts of the past; here under a six-century-old cypress was
perhaps the trysting place of the Sultana and Hamet, head of
the noblest family of the kingdom. A tryst which, like that of
Tristan and Isolde, was destined to cost the life of the King's
trusted courtier. Here —

But the music comes to a pause, and we are transported to
another garden for the second part of the suite — " Dance in the
Distance." About us again are the orange trees, the myrtles and
the palms, the rushing and splashing of water. In the distance

we hear the music which accompanies a series of dances, the mandolins sounding scraps of Oriental tunes. One dance follows another, the rhythmic figures changing in quick succession and whirling to an excited close.

Suddenly — this time without any break in the music — we are " In the Gardens of the Sierra at Cordova." The owners of the gardens are hosts to a gay party: a *zambra* of gypsy musicians plays, sings, and dances. (It is interesting to recall the fact that the gypsies came into Spain from the East at about the time the Catholic sovereigns were trying to force out the Moors — the fifteenth century.) Happy shadows flit about under the trees; the wines, set out on the long tables, flow freely. There are wild rhythms, rude songs; a dancer steps out, her stamping feet and suggestive gestures flash in the moonlight. Although very few of us have experienced a night like this, we are like the sleeper awakened in *The Arabian Nights*, for we are caught up to hear things and see things with other senses than our own, and yet with senses which we realize all the time to be our own. It is a dream, and yet we know it to be real, brought to us by the magic of this composer who has made his music able to circumvent the barriers of time and space, and has brought us directly into touch with the beauty of his own people, a beauty which will last as long as romance holds its spell.

LIST OF SUGGESTED MUSIC

Here are some of the most interesting works of the three composers treated in this chapter; compare them and notice the difference in the styles of writing.

Debussy

Piano Works

> *Two Arabesques*
> *Suite Bergamasque*
> *Estampes*
> *Reflets dans l'eau*
> *Préludes*, Books I and II

Orchestral Works

    Prélude à l'après-midi d'un faune
    Nocturnes — *Nuages, Fêtes, Sirènes*
    Iberia
    La mer

Choral Works

    La Damoiselle élue (Poème lyrique)
    Pelléas et Mélisande (Opera)

Chamber Music

    Quartet in G Minor, Op. 10
    Sonata for flute, viola, and harp

Ravel

Piano Works

    Jeux d'eau
    Sonatine
    Gaspard de la nuit (*Ondine, Le gibet, Scarbo*)
    Valses nobles et sentimentales
    Concertos (for piano and orchestra)

Orchestral Works

    Rapsodie espagnole
    Ma mère de l'oye (*Mother Goose* Suite)
    Daphnis et Chloé Suites No. 1 and 2
    Le tombeau de Couperin
    La valse
    Bolero

Chamber Music

    Quartet in F Major

Falla

Orchestral Works

    El amor brujo (Ballet)
    The Three-cornered Hat (Ballet)

Andaluza
Nights in the Gardens of Spain

Chamber Music

 Concerto for harpsichord, flute, oboe, clarinet, violin, and cello

TOPICS FOR FURTHER DISCUSSION

Compare, according to your knowledge of their works, the aims, styles, and values of the music of Debussy and Ravel. Which do you think most representative of French culture and of the French mind? Does one look forward and the other backward? Has either ceased, wholly or partially, to represent the artistic " movement " of his period?

What are the special attractions of the art of Falla? Are there, in your opinion, any weaknesses in his and other composers' cult of Spanish nationalism? And are these inherent in that country's folk music, or in the composers' treatment of it?

Why did Spanish music linger so long in semi-obscurity, after the great days of Victoria, of the Palestrinian age?

An English critic has said: " It matters not that we can transpose the titles of *Nuages* and *Fêtes* (two of the orchestral Nocturnes), call each by the other's name and see in the magical fanfares of the second the pageant of cloud and sky or hear the echoes of rejoicing in the first." Discuss, in this connection, the value and meaning of attaching definite titles to such movements.

SUGGESTIONS FOR READING

Theories of Claude Debussy, Vallas. (New York and London: Oxford)
Debussy, Man and Artist, Thompson. (New York: Dodd, Mead)
Claude Debussy, His Life and Works, Vallas. (New York and London: Oxford)
Debussy, Lockspeiser. (New York: Dutton)
Bolero. The Life of Maurice Ravel, Goss. (New York: Holt)
Manuel de Falla and Spanish Music, Trend. (New York: Knopf)
The Music of Spain, Chase. (New York: Norton)

CHAPTER XXV

British Nationalism

BRITISH MUSIC IN THE PAST

IF this were a history of music, it would have much to say about the days when British musicians led the world: when William Byrd was admired all over Europe, and the great Dr. John Bull carried abroad the fame of English virtuosity in keyboard playing. The great Tudor school of madrigalists and church composers — Tye, Tallis, Gibbons, Morley, Weelkes, and the rest — paralleled the movement in the Netherlands (where it began) and in Italy; but about the time the Puritans landed in New England, the impetus was disappearing, partly in the face of the new solo-song movement, partly because every great " school " gives way, in time, to the next stage — though nobody, at the time of change, may know what is happening or where things are going.

Then there was a dull time, comparatively, with graceful masque music by the Lawes brothers, some writing for strings, and the like; in Purcell (1658 to, alas, only 1695) we have pure genius again, in opera, in church and chamber music, powerful, forward-looking songs (for example, the lovely " Lament of Dido "), and dance music. Then Handel overshaded all, and not in England alone; and though Arne (of " Rule, Britannia " fame) held the fort pluckily in the first half of the eighteenth century, the great foreigners — first Handel, then Spohr, Mendelssohn, Gounod, and all sorts — were cultivated to the neglect of such mild masters as England could show. In the later nineteenth century, English composers began to be more conscious of their great heritage. Sir Alexander Mackenzie, Sir Charles Stanford, Sir Hubert Parry, and Sir Arthur Sullivan stood for classic values in Victorian England, while attempting to seek out something of a national spirit. They prepared the way for Sir Edward Elgar.

DEFINE BRITISH MUSIC!

If one asks, " What is *British* music? " the experienced critic in England replies, " Why, that of Elgar and Vaughan Williams — and Delius — and Holst — and of course, on the Irish side, Bax — " And one has to cry, " Stop! What on earth have all these men in common? Surely they are all antipodal? " So they are, largely; but so are the elements of British character. And that is the first step towards understanding the British, if anyone wants to try that not-easy exercise!

All these composers have *some* English traits strongly developed, and all differ widely. No British musician could mistake one for the other, or fail to " place " a piece by any of them. There is an essence of each, and few foreigners can distill it. Newman, in commenting on a performance by the famous Toscanini of the *Enigma Variations* by Elgar, said: " We were left with the puzzled feeling that in some curious unanalyzable way this was not Elgar, that something in the blood of the music had been left out of it." And again, writing of Menuhin's playing of the Elgar violin concerto, Newman said: " I feel that now and then the thing was not English, and therefore not ideal Elgar."

SOME SAMPLES: ELGAR'S " ENIGMA VARIATIONS "

Of the group named above, Elgar, whom the British deem their greatest composer, is the easiest to understand as far as the style of his writing goes. He is a classical-romantic builder, a good link with Brahms, for instance; though his building material is often much more extensive than any former composer's, and he has carried the use of leading themes further than anyone except Wagner. Elgar (1857–1934) stands as by far the greatest English composer since Purcell — the first real world figure. In many ways he is the typical nineteenth-century Englishman; in others he transcends typical British traits as far as Shakespeare did (and when we think of " typical " Englishmen, we have to remember Shakespeare as well as the florid John Bull of the cartoons, who really never did represent England particularly well). Elgar is the consummate craftsman, the reserved, proud, thorough gentleman. Underneath his reserve, however, there is a

vein of deep and often noble sentiment — when he allows us to
see it. To a listener of another nation, this characteristic reserve
and careful husbanding of emotional resources is one of the most
puzzling attributes in Elgar's music. The emotional motivation
is so clearly present in all the best things he has written; and a foreigner cannot but wish that he would sometimes infuse a greater
warmth and poignancy into his writing. It is worth emphasizing
that he is (like more Englishmen than you might imagine) a
character full of contradictions.

But in hearing such a work as his *Enigma Variations* we are
convinced that, taking the personal and nationalistic traits for
what they are worth, it is great music. Elgar's pride of workmanship stands him in good stead here, for he is largely concerned in
a specifically musical problem — the writing of a number of
variants of a single theme. The theme-and-variation form became
unfortunately hackneyed and stylized during the eighteenth
century. Elgar, writing in the latter part of the nineteenth century, did not hesitate to employ this old form, and handled it
with such consummate mastery as to produce an outstanding
masterpiece. We need not be particularly concerned about the
fact that the composer contrived each of his variations (there
are fourteen in all) to represent a friend of his, making them
musical character sketches, so to speak; in so doing, he achieved
a combination of one of the formal devices of absolute music and
a programmatic manner of treatment. At the time of the first
performance of this music, the composer announced that he had
invented his theme so that it always fits another and greater
theme, this latter always remaining unheard — hence the title,
Enigma. The composer never divulged this theme. An amateur
detective declares that it is " Auld Lang Syne " (see *Music and
Letters*, July, 1934), but many doubt this. It matters little; what
we are interested in is the music itself, and we find this to have
vigor and full-bodied strength; there is a cleanness of structure,
a straightforward hewing-to-the-line quality that is refreshing.
The theme that we hear at the beginning, with its slightly melancholy, serious, reserved character, is real Elgar; we are immediately conscious that here is an orchestral master speaking. We
realize that this is not a tune thought of abstractly and then
clothed in orchestral dress; it was born complete, springing full-
armed from the composer's head.

The variations are as different in substance as the idiosyncrasies of the friends they portray; but in all of them we can recognize the contour of the main theme shaping and molding the music, though at times its influence is felt rather than clearly heard. How masterful is the composer's contrast of musical detail — rhythmic differences, key relationship, orchestration, power; the sensitive change of mood in each variation places the portraits in artistic relationship with one another. In some of the variations, notably the second and fourth, it seems as if Elgar was largely concerned with solving the musical side of his problem; others, notably the first, identified with the initials of the composer's wife, and the set of three which seem to fit closely together — the fifth, sixth, and seventh — contain tender feeling and deep sentiment. The ninth shows the composer at his best; it is the result of a long summer evening's talk, Elgar tells us, when "my friend grew eloquent — as only he could — on the grandeur of Beethoven and especially of his slow movements." This music is of noble, heroic stature, certainly an embodiment of the best that there is in the Anglo-Saxon heritage. The eighth and tenth variations are a bit more formal, the latter, headed "Dorabella," in a delicately charming way. Variation Eleven shows that Elgar is able to achieve an orchestral *tour de force* with great brilliance: the subject was the frolicking of a dog owned by Dr. G. R. Sinclair, organist friend of the composer. The friend of Variation Twelve was very close to Elgar, for this section contains some of his tenderest music — the sort of open-hearted, frank sincerity that many of his admirers wish he had indulged in more frequently. Without pause the thirteenth variation follows immediately, a happy flowing romance which contains a quotation from Mendelssohn's overture, *Calm Sea and Prosperous Voyage.* This was Elgar's happy salutation to a friend to whom the variation is dedicated, who was on the sea when it was written.

We might be excused for thinking that in the final variation (fourteen) Elgar the tone poet seems to have become Elgar the imperialist, in his effort to bring the work to an impressive climax. Although the movement is not his best work, we feel more sympathetic when we hear from him that, written at a time "when friends were dubious and generally discouraging as to the composer's musical future" (and we must remember that he was about forty then), it expresses his determination to win out somehow. So we might describe it as the "bulldog spirit variation."

Elgar's other outstanding works are two magnificent symphonies, concertos for violin and cello, and one of the finest, most complex of tone poems, *Falstaff*. These represent the greatest musical glories of modern Britain.

DELIUS THE RHAPSODIST

Nothing could be further removed from the martial side of Elgar's spirit, with which the *Enigma* takes its leave, than the fragrant, delicate beauty of such a work as Delius's *On Hearing the First Cuckoo in Spring*, or *The Walk to the Paradise Garden*, an extract from an opera. Here we are in the midst of natural loveliness, distilled into music. English people find that this composer and Vaughan Williams reflect aspects of their own countryside; but the charm of Delius is universal. His music is emotionally reflective, suggestive of the poetic retrospection that is inherent in every sensitive person, of spiritual self-communion. As Heseltine, Delius's understanding biographer, put it, "One feels that all his music is evolved out of the emotions of a past that was never fully realized when it was present, emotions which only become real after they have ceased to be experienced. The message of his music is one of ultimate assurance and peace. It is full of a great kindliness which makes us feel akin to all things living, and gives us an almost conscious sense of our part in the great rhythm of the universe."

The beautiful rhapsody *On Hearing the First Cuckoo in Spring* is one of Delius's finest achievements. The musician-poet needs only the title to suggest to us what evoked this mood in his creative consciousness, and we need no further program in order to respond immediately and fully to his haunting suggestions. There is no concern here over particularized events, details of thematic structure, or other exterior considerations; we are within the true domains of music. How marvelously its magic images are communicated! With the opening measures Delius evokes immediately the mood of early spring, and by the folkish character of the tune he sings, suggests a northern spring, loveliest of all seasons. The hedgerows are wet with early morning dew, glittering in the warm sunlight; we are greeted with the sweet smell of awakening earth, and from far off in the distance comes the sound of the first cuckoo. By means of the constantly shifting harmonies which he supplies to the folk tune Delius works his spell, and we listen entranced, forgetting to be concerned with the minutiae of musical structure. A note of homesickness creeps into the music; these seem to be " home thoughts, from abroad," to use Browning's phrase. There is a suggestion of melancholy, too, as if the composer would hint, with a subtlety beyond the power of words, at that *memento mori* so peculiar to spring — the reminder, in the midst of all the growing strength, of the transitoriness of life. It is the melancholy reflected by Housman:

> Loveliest of trees, the cherry now
> Is hung with bloom along the bough,
> And stands about the woodland ride
> Wearing white for Eastertide.
>
> Now, of my threescore years and ten
> Twenty will not come again,
> And take from seventy springs a score,
> It only leaves me fifty more.
>
> And since to look at things in bloom
> Fifty springs are little room,
> About the woodlands I will go
> To see the cherry hung with snow.

This is simple, haunting melody which within its particular milieu is unequaled; when we tire of the soul-stirring struggles and seek relief from the majestic utterances of the Titans of music, it is refreshing to walk for a while the quiet, dreamy ways with Delius and delight our souls in his fragile, tender beauty. Perhaps the only detail necessary to note is the surety of this composer's expression. Delius does not give the slightest feeling of hesitancy either in the way he repeats his charming melody or in the way he makes it sing from the orchestra. All is carefully and competently ordered, though there is not the least sign of preoccupation with intellectual manipulation; here we have a happy blending of *sensibilité* and intelligence — a perfect interpretation of the idyllic in terms of music.

CONTRASTED TYPES

Vaughan Williams (born in Gloucestershire in 1872) has been compared to Wordsworth, but he might almost be likened to any poet of nature and philosophy; and in his music for the masque of *Job* can be discerned something of Miltonic power. Not much of his music has been recorded. There is a *London Symphony;* but the *Sea Symphony,* a choral and instrumental work to Whitman's words, has perhaps the most universal appeal. His *Pastoral Symphony,* consistently cast in reflective mood, has given great pleasure to lovers of nature and of the kind of music that poses no problems, whilst bearing imaginative intimations of timeless beauty. This composer has not hesitated to carry the use of folk idioms over into the field of opera, where he has achieved considerable success with his interesting and bustling *Hugh the Drover.*

A friend of Vaughan Williams's once said that the very pains that this composer took to shed convention and express his innermost feelings tend to limit the appeal of his music to people of like feelings with his own. This is true of his work up to 1934; then came a radical change with his *Symphony in F Minor.* This is a work of tremendous violence, harsh, bitter, with tremendous drive, as if the composer would repudiate everything he had written up to this period. Certainly the temper of the times had a great deal to do with its style; its fighting challenge seems part and parcel of the epoch which foisted Fascism and Naziism upon an unwitting world. Some critics consider this to be Vaughan Williams's greatest work and one of the greatest of its period.

Gustav Holst (1874–1934), British in spite of his name, is considered by a few a peer of Vaughan Williams, Bax, and Delius. His music is often austere, sometimes astringent, though at his broadest he sounds a strongly tuneful British note. He was a lover of the Elizabethans, modeled his music on no very obvious plans of the past, and at his best combined austerity with wonderful spiritual insight, as in his chorale, *Hymn of Jesus. The Planets,* a large-scale suite for orchestra, brought him fame. One wonders if these suite movements wear well. In his late years Holst wrote little, and his austerity grew; so, in the eyes of some, did beauty, but there are doubters. Nobody ever doubted the sincerity and high artistic integrity of the man.

A CELTIC TONE POET

His contemporary Arnold Bax (1883–   ) represents the Celtic side of the biggest modern British music. There is in him a certain expansiveness, an efflorescence of, at its best, subtly expressive ornamentation, a length of wind that sometimes seems excessive, and an informing richness of spirit. He has composed much chamber music, and several symphonies. Every now and then comes out a really fine tune, generally with an Irish scent; and Bax can be gay, as the jig finale of his oboe quartet and two of the movements in the *G Major Quartet* (to name only a couple of examples) readily prove.

A good idea of his style may be gained from the *Nonet* for flute, bass clarinet, oboe, harp, and string quartet, one of the loveliest works in all chamber-music literature; this has had an authoritative interpretation and a beautiful recording.

OTHER COMPOSERS

Mention should also be made of Frank Bridge (1879–1941), a prolific writer of chamber music, and the later Arthur Bliss (1891–   ), the latter a composer with ideas of his own. He was one of the first English composers to write good music for the films, and his suite from the music for H. G. Wells's famous film *Things to Come* is typical of his vigorous style.

Perhaps the most talented of the younger English composers is William Walton (1902–   ). His skittish *Façade*, written in 1923 when he was looked upon as one of the bright young men of music, is hardly typical. Much more significant are his *Viola Concerto* (1929), his *First Symphony* (1935), and his *Violin Concerto* (1939). Lesser known are Ernest J. Moeran, Edmund Duncan Rubbra, Edward Benjamin Britten, and Alan Rawsthorne. Some of these younger Englishmen, to use the phrase of one of their compatriots, have " sought after Stravinskian gods, others have tried the thin-lipped French wines of neoclassic brands; they have produced little strong stuff of their own." What effect the second World War will have on talents such as theirs, only time can tell; since it has shut them off from many of their former sources of inspiration, it may well prove disastrous.

We have not tried to make this an inclusive catalogue of British musicians but have simply given a few words about some of the acknowledged path-seekers of the new century. The keynote of the British mind is individuality, sometimes carried to the cheerful length of " Mind your own business and I'll mind mine " — not unkindly meant, but simply implying that the Englishman expects everybody to be different. Logic is not his long suit, though the best British music shows fine organization in its reasoning, as all great music must. But no one must expect " a " British style; as we have seen in the case of Elgar, the character — national, as well as individual — is full of contradictions.

LIST OF SUGGESTED MUSIC

Enigma Variations	Elgar
On Hearing the First Cuckoo in Spring	Delius
The Walk to the Paradise Garden from the opera *A Village Romeo and Juliet*	Delius
A London Symphony	Vaughan Williams
Symphony in F Minor	Vaughan Williams
The Planets	Holst
Nonet	Bax
Things to Come, Suite	Bliss
Façade	Walton
Symphony No. 1	Walton
Concerto for Violin and Orchestra	Walton

Further Recorded Examples of British Music

Concerto for Violin and Orchestra in B Minor	Elgar
Introduction and Allegro for Strings	Elgar
Brigg Fair, An English Rhapsody	Delius
Summer Night on the River	Delius
In a Summer Garden	Delius

Appalachia: Variations on an Old Slave Song	Delius
Sea Drift	Delius
Fantasia on a Theme by Tallis	Vaughan Williams
Suite: English Folk Songs	Vaughan Williams
St. Paul's Suite	Holst
Phantasie in C Minor	Bridge
Music for Strings	Bliss
Portsmouth Point, Overture	Walton

(The orchestral score of Elgar's *Enigma Variations* [miniature edition] is available in the Novello Edition; of Vaughan Williams's *Symphony in F Minor* and Walton's *Concerto for Viola and Orchestra* and *Symphony No. 1* in the edition of the Oxford University Press.)

TOPICS FOR FURTHER DISCUSSION

Do you find much, or little, correspondence between your impressions of British national character and British musical character? What strikes you most about British music in general?

Sometimes the charge of " vulgarity " is brought against such works of Elgar's as *Salut d'amour*, and the set of *Pomp and Circumstance Marches*. Do you think there is basis for the charge?

Dr. A. Einstein, a distinguished German critic, says that the characteristics of the older type of British music appear to the continental observer " to consist in the subdued rendering of rich and powerful sentiments — the open exhibition of sentiment is not permitted in England." Discuss this in the light of any knowledge you may have of English national types.

SUGGESTIONS FOR READING

Elgar: His Life and Works, Maine. (London: Bell)
    (Two volumes, one *Life* and one *Works* — obtainable separately)
Elgar as I Knew Him, Reed. (London: Gollancz)
Edward Elgar; Memories of a Variation, Powell. (London and New York: Oxford)

Frederick Delius: Memories of My Brother, Clare Delius. (London: Nicholson & Watson)

Delius as I Knew Him, Fenby. (London: Bell)

Delius, Heseltine. (London: John Lane)

A Survey of Contemporary Music, Gray. (New York and London: Oxford)

    These stimulating studies are not always in true perspective.

A History of Music in England, Walker. (New York and London: Oxford)

    The book is the standard work of its kind. Get the 1924 edition.

The Land without Music, Schmitz. (London: Jarrolds)

    Here is a notorious attack.

National Music, Vaughan Williams. (New York: Oxford)

CHAPTER XXVI

Stravinsky's " Petrouchka "

STRAVINSKY, A BORN BALLET COMPOSER

MUSICIANS, as well as poets and novelists, have looked at life and wrought their philosophy of it into their art. In Beethoven's *Coriolanus Overture* or Brahms's *Tragic Overture* we feel, avowed or tacit, the drama of conflict. In Liszt's *Les Préludes* we have another view of life. It remained for some of the Russian composers in the last century to escape, in their music, into the puppet world of the folk tale and to draw after them the child that is in all of us, as the Pied Piper drew the children of Hamelin. Perhaps, in our Western sophistication, we soon tire of some of this gaily colored music; but whilst its spell works, how delightful to forgo the realities of life and follow the Russian piper!

The music now to be considered, Stravinsky's *Petrouchka*, is a gorgeous specimen of this type of art, showing the composer at his best. It might be said of him, as Newman said of Strauss, that he is a clever man who was once a genius. Those who may have disliked his later works, but missed *Petrouchka* and *The Firebird*, will have an altogether different idea of him after listening to these two works, masterpieces in their curious way. In *Petrouchka* the composer identifies himself with the inventor of the folk tale in looking at life with the detached observation of the cynic, amusedly watching the futile, puppetlike activities of the human race. The composer, who wrote this music in 1912, is a typical artist of his time, as all great artists must be. Anti-romantic, realistic, his music is a product of the Machine Age in revolt against the emotional softness and intellectual haziness of its predecessors. Stravinsky, like the contemporary painters, sculptors, and writers, tried to produce an art as free as possible from emotion, an art concerned chiefly with the delivery of its message in the most lucid way possible, adapting its style to the

231

necessities of the occasion and paying little attention to older methods of expression.

This vignette from the hand of a master is a striking commentary on man, the machine, as viewed from the vantage point of the twentieth century; no other time could possibly have produced it. It is engraved with real understanding of the human's essential futility, full of laughter at his unconscious comedy and tinged with pity at his inevitable fate. As we might expect, the music is as different in its sound from anything we have heard up to this point as the idea back of its conception was different from anything felt or expressed by the romanticists or the impressionists. The older ideas of harmonic and orchestral combination are entirely cast aside; new types of dissonant chords, often frantically and forcefully emphasized, scrappy melodies that are terribly banal in their awkward simplicity (melodies that are in character in *Petrouchka,* but which are Stravinsky's outstanding weakness in his other large works), both melodies and chords in different keys at the same time, pungent rhythms which, like the chords and melodies, are repeated and repeated — all these are characteristic of Stravinsky's style and are used to suit his particular purpose here. There is seemingly no sense of continuity throughout the whole work — everything is reduced to the idea of the moment, without relation to what has preceded or what is to follow.

MUSIC FOR THE RUSSIAN BALLET

Like so much of this composer's other music, *Petrouchka* was designed originally as music to accompany one of the colorful Russian ballets directed by Fokine. But the music is so picturesque, so self-sufficient, that only a general idea of the scenario is necessary for complete enjoyment of the work. The three principals, the half-wit Petrouchka, the enticing Ballerina whom he loves, and his gaudy and brilliant rival the Blackamoor, are three puppets of an old showman who sets up his booth in the midst of a Russian fair. The scenes which tell of the living, wooing, and dying of these characters are interspersed with those which give the atmosphere of the fair in which the little tragicomedy is played out. At the end, after a bitter fight, the Moor kills

Petrouchka, and the latter's ghost appears above the onlookers as if gleefully to refute the protestations of the showman trying to convince the onlookers that after all his actors were but puppets, and not humans. All this is told vividly, realistically, by the music, with no superfluous touches, no unnecessary details. There is little grace or charm in this music of Stravinsky's; all its hard, brittle details stand off sharply from one another, but they are nevertheless magnificently effective. As Rosenfeld (in his *Musical Portraits*) says, the angular, wooden gestures of dolls, their smudged faces, their entrails of sawdust, are present in this music just as they were present in the stage ballet that was designed to go with it. The scene makes a complete picture for those who are able to see the man-machine in all his comedy. The music was written to depict the scenes at a Russian Shrovetide fair of a hundred years ago, but the scene might just as well be that of a contemporary amusement park. For there is an essential crudeness about this music, a piety of " servant-girl grace and coachman ardor," a spirit of humanity unloosed from its fetters, that makes it timeless.

THE VARIOUS EPISODES OF "PETROUCHKA" [1]

It begins with a realistic suggestion of the bustle and confusion attendant on the fair. A constantly repeated figure suggests the pathetic tawdriness of it all; from this undulating tonal background there stand out little whiffs of flute melody and a countertune on the cellos, the whole finally crystallizing into a real march tune. Presently, in the midst of the excitement, there sound the first wheezes of an organ-grinder's tune (played by four clarinets), and soon we hear the whole tune, with the piccolo and the flute adding appropriate gasps. A danseuse comes tripping up, marking the rhythm of the organ-grinder's tune with a triangle. Soon another tune from the opposite side of the stage is heard on a music box, all three tunes joining in intermingling counterpoint. But in spite of the excitement, what a world of pathos there is in these cheap organ tunes! The uproar recommences and continues until a drum roll introduces us to

---

[1] The orchestral score (miniature edition) of Stravinsky's *Petrouchka* is available in the Kalmus Edition No. 79.

the Showman. Grunts from the bassoons and contrabassoons, followed by some excruciating chords on the clarinets, horns, celesta, harp, and strings, place him on the scene. He stands in front of his little booth and plays some charming and quite ineffectual arpeggios on his flute. The harsh chords are again heard as he pulls up the curtain and reveals the inanimate forms of his three puppets. Three quirks on his flute summon them to life, and they immediately start off in a terrific swirling dance that is full of all sorts of ingenious rhythms. How mechanized the whole dance, the same little tune appearing over and over again, hard and percussive through all its brilliance! The pages of the score here are black with notes: two piccolos, two flutes, three oboes, *cor anglais,* three clarinets, three bassoons, four horns, two trumpets, two trombones, xylophone, bells, two harps, piano, in addition to the usual strings, are all kept busy in the mad whirls of this dance. Little scraps of a new tune are heard and reheard, the piano taking up the rhythm alone, and the whole thing suddenly ending in three outlandish chords.

The next scene introduces us to Petrouchka's apartments. Sharp chords from the wood winds, a hard percussive piano part, and two clarinets with a terribly dissonant melody serve to characterize the poor chucklehead. He evidently realizes his own folly, for the trumpets have a bitter railing passage, *fff.* The dainty Ballerina minces in to the sort of inane melody to which ballerinas have grown accustomed; Petrouchka advances timidly and is, of course, repulsed — to a gorgeous clarinet cadenza. The following section, marked *Désespoir de Petrouchka* (" Petrouchka's Despair ") in the score, is amazingly effective and full of real feeling. Everything is again clearly drawn, with perfect understanding but with no wasted sympathy. We feel somehow that Petrouchka represents not a single individual but all masculinity crying its foolish head off for the worthless attentions of some female.

The third tableau, *Chez le Maure* (" At the Moor's House "), gives an excellent portrayal of this forceful gentleman, and it is little wonder that the Ballerina prefers him to the impotent Petrouchka! The episode is largely given over to a long characteristic dance to an Oriental-like melody. Unfortunately the incidents following this are omitted from the concert version. A little trumpet melody, with drum accompaniment, suggests the flirta-

tion of the Ballerina and the Moor; this Stravinsky follows with
a neat parody on the usual musical *langue d'amour*. Petrouchka,
mad with jealousy, tries to interrupt this amorous discourse, but
is pushed aside by the imperious Moor. The whole is a perfect
translation of satire into the terms of music.

Suddenly we are again in the midst of the fair. The familiar
din has recommenced and grows even louder as the excitement
reaches its height in a merry dance of Nursemaids. The oboe, followed by a horn and then by the strings, plays the infectious
tune; a trumpet is heard in another typical Stravinskian melody.
At the climax of the merriment a performing bear comes on
(this incident omitted in some versions) with a high tune for the
clarinets answered by growls from the tuba. The festivities are
resumed after this momentary interruption: there are other
square-cut tunes and heavy peasant rhythms, cheap and tawdry
as the rabble they delineate. The Grooms and the Coachmen
dance a stolid rhythm, to which is later added the bright tune of
the Nursemaids as they join in the fun. The mirth grows more
and more frenzied as a troupe of mummers joins the mad circle.
Wild, whirling wood-wind and string figures suggest the antics
of these new arrivals, and the concert version of the suite ends
on this note. In the complete version, Stravinsky does not have
to maintain the fetish of the happy ending and proves himself a
greater artist. He uses this frenzy of excitement as the prelude
to the final tragedy; a sudden cry from a muted trumpet stops all
the excitement, Petrouchka dashes out of the little theater followed by the angry Moor, there is a brief, terrible struggle and
poor Petrouchka's head is banged in with a loud cymbal stroke.
A charming little lamentation follows from the whole orchestra
as the showman demonstrates to the dismayed crowd that the
puppet is but a creature of sawdust. The crowd, not at all satisfied, disperses, and suddenly, to a piercing trumpet melody, the
ghost of Petrouchka appears above the booth and fingers his nose
at the Showman, who rushes off the stage, terrified. The curtain
falls to a mere suggestion by three horns of the repeated figure
heard at the beginning. This strange and yet extremely effective
ending to a beautiful work is characteristically Russian, a fitting
climax to the comedic existence which the man-machine leads
in a world that is for the most part disinterested in him and his
actions.

LIST OF SUGGESTED MUSIC

One of the most interesting studies in the development of a composer's style may be made with Stravinsky. Here is a list of compositions which will aid in such a study, arranged in chronological order.

> *Fireworks* — 1908
> *The Firebird* — 1910
> *Petrouchka* — 1912
> *Le sacre du printemps* (*The Rite of Spring*) — 1913
> *Les Noces* — 1917
> *L'Histoire d'un soldat* (*The Tale of the Soldier*) — 1917
> *Pulcinella* — 1920
> *Apollon Musagètes* — 1928
> *Capriccio for Piano and Orchestra* — 1929
> *Symphony of Psalms* — 1930
> *Jeu de Cartes* (*Game of Cards*) — 1937

TOPICS FOR FURTHER DISCUSSION

What are the differences between the Russian mind of *Petrouchka* and that of Rimsky-Korsakoff's *Scheherazade*?

Do you think that Stravinsky represents more than a mere national spirit of his age? Will this endure, and do you think that it ought to?

If you have heard other music by Stravinsky, discuss the statement by an English critic that his nickname might well be " What-shall-I-do-to-be-saved? "

What is Stravinsky's philosophy about emotion in music? Discuss his mastery of the technic of composition.

SUGGESTIONS FOR READING

Musical Portraits, Rosenfeld. (New York: Harcourt, Brace)
  (Out of print)
  Somewhat over-rhapsodic in nature, Rosenfeld's portrait of Stravinsky contains many Stravinsky ideas.
Modern Russian Composers, Sabaneev. (New York: International Publishers; London: Lawrence)
Twentieth Century Music, Bauer. (New York: Putnam)

Nijinsky, Madame Nijinsky. (New York: Simon & Schuster)
  The book is a fascinating popular story of the greatest Russian dancer and of the first production of some of Stravinsky's ballets.

Stravinsky; an Autobiography, Stravinsky. (New York: Simon & Schuster)
Chronicle of My Life, Stravinsky. (London: Gollancz)
  Stravinsky's own book, published under the two titles, is invaluable for obtaining his views on music and composition.

Stravinsky's Sacrifice to Apollo, White. (London: Hogarth Press)
  This contains a general sketch of the composer's career, up to 1930.

CHAPTER XXVII

"This Modern Stuff"

WHITHER, AND WHY?

THE works of Igor Stravinsky (born in Russia in 1882) and his most important contemporary, Arnold Schönberg (born in Vienna 1874), are for us important landmarks in music. Both these men stand at the parting of the ways. Stretching back from them on the one hand we have the line of the past, a heritage that contains all which we consider great in music; beginning with them on the other hand is the line which stretches out uncertainly into the future, tenuous and indistinct, yet holding promise . . . or threats . . . of developments as yet undreamed of. The early works of these composers — things like Stravinsky's *Fireworks* and his *Firebird* Suite, and Schönberg's beautiful *Verklärte Nacht* and *Gurrelieder* — may be said to belong to the era of the past. In fact in point of time, though certainly not as regards importance, these works represent the climax, the peak of the whole development out of the past. Their later works (Stravinsky's *Le sacre du printemps* and *Oedipus Rex* and Schönberg's *Pierrot Lunaire*) are examples of the opening of another era — extremist works, in the real sense of the term.

The listener who is trying to familiarize himself with the masterpieces of music halts abruptly and becomes hesitant about trying to go on further when confronted with some of this modern music. The works to which he has become somewhat accustomed, be they Bach's, Wagner's, or Debussy's, may have seemed strange to him at first; but they gave him a certain sense of security, nevertheless, and of hope that, when he had become somewhat better oriented, he would be able to understand and to appreciate their beauty. But " this modern stuff " baffles him; he feels himself at a disadvantage, like a person lost in a fog, without any communication with familiar things. The novice listener

Photo by Gottscho; Eggers and Higgins, Architects

FUNCTIONAL ARCHITECTURE — TRIBORO HOSPITAL, NEW YORK

KARL SCHLAGETER: CROSSING

"Non-commenting" art. The artist makes no attempt to tell a story or enlist our sympathy for any of his fancies about the scene.

may well be advised to avoid this newer music, as far as possible, until he has acquired a fairly representative background of experience against which to place it. But we cannot always choose the music we hear, and a few aids may serve to acquaint the listener with some of the most outstanding differences between the music of the past and that of the future: so that he may not feel entirely intimidated when confronted with a work by Hindemith, Bartók, Schönberg, or Varèse. A useful description, fuller than can be undertaken here, will be found in a little book by Gerald Abraham, *This Modern Stuff*.

MODERN TRENDS IN ART

In its most recent developments music of course has followed the general trend of the arts and turned resolutely away from things connected with the past. The modern tendency in what were formerly called the " representational " arts — painting and sculpture — is away from storytelling and also from trying to represent things as the camera does. These arts, of course, always held the higher possibilities of arousing emotion in the observer, and the finest paintings and sculptures have those qualities of balance and " rhythm " (here they borrow a term from music) which delight the artistic sense, apart from the subject chosen. In much modern art these qualities have taken the foremost place, blended with attempts to carry out various theories of what non-representational art ought to be and do. In painting, for example, we have had all kinds of " isms " since the days of the impressionists — Manet, Monet, Pissarro, Sisley, and the rest. There were post-impressionism, Fauvism, naturalism, cubism, futurism, symbolism, eclecticism, orphism, purism, Dadaism, surrealism, and heaven knows how many other " schools," many of them lasting but a few years. It is difficult to know what some modernists are after, since (as might be expected) a good many artists can express their ideas in paint or stone but not well in words. Whatever these varieties of art attempt, they all appear to have one thing in common — they will have nothing to do with storytelling. In music there has been something of the same trend, away from program and towards " pure music." As Sir John McEwen has well said, literature seeks to express meaning through words; but music " is itself the meaning."

Yet surely a Brahms symphony is "pure music"! What better is wanted? It is when we ask this that the weakness of much theory-founded modernism appears. Granted that no composer need write in the manner of any predecessor, if he does not want to do so; the only thing we have to demand is that if he deliberately avoids putting into his art what the Classical writers sought to put into theirs, then the things he puts into it instead of these shall be as interesting and valuable as *their* offerings. If he wants to avoid sentiment and emotion, then he must replace these qualities by others which will give us equal satisfaction. It is obviously not enough merely to be anti-this-or-that classic; the modernist must be a provider of positive beauties, for in the long run the mass of music lovers will never cleave to any art that does not give them pleasure. No amount of earnestness about "schools," theories, systems, or the listener's alleged "duty" to art will have the slightest effect. If people like any art sufficiently to want to live with it, they will support it, pay for it, and ask its provider for more. That is the way of mankind, the way of life — however hard it may seem to some composers. Innovators, unfortunately (as history teaches us), have rarely been the greatest men. The greatest have been those who first, and often for long, built on the foundations of the past and then added the original beauties that heaven made them create. Such outstanding composers as Beethoven, Debussy, and even Schönberg showed that they had thoroughly mastered the technique of their predecessors and did not hesitate to employ it in their earlier works. The best of the modernists make their way, even in a period of cheap music.

Out of this welter of seemingly incoherent experimentation there has come serious work from some creative artists with which every music lover must reckon. But nevertheless we must remind ourselves that probably in no period of the world's artistic development has there been so little straight thinking on the whole subject of art. Because the first World War brought about a realization that old standards are not necessarily valid ones, we have had produced a lot of sad junk with the little treasure that the painters, sculptors, writers, and musicians have given us.

MUSICAL MODERNISM

It is a commonplace aphorism, and one that the fakir is quick to use to further his own ends, that every generation finds the art of its contemporaries difficult of comprehension, and that later periods are likely to give quite a different verdict upon the quality of these " modern " works. The history of music is crowded with examples of this: thousands of music lovers today remember the time, not so far distant, when the music of composers like Debussy and Ravel seemed impossibly dissonant and incomprehensible; a book published not so many years ago on the music of Richard Strauss devotes considerable space to condoning his daring harmonic extravagances. Yet these composers are everywhere accepted today as perfectly understandable to the average music lover. They may not be liked, but their language is capable of being understood. Wagner and Beethoven were both considered modern and difficult (though well worth while) by some of their contemporaries, and Mozart, who seems to us today to be the crystal-clear exponent of the Rococo spirit of his time, was spoken of as an advanced thinker by some of the outstanding musicians of the eighteenth century. Obviously " advanced " is always a relative word; " movement " would be better, for we can move backward as well as forward! For the best large-scale discussion of facts and fallacies of this kind, read Ernest Newman's *A Music Critic's Holiday.*

POLYTONALITY AND ATONALITY

Yet the listener of today, although he probably does not realize just what his trouble is, has more reason for his pronounced distrust of and disturbed convictions regarding modern music than had the contemporaries of Strauss, Wagner, Beethoven, or Mozart. For we are living in a time of radical change in both musical theory and practice; there has been none like it since 1600 — the time of the ushering in of the era that we have just now completed. During this whole time, from Gesualdo (1560–1613) and Monteverdi (1567–1643), the ultra-modernists of their day, down to Debussy and Ravel, there has been one principle governing the practice of all composers — that of keeping their music in one key at a time. No matter how far astray from the original key the music might wander, or what dissonant shape it might assume, it is evident what modernists like Monteverdi, Bach, Haydn, Mozart, Beethoven, Liszt, Wagner, Strauss, Debussy (with only a few exceptional cases that prove the rule) had in mind when they were writing in only one key at a time. With these writers we can say, for instance, that music in certain measures is in the key of C, or is definitely related in some way to this key. But the extremists — the Milhauds, Stravinskys, Bartóks, and Bergs — are no longer satisfied with singleness of key; they demand that two, or even more, tonalities go on at the same time. An approximate idea of this polytonality which they reach may be gained by considering a certain measure to be in the keys of C and C sharp simultaneously, a practice which Milhaud actually employs in his *Sonata*:

There are others in this liberal group, notably Schönberg and his disciples, who have thrown over any alliance whatsoever with keys, and therefore call themselves " atonalists." Instead of having one or perhaps two or three key centers around which to group their music, they have twelve: C, C sharp, D, D sharp, E, F, F sharp, G, G sharp, A, A sharp, B. It is readily seen — and could more readily be heard — that the music these atonalists write, while it can be theoretically in twelve keys at once, has no relationship of tonality at all. Listening to these few measures of Křenek's *Toccata und Chaconne* will quickly convince you of this!

Schönberg, who is the outstanding exponent of atonality, says that the relinquishment of the scheme of tonality implies a corresponding relinquishment of the structural processes that were founded upon the principle of tonality. So we have not only our old concepts of tonality brushed aside by the atonalists, but like-

A MODERN ROOM INTERIOR

Photo by Paul Davis, Boston

RELIEF FOR A GRAVESTONE (1930)
BY KARL SCHMIDT-DIETFURTH

The extraordinary economy of line of this figure may well be compared with the " elimination of the unessentials in modern music."

wise all our ideas of musical construction that have been used
by composers from Bach to Debussy. And, in addition, there
will be other poly-devices used — polyharmonies, polyrhythms,
and so on — different harmonies and rhythms superimposed and
heard simultaneously. Little wonder that we are somewhat confused and keep wondering where all these new ideas will finally
lead us!

But this is not all. As if to make confusion worse confounded, there are other difficulties to make trouble for the
present-day listener. We have been accustomed to consider all
art, and especially the art of music, as something wrought by
the imagination — the result of an imaginative experience in
beauty that has not been apparent to us until it was made significant through its expression in art. And so art has concerned
itself with communicating emotions or experiences that are common to us all; it has not hesitated to deal with such immensities
as Life and Death, Man's relation to the Infinite, his struggle
with Destiny, his rhapsodies of love, or his adventures in search
of the Ideal. All this preoccupation with concepts so far removed
from practical experience has been brushed aside impatiently
by the creators of today. For them no visionary adventurings of
the dead days of Romanticism, but rather the cold, hard glint of
present reality. Bach's titanic flights of religious ecstasy, Mozart's
careful concern with perfection of style, Beethoven's great passion for the rights of the individual, Brahms's reflective meditations on the transitoriness of worldly things, Wagner's flaming
power, all these are considered as manifestations of a vanished
past, good enough in themselves, perhaps, but with no interest
for the artist of the present. This new music must be like the
period, inexorable, practical, unbelieving, a travesty of things
as they exist, a constant search for new sensations and fresh impulses, no matter how primitive or ludicrous they may be. Such
a spirit has given us works like Schönberg's *Die glückliche Hand*,
Berg's *Wozzeck* (a subtle, powerful, realistic, neurotic, intensely
human drama, with music that is both tortured and exalted),
Stravinsky's *Symphony of Wind Instruments*, in which he definitely sets out to avoid emotional expression of any sort and seeks
to divorce tone from any suspicion of association with sentiment, and his *Symphony of Psalms*, written *à la gloire de Dieu*,
one might well ask, in veneration or in travesty?

QUARTER TONES

Finally the harassed music lover is faced with the possibility of the destruction of the one fundamental principle still left to him in a changing world — the fact that our music system is based upon the unit of the half tone as the smallest unit. It was the Greeks who gave us our present system of scales based upon a certain arrangement of tones and half tones, although they recognized the possibility of using smaller intervals as well; both the Hindus and the Arabs used quarter tones and even smaller intervals in their scales. Today composers have again turned to these smaller divisions in their search for novelty, and considerable experimental work has been done both in writing music according to intervals smaller than the half tone and in manufacturing instruments that will play this music. Alois Hába in Europe, Hans Barth in America, and Julian Carrillo in Mexico have written in this new manner, the latter making use of both eighth and sixteenth tones. But the experiments in these enlarged scales are hardly likely to assume the importance of the work that is being done along the line of polyrhythms and polytonalities. Though individual composers may be attracted to the quarter tone, decades will pass before the possibilities of our present scale system are exhausted.

OUR ATTITUDE

What should be our attitude towards these novel changes and experiments? Realizing that there has been and will be more " faking " by innovators who wish to attract attention to themselves, we must nevertheless keep an open mind on the whole question, especially since the employing of so many new and as yet unproved resources makes the truth hard to get at. Dr. Buck's admonition, in his admirable little *History of Music,* needs to be heeded: " We must remember that what we call ' ugliness ' is merely a convenient name for things at the moment outside the cluster of the things that we are accustomed to call ' beautiful,' and that the life of music depends upon our keeping that cluster elastic." It may be suggested that, while a first necessity in judging any piece of work is to avoid blaming its maker for not doing something that he never set out to do, an equal responsibility is upon us to decide whether what he set out to do is worth doing at all. The music lover's task is to consider how far music can get away from (*a*) the formal strengths and beauties of the " Classics," and (*b*) the emotional suggestiveness of the " Romantics," without losing its hold on us. If an extremist throws over old forms and " development," he must invent new forms and means of keeping up the interest of his music, which shall grip us as strongly as the old ways did. As suggested before, if he casts off the beauties that Romanticism created, he must substitute equally compelling beauties of his own, however different they may be.

A THIRTY-YEAR-OLD ATTEMPT

It is difficult for a listener to make a fair assessment of the music of his own time, for he is too much a part of the period which produced it to enable him to listen to it objectively. There are certain pertinent facts, however, that should be taken into consideration if we attempt any appraisal of this era of change.

First, and most significant, is the fact that the music originating in this period has failed to obtain any permanent hold on the affections of contemporary audiences. In spite of the fact that the average listener today probably absorbs more good music in a week than his ancestors did in a year, and has a correspondingly greater acquaintance with music of all types than did his predecessors of the nineteenth century, there seems to be no real hunger for the works of contemporary composers. As one writer has put it, contemporary music has become a " thing apart from what the public thinks of as music — a thing to be listened to with polite fortitude when it makes its infrequent appearances, something that aesthetes and professors discuss, that composers argue about academically, that foundations support with fellowships and that small *avant garde* societies are always being formed to propagate; something that, despite a generation of fervent support by various societies, leagues, and guilds, remains a thirty-year-old flop." [1]

Anyone at all familiar with the present-day situation will concede the truth of these statements. The reason that they are

[1] Winthrop Sargent in *The American Mercury*, September, 1941.

true is not difficult to ascertain. Since the end of the first decade of this century, at which time Debussy, Strauss, and Stravinsky had completed their most significant works, composers have been so occupied with experiments, with trying to be different, with avoiding any semblance of eclectic relationship with their predecessors, that they have forgotten the primary function of art — that of communication. They have looked upon composing as a complex problem in musical structure or as an act of arranging sounds in some sort of intriguing, provocative manner, rather than as a means for expressing experience. They have forsworn the whole range of poetic, religious, legendary, and erotic emotions, to express which was the ideal of so many of the composers who preceded them. Rather have they uncritically followed the dictum of Stravinsky, who announced blandly that music essentially is incapable of expressing anything — " if it seems to express anything, it is an illusion." The approval of the cliques rather than the genuine understanding of the public has been sought. Instead of being truly inspired to produce music, many of these modern composers have been motivated by an attempt to outsmart their fellows and to surpass them as audacious experimenters. They have generated a great deal of luminous vacuity but very little genuine warmth, and so the great listening public, baffled and unconvinced, has remained aloof.

Second, it is becoming obvious that modern music, like modern art in general, is a sad revelation of the spiritual bankruptcy of the period which produced it. Nothing could better show the emotional paralysis which swept over Europe, the deficiency in spiritual ideals, the tolerance of compromise, the tremendous concern with concepts of a mechanistic, material character, the avoidance of those fundamental issues that must be met if man is to live on a plane above that of the beasts, the general lack of direction and conviction that marks the period between the two great World Wars. The art which the twentieth century has produced so far seems largely to have lost touch with human reality; we need but to examine it and mark its characteristics to know why European civilization of its era perished in the consuming flames of revolution and war. A culture such as this, which showed itself so afraid to face reality, cannot but wither at the root because of the sterility and affectation of the soil from which it grows.

The work which marked the beginning of this trend toward aesthetic decadence was Schönberg's *Pierrot Lunaire,* written in 1912. Whether or not its composer intended to express the intellectual and spiritual atmosphere of this time when the old romantic world of imperialism began to break up, this significant work is certainly prophetic of the bitterness and disillusion of the years to come. Set to twenty-one short poems by Albert Giraud, poems that are highly romantic in character, this score calls for only a small complement of interpreters: a vocalist who neither sings nor declaims, but " recites in song-speech," a violin or viola, a cello, a piano, a flute or a piccolo, and a clarinet or a bass clarinet. Out of this combination Schönberg has wrought a work that stabs with color, sears with dissonance, but which lingers in the memory. We may or may not like it, but we have to acknowledge that it communicates something that is part and parcel of its time.

Stravinsky's contemporary work, *Le sacre du printemps,* called by some of the extremists music's Declaration of Independence, showed the same general tendencies as developed in another milieu, that of Paris and its Bohemia of writers, painters, and libertarian intellectuals. As we have shown, the revolution proclaimed by these two works swept the musical world, affecting all composers in one way or another. Yet the net result has so far been almost negligible. The few arresting works that have been written since (some of them mentioned earlier in this chapter) simply serve as the exceptions that prove the truth of the statement, made by the critic already quoted, to the effect that there is little, even in the best music written during the past thirty years, that indicates a revival of the tremendous affirmative fecundity that characterized European music during the eighteenth and nineteenth centuries. The contemporary composer, unfortunately for him and for the world in which he lives, seems to have ceased being a vital factor in musical life.

The third fact that stands out strongly in a consideration of modern trends is that since 1930 there has been a tendency on the part of many composers to move away from this earlier extremist position towards a new creative synthesis that seems to show more promise for the future. This new tendency does not hesitate to acknowledge the falsity of recent attempts to do away with tradition — that slowly evolved means of communication between composer and listener. Nor does it try to deny the necessity of what has come to be known as the romantic, or better, subjective, point of view.[2] Without attempting to use the outmoded elements of a foreign culture, or to summon from the past a vision that has departed forever, and basing its ideals firmly on the verities that have proved themselves so abundantly in the past, such a synthesis of old and new, such a carrying-on of the traditions of the greatest music, should be able to heal the unfortunate schism that has developed between the contemporary composer and his public.

One thing is sure, that when the man arrives who can make the act of composing of major importance in the life of his time, who can write music the positive beauties and compulsions of which impels us back to it time and time again, we shall quickly be aware of the fact. We may have to wait years, generations perhaps, for such music; but when it is written there is no doubt that we shall in the end recognize it. For if the history of music teaches anything, it teaches that the only considerations that have value in so far as a work of art is concerned are the quality of the artist and the sincerity with which his work is produced. All else is secondary — questions of technique, style, school, and so on. Those who become deeply involved in matters of formulas and systems are apt to forget this. Aesthetes can talk, writers can propagandize, societies can be formed, intellectuals can theorize, all to little avail. Ultimately it is the response of the public that determines the worth of a piece of music. Granted that public taste is inclined to be conservative and that new developments are at first appreciated by a small minority, in the end the public has never failed to recognize the full value of a work of real genius. There is no reason to suppose that the present will be any exception.

LIST OF SUGGESTED MUSIC

The Firebird Suite	Stravinsky
Le sacre du printemps	Stravinsky
L'Histoire d'un soldat (Septet)	Stravinsky

[2] See articles by Roy Harris and Oscar Thompson in *The Bases of Artistic Creation* (New Brunswick: Rutgers University Press).

SCHÖNBERG AT REHEARSAL

PAUL SAMPLE: JANITOR'S HOLIDAY (1936)

In this picture Paul Sample gives an answer to " What is American? "

Symphonie des psaumes	Stravinsky
Octet for Wind Instruments	Stravinsky
Capriccio for Piano and Orchestra	Stravinsky
Game of Cards — Ballet Suite	Stravinsky

These works show characteristic trends in their composer's career. Where would you place the climax of this career? Why?

Verklärte Nacht	Schönberg
Gurrelieder	Schönberg

Both of these show strong Wagnerian tendencies.

Pierrot Lunaire	Schönberg
Piano Pieces, Op. 11	Schönberg
Six Little Piano Pieces, Op. 19	Schönberg
Symphony No. 1, Op. 10	Shostakovich
Symphony No. 5, Op. 47	Shostakovich

Born in Leningrad in 1906, this composer is one of the few moderns who has learned to speak directly and effectively to the musical public of all countries. His works (he has written operas, ballets, and chamber works, in addition to his symphonies) are supposed to have political significance; he has often been spoken of as the " composer-laureate of the Soviet state." Their most striking characteristic for most listeners, however, is the revelation of a distinctive personality who seems to have something worth while to say. This may not always seem to be of the utmost importance, but Shostakovich is able to say it simply, and in an idiom that all can understand — no mean achievement in a period marked by so much cerebral and affected writing.

Suite Lyrique	Alban Berg
Violin Concerto	Alban Berg

The most human of all the pupils and disciples of Schönberg, Berg has often used the style of his master with magical results. He died in 1936, and it is doubtful that anyone else will carry the atonal idiom further. Already even such works as these two of Berg's seem dated.

Concerto for Violin and Orchestra	Prokofiev
Preludio a Cristobal Colon	Carrillo
Sonata for Viola and Piano, Op. 11, No. 4	Hindemith
Quartet No. 3 (atonal)	Hindemith
Symphony, *Mathis der Maler*	Hindemith

One of the most easily appreciated of this composer's works, this deeply felt and finely expressed work is an attempt to recapture something of the spirit of a Gothic painter in the musical language of today. This composition, together with his music written for a ballet based on the life of St. Francis of Assisi, marks Hindemith as one of the truly characteristic composers of this century.

Scaramouche — Suite for Two Pianos	Milhaud
Concerto for Piano and Orchestra	Milhaud
La création du monde — Ballet Suite	Milhaud

The first of these works by the leading French modernist shows that he, unlike some of his contemporaries, does not take himself too seriously. The last shows his preoccupation with the American jazz idiom.

TOPICS FOR FURTHER DISCUSSION

Discuss the charge that when rhythmic subtleties are carried as far as Stravinsky takes them in *Le sacre du printemps* they come to exist only on paper, being too subtle for the hearer to follow.

Continuing this idea, discuss the extreme stress that is being laid upon rhythm by certain modern composers and the broad declaration by some enthusiasts that rhythm is taking on a new significance. Has this any relation to present-day modes of living?

Do you agree that the older means of expression have been exhausted by composers and that it is necessary for modern men to employ different ones?

SUGGESTIONS FOR READING

This Modern Stuff, Abraham. (London: Duckworth)
A Music Critic's Holiday, Newman. (London: Cassell)
The Problems of Modern Music, Weissmann. (New York: Dutton)

Music Here and Now, Křenek. (New York: Norton)

Our New Music, Copland. (New York: McGraw-Hill)

Stravinsky; an Autobiography, Stravinsky. (New York: Simon & Schuster)

The Art in Painting, Barnes. (New York: Harcourt, Brace)

> An enthusiast in modern art, Mr. Barnes in this book tries to show that modern painters use the same means and attain the same ends as the great masters.

Art Now, Read. (New York: Harcourt, Brace; London: Faber)

Modern Art, Craven. (New York: Simon & Schuster)

> This is an excellent summary of the whole subject, with special emphasis upon the art of painting.

Sense and Poetry, Sparrow. (New Haven, Conn.: Yale University Press; London: Constable)

> Here is a clear attempt to find the principles behind modern poetry and to separate wheat from chaff. It contains ideas that can be valuably applied to modern music.

CHAPTER XXVIII

Music in the Americas, North and South

TWO DIFFICULT QUESTIONS

JOHN TASKER HOWARD has written a book on American music (*Our American Music*); it is a good book, and one that should be consulted by all those who would be informed as to the details of the development of music within the United States of America. In the course of its seven hundred pages Mr. Howard does not succeed in answering, however, the two questions which have always confounded writers on this subject, namely: " Who are the American composers, and why? " and " What can legitimately be called *American* music? " Probably no definite answer to these can ever be made, but some consideration of them is necessary if we are to come to a conclusion regarding the present status and the future hopes of music in America.

AMERICAN MUSIC HISTORY

The history of music in the United States is a comparatively brief one, covering only three hundred years. At the time when Elizabethan England was a " nest of singing birds," when Palestrina and Di Lasso were carrying Italian music to its greatest heights, and when Schütz was laying the foundations for the future greatness of German music, America had not yet even been settled. New Amsterdam, the Dutch colony, became New York, the English possession, at about the time two of the greatest of the German composers, Handel and Bach, were born. The embattled farmers at Lexington fired their famous shot at the time when Haydn and Mozart were at the height of their brilliant careers, and when Beethoven was just starting his stormy life. The end of the first decade of the nineteenth century witnessed the birth of the great men of the German Romantic movement — Chopin in 1810, Liszt in 1811, Schumann in 1810, and Wagner in 1813, as well as that of the man responsible for the establishment of the permanent American union — Abraham Lincoln in 1809. During the great years of the flowering of European music, America was largely concerned with the basic work of pioneering and economic expansion; and it is little wonder that music, as well as all the other arts, led rather a pitiful and meager existence during that time.

Howard divides American musical history into the conventional three periods: (1) that from 1620 to 1800, in which " Euterpe came to the wilderness " and made the best of a rather bad situation; (2) from 1800 to 1860 when " Euterpe made up her mind to stay " and the alien tides of immigration, particularly that from Germany, gave a tremendous stimulus to the arts; (3) from 1860 to the present day, during which time " Euterpe makes a home in America "; native-born composers received encouragement and an attempt was made to determine just what the " American idiom " should be.

Seeking a Definition

The definition of the term " American composer " is difficult. Some writers insist that any man, whether born in the United States or coming from abroad, who is trying to express in his music what he feels to be the spirit of the country, and using materials that are largely indigenous, is a real American composer. Others feel that native-born composers, whether or not they pay homage to the national spirit, have sole right to this title but only as long as they follow modern tendencies. It has been maintained that the composer, whether born in the United States or elsewhere, who takes the materials he finds to hand (Indian or Negro folk music, jazz, and so on) and adapts these to suit his purpose is an American composer. The view of the conservatives is that any resident composer who is writing good music may be called an American composer, though his work be based on the conventional European types without attempting to be new or startlingly national in spirit.

And what determines the characteristics of American music? Should it be based on the native folk idioms? Is it American sim-

ply because the composer has passed part of his physical existence within the country? Must it express some phase of life, some
aspect of feeling that can be definitely recognized as American?
Or is music American because it contains new ideas created by an
American resident or peculiar to the American people? Can the
men who have infused native feeling into the conservative idioms
be called American composers?

Howard's definition of both American composer and music
is helpful in trying to answer such perplexing questions. He says
that a composer is an American if by birth or choice of residence
he becomes identified with our life and institutions *before his
talents have had their greatest outlet;* and the music he writes is
American if it makes a genuine contribution to the country's
cultural development. This will not do for Roy Harris, however,
who, in an essay on " The Problems of the American Composer,"
insists that an American composer must be able to be recognized
as belonging to that race which the peculiar climatic, social, political, and economic conditions of the United States have produced. His moods must not be the warmed-over ones of eighteenth-century and nineteenth-century European society, nor his
material merely the rearranged formulas of the conventional
type. Still another writer on the subject, Lazare Saminsky, says
that any music that is born of, or at least with, the creator's conviction that America is his native soil is American music.

THE INDIVIDUAL AMERICAN QUALITY GROWS

It is difficult for the European to envisage Americans as being anything but transplanted Europeans of various types and
differing qualities, and thus incapable of producing anything in
the way of an indigenous art. It is almost impossible for anyone
not on the immediate scene to realize that there is gradually
coming into being in the United States a population which, because of its past and present experiences, its geographical surroundings and its future hopes, is sharply different from that
of any European country. Frank Ernest Hill in his book *What
Is American?* states this clearly: " We have thought of the American quality as a modification of the European. If we are to realize
it fully we shall perhaps give it as definite and separate a place

as we give to ' African ' or ' Oriental.' " This being the case, why should it not lead eventually to the production of a really national art?

There are a number of factors that have contributed to forming the background of this American race. Prominent among them has been the constant absorption with the problems of frontier, a factor which we have already mentioned. The tremendously pressing business of gaining a living left little time for any consideration of art. The American has therefore no ripened and matured civilization to serve as a ready soil from which his art can flower. As Mr. Hill puts it, the frontier has no place for a Michelangelo or a Shakespeare (or for a Bach!), although it may conceivably produce a Lincoln. And unfortunately the Puritan attitude of mind did not concentrate upon artistic life, since it viewed cultivation of the arts as a ministration to that pleasure which should not take up much of man's time. Then, too, the dominance of the Machine Age, which seems to be able so effectively to outlaw beauty and romance as well as that " priceless thing, true individuality," has had a strong influence upon the art life of America. These things, together with the generally unstable influence of American life, have been largely responsible for the fact that the Americans as a people have as yet produced no great art.

Yet there are elements in the American character at present which give promise of a richer future. The dominating moralistic influences which so long played havoc with the country's artistic possibilities have been strikingly mitigated. The American melting pot is gradually integrating bloods of a widely differing character, and the science of genetics teaches that genius is more likely to spring from a hybrid race than from a pure strain. The courage, resourcefulness, and energy of the people, features which always impress Europeans, have been healthfully tempered by a forced realization that the material aspect of life is not necessarily all-important; the very wealth and leisure which the machine has made possible have given a wider and more understanding interest in art, an interest that has dynamic possibilities for the future. When the American has learned, as Hill says, to integrate art and life, to blend practical life with imaginative creation, there are good reasons for thinking that he will be able to produce native art that can be called great.

A treatment of American music, no matter how brief, should include a discussion of its three aspects — folk, popular, and serious music; up until the present the first two of these have been of greater importance and have secured wider recognition than the third. Evidence is accumulating, however, that during the last twenty years the creation of serious music in the United States has entered upon a new phase. Indeed, the political, economic, and social conditions of the present-day world seem to indicate that the future of this type of music, for a great many years at least, lies largely in this country.

AMERICAN FOLK MUSIC

Anton Dvořák, who came to New York in 1892, was the first well-known composer to recognize the individual character and importance of American folk music. He believed, and there are students of the subject who agree with him, that the so-called American Negro music is in reality a representative American folk music, a mixture of the musics of the white, black, and Amerind races, something that is entirely indigenous to this continent.[1] Most authorities agree that the Negro spirituals and plantation songs as they are used today are an adaptation by the Negro of the traditional hymns and songs of the whites with which he became familiar; in adapting this music to his idiom, the melodic and rhythmic peculiarities of his race, brought with him perhaps from Africa, played an important role. The result, together with some characteristics taken from the music of the American Indian, is a folk music different from that of any other country. Whether or not it is representatively American, this folk music has become known the world over and was the prototype for the characteristic songs of Stephen Foster, written originally for the troupes of Negro minstrels that were popular in the second half of the nineteenth century.[2] These Foster songs have

[1] See an article which was published by Dvořák in 1895 in *Harper's Magazine*.
[2] According to tradition, it was " Daddy Rice " who first started the minstrel vogue in Louisville, Kentucky, when he put on a " Jump Jim Crow " act there in 1830. The most famous of all the troupes was the Christy Minstrels, for whom Foster wrote his best songs. When these were first published they were attributed, with Foster's consent, to Christy. But in 1852, Foster asked the band leader that he be given proper credit in the future: " I find I cannot write at all unless I write for public approbation and get credit for what I write."

THOMAS HART BENTON: THRESHING WHEAT

Another well-known American artist gives his idea of " What is American? " in this lithograph.

GEORGE BELLOWS: FORTY-TWO KIDS

Still another artist's answer to the question "What is American?"

become so integral a part of American tradition that " My Old Kentucky Home " and " Old Folks at Home " are considered the world over to be American folk songs.

Another source of American folk music, the richness of which is only now beginning to be realized, is the music brought over by the settlers of this huge continent and preserved, with or without alteration, by them from generation to generation. Sometimes this traditional music has survived almost intact, as in the case of the Scotch-Irish settlers who, coming to the South and finding the best of the land already occupied, moved into the hills of Kentucky and Tennessee. Their descendants, isolated for more than a century from the rest of the continent, still sing the old country songs with pristine purity, at a time when the original forms have vanished from the land which gave them birth.

Most of the transplanted European folk songs have been altered and fitted to suit local conditions and American customs; oftentimes their form and subject matter is so changed that it is difficult to recognize their original source.[3] Thus there has grown up a great body of ballads, pioneer songs, sea chanteys, drinking songs, and the like, songs that are American in the real sense; no matter what their origins, these folk songs have so assimilated the American spirit as to make them expressive of a whole culture, and they reflect a democratic community of thought so perfectly as to make them adaptable to every type of citizen and singable by every sort of people. In this way they are unique.

Americans have always been a hard-working people and as such have always sung; each new frontier has created its own music. The cowboys on the prairie,[4] the roustabouts on the riv-

---

[3] John Lomax, who has collected hundreds of American folk songs and preserved them in the Library of Congress, Washington, tells of recognizing the lovely Scotch ballad, "Barbara Allen," in the Negro convict song " Bobby," the subject of which the Negro ships as a corpse out of the railway depot at Dallas, Texas, leaving her relations " squallin' an' holl'rin' with grief."

[4] Illustrating the fact that there can be a modern growth of folk song, Lomax thus describes the origin of cowboy songs:

" Not only were sharp, rhythmic yells (sometimes beaten into verse) employed to stir up lagging cattle, but also during the long watches the nightguards, as they rode round and round the herd, improvised cattle lullabies which quieted the animals and soothed them to sleep. Some of the best of the so-called ' dogie songs ' seem to have been created for the purpose of preventing cattle stampedes — such songs coming straight from the heart of the cowboy, speaking familiarly to his herd in the stillness of the night."

ers, the workers on the canals and railroads, the soldiers fighting
the country's wars, the backwoods pioneers bent on relaxation, all
have made original and unique contributions to American folk
song, contributions that are as native as " corn pone, chewing
tobacco, or Boston baked beans." Recent research has shown that
these native songs, instead of being confined to a few types such
as hillbilly ballads or cowboy songs, have been produced everywhere, from Vermont to Florida, from Michigan to Texas. The
Library of Congress has many thousands of recorded disks of these
native songs — play, party, and square dances, prison wails, work
songs, folk hymns, and the like. These embody the very spirit of
the country, a youthfulness, gaiety, crudeness, sentimentality,
cocksure braggadocio, and homespun sincerity that is far more
genuine than most of the intellectual and serious music as yet
produced in America.

POPULAR MUSIC

Like folk music, popular music in America has had various
origins. The early settlers had little time for what they called
" amusements "; life with them was grim and serious, and the
use of music was largely confined to occasions of religious worship or social intercourse. The first native form of amusement
music to thrive in the United States was that connected with the
Negro minstrel show (already mentioned in connection with
Foster's songs); this was popular throughout the country for
over sixty years. Then followed the more sophisticated variety
and burlesque shows, patterned after continental models and
flourishing in the larger seaboard towns. The Gilbert and Sullivan comic operas became almost as well liked here as they were
in England, and native composers imitated them as well as their
French and Viennese counterparts. Victor Herbert's graceful
works in this genre, while based on European types, are definitely
American in the lilt of their melodies, the verve of their rhythms,
and the sparkle of their wit. Even more nationalistic are the
marches of John Philip Sousa, known the world over; nothing
better characterizes the " youthful spirit, optimism, and patriotic fervor " of the United States of their day.

The heyday of the Herbert operettas and the Sousa marches

witnessed the development of the peculiarly American coon
songs and ragtime, music marked by a strongly accented melody
superimposed on a regularly accented accompaniment. This is
an African characteristic, brought to America by the slaves and
used by their descendants in their dance music; during the latter part of the nineteenth century it was imitated by white
composers because of its happy, infectious rhythm, and developed, through the infusion of other folk elements, into jazz and
then into swing.

There have been a number of contributions to this evolution; among them may be mentioned the intensely felt, everyday,
worldly disillusioned songs of the Negro — the Blues[5]; the
groups of Jewish composers steeped in the curious metropolitan
traditions of New York, among them Irving Berlin,[6] whose
" Alexander's Ragtime Band " was the first published ragtime
number to become widely recognized, and George Gershwin,
perhaps the best known of all American popular composers; the
musically accomplished arrangers who carried over the principles
and ideas of some of the standard composers into their scoring
for jazz and swing bands; and finally the well-known bandstand
gods of today and yesterday in New York and Hollywood —
King Oliver, Louis Armstrong, Duke Ellington, Benny Good-
man, the Dorseys, Bob Crosby, and the rest.[7]

It was Paul Whiteman who first tried to popularize what
he called " symphonic jazz " — music written for the theater
and concert hall rather than for the dance band. In as late an

---

[5] The difference between the religious spirituals and the secular blues has thus
been characterized by a Negro writer: " To the spiritual writers, a great flood would
have been considered as a visitation of a wrathful God upon a sinful people; the blues
singer would simply have raised the question, ' Where can a po' girl go? ' "

It was W. C. Handy who first caught the spirit of this Negro form and who
made it a vital part of American dance music with his " Memphis Blues " (1912) and
the even more famous " St. Louis Blues " (1914).

[6] Osgood, in his book *So This Is Jazz*, calls Berlin the " Bach, Haydn, Mozart,
and Beethoven of jazz — all the old masters in one."

[7] None of the authorities on the subject seem to be clear as to the exact differences between jazz and swing; all agree, however, that swing's outstanding characteristic is its driving rhythm over which soloists improvise as they play. The terms
" straight " (or sweet) jazz and " hot " jazz are generally used to designate the difference between jazz played as written and jazz that is largely improvised. Louis
Armstrong puts it this way: " There'll probably be new names for the same music.
There have been several names since I remember the good old days in New Orleans,
when hot music was called ' ragtime music.' So you see instead of dying out it only
gets new names."

Americana item as one published in 1926, Whiteman was given first and Beethoven second place in a plebiscite taken of the students in an American university to determine the identity of the world's greatest musician. Such fame probably came from his commissioning and playing Gershwin's famous *Rhapsody in Blue,* a work which certainly owes some of its success to its scoring by other men. In addition to this work, Gershwin made other experiments in symphonic jazz, none of them very successful, even though they were played by some of the country's most famous orchestras: a *Second Rhapsody* and a *Piano Concerto in F.* Other American and European composers (for this music is popular not only in America, it has swept the world) who have been influenced by the ragtime and jazz idiom are Debussy, Stravinsky, Hindemith, Kurt Weill, Křenek, Constant Lambert, Sowerby, Carpenter, Gruenberg, and Copland. But the serious composer is greatly hampered by the monotonous harmonic schemes and the necessity for constant violent rhythmic disturbances to feel at all at home in this medium. Jazz is, as has so often been pointed out, largely a bag of tricks, and the composer who tries to develop this type of writing is on the horns of a dilemma, as Ernest Newman has pointed out. If he makes use of the tricks, he is likely to lose his individuality; if he does not, he ceases to write jazz. Perhaps the only contribution which this style of American writing can make to the general idiom lies in new methods of exploiting musical instruments and of producing tone color and the possibility of making different orchestral combinations.

The future will probably know jazz as the typical amusement music of its period. For it is a characteristic phenomenon of escape, this bizarre, exaggerated, oversentimental, violently rhythmic, mechanistically constructed, patently commercialized music. It is the popular folk art of a world gone pleasure-mad, a world not too much concerned with realities, shutting its eyes to unpleasantness, and yet cynical and pretty well disillusioned. Jazz is too fixed in its limitations and too narrow in the variety and quality of its content to be able to maintain itself long in a world of flux and change. Influential as it has been as a factor in the cultivation of present-day taste, it can hardly be looked upon as a real basis for the development of an American musical idiom.

Acme Newspictures, Inc.

GEORGE GERSHWIN

Philip Gendreau, N.Y.

THE VOICE OF SWING

AMERICAN SERIOUS MUSIC

The reading of any account of American music of this type is both an inspiring and a depressing experience — inspiring because there has been so much activity, depressing because this activity has produced no works that can honestly be called first-rate.

Although, contrary to general opinion, there was no widespread and deeply felt objection to music and dancing among the New England Puritans, the fact that a pioneering and largely rural people has little opportunity for developing interest in art accounts for the lack of evidence of musical activity amongst the early English settlers in America. Most of the musical programs during colonial times were simple ones, largely devoted to religious music; a love of singing developed from the custom of singing metrical versions of the psalms in the churches, particularly in New England. William Billings, born in Boston in 1746 of humble parents, and apprenticed as a tanner, was one of the few original native composers of the eighteenth century; from 1770, the year of Beethoven's birth, Billings issued a number of church tunes of a lively " fuguing " style, and started classes and societies for teaching people how to sing this music.[8] Another genuinely American composer was Francis Hopkinson (1737–1791), who wrote a number of songs and insisted that he was the " first native of the United States who has produced a Musical Composition." A third prominent figure in early American music was Anthony Philip Heinrich, a rich Bohemian merchant who settled in Kentucky from 1818 to 1823, and who later, in New York and Boston, wrote a large number of huge orchestral compositions. Although these are never played today, their composer was the most commanding figure of his time.

SOME COMPOSERS

The earliest group of American composers able to stand on their feet in comparison with contemporary Europeans centered

[8] One historian has called Billings the father of American church choirs and singing schools, a teacher and composer whose work " provided the spark that set America's dormant musical life going."

largely in New England. Prominent names were those of John
K. Paine, Edward MacDowell, Arthur Foote, George W. Chadwick, and Horatio Parker; of these only the music of MacDowell
survives. It has a characteristic refreshing quality that keeps it
alive, but it can by no means be called original or great. Nor
does it echo in any strikingly individual or national idiom, what
MacDowell himself suggested he would like to feel in American
music — " the youthful, optimistic vitality and the undaunted
tenacity of spirit that characterizes the American." The other
men of the period wrote good music, which was unfortunately
unoriginal. Later writers in the larger forms (symphonies, operas,
quartets, and so on) who would conform to Mr. Howard's requirements but hardly to Mr. Harris's, include Edgar Stillman
Kelley, Daniel Gregory Mason, John Alden Carpenter, Deems
Taylor (whose two operas were the most successful of a long
list of native works produced by the Metropolitan Opera in New
York). Writers who have employed folk idioms in their compositions include Henry F. Gilbert, Harvey W. Loomis, Charles W.
Cadman, John Powell. A severe loss was the early death of Charles
T. Griffes in 1920, one of the most promising of the younger
men. Whether or not Ernest Bloch can be called an American
composer is a question, but there is little doubt that he has produced the most significant music of any man who has lived and
worked in America. A Swiss Jew, Bloch did not come to the
United States until 1916, and some of his important things were
written previous to this; but Americans have given him more encouragement than have any other people, and he has become a
naturalized citizen, with a liberal subsidy provided through
American generosity so that he can pursue his composing unham-
pered. Another gifted foreign-born composer who spent his best
creative years in the United States was Charles M. Loeffler, who
wrote a number of important orchestral works.

There is at present a virile and immensely active group of
composers in the United States. These come from various backgrounds and show different tendencies: some of them are conservatives, others lean rather heavily to the musical left; some are
romantic, others neoclassic [9] in their predilections; some are

⎯⎯⎯⎯⎯⎯⎯

[9] Roger Sessions sums up the ideals of this group as he sees them:
" Younger men are dreaming of an entirely different kind of music — a music
which derives its power from forms beautiful and significant by virtue of inherent

frankly nationalistic, others make no attempt to be American in content. Here is a list of them as selected by Aaron Copland:

The older generation of " young " composers:
Gruenberg, Ives, Jacobi, Morris, Ornstein, Riegger, Ruggles, Salzedo, Saminsky, Varèse, Whithorne.

A contemporary generation of new composers:
Antheil, Bennett, Berezovsky, Blitzstein, Copland, Cowell, Hanson, Harris, McPhee, Moore, Piston, Porter, Sessions, Sowerby, Still, Randall Thompson, Virgil Thomson, Wagenaar.

Still younger men are Samuel Barber, Paul Bowles, Henry Brant, Israel Citkowitz, Paul Creston, Dave Diamond, Lehman Engel, Alvin Etler, Bernard Herrmann, Hunter Johnson, Boris Koutzen, Oscar Levant, Robert McBride, Jerome Moross, Earl Robinson, William Schuman, Elie Siegmeister.

Among the most representative men of the older generation is Charles Ives; it is difficult to come to an honest opinion regarding his complex and lengthy scores, for they are seldom played; all that is accessible to the ordinary listener is a group of his songs. Roy Harris, on the other hand, has been most fortunate in having his music heard; it has been played by many of the great American orchestras, and a surprising amount of it has been recorded, so that every listener can form his own opinion regarding this vital, completely indigenous music. Sessions is a difficult composer to understand, for his music is thoroughly neoclassic in style and makes no concessions to the listener; there is a sincerity and an honesty about it that impress. Piston, a composer of marked technical aptitude, is a full-fledged member of the international school of dissonant counterpoint. Virgil Thomson and Marc Blitzstein have achieved notoriety through their stage works. Thomson's *Four Saints in Three Acts*, a setting of a libretto by Gertrude Stein, is typical of the time and place of its origin, Paris of the 1920's. Blitzstein's two works *The Cradle Will Rock* and *No for an Answer* are theater hybrids, partaking of the characteristics of social drama, revue, and opera. Both show strong leftist tendencies, and, in their own vernacular,

musical weight rather than intensity of utterance; a music whose impersonality and self-sufficiency preclude the exotic; which takes its impulse from the realities of a passionate logic; which, in the authentic freshness of its moods, is the reverse of ironic and, in its very aloofness from the concrete preoccupations of life, strives rather to contribute form, design, a vision of order and harmony." (Reprinted by permission of the quarterly review *Modern Music*, November–December, 1927.)

" pack a terrific wallop "; they point definitely towards a living, really American form of musico-dramatic expression. There is a great deal of coarse stridency and terrific drive in Copland's music which, according to Saminsky, shows him to be a typically Jewish composer. To be numbered among those who have not forgotten that the *raison d'etre* of all music is *communication,* the establishment of a common meeting point between composer and listener, are Howard Hanson and Samuel Barber. There is a beautiful northern aura to Hanson's work, natural enough, since he is of Scandinavian ancestry; but some of it shows a curious predilection for overstatement and bombast. The sincerity, deep imaginative content, and directness of utterance in Barber's music marks him out as one of the most significant of all the younger American composers.

The second World War has peculiarly accelerated the growth of the United States as a musical nation; for all of Europe's outstanding composers, performers, conductors, critics, and scholars who could get away have come to this country and are becoming integral parts of American musical life. What will come of this new amalgamation of cultural influences only time can tell; there can be little doubt, however, that the center of the world's creative activity in music has moved from Europe to the Western Hemisphere and that the future history of the art will be closely identified with whatever is accomplished in the United States of America. It is this fact that makes American music of such significance today.

MUSIC IN THE AMERICAS SOUTH OF THE UNITED STATES

In our treatment of this subject up to this point we have used the word *American* in its usual connotation, as pertaining to the inhabitants of the United States. We are beginning to realize more and more, however, that this nomenclature is unfair and incomplete, and that there are other Americans of importance that should be included in such a term — the peoples of Mexico and Central America and those inhabiting the South American continent. This is especially true in a discussion of music, for some of these lands had developed important and extensive musical systems long before the European settlers arrived.

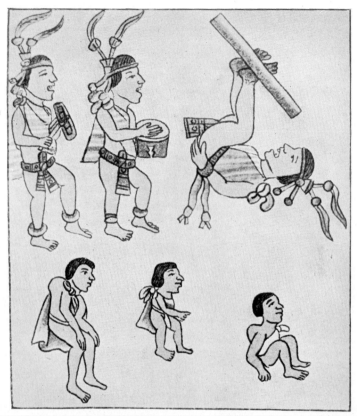

ANCIENT AZTEC MUSICIANS, FROM THE CODEX FLORENTINUS

N. C. WYETH: BEETHOVEN AND NATURE

The composer's close contact with the beauties of nature was the source of some of his finest music. The painter has depicted him here in the mood of the *Pastoral* (*Sixth*) *Symphony*.

In pre-Columbian days, for example, there flourished in Mexico several civilizations which cultivated the arts extensively. Recent archaeological research has shown precisely the degrees of progress achieved by these Aztec cultures; and there are irrefutable proofs that music played a role of real importance in government, religion, and war and that it was the object of special study and cultivation by the state.

Basing his materials not on archaeological melodies or quotations from pre-Conquest music, for no such records exist, but on a study of Aztec instruments and the way they must have sounded, Carlos Chavez, a modern Mexican composer, has given us an impression of how he believes this ancient Mexican music must have sounded in his *Xochipili Macuilxochitl*. In addition to the influence of these ancient American cultures, present-day Mexican music has been affected by the music of Spanish and other origins that has come into the country from the four corners of the globe, together with the influence of the peculiar native admixture resulting from these elements. A great deal of this interesting folk music, the result of blending Indo-Spanish elements with Italian, German, French, Moorish-Arabic, and Negro slave music, is readily available. It takes the names *corridos, sones, canciones,* and is worthy of considerable study.

The most important figure in the modern Mexican scene is the aforementioned Carlos Chavez, conductor and composer, whose music achieves a real indigenous blend of the influences that have gone into the folk music of his country. But this is likewise music that has been affected by the developments of the composer's generation, as is evident in its linear contrapuntal lines and its stark objectivity. At one moment it seems to express a primitive barbarism, in the next a machine-age spirit. The list of other Mexican composers of serious music includes Silvestre Revueltas [10] (who based his work on the popular music of his

---

[10] Mayer-Serra, in his book *Panorama de la Música Mexicana — desde la Independencia hasta la Actualidad* (published by El Collegio de México in 1941) makes this distinction between the two leading Mexican composers:

"For Chavez the aboriginal musical culture is the most important in the history of Mexican music; he tries to reconstruct musically this atmosphere of primitive purity, thinking to find in it the true Mexican character; for Revueltas, on the other hand, Mexico is genuinely represented by the remains of primitive cultures as well as by the surprising results of that mixture of races and civilizations that is so characteristic of modern Mexico."

country's fairs and taverns and whose tragic death in 1940 robbed Latin-American music of one of its finest and most individual talents), Luis Sandi, Daniel Ayala, Salvador Contreras, and Blas Galindo.

Small but active groups of composers have been functioning in the South American countries of Brazil, Chile, Argentina, and Uruguay. Here, as in Mexico, there has been a peculiar blending of many diverse elements and resources — chiefly Portuguese, Indian, and African. Of all these countries, Brazil has had the richest and most important musical development; by the middle of the nineteenth century its greatest city, Rio de Janeiro, had a cosmopolitan music culture comparable to that of the great European centers, supporting first-class operatic and concert performances and a good national conservatory. The first Brazilian composer to win universal renown was the nineteenth-century Carlos Gomes, who was the first opera composer of the Americas to win European recognition. Alberto Nepomuceno was a strong nationalist and sponsor of Brazil's greatest composer to date, Hector Villa-Lobos. A genius with an insatiable curiosity and seemingly inexhaustible energy, Villa-Lobos is almost an entirely self-taught composer. He has written over fourteen hundred works in every musical idiom; the best of these show great ingenuity, strong individuality, and real originality. Such a thing as his major chamber-music work, the *Nonetto* for chamber orchestra and chorus, could have been written by no other composer. His great suites, the *Bachianas Brasileiras*, attempt to " transmit the spirit of Bach — a universal spirit, source, and end in itself " — into the soul of Brazil, and are worth careful study.

Other leading Brazilian composers who are trying to build a contemporary national school are Oscar Lorenzo Fernandez, Francisco Mignone, and M. Carmargo Guarnieri.

In the Argentine, the best-known name seems to be that of Juan José Castro, conductor of the Colon opera, Buenos Aires, a brilliant and very successful composer as well as conductor; his brother, a composer of even greater talent, José Mario Castro, is not so well known outside his native country. Juan Carlos Paz seems to have become enamored of Schönbergian twelve-tone ideals, while the young Alberto Ginastera is looked upon by the Argentine musicians as their most promising composer. Prominent progressives in Uruguay include Carlos Estrada and Vincente Ascone.

In general it must be stated that, with one or two outstanding exceptions, these South and Central American composers, like so many of their contemporary brothers to the north, have shown a tendency to ignore their own birthright and imitate European music that was modern some years ago. The resulting music is both unfertile and unrepresentative.

In most of the South American countries there are folklorists who conduct important research work along the line of native songs and dances, as well as scholars who try to piece together these valuable finds in pre-Columbian music. Chief among these are Carlos Vega of Argentina and Dr. Luiz de Azevedo of Brazil.

It seems strange that it has taken a world war to awaken the curiosity of the people of the United States to the activities of their neighbors to the south. All signs point to an increasingly active and profitable interchange of ideas between the countries of the American hemisphere in the years that lie ahead. In this, music is bound to play an important part.

LIST OF SUGGESTED MUSIC

We have prepared the following list of American recorded music; it makes no pretense of being complete, but it shows the great interest in American composers displayed by the recording companies in recent years. (The asterisk * refers to Album of Collected Items.)

American Folk Music

American Indian Music

Indian Music of the Southwest by Laura Boulton *	V
Sun Dance; War Song; Funeral Song	Decca

Negro Spirituals

Favorite Negro Spirituals by Hampton Quartet	Musicraft
Crucifixion	Col
Hear de Lambs Acryin'	Col
Standin' by the Bedside; My Poor Mother Died	Col

Negro " Sinful Songs "

Sinful Songs by Lead Belly *	Musicraft
John Henry; Grey Goose	Timley

Folk Songs

Foster Gallery by Morton Gould	V
(An orchestral arrangement of some Foster songs in rather sophisticated manner)	
Early American Ballads *	V
Drill, Ye Tarriers, Drill; Kevin Barry	Timley
From the American Songbag by Carl Sandburg *	Musicraft
Folk Songs, Religious and Worldly *	Musicraft
Southern Prison Songs *	V
Bayou Ballads of the Louisiana Plantations *	V
Early American Carols and Folk Songs *	V
Two Centuries of American Folk Songs *	V
The Wayfaring Stranger *	Okeh
The Old Chisholm Trail *	Keynote
A Program of Mexican Music by Chavez *	Col
Indian Melodies of Peru *	Col
Brazilian Folk Songs by Elsie Houston *	V
Carlos Gardel Tango Cancion Album *	V

American Popular Music

American Fantasy — Victor Herbert		V
Semper Fidelis; " The Stars and Stripes Forever " — Sousa		V
Naughty Marietta — Victor Herbert (Selections) *		V
" Ol' Man River " — Jerome Kern		V
Rhapsody in Blue		V
An American in Paris	— George Gershwin	Decca
Songs of George Gershwin *		Decca
A Louis Armstrong Album *		Col
A Bix Beiderbecke Album *		Col
" Black and Tan Fantasy "		V
" Reminiscing in Tempo "	— Ellington	Brunswick
" St. Louis Blues " (Handy)		V
Lonesome Blues by Blue Note Quartet *		Blue Note
" Twilight in Turkey " — Scott		Brunswick
From Bach to Boogie-Woogie *		General
Grand Canyon Suite — Grofe		Col
Scenario from *Showboat* — Jerome Kern		Col

American Serious Music

Fuguing Tunes — William Billings *	Col
Prelude to *Œdipus Tyrannus* — Paine	V
" Jubilee " — Chadwick	V
" Night Piece " (for flute and strings) — Foote	Col
" Piano Concerto in D Minor " — MacDowell	V
" Suite No. 2 (Indian) " — MacDowell	Col
" Piano Sonata " — Griffes	Friends Rec. M.
" The Pleasure Dome of Kubla Khan " — Griffes	V
Three Pieces for Harp, Flute, String Quartet — Mason	Royale
" Concerto for Violin and Orchestra " — Bloch	Col
Schelomo (Hebrew Rhapsody) — Bloch	V
Baal Shem — Bloch	Col
" Skyscrapers " — Carpenter	V
" Music for Four Stringed Instruments " — Loeffler	V
" Six Songs " — Charles Ives	New M. Quarterly Rec.
Through the Looking-Glass Suite — Deems Taylor	Col
Scherzo from *Afro-American Symphony* — Still	V
Romantic Symphony (No. 2) — Hanson	V
Third Symphony — Hanson	V
" When Johnny Comes Marching Home " — Harris	V
Symphony 1933 — Harris	Col
" Quintet for Piano and Strings " — Harris	V
" Quartet in E Minor " — Sessions	Guild Recordings
" The Incredible Flutist " — Piston	V
" String Quartet No. 1 " — Piston	Col
Music for Theater — Copland	V
El Salon Mexico — Copland	V
Essay for Orchestra — Barber	V
The Cradle Will Rock — Blitzstein *	Musicraft
No for an Answer — Blitzstein *	Keynote
Piano Music by American Composers *	V
Sinfonia di Antigona — Chavez	V
Sinfonia India — Chavez	V
Isle of the Ceibos; The Country — Fabini	V
A Festival of Brazilian Music — Villa-Lobos *	V
South American Chamber Music	Col

TOPICS FOR FURTHER DISCUSSION

Name some of the American writers who have infused a native feeling into the older idioms. What are some of their works?

What is your opinion regarding the essential characteristics of American art? What are its possibilities for the future?

Why has American " jazz " become so popular in Europe? Do you think its influence is important for the development of music?

Have you ever heard any music which fulfills Harris's qualifications for American music?

How can improvement in cultural relationships between North and South America best be brought about in so far as music is concerned?

SUGGESTIONS FOR READING

What Is American? Hill. (New York: John Day)
> Here is an excellent discussion of the general American scene. It should be read by all who wish to understand the spiritual backgrounds of American art and its possibilities for the future.

Our American Music, Howard. (New York: Crowell)
> This book is an enormously detailed (700 pages) and accurate account (except as to the Puritan attitude) of the development of American music. It likewise contains a representative list of published orchestral and chamber-music compositions by American composers.

Our Contemporary Composers, Howard. (New York: Crowell)

Twentieth Century Music, Bauer. (New York: Putnam)
> A good chapter on jazz and American music will be found in this book.

American Composers on American Music, A Symposium, edited by Henry Cowell. (Stanford Univ., Calif.: Stanford University Press; London: Oxford)
> Mr. Cowell has followed the idea — not so new or original as he seems to consider it — of letting composers express themselves on the works of their fellows. The title is misleading, for the book contains only an account of the " modern " men.

Modern Composers, Pannain. (New York: Dutton)
> This book contains a survey of American music by a European and is interesting from that angle.

Music of Our Day, Saminsky. (New York: Crowell)

Our New Music, Copland. (New York: McGraw-Hill)

A Treasury of American Song, Downes and Siegmeister. (New York: Howell, Soskin)
> Here we have a representative collection of Americana, harmonized, with piano accompaniments.

American Ballads and Folk Songs, John and Alan Lomax. (New York: Macmillan)

Our Singing Country, John and Alan Lomax. (New York: Macmillan)
These two excellent collections were made by men who have worked in the field.

Traditional Music of America, Ford. (New York: Dutton)
This gives a picture of America's early social and work activities, expressed in some of its unwritten traditional music and history.

Jazz: From the Congo to the Metropolitan, Goffin. (New York: Doubleday, Doran)

Jazzmen, Ramsey and Smith. (New York: Harcourt, Brace)

American Jazz Music, Wilder Hobson. (New York: Norton; London: Dent)
These are three of the best books on the subject.

The Jazz Record Book, Smith and others. (New York: Smith & Durrell)

Mexican Music, Weinstock. (New York: Museum of Modern Art)

CHAPTER XXIX

Beethoven's "Fifth Symphony"

BEETHOVEN'S EXCITING BACKGROUND

A REGRESSION from the study of modern trends to a consideration of the *Fifth Symphony* of Beethoven is not so abrupt as it first seems. We have suggested that the leaders of musical thought of the first two decades of the twentieth century have been looking for a new freedom from the older conventions. During a period marked by violent changes — physical, spiritual, and economic — these composers have demanded that music be permitted to cast off the fetters of the past and develop along the abstract lines of musical design. We have likewise suggested that the process of experimentation in these new fields, even though it has not yet produced figures which approximate the great masters of the past, deserves our attention even if we cannot give it our sympathy. But the weaknesses of the results that have followed the practice of these modern ideals show up in rather unfortunate relief against the striking work of the Titan who lived and composed in a period of upheaval almost exactly like that which has given us our present-day conditions.

Ludwig van Beethoven wrote during the period of unsettlement and doubt that followed the French Revolution; he was born in 1770 and died in 1827, and the fall of the Bastille occurred, you remember, in 1789. It was Beethoven who voiced the thoughts and emotions of that great time as did no other, raising himself and his music into the very " realms of the sunlight itself." His music is the incarnation of Taine's description of the period; it is filled with discontent with the present, a vague desire for a higher beauty and a more ideal happiness, the painful aspiration for the infinite. But it was because of the manner in which he sang of these desires and aspirations that we listen to him today; he spoke a universal language, and his message has

reached the whole cultured world. He was not merely content
with a garrulous protest against things as they existed. The music of the time had reached heights, under the genius of Haydn
and Mozart, that seemed to make any further progress difficult,
if not impossible. But, building firmly on the past, realizing that
ideas are best communicated through music that follows fundamentals of design, Beethoven gathered up the surging discon-
tents, strivings, and aspirations of his time, and voiced them
through a universally understood medium, charging them with
a vitality and emotional power that is as strong today as it was
in the early part of the nineteenth century. And so he remains a
man, not of historical yesterdays, but of today, and for all time.
Shall we be able to say the same of the Stravinskys, Schönbergs,
and their like a hundred years hence?

Some of the music that Beethoven wrote has become dated
and old-fashioned. The quality of his work is uneven, for he had
to live from the practice of his art and sometimes wrote things
that were obviously designed for immediate consumption. While
all of his work is filled with what one writer has called " moral intensity " — that is, with a struggle to express the infinite — this
intention is not always realized and we have music that is grandiose and impressive rather than really great. But in his best works,
things like the *Eroica Symphony*, the *Fifth Symphony*, the *Ninth
Symphony*, and the last string quartets, he stands unequaled both
in the force of his thought and in the quality of its expression.

THE " C MINOR SYMPHONY ": A DRAMA IN PURE MUSIC

It is unfortunate, but perhaps inevitable, that the *C Minor*
(*Fifth*) *Symphony* of Beethoven, one of the most epochal of his
works, has suffered from overplaying almost from the day of
its first performance. Sir George Grove tells us that the conductor who first introduced orchestral music into England played
this symphony week after week; and it was his opinion that the
tremendous hold which this work had upon audiences is due to
its " prodigious originality, form, and conciseness." The very
qualifications that have made its popularity are those which have
given it staying power; present-day writers might well ponder
these two characteristics, popularity and staying power! They

might, if the task is not too obvious for them, try to realize how
Beethoven achieved this popularity and staying power.

For it is this work that stands above all others as a triumphant demonstration of the eternal necessity of shaping expressive materials according to fundamental laws of design. It proves,
as does no other single piece of music, that only if various elements at the disposal of the composer are combined according to
organized plan will the final appeal of the whole be realized.
No one knew better than did Beethoven that the formal principles of music are not arbitrary rules laid down by authoritative
fiat. Rather were they the result of continued experimentation
from the early unidentified writers of simple songs down to the
composers of his own day. The final object of experimentation
was to find the best method of composing music so that it could
give the hearer a feeling of definiteness, clarity, and unity of
expression.

BEETHOVEN'S SHAPING OF FORM

We have already said what the most usual forms available
to the composer of Beethoven's day were; in view of what we
have just stated, it will be no surprise then to find that he employed them all. As Grove says: " The *C Minor Symphony* is from
the beginning to the end as strictly in accordance with the rules
that govern the structure of musical composition as any symphony of Haydn." But the important thing is that while the
symphonic form as he used it was rigidly definite in outline, his
method permitted the widest liberties of style and idiom. While
the music is conceived in the most rigorous of intellectual methods, it nevertheless is incandescent with fiery emotion. In this
Fifth Symphony Beethoven brought the organization of form to
a state of perfection, but he was " no theorist endeavoring to
demonstrate the validity of his innovations. He was working in
obedience to the dictates of his artistic soul " (Henderson in the
New York Sun).

This work is a most significant example of the necessary in-
terrelationship of form and substance. It is perfectly easy to dis-
sect the first movement, for example, and show that it is written
almost exactly according to the strictest pattern of sonata form.
This is interesting — and helpful, if we are trying to arrive at an

understanding of the demands that this form makes upon the composer. But what is significant is that the substance of this music grows inexorably out of the formal design — that one would be unthinkable without the other. Beethoven could have produced neither the logical coherence nor the dramatic intensity of this movement if he had not observed the necessities of formal design. On the other hand, the obedience to all the laws of structure known to artists would have been of little avail if Beethoven's thoughts had not been so original and the glow of their emotional power had not been so intense.

THE EMOTIONAL BACKGROUND

The emotional stimulus for writing this music is not difficult to discern. It was composed during an active and fervid period of Beethoven's life, in the summer of 1808, and the composer is supposed to have said of its first theme: " Thus it is that Fate knocks at the door." (This is according to Schindler, a biographer whose statements have been somewhat discredited today.) But Beethoven might well have said it. What did he mean? We can find the answer readily enough in some of his writings of the time. In his diary, written on his twenty-fifth birthday, he says in apprehension over his sickness and increasing deafness: " Courage, my mind shall triumph over all the weaknesses of the body! " To a friend in 1801 he wrote: " Your Beethoven leads an unhappy life, in conflict with Nature and Creator; more than once have I cursed him that exposes his creatures to the meanest accident, so that even the most beautiful flower is destroyed and crushed. I will take Fate by the throat; surely it cannot bend me down completely." In addition to realizing that he was growing deaf and consequently more and more isolated from the world, Beethoven was constantly and bitterly disappointed in love. He appealed anxiously for feminine love and sympathy, proposing to Countess Guicciardi in 1800 and being summarily rejected; falling in love successively with Countess Brunswick, Theresa Malfatti, Amalie Sebald, he was unable to find a woman willing to share his stormy life.

It is hardly presuming on fancy, then, to suggest that this whole symphony is a glorious protraction of Beethoven's bitter struggle and final triumph. The music certainly suggests it, and we have plenty of documentary evidence to support such an idea. Beethoven the individual in bitter struggle with life is sublimated into Man battling with his Destiny. And as Beethoven the individual triumphed (" Everything which pertains to life, let it be consecrated to Art the sublime and be her sanctuary — Let me live! ") through his ability to create, so does Man, his counterpart, triumph through his ability to rise again out of the shadow of torment to rule in dignity and power.

The First Movement [1]

The first movement, as in every great symphony, gives the clue for the whole work. It is tensely dramatic — one of the few movements in all music, as a great contemporary composer has said, that we feel to be absolutely perfect, every note of it being incapable of change. The gist of the movement, and for that matter of the whole symphony, lies in the first theme, Fate knocking at the door, hammered out on the whole orchestra.

Worth noting and delighting in is the passage which immediately grows out of this opening summons, the bridge passage leading over from the first to the second theme. This was a master stroke in 1808; and no one has yet produced a finer growth from a tiny seed. During it all, the first theme is driven home to our minds, and its rhythm and mood pushed onward for some sixty measures. Just as we are ready for the second theme, we hear the first once more on the horns (59–62). And while the second theme is being given out by the strings and the wood winds, in a sudden change of key and mood, we hear the first softly reflected by the basses (63–76).

[1] The piano score of Beethoven's *Fifth Symphony* is available in the following editions: Universal (in a volume with the other symphonies) No. 525; Breitkopf No. 36665; Schirmer (edited by Daniel Gregory Mason); Ditson (edited by Percy Goetschius) No. 3. The orchestral score (miniature size) is available in Kalmus Edition No. 5.

There is a short third theme,

and then Beethoven rushes onward impetuously to finish the first section (the Statement, or Exposition) of 124 measures. In the old-fashioned, leisurely eighteenth-century manner, Beethoven there draws a double bar and marks these measures for repetition. The chief object of that procedure was to enable the hearer to get the themes well in mind. But in the hurrying tempo of modern life, this repetition is not often carried out.

The development, or "working-out," is short, only 123 measures to be exact. The perhaps overenthusiastic Berlioz suggested that in it Beethoven revealed all the secrets of his being, his private griefs, his lonely meditations, his bursts of enthusiasm, his anxious search for love. The gentle second theme has no place in this emotional display; practically all the material is drawn out of the first theme, even the dramatic series of alternating high and low chords between the strings and the wood winds. The development section ends with an insistent hammering out of the rhythm of the opening, leading directly into the Restatement, or Recapitulation, with a typically Beethovenish turn just after the first theme is heard again. At the moment we are all ready for the bridge passage that will lead us from the first to the second theme, a curious little oboe cadenza is interpolated (269), the sort of surprise that Beethoven so often uses to give added piquancy. It lasts for just a moment, and then we are off again. The Restatement is almost an exact replica of the Statement (there are 126 measures), but instead of ending it abruptly as he did the first time, Beethoven adds a long coda of 129 measures in order that he may pile up a bigger and more impressive climax. This is almost like another development; it seems here as if Beethoven felt that he had more material at hand than he could logically crowd into his development section; the motto theme is again the predominating feature, but there is also a new theme (424). The coda is as well built as the rest; indeed, we may well

ask whether there is a more keenly knit half-a-thousand bars in
all music. It moves as an organic whole, bound together by the
masterful motto theme, and drawn to its logical end with inexorable force.

THE SECOND MOVEMENT, A THEME WITH VARIATIONS

The second movement is necessarily a relief, and through
it runs a note of quiet resignation and strength. It follows the
general formal scheme that we know as the Theme and Variations, but Beethoven adds some passages that are developed out
of the main theme instead of being merely variants of it. This
freedom displayed in the treatment of accepted and traditional
formal schemes is another characteristic of Beethoven. The main
theme

of this movement is gracious, leisurely, kindly; it comprises three
divisions of unequal length: 1–10, 11–19, 29–31, and ends with
a little coda of its own, 40–48. Thus we have the main section
of forty-eight bars complete; this is followed immediately by a
variation of the material, the general scheme employed being the
use of an accompaniment with notes twice as quick as those in the
original statement. In the second variation (commencing at 98)
the motion is sustained in still shorter notes. After this second
variation come several interpolated ideas that Beethoven developed out of the main theme; particularly effective are twelve
humorous bars of duet by the wood winds (flute, oboe, and clarinets), interrupted by a loud insistence upon the third part of the
main theme by the whole orchestra (148). And this is again
interrupted by a passage where everything seems to stop, as if
the composer were hesitating to decide in which direction he
would go. Finally (at 185) we come to the last variation, to
which is again added a coda, giving a touch of beautiful pathos.
Beethoven ends the movement suddenly.

The Third Movement

It is important to note that Beethoven did not label the third movement a *scherzo:* he merely marked it *allegro*. For this is not a joking movement, nor a humorous interlude; we feel rather that Fate's grim pursuit has again begun. The first whisperings of the basses,

are sinister enough; the upper strings take up the same figure and pause. Then we are left in no doubt of the composer's intent; the main motto theme is again heard here as the second theme,

but now in a rhythmic pattern of threes — notice the difference in effect. These two themes are alternated and somewhat developed for the remainder of the first part of the movement. The second section (usually called the Trio) is, in contrast to the first, in major, and in it we feel that Beethoven has indulged in the kind of writing more in the usual mood of his third movements. The opening section, quick and staccato, is given to the double basses,

the instruments least fitted by nature to deal with this type of music, but they manage it, and then the violas, second violins, and finally the firsts have a try at the same theme, as if they would show how easy it really is. The whole section is repeated, and the second part of the Trio appears. It is introduced by several false starts on the part of the basses; they finally dash off, inviting the rest of the orchestra to join them. Instead of going back, as was customary, to the opening section of the Trio, Beethoven repeats the second part and then leads us directly back to the beginning mood of the movement — but this time with what a difference! Now it is more eerie than ever; the wood winds alternate with plucked strings and everything is rushed along, faster and faster. Suddenly there is an interruption — everything stops, the rhythm being continued only by a kettledrum beating against a strange low note held by the strings. Gradually this astonishing interlude gathers pace, increases in volume, and before we realize what is really happening, there come those three glorious crashes that usher in the greatest finale devised up to that time, one that has hardly been equaled since.

THE TRIUMPH OF THE LAST MOVEMENT

What strength and conviction and everlasting ardor breathe through this last movement! There is no doubt here of the composer's intent; this is triumph — " Oh, life is so beautiful, let me live, live! " If one has had many years' experience in listening, this music, if properly interpreted, never seems to lose the thrill which will lift one out of one's seat. Between the first and second themes,

(at measure 26) there is introduced a subsidiary theme,

which leads in turn to another secondary tune,

in triplets (45), before we are formally introduced to the second main theme. Both these secondary themes are used later in the development section. At measures 62–63 there is a change of key, after which the second theme is heard, and shortly after the exposition section comes to a close. Again, as in the first movement, this is marked for repetition, but is rarely so played. The development uses the subsidiary themes almost entirely, a fact which

again shows Beethoven's unconventional freedom of treatment
when he finds such will suit his purpose. In this last movement
the orchestra has had added to it a piccolo, three trombones, and
a double (bass) bassoon, and their additional weight shows. Just
at the climax of the development, there comes a dramatic pause,
a change of time from two's to three's, and an astonishing appearance of the ghost of the motto theme, as if the composer would
suggest that even in the midst of joyful triumph the specter
of man's inevitable fate lurks in the background. But this " flash-
back," played by strings and wood wind, is a most effective dramatic device for providing contrast before the return of the first
theme in the Restatement section. It quickly fades into the background, there is a short, sharp crescendo, and we are back again
at the opening theme of the movement, all the more brilliant now
for it comes like the sun bursting from behind a cloud. The
themes we have heard before are again presented, now in the
key unity of C major. When we are more than a hundred bars
from the end, the grand coda begins (318) with an exultant
little fanfare. More and more intense, faster and faster, higher
and higher grows the music; Beethoven working up the excitement until the final chord, which he hammers almost as if de-
mented. But the cool head is in command of the warm heart all
the way through, and this glorious rampage is carefully calculated and controlled down to the smallest detail. In the manner
of a great artist, every detail is closely watched and designed,
even when the music seems most free; and so the resultant effects
are sure, beyond peradventure. Here, as in almost everything he
did, Beethoven was absolutely individual, unlike anyone before
or since.

This symphony piles up, as all great works should. It begins with astonishing freedom of expression, achieved through
strictness of structural detail, goes on to Variations, again with
spacious freedom and emotion in them, something quite different
from the brief, rather stilted variations written by the older
composers. Then there is the third movement, with its touch of
the demonic, running without interruption into the magnificent
finale. Masterful construction, magnificent tunes which everyone
can remember, and the authentic thrill of music that cumulates
in power and repose — no wonder the *Fifth Symphony* stands,
a world's masterpiece for all time!

TOPICS FOR FURTHER DISCUSSION

What is your opinion of the remark, "Thus Fate knocks at the door," which Beethoven made in answer to an inquiry as to the meaning of the four-note motive which opens the *Fifth Symphony*? Did the composer necessarily mean that when he wrote he had Fate in mind?

Is there any reason, in general, why we should look for the "meaning" of symphonies? Discuss, in this connection, Sir John McEwen's saying: "While language seeks to express a meaning, *music is itself the meaning*."

SUGGESTIONS FOR READING

Beethoven, the Man Who Freed Music, Schauffler. (New York: Double-day, Doran)
> This is an interesting biography, unfortunately interspersed with too many references to and speculations on Beethoven's music, a fact which makes it hard reading for the amateur.

Beethoven: Impressions of Contemporaries. (New York: Schirmer)

Beethoven and His Forerunners, Mason. (New York: Macmillan; London: Gollancz)

Beethoven the Creator, Rolland. (New York: Harper)

Beethoven, His Spiritual Development, Sullivan. (New York: Knopf)
> The book contains an extended study of the composer's later works, particularly the last quartets.

Beethoven, Dickinson. (New York and London: Nelson)
> Here is a good, brief work.

CHAPTER XXX

Brahms's "First Symphony"

MAKING THE BEST OF BOTH WORLDS

JOHANNES BRAHMS (1833–1897) has of late years become popular because he made the best of both the " Classic " and the " Romantic " world. And so, when people want to go back to something satisfying, they find that Brahms enriches both the mental and the emotional life. In early days he foolishly signed a manifesto against the sort of " new music " that Wagner was supposed to have brought in. So he was thought of as a stern defender of the classics and was labeled for life. But he really was at heart a Romantic, and a pretty wild one, as his first *Piano Concerto* shows. He was a superb lyricist, as his songs prove; and he could build on the big forty-minute-symphony scale. Some think that he lacked " passion "; he had it, and sometimes it comes out, all the stronger and sweeter because it is not thrown about all over his music. There is no lack of deep feeling in Brahms's music, even if he keeps " passion " under most of the time; and music lovers cherish his pages as the purest quintessence of German Romanticism. The *First Symphony* [1] shall stand as our example of Brahms, for admiration and brief analysis. Although this was the first big work he wrote for orchestra alone, he was forty-three when it appeared, and thus finely mature.

FIRST MOVEMENT

A slow introduction sets the scene — for what? Everyone can make his own background, provided he remembers that the composer meant his work to be listened to in terms of the dra-

[1] The piano score of Brahms's *First Symphony* is available in the following editions: Universal No. 2105; Schirmer (edited by Daniel Gregory Mason); Ditson No. 20. The orchestral score (miniature size) is available in Kalmus No. 12.

matic life of music itself, not of the other arts. If we like to
think again of Life *vs.* Destiny, well and good, but it is music's
life, not just man's. The bass throbs; it binds the music — perhaps to earth. The first theme

of the main movement (42, hinted at in measure 21 of the Introduction) soars in arpeggio, as do so many of Brahms's tunes.
This and the second theme,

given to the oboe (121), a theme which is again evolved from
the introduction, form the chief material from which the movement grows. It never loses the cast of melancholy, or pathos;
indeed, that mood is never altogether absent, in some form or
other, from the next two movements also. Brahms has lovely
taste in allowing the varying shades of musical feeling to follow
each other with the maximum of emotional effect, and in the
meantime sustaining the flow of the music and its argument and
interest; so that one feels each mood transition to be at once refreshing, since it comes at just the right moment, and vital to
the continuity of the work — woven into its texture. Therein,
of course, lies one of the greatest qualities in any composer. In
this movement he may be said to attain even a tragic mood, but
restrained, reflective pathos (suggested by the descending chromatic harmony he so often uses) is perhaps the emotional keynote.

SECOND MOVEMENT

The second movement is a fine example of Brahms's power
of varying his emotional stresses, while maintaining something of
the same atmosphere as in the first movement. Yet here we have
lyrical expansion instead of the keen, close development of semi-
nal motives. There is something of Beethoven's breadth of spirit

BRAHMS IN HEAVEN

Silhouette by Otto Böhler

Haydn. Weber. Wagner. Bach. Beethoven. Mozart.
Gluck. Handel (?)
Brahms. Schumann. Bruckner. Mendelssohn. Schubert. Liszt. Bülow. Berlioz.

BRAHMS AS PIANIST
From a contemporary print.

here, as for example in measure 27, where one of the arpeggio themes

is begun by the violins. Before this, notice how the oboe (17), in replying to the strings' enunciation of the first idea in the movement,

is taken up by the strings before it has had the opportunity of finishing its theme (22), as if they were eager to add sweet strength to the tranquillity of the oboe theme. After a section in which the solo parts for both oboe and clarinet predominate — very typical of Brahms's manner of writing for the orchestra — comes the repetition, freshly scored, of the original theme, followed by a leisurely, gently pathetic coda, with a final cadence. This is reminiscent of the opening of the first movement and, with its flattened sixth of the scale, has become only too well known in vulgarized forms, at the tail end of cheap ballads, since the days of its fully expressive use by real composers.

THIRD MOVEMENT

Brahms's scherzos are much meatier and more solid in style and a bit slower in tempo than those of the other writers of symphonies. This one shows a feeling of German hominess most charmingly interpreted in terms of art music. The general structural scheme of the scherzo-trio-scherzo is carried out. There are three main themes in the scherzo section: the one on the clarinets at the very beginning,

the one heard on the combined wood winds which follows shortly after (11),

gracefully descending its melodic way; and the clarinet tune which comes shortly before the trio section is introduced (45):

Brahms loved the warm, rich quality of the clarinet and used it frequently in solo parts. The trio has a 6/8 swing, is a bit faster, and is almost entirely given over to discussions between the wood wind and the strings. When the first section returns, the themes have a little more elaborate accompaniment, some of them borrowed from the trio; Brahms never wastes material, but loves to tie his whole structure by interrelating themes in this fashion.

Fourth Movement

Brahms followed Beethoven's example (in his *Fifth Symphony*) in using the trombones in the last movement for the first time in this work. Again a slow introduction, deeply dramatic. The violins and the horn (1) hint at the great tune that is to follow; the chromatic element, so prominent in the first movement, is again noticed. The exciting plucked-string working up that begins at measure 5 is extremely brief; it leads to higher agitation, finally leading (29) into a magnificent horn theme,

one which Brahms tells us he heard first from the Alpine-horn players in Switzerland. In this introduction, we might figure a giant's heavy sigh as he strives to throw off a mood of depression.

Then comes the horn's peaceful entry. One could not wish a more beautiful example of this composer's evoking with serene surety a new mood at a vital moment; this is a true stroke of fine art, in its swaying of the balance of emotion. We realize again, as David Stanley Smith succinctly puts it, that " technical subtlety is the prime quality of great music "; and we understand more deeply how worth while is the closest study we can make of the thousand subtleties of a great composer's technic. After the horn theme, a short hymnlike section on the brass,

one of the finest bits of the whole work (46), leads to the entrance of the *Allegro* (60), with one of the world's great tunes,

bracing the nerve and warming the heart. This, with succeeding passages that keep up the feeling of exhilaration, forms a splendid foundation for the movement, which, although fairly complex, carries us along in a tide of powerful rhythms and glorious harmony. The second subject (117)

and another theme later on (147),

build up the movement's life. Near the end, in a Beethovenish coda, the solemn brass tune of the introduction arises in the full glory of its strength (406); and so the magnificent work takes its leave.

The man who is fit for big music does not come out from hearing the best of Brahms at the same door of the spirit in which he went. Few of us win at once to the heart of this composer; we have to grow up to him, and that means work and time; but how often will equal labor give greater joy, and expense of time so great a satisfaction? The biggest, broadest art seeks for its service devotion and the refreshment of one's faculties. The man who makes music such as this symphony one of the broad bases of his experience and one of the touchstones of his taste wins something that he will never willingly let go, something that in the truest and deepest sense will gladden and enrich the rest of his life.

TOPICS FOR FURTHER DISCUSSION

What distinctions of style come to mind between Beethoven's *Fifth Symphony* and Brahms's *First?* Which makes the more immediate appeal to you, and why?

The *First Symphony* of Brahms has been referred to as the *tenth*, meaning that it is a logical successor to Beethoven's nine symphonies. Do you think this a wise statement?

SUGGESTIONS FOR READING

The Unknown Brahms, Schauffler. (New York: Dodd, Mead)
   This work is not only a thoroughly reliable biography but it makes exciting reading for the lovers of Brahms's music. It is to be highly recommended.
Johannes Brahms, Specht. (New York: Dutton; London: Dent)
   (Translated by Blom)
Brahms, Niemann. (New York: Knopf; London: Allen & Unwin)
   (Translated by Catherine Phillips)

CHAPTER XXXI

Three Later Symphonies

AFTER two of the great masterworks of symphonic literature have been studied, it is important to see what later composers did with the form, and to realize that, although they may have followed in general the formal schemes of Beethoven and Brahms, these men made contributions that mark their works as distinctly individual and characteristic of the periods in which they lived. We have seen that Beethoven used the fundamental structural ideas of his predecessors in such a way as to make them his own; and that Brahms's intense preoccupation with the problems of symphonic form was due to a realization of his debt, as he expressed it, to the " giant whose steps he always heard behind himself " — Beethoven. So, too, the works of the best symphonists of the latter part of the nineteenth and the early years of the twentieth century owe much to the towering structures which preceded them; yet even a brief study of such representative works as Tchaikovsky's *Fifth Symphony*, Sibelius's *Second*, and Shostakovich's *Fifth* [1] will show that their composers were men of genius, with ideas of their own and an ability to express them clearly and idiomatically.

TCHAIKOVSKY'S " FIFTH SYMPHONY IN E MINOR "

In this symphony, written twelve years after Brahms's *First Symphony*, we find the Russian composer achieving a unique uniformity of mood and structure through the employment of a theme common to all four movements, what he called a " motto theme." It is almost as though Tchaikovsky had said to himself: " In this symphony at least I will rid myself of my tendency to

[1] The miniature scores of these works are available in the following editions: Tchaikovsky's *Fifth Symphony*, Kalmus Edition; Sibelius's *Second Symphony*, British Edition; Shostakovich's *Fifth Symphony*, Musicus Edition.

rhapsodize [this composer was a severe self-critic] and will choose one theme around which my whole work can revolve. This symphony must and shall be homogenous." This is the theme he used:

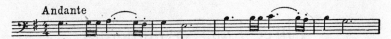

In carrying out his plans, Tchaikovsky employs the usual four movements, through all of which this theme runs like a dark thread through a gorgeous tapestry.

In the first movement there are two main subjects, the first (42–48), obviously influenced by the character of the motto theme, sad and reflective:

The second, in contrast, is full of brightness and vitality (116–120):

Two subsidiary themes are immediately introduced, the first (154–157):

the second (170–174):

The composer, in his development section, considers these equally as important as his main subjects; in fact, the introduction of so much thematic material robs the development of the particular importance it possesses in the Beethoven and Brahms works. But there is much brilliance and animation, with plenty of repetition of themes and those peculiar rushing passages so characteristic of this composer. Then the main and subsidiary themes are restated, the first in rather shortened form; suddenly, in the midst of the brilliant coda (which begins at 471), the first theme appears, the mood of the music grows somber and dies away in Tchaikovsky's mournful manner, down and down to lower strings and bassoon, on this melody.

The second movement — *Andante cantabile, con alcuna licenza* [2] — takes the form of a songlike romanza, the first section of which (1–65) is based on a lovely horn theme with string accompaniment (8–12):

The middle section is of a quicker character (66–107) with this theme, first given to the clarinet and then answered by the bassoon:

In the third section (108–157) of this song form, the first theme is assigned to the strings, with a charming wood-wind embroidery. Everything quickens and strengthens until the coda, when suddenly the motto theme is heard again, *fff* (159), breaking in upon the prevailing happy mood of the movement. From this point there is a decrescendo until the end, marked *pppp*.

The third movement is a graceful one in 3/4, to which the composer has given the name *valse*, based on this theme:

[2] Slowly, in a singing manner, with some license.

A sprightly, trio-like middle portion (73–144) stands out in fine contrast. After a restatement of almost exactly the same length as the first section, there follows a short coda of 52 measures, at the end of which occurs a weak citation of the motto theme in 3/4 time, its only appearance in the whole symphony which does not seem spontaneous.

In the finale the motto theme comes into its own; the impressive introduction to this last movement (1–57) is entirely based on it, in major, and we feel that this must have been the form of the origin of the theme. The movement grows clearer as it proceeds, as though " the heart had cast off a load of suffering and God's world shone out bright once more." The exposition is based on the following themes:

(58–62)

Allegro vivace

(128–136)

Espr.

There is a development of some 120 measures and a restatement that is of approximately the same length as the exposition. The coda (426–565), the most important factor in the whole movement, heralds the final entry of the motto theme against a whirling wood-wind background; the clouds lift, the skies clear in this grandiose setting. Here is a fine example of this composer's Byronic power of becoming momentous and eloquent on slight provocation. Like the popular romantic poet, Tchaikovsky assumes on slight occasion a more tragic mien than the average Englishman does (to use Bernard Shaw's words) when he is going to be executed. Here the composer whips himself into a frenzy and proclaims this last utterance of his generative theme with tremendous power and impressiveness. Yet all the frenetic energy does not impress or move us as do the finales of the Beethoven and Brahms symphonies; in comparison, Tchaikovsky's seems too obvious and unmotivated.

Yet one need not pretend that this work is Jovian in order to enjoy it. It has its own color, due to consummate orchestral draftsmanship; it alternates romance and revelry; it delights in melancholy, yet in the end hope triumphs over despair. Tchaikovsky does not need to indulge in bizarre effects or violate accepted canons of form to make his work distinctive; yet he did not hesitate to use whatever means his muse seemed to require in order to secure the effect desired, regardless of custom or convention. A stirring work, and one that is bound to occupy an important place among late romantic compositions.

SIBELIUS'S " SECOND SYMPHONY IN D MAJOR "

It is natural that a composer who wrote almost a century later than Beethoven would display a tendency to rebel against many of the conventionalities and clichés that had become an essential part of romantic expression. In many ways the seven symphonies of Sibelius are the record of such a revolt. In them Sibelius, a composer who kept himself isolated from the many fads and poses of his time, a man of incorrigible sincerity and real genius, gradually freed himself from what he felt to be the spirit of German dominance in music. The later symphonies, particularly the Fourth, Sixth, and Seventh, reveal this composer at the height of his individualistic expressive powers; the Second, written during his exuberant thirties, is a full, rounded expression of his virile talent, even though it contains obvious connections with the past. In it, as one of his ardent admirers says, Sibelius already shows himself a giant among men, composing with a seven-league stride that his fellows never knew or conceived, gifted with a fresh northern sense of beauty as well as a power of form denied " punier though wishful colleagues " (Olin Downes).

The name of this composer has become inseparably connected with Finnish nationalism. And quite rightly so, for his music is full of the spirit of the north, colored with an austere, often ascetic, hue, shot through with faërie fantasy, born of the same blood as the stirring northern sagas. There is a dark and somber character to much of the music Sibelius has written, a certain powerful, granite strength and uncompromising austerity; with it all, however, is a sincerity and spontaneity not excelled by any of his contemporaries, a warmth of emotion all the more moving in that it is so well controlled.

This *Second Symphony* corresponds in its composer's career to the *Eroica* in Beethoven's or the Fourth in Tchaikovsky's; all three works represent their creators as young men girding their loins for the race ahead of them, fully conscious of their irrepressible genius and teeming with ideas. It shows many of the most characteristic traits of Sibelius's symphonic style: his choice of short fertile melodic fragments as thematic materials; his method of working these fragments into a full-sized theme that finally arrives as a supreme climax, rather than working them out on principles of exposition, development, and recapitulation; the use of peculiarly built whirring accompanimental passages, out of which coherent ideas suddenly crystallize; and the repetition of melodic ideas and rhythmic patterns, sometimes almost to the point of satiety.

Even in such an early work as this *Second Symphony,* we should not try to look for the ordinary structural patterns in Sibelius's writing. Although he follows the general ideals of symphonic form, the first movement is based upon the following generative fragments, without any hint of a first and second theme in the accepted manner:

1. A series of detached chords for the strings

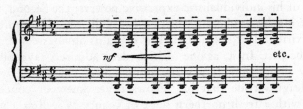

2. A six-measure melody for the wood winds over a detached string accompaniment

JEAN SIBELIUS

DMITRI SHOSTAKOVICH
In the uniform of a fire warden, 1941.

3. A theme given out by the bassoons

4. An epic-like proclamation by the violins alone, as virile as one of the heroes in the *Kalevala*, Finland's great national poem

5. The most potent phrase of all, consisting largely of one high, long-held note for the wood winds, followed by a sort of shake, and a sudden drop of a fifth, thus:

These fragments succeed each other simply, with no transitions or connecting materials; they are gradually combined and gather meaning, the whole musical fabric unfolding without break and mounting toward inevitable climax. Sibelius's constructive process here is one of gradual fusion of material, rather than the usual dissection and reassembling of themes; it can be felt more easily than analyzed and " bespeaks a full heart, magnificent fertility, an absorption which pervades all things and directs them to a single end."

Again in the second movement thematic snatches follow one another with poignant effect; they are dramatically contrasted and presented with a skill which never deviates from a single purpose, that of arousing expectation and of slow shaping toward a climax. Here are the materials out of which the movement is made:

1. A sad tune for the bassoons

2. An intense dramatic bit in accelerated pace

3. A lovely lyric string theme

4. Another lyric bit, this time played by oboes and clarinets

The two large contrasting sections that go to make up the third movement can be considered in the light of a scherzo and trio movement. The pace of the scherzo is swift — *vivacissimo* — the time, 6/8. A soft series of drum taps introduces the lovely trio, built on this simple oboe melody:

Both sections are repeated with a change of orchestration, and then a dramatic transition leads into the *Finale*, in which Sibelius yields to orthodoxy, for there are two principal theme groups:

1.

2.

Development, with plenty of spinning, whirring accompanimental figures, follows; heading back to the restatement is a long-breathed, wonderfully sustained crescendo of 91 measures, after which the themes are dramatically reheard with magnificent accretion of instrumental power and color. A triumphant coda over a throbbing kettledrum bass brings the work to a clarion conclusion.

Coming from the composer's early period, this symphony is surprisingly effective and moving today, some forty years after it was written, in spite of certain conventional idioms and derivations and a few close approaches to banality. For it speaks of things that eternally matter, with a greatness of manner and a sincerity of utterance that raise it high above so much of the music that has been written since. Its composer has shown himself to be completely independent of the cliques and schools that grew up all about him in the early decades of the twentieth century, cliques and schools that have sunk deeper and deeper into a morass of " chauvinism, self-deception, and evasion of emotional reality." Built firmly upon the past, with no aim of overthrowing the great traditions of art, this music nevertheless points steadfastly towards the future; its composer, like Dante, is a revolutionary by temperament but a conservative by opinion. Above all else, he is a man, at least in this work, who thinks clearly and feels deeply, who does not hesitate to say simple and sometimes obvious things in a simple and direct way. We may well leave judgment as to the result in the lap of the future.

SHOSTAKOVICH'S "FIFTH SYMPHONY," OP. 47

Written for performance in celebration of the twentieth anniversary of the Republic of Soviet Russia, this important work was first heard in Leningrad on November 21, 1937. At that time its composer was 31 years old, and had a formidable number of compositions to his credit; he had come to the conclusion, " not acquired without travail, that music is not merely a combination of sounds arranged in a certain order, but an art capable of expressing by its own means the most diverse ideas or sentiments," as he himself put it [3] in an article written just before the performance of this symphony. " Working ceaselessly to master my art," he goes on to say, " I am endeavoring to create my own musical style, which I am seeking to make simple and expressive. I cannot think of my further progress apart from our socialist structure, and the end which I set to my work is to contribute at every point toward the growth of our remarkable country. There can be no greater joy for a composer than the inner assurance of having assisted by his works in the elevation of Soviet musical culture, of having been called upon to play a leading role in the recasting of human perception."

All of which accounts for the directness and simplicity of this symphony; Shostakovich does not hesitate to use, in the broadest of ways, the abstract historical forms hallowed by the past; neither does he hesitate to use, and very effectively, some of the newer devices of " modernism." The point is that, however he writes, he says something — he is a man with life and imagination and real musical consciousness, not a mere conjurer of notes or designer of tonal patterns. The design of this symphony is strikingly simple and unaffected; there is nothing here that need bother anyone who is willing to concede the prolonged use of dissonance as an effective means of musical communica-

[3] *La Revue Musicale*, December, 1936.

tion. In contradistinction to so many of his contemporaries, Shostakovich has been wise enough to simplify and clarify his style so as to meet the needs of the large mass public for which he writes. The result is striking and impressive, if the hearer is not too far removed from life to appreciate the earthy, bourgeois tang of this music.

The first movement opens with a wide-jumping theme stated antiphonally between the high and low strings:

The second theme is lyric and expressive; it is a fine example of this composer's ability to write a tune of sustained melodic power:

There follows an extended development in which the tempo is quickened, the rhythms tightened, and the melodies made even more eloquent. With the restatement, the *largamente* mood of the opening theme is restored; the second theme is beautifully exploited by the wood winds over a throbbing string accompaniment. The end comes peacefully. The whole movement is taut and clear — there are only 305 measures in it — with little waste in thematic material or instrumental sonorities.

There is an ironic, gamin-like spirit to the second movement which has made it seem cheap to some ears. It is in the traditional scherzo form, all the elements of which are clearly discernible: after the opening allegretto section based on two themes, there comes a contrasting trio, and then the first part is repeated *da capo*. This vivacious dance movement serves as a perfect link between, and a necessary contrast to, the sustained mood of the first and third movements.

The third movement, marked *largo*, is one of slow melodic growth from simple beginnings that are again announced by the strings:

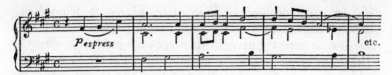

The mood of the whole is dark and brooding, as if the composer would reveal the melancholy searchings of his Russian soul; gradually more and more voices enter; the tension increases and then subsides as the ecstatic melodies are sung once more muted and in high register. A stab of harp and celesta color brings the movement to a close.

The theme of the last movement *rondo* is strongly Russian in flavor, an uncouth but buoyant march rhythm:

There is a slower section during which the lyric qualities of the earlier movements are recalled, and the whole winds up with an impressive and broadened reappearance of the rondo theme.

According to the modern Soviet conception, the "*avant garde* can express progressive ideas only when it talks to the people in a new, powerful, and intelligible language. The demands of the wide masses of the people, their artistic tastes, grow from day to day. The 'advanced' composer is therefore one who plunges into the social currents around him, and, with his creative work, serves the progress of mankind." [4] This being the case, it is no wonder that the performance of this *Fifth Symphony* of Shostakovich met with such acclaim in Russia. For if ever music speaks with a " new, powerful, and intelligible " language, it does so here. The playing of this music was hailed everywhere as an occasion of utmost importance. " Tickets for the concerts at which it was played were sold out in the course of three hours, long before the official announcement, and Symphony Hall of the Moscow Conservatory was filled to overflowing. The composer submitted his creative report, as it were, to a very exacting judge; and from the ovation he received his triumph was obvious." [4]

    [4] Grigori Schneerson; reprinted by permission of the quarterly review *Modern Music*, March–April, 1938.

LIST OF SUGGESTED MUSIC

Symphony Number Five in E Minor, Op. 64   Tchaikovsky

There are a number of recordings of this, one of the most popular of Tchaikovsky's symphonies; so far, there exists no " ideal version." Mengelberg and the Amsterdam Concertgebouw Orchestra give a good account of the music, but the recording is old; Stokowski's version with the Philadelphia Orchestra is apt to be oversentimental in many spots; Rodzinski and the Cleveland Orchestra, on the other hand, lean to overexcitement. A good compromise is Beecham's interpretation with the London Philharmonic Orchestra, a rendering that is balanced and wears well in repeated hearings. A rendition by Ormandy and the Philadelphia Orchestra contains many of the defects of the Stokowski version, but is, of course, better recorded.

Symphony Number Two in D Major, Op. 43   Sibelius

Years ago an excellent recording of this work was made by the composer's friend, Robert Kajanus; in many respects, in spite of the old recording, this is still very satisfactory. Koussevitzky and the Boston Symphony Orchestra have made an opulent and thrilling version of this popular symphony; and recently Barbirolli and the New York Philharmonic Orchestra have added theirs. This latter is not to be recommended if one would obtain a real idea of the quality of the music.

Symphony Number Five, Op. 47   Shostakovich

The recorded version of this symphony by Stokowski and the Philadelphia Orchestra is highly satisfactory, for it is evident that the young Russian is a man after Stokowski's own heart — " a master, ever growing, ever expanding," to use the conductor's own words.

TOPICS FOR FURTHER DISCUSSION

Which of these three works makes the deepest impression on you? Why?

Can you trace any derivations in the works of the two later composers from the style of Tchaikovsky? If so, where?

One enthusiast regarding Sibelius calls him the " greatest symphonist since Beethoven "; another critic says that his music is " excellently put together by a man with nothing profound to say "; still a third maintains that his music does not come to grips with the problems of our own world, and so the attempt to set this composer up as the " great modern composer of our day " is certain to fail. How much truth do you think there is in these statements?

Speaking of the Shostakovich symphony, a recent critic has asked, " Who else among the contemporaries has composed a work lasting fifty minutes that is so consistently interesting and stimulating? " Can you answer?

SUGGESTIONS FOR READING

Tchaikovsky, Newmarch. (New York: Scribner)
Tchaikovsky, Evans. (New York: Dutton)
Beloved Friend; the Story of Tchaikovsky and Nadejda von Meck,
        Bowen and Meck. (New York: Random; London: Hutchinson)
Jean Sibelius, His Life and Personality, Ekman. (New York: Knopf)
Sibelius, Gray. (New York: Oxford)
Music of Our Day, Saminsky. (New York: Crowell)
Our New Music, Copland. (New York: McGraw-Hill)

CHAPTER XXXII

The Rococo Age

CLASSIC AND ROMANTIC

THE two eighteenth-century predecessors of Beethoven,
Mozart and Haydn, are best understood if their music is
heard in direct contrast with the later Romanticism.
These three composers may be said to have been the first to show
us the full glories of the modern art of music. Their compositions breathe much the same spirit — that of a deep understanding of the essential property of art — but there is a wide difference in the character of their work. Compare the *Fifth
Symphony*, for instance, with the *C Major Symphony* of Mozart
(No. 34) or the *Oxford Symphony* of Haydn. In place of the
striving, the striking individualism, the intense feeling, the vivid
and abrupt changes of mood that we find so constantly present in
the Beethoven music, there is a certain serenity in Haydn and
Mozart, a serenity of detachment from the realities of life, something that lies beyond its transient joys and sorrows. These eighteenth-century men seem largely concerned with the molding of
their materials in the most artistic and well-balanced manner
possible. The music of Beethoven delights because of its communication of ideas and emotions, to which we so readily and fully respond. There is in addition, of course, a sturdy and suitable structure which grows out of the emotional need of the composer's
expression. With Haydn and Mozart, we cannot but feel that
the position is reversed; our pleasure is first of all an aesthetic one,
less connected with the outside world and more concerned with
the adjustment of abstract ideas of proportion. The one style we
call Romantic — the composer expressing his individual experiences, sometimes out of the white heat of his own crises, sometimes shaped by calmer reflection and intellectual manipulation;
but, in any case, the music is always personal and impassioned.
The other style we call Classic: here the composer's emotion seems

303

cleared of circumstances, cleansed of personalities, assimilated and purified, an "emotion not only recollected in tranquillity, but also generalized from humanity." Dr. Nicholas Murray Butler's definition of the classic spirit is an excellent one: " It is the search for perfection, the law of clearness and reasonableness and self-control. It is also the love of permanence and of continuity. It seeks not merely to express individuality and emotion, but to express disciplined emotion and individuality restrained by law."

THE EIGHTEENTH-CENTURY SPIRIT

A consideration of the difference in the periods in which these composers lived and worked will give an excellent idea of the reasons for these differences in their music. All three men were typical of their time: Beethoven a man of the nineteenth century; Haydn (1732–1809) and Mozart (1756–1791) of the eighteenth. Today, as we look back from the vantage point of the present, we can see these centuries in just perspective. The seventeenth century had been a period of brilliant activity, of intellectual, artistic, and material achievement; Europe was beginning to experience the full power of the tremendous forces which had been set in motion by the Renaissance. This century was a time of fierce and joyous pride in national life. Under Elizabeth, James I, Charles I, and Cromwell, and under Richelieu and Louis XIV, England and France became conscious of new powers and struggled towards new destinies. There were great discoveries in physical science: this was the time of Francis Bacon and his turning of the current of man's thought towards material things, of Galileo and his telescope, of Isaac Newton and his law of universal gravitation. New lands had been discovered and opened up, England reaching out towards India on the one hand and the New World on the other. There had come a complete revaluation of literature and art: it was the time of Shakespeare and Bacon, of Corneille and Molière, of Rubens, Rembrandt, Velásquez, and Van Dyck — these latter carrying on the traditions instituted by the sixteenth-century Renaissance painters. And last, but by no means least, there had developed new and rather unaccustomed ideas of religious tolerance and freedom. Music, during this time, had come out from under the protection of the Church and had developed an entirely new method of expression — that of the more personal instrumental style. " At the end of the sixteenth century, a composer was a man who wrote church music in the accepted tradition . . . but before the seventeenth century was very old, a composer had almost as many fields in which to work as would be open to him at the present time " (Buck).

ROCOCO ART

But there came an end to this glorious period. After all this enthusiasm, these strong opinions, these great discoveries, this tremendous activity in the arts, and these many wars, there came complete exhaustion. The next century was a period of natural and inevitable reaction. After an epoch of great creative forces, it seems necessary for nature and man to recoup their strength and regain their balance. And so in this new century, the people, weary and disillusioned, no longer pursued their ideals of religious, political, and intellectual life. " There could be no wars of religion now, for men had not much faith in anything. The intellectual outlook was frank and tolerant, but not serious. Life was an art, to be pursued gracefully by all who had the means to live like educated people " (Mowat). The strong feelings of nationalism had degenerated into political bickerings, the earlier enthusiasms for scientific discovery into a period of research. Instead of the universal curiosity and burning enthusiasms of the earlier time, artists of the eighteenth century reflect the grace and intelligence of their period. It was, of course, the era of the great French domination, and Louis XIV, the Sun King (who lived well into this century of which we speak), and his successor Louis XV, became models for all Europe; their luxurious court at Versailles was the envy and pattern of every king, prince, and courtier. The society of this century was, as Strachey observes, the most civilized that history has ever known. Art, religion, intellectual activities, economic conditions — everything was organized and disciplined for the advantage of the absolute monarchs who ruled in the different European countries.

All the arts catered to the manifest desire of the times for the enjoyment of life in the most aristocratic manner possible; the century has come to be known as the Rococo period. In real-

ity the art of the Rococo period derived from that of the earlier
Baroque (discussed in a later chapter), being a graceful refinement and an aristocratic adaptation of its rich strength and buoyant vitality. Rococo architecture was of harmonious, gracefully
flowing lines; the interior decorations, dainty in style, made use
of gay draperies and formal furniture. These provided an ideal
setting for the gorgeous dresses, formal wigs, and laced jabots affected by the *haute monde*. Against this gleaming background
the polished and stilted manners of the period, the carefully stylized diversions and the witty, malicious conversations are easily
understandable. Writers and composers paid less attention to
spontaneous and inspired creation, and more to the development
of craftsmanship and skill for the delectation of their princely
patrons. Painters filled their pictures with distinguished figures in
ravishing colors, ladies and gentlemen in glistening silks, or lovers
ensconced in Fairy Islands of the Blest — dainty fantasies of
luxurious idleness as well as of tender love. Sculptors, jewelers,
wood carvers, iron workers, even chinaware makers catered to
this passion for decorative grace. Everything and everybody, in
so far as the creative world was concerned, combined to form a
fitting setting for the existence of superlative luxury. In this
ostentatious setting there was little tolerance for the bold expression of emotion in art.

But because this Rococo art of the eighteenth century was
created to frame the social graces of the period, and so possesses a
stylized, formal aspect, it should not be thought of as being only
artificially conventional and pleasingly correct. The artists of the
time used mediums of expression that were natural and logical
for their purpose, and used these mediums with an almost unbelievable ease and fluency. But underneath all this seeming ease
and natural complexity there exists a profound art; the effects
that were attained were the results of the most skillful manipulation of materials. Accent and quantity and proper stressing of
syllables; ornaments and scrolls and harmoniously curving lines;
gilded scale passages, lovely in their thin airiness, lightly curving
melodies, and exquisite harmonies — all were molded by the artists
of the century into an art of real significance. And if we learn
to know the achievements of one type of artist in this luxurious
period, we can better understand the others. The writings of
Pope and Collins will help us to appreciate the paintings of Wat-

MOZART'S MUSIC IN ARCHITECTURE

Probably the finest example of Rococo in Europe — the Amalienburg
in Munich, built 1734–1739 after plans by Cuvillies. Here are the molded
curves and the facile ornaments of the eighteenth century at their best.

THE GRAND STAIRWAY IN THE CASTLE AT WÜRZBURG
One of the finest examples of Baroque art in Germany.

teau, Boucher, and Chardin. The creations of Cuvillies, Neumann, and the Brothers Asam are the architectural counterparts of the music of the younger Scarlatti and the youthful Mozart.

THE VIEWPOINTS OF TWO POETS

If we examine the treatments given similar themes by poets of this period and of the Romantic epoch, we can see these eighteenth-century characteristics very clearly. In his " Ode to Evening," William Collins (1721–1759) uses this manner of treatment, a manner that is most characteristic of the whole century under discussion:

> If aught of oaten stop, or pastoral song,
> May hope, chaste Eve, to soothe thy modest ear,
> Like thy own solemn springs,
> Thy springs and dying gales;
>
> O Nymph reserved, while now the bright-haired sun
> Sits in yon western tent, whose cloudy skirts,
> With brede ethereal wove,
> O'erhang his wavy bed:
>
> Now air is hushed, save where the weak-eyed bat
> With short shrill shriek flits by on leathern wing,
> Or where the beetle winds
> His small but sullen horn,
>
> As oft he rises, 'midst the twilight path
> Against the pilgrim borne in heedless hum:
> Now teach me, maid composed,
> To breathe some softened strain,
>
> Whose numbers, stealing through thy darkening vale,
> May not unseemly with its stillness suit,
> As, musing slow, I hail
> Thy genial loved return!

Shelley — an ardent Romanticist if there ever was one — thus expresses himself on the same theme:

> I arise from dreams of thee
> In the first sweet sleep of night,

When the winds are breathing low,
And the stars are shining bright.
I arise from dreams of thee,
And a spirit in my feet
Hath led me — who knows how?
To thy chamber window, Sweet!

The wandering airs they faint
On the dark, the silent stream —
And the Champak odors fail
Like sweet thoughts in a dream;
The nightingale's complaint,
It dies upon her heart
As I must on thine,
O! belovèd as thou art!

Oh lift me from the grass!
I die! I faint! I fail!
Let thy love in kisses rain
On my lips and eyelids pale.
My cheek is cold and white, alas!
My heart beats loud and fast;
Oh! press it to thine own again,
Where it will break at last.

It is easy to realize the comparative restraint, the insistence upon balance and clarity of structure, the deft manipulation of expressive means for their own sake found in the first poem, especially when placed in immediate juxtaposition with the second. But we can hardly say that the Collins ode lacks feeling because it is so restrained in expression and so balanced and clear in its structure, or because often the words are used just for the sound they convey. There is emotion in the first poem, certainly; but it is the emotion that has little to do with the immediate individuality of the writer, emotion that is cleared of the violent personality of the second writer. In the words already quoted, Collins's emotion is " recollected in tranquillity and generalized from humanity." In reading the first poem we are not so much impressed with the fact that we ourselves have felt exactly the emotion contained therein, as we are with " clearness, reasonableness, and self-control " so evidently present. When Romantic poetry or music is concerned with its intensity of personalized emotion, we are often tempted to say: " Why, that is exactly how I have often felt!'" With the composers and artists of the Classic period, on the other hand, we have a sort of subconscious feeling that what they have expressed for us is the very essence of what humanity in general has experienced throughout its development.

LIST OF SUGGESTED MUSIC

Romantic Music

Fifth Symphony in C Minor	Beethoven
Third Symphony in E Flat Major	Beethoven
Symphony in C Major	Schubert

Classic Music

Symphony in C Major (Jupiter)	Mozart
Quintet in G Minor	Mozart
Symphony in G Major, No. 92 (Oxford)	Haydn
Quartet in D Major, Op. 64, No. 5 (Lark)	Haydn

TOPICS FOR FURTHER DISCUSSION

It is sometimes charged that a great deal of the music of the eighteenth century — even Mozart's — is too much according to formula: that one familiar with it often can predict what is coming, since the same turns of phrase constantly recur. Discuss the weight of formalism in this period and its influence, as far as you have noted it in the above sense.

Jan Gordon, art critic of the London *Observer*, has said: "The product of love and leisure is almost always embellishment." Discuss this in connection with Rococo art.

The distinction customarily made between Classic and Romantic art is this: by *Classic* and *Romantic* we mean art in which emphasis is largely on design and emotion respectively. Is this true? If so, where would we place Bach?

Discuss the statement that every "Classicist" was a "Romanticist" when alive.

Discuss Lowell's definition of a classic — that which "maintains itself by that happy coalescence of matter and style, that innate and requisite sympathy between the thought that gives life and the form that consents to every mood of grace and dignity, and which is something neither ancient nor modern, always new and incapable of growing old."

SUGGESTIONS FOR READING

The Romantic Composers, Mason. (New York: Macmillan)
    Introductory Chapter
Art through the Ages, Gardner. (New York: Harcourt, Brace)
Music: an Art and a Language, Spalding. (Boston: Schmidt)
    Chapter XII
"Romantic *vs.* Classic," Grew, *The British Musician*, Feb., 1934
A History of Modern Culture, Smith. (New York: Holt)
    Vol. II, 1687–1776

CHAPTER XXXIII

Mozart and Haydn

A Mirror of the Eighteenth Century

IT is in the works of Haydn and Mozart, especially the latter, that we find the musical incarnation of the eighteenth-century spirit. Both these composers were affected by the intellectual and spiritual characteristics of the period in which they lived, and there is much in their music that suggests the airs and graces, the molded curves and facile ornaments of the eighteenth century. Yet we are coming to realize that there is much more than this mere suggestiveness of the elegancy of a minor age in their works, or they would have passed into oblivion long ago. Haydn is not merely an individual who wrote jolly, conventional, light-hearted, but rather meaningless music; and Mozart's hold on posterity is the result of far more than the limpid clarity and perfection of his style. Both these men were composers who were able to feel deeply as well as to write clearly: they were not merely periwigged " Classicists," buried under the patronage of dukes and bishops; they were living, sensitive individuals. Haydn, for all his rugged simplicity and straightforward spontaneity, has a depth of feeling in some of his slow movements that anticipated Beethoven. Underneath much of the intuitive grace, the melodic charm, and the refined perfection of Mozart's music we can surely feel a peculiar sadness which suggests that he, like Beethoven and Brahms who were to follow him, realized the tragic futility of all human activity — that he could feel the taste of death on his tongue, as he himself phrased it.

The Classical Composer at Work

Mozart's compositions group themselves naturally into two great divisions: first the " gallant " works, strongly eighteenth-century in spirit; and second, the greater compositions which

311

transcend time, place, and circumstance. Much of his chamber music, his sonatas and concertos, his church music (strangely enough), his serenades, and some of his earlier operas belong to the first group. His great symphonies, notably those in G minor, E flat major, and C major, the six quartets that he dedicated to Haydn, his *G Minor Quintet,* the operas *The Marriage of Figaro* and *Don Giovanni,* can be classed together in the second group.

No better introduction to the beauties of the works of the first type can possibly be found than the charming serenade *Eine kleine Nachtmusik,* written for performance at some courtly, out-of-door occasion. Holmes, one of the early Mozart biographers, has this to say of the Mozart serenades:

> Sunday garden fetes in the spring and early summer are peculiarly characteristic of life in Vienna, where the pleasure of the promenade and the enjoyment of the air and sunshine regularly succeed the observances of religion. In such a scene, where all the beauty, rank, and talent of the capital are assembled, the spirit of the season is irresistible. And there is the music. An orchestra is erected in some green walk among the trees; and the first sound is the signal to suspend conversation, to sit quietly, or to cluster round the musicians. . . . A style of instrumental music at once light and ariose — somewhat between the symphony and the dance, but calculated to give elegance and tenderness of sentiment to the promenaders — was at any time attractive to Mozart and among his easiest work. His serenades were not such as the starved lover sings, but imbued with all the genius of the South; in fact, when we consider the emotions aroused by his instrumental music, and by the *adagios* of his symphonies in particular, the imagination of the author may be compared to a Mohammedan paradise; for in no other element can such refined voluptuousness and elegance be conceived to originate.

The four short movements of this work well illustrate Holmes's description: this miniature symphony is frankly meant to delight the senses, and we should listen to it with this in mind.

The *Symphony in D Major* is another fine example of the gallant Mozart style. This astonishing work, sometimes called the *Haffner Symphony,* was written in the almost incredible time of two weeks, at a time in Mozart's life when his attention was largely occupied with other matters. He did it at the request of his father for the Haffner family in Salzburg, the town of his birth, during the summer of his twenty-sixth year. Six months afterwards, when Wolfgang was arranging for its rehearsal and first performance, he had so completely forgotten the contents of the score as to write to his father, " the new Haffner symphony has quite astonished me, for I do not remember a note of it. It must be very effective."

And very effective it certainly is, especially if we can listen to it interpreted for us by some Mozart specialist, Beecham or Bruno Walter, for instance. The slow movement again suggests the serenade style of " refined voluptuousness and elegant repose." The last movement, in rondo form, is full of high spirits and keen wit; but there is none of the vigorous boisterousness that we so often find in the last movements of the Haydn symphonies.

MOZART'S " G MINOR SYMPHONY "

To turn to Mozart's *G Minor Symphony* from some of his earlier works is to realize the depth and range of his mind, whose ultimate richness was so far above the somewhat superficial Rococo graces of his time, as expressed in some of the works already considered. It is amazing to consider what must have been his mental concentration and illumination in the summer of 1788, when within a couple of months he produced three of his greatest symphonies, each of them as different from the others, emotionally, as it could possibly be, works happy, noble, and troubled. Truly that " heart of fire and brain of ice " that Wagner speaks of as the vital necessities for a composer were Mozart's.

There is a breath as of foreboding in the *G Minor Symphony*, a more somber feeling than that of the other two works in this group. It is music peculiarly meet for study in the waning days of the year, when the face of nature has changed from summer pride to autumn brooding. The dignity and power of nature are in the music, too, the dignity that suggests the unchanging processes of life, that in right contemplation are noble, however sad.

The orchestration suits the work's mood — strings, wood wind, and horns only. The blare of the heavier brass would be out of place. The gravity of the horns alone is required. It may be noted that although no clarinets are found in the first version of this work, they are used in the second which Mozart prepared. A note upon this will be found in the Philharmonia score.

FIRST MOVEMENT

Over a soft, impassioned pulsating viola figure is given out
the first theme, *Allegro molto:*

In the second theme (44),

we may feel sweetness and a faint sadness, in a gliding chromatic
movement. The magnificent dramatic life of the whole movement is lived in the spirit of the first theme only, with the inter-
weaving of parts suggesting the complexity of life. A wistful
dialogue for wind and strings (138) leads back to the recapitulation (164). Here the first theme is extended, and there is an
urgent coda (281), mounting upwards and ending on the heights
of dramatic tension.

SECOND MOVEMENT

This is in regular " first-movement form," like the first and
the finale. It may be that Mozart felt this form, with its possibilities of conflict and working-up of tension in the development,
to be peculiarly fitted as the stage for his drama in music. The
first theme of the *Andante* seeks comfort, and finds it within.
Soon after the second subject has begun (at 37), there is a poignant chord (44) that hints at much behind the self-control of
the opening. Throughout the movement the modulations, and the
calling and answering of the themes, are emotionally suggestive
and artistically masterly.

MINUET

Is there spiritual conflict here also? Its firmness is curiously
austere, in the first part. The Trio (43) brings a softer mood,

when strings and wind graciously bow to each other. The return
of the first section, with its earnest, even stern urgency, empha-
sizes the feeling that Mozart has departed from the usual Minuet
spirit because he so strongly felt the work as an organic whole.
Between its four movements there is a rare consonance in moods
and power.

FINALE

Restlessness, anxiety, a going to and fro in the mind, with
searching of the spirit. Here is something of the first movement's
imperiousness, in the sweeps of the strings and the chordal inter-
jections of the wind. The first theme

enters at once, the second

at 71. Here again is the chromatic hint of noble melancholy that
we found in the earlier movements. At 125 Mozart begins to
work out his thoughts by declaiming the first in interrupted
sentences, before settling down to tear the heart out of it in impassioned exhortation and the weaving of argument, moving
masterfully from key to key and leaving the issue uncertain
when he turns to the recapitulation (207). The change in the
latter portion of the second theme (twice, at 251 and following)
will not escape attention. It is as if at the last the composer
sought to make even more urgent the poignancy of his thought.

BERNARD SHAW ON MOZART

In one of the best descriptions of the Mozart style ever written, Bernard Shaw [1] says that nothing but the finest execution —

---

[1] *Music in London — 1890–1894* (London: Constable).

beautiful, expressive, and intelligent — will serve for this music. The phrases look straightforward and clear, but a deviation of a hair's breadth from perfection shows up immediately, though the music sounds so obvious that it seems as if anyone could do it. But it is " impossible to make an effect with Mozart, to work up an audience by playing on their hysterical susceptibilities. It is still as true as it was before the *Eroica Symphony* existed that there is nothing better in art than Mozart's best. We have had Beethoven, Schubert, Mendelssohn, Schumann, and Brahms since his time . . . but the more they have left the Mozart quartet or quintet behind, the further it comes out ahead in its perfection of temper and refinement of consciousness. In the ardent regions where all the rest are excited and vehement, Mozart alone is completely self-possessed: where they are clutching their bars with a grip of iron and forging them with Cyclopean blows, his gentleness of touch never deserts him: he is considerate, economical, practical, under the same pressure that throws your Titan into convulsions. We all in our barbarism have a relish for the strenuous: your tenor whose B flat is like the bursting of a boiler always brings down the house, even when the note brutally effaces the song; and the composer who can artistically express in music a transport of vigor and passion of the more muscular kind, such as the Finale to the *Seventh Symphony* of Beethoven, or the *Ride of the Valkyrie* of Wagner, is always a hero with the interpreter in music. . . . With Mozart you are safe from inebriety. Hurry, excitement, eagerness, loss of consideration are to him purely comic or vicious states of mind. . . . Give me the artist who breathes the true Parnassian air like a native and goes about his work in it as quietly as a common man goes about his ordinary business. Mozart did so; and that is why I like him. Even if I did not, I should pretend to; for a taste for his music is a mark of caste among musicians, and should be worn, like a tall hat, by the amateur who wishes to pass for a true Brahmin."

While it is hardly necessary to follow Shaw's whimsical suggestion and feign a liking and understanding of Mozart's music, this will gradually assume its proper place in the repertoire of the listening amateur if we give it a chance. Acquiring a taste for Mozart is an invaluable experience, if for no other reason than the sensing of the value of a consummate perfection of workmanship in art.

HAYDN THE PATHFINDER

It was Haydn who gave Mozart the form of the quartet and symphony that he was so quickly to make his own. We cannot remind ourselves too often that Haydn was the composer who first used the orchestra in its modern sense and who developed the general type of music which it was to play. Basing his work on the experiments carried out by earlier men (notably Carl Philip Emanuel Bach, a son of the great Johann Sebastian Bach, and the various conductors of the orchestra at the ducal court at Mannheim), Haydn laid out a plan for the symphony which we still use today — that of writing it in four movements, each with a different form. Particularly important was his scheme for the working out of a plan for the first movement — the sonata form, as we have come to call it. He it was who introduced the Minuet, a dance in great favor with court circles at the time, into the symphony as its third movement. The type of orchestration which he adopted after long experimentation has remained in general use up to the present: instead of arranging his orchestra as a general unit and giving parts rather indiscriminately to all the instruments, no matter what their individual tone might be, Haydn separated his band into groups (we call them " choirs "), each of them having a special significance in the make-up of the whole. And he uses these " choirs " according to their significance: strings alternate with wood winds for special dialogue effects, for instance, instead of always combining with them as they did in the orchestra of Johann Sebastian Bach; contrasts of timbre and tone are frequent, with many sudden changes and rather whimsical turns throughout the music. It was this general scheme which Mozart adopted, adding some instruments to it and polishing it up as to style and finish; Beethoven took it up in turn and passed it on to the later composers — Liszt, Berlioz, Wagner, and Strauss — for their further development. We could also call Haydn the father of the string quartet, for he chose the four instruments that are used in this combination and marked out for them a type of music well suited to the display of their essential traits.

Naturally when compared to the heaven-storming work of his followers, Beethoven and Brahms, or even the more perfect compositions of his friend and contemporary, Mozart, Haydn's

writing sounds a bit uneven and experimental, especially in those
passages which we call " bridge passages," uniting the themes in
the various movements. He had not learned how to lead gradually and almost imperceptibly from one theme to another, as
Beethoven knew so well how to do. Some of Haydn's phrases lack
the concentrated perfection of Mozart's writing; but there is
always a fresh, spontaneous quality about Haydn's work that
makes it most acceptable to us today. Born of Slavonic rather
than of Teutonic stock, he was brought up in an humble atmosphere abounding in folk songs with plenty of rhythm and gracious melody; and it was natural that he should introduce the
idiom of these songs into his music. There is a certain sincerity
and often a depth of feeling in his work that is suggestive of the
great Romanticist, Beethoven. Haydn perhaps may have been
somewhat more of a " common " man than was Mozart, but for
that reason he is often a very likable one.

Haydn's Humanism

He shows this likable quality in a remarkable degree in his
Surprise Symphony. Written in the usual form, the first movement has a rather long introduction before the first theme is
heard at all. This is typical of the eighteenth century, that period
of leisure when composer and audience had more time at their
disposal than we of today. Nowadays such passages seem a bit
tiresomely drawn out. After this introduction everything proceeds according to the usual plan; contained in this movement are
some of the rather insignificant bridge passages referred to above,
which Wagner called the " rattle of dishes at the royal feast."
But the movement, as indeed the whole symphony, possesses
charm and freshness. The slow movement containing the " surprise " — a loud chord to awake the sleepy London audiences
for whom the work was originally written, just as they would be
settling down for a nice after-dinner snooze — is a good example
of the Theme and Variations. The Minuet is characteristically
solid, and the last movement — a Rondo — is full of the zest in
life that was one of Haydn's chief traits. Its principal theme
sounds like a vigorous dance tune, and its treatment is full of
strength and spontaneity.

In the slow introduction to the *Clock Symphony* (a work also written for the London concerts of the impresario Salomon) we have an opportunity for observing the depth of feeling that has been suggested as characteristic of Haydn at times. This introduction is full of a grave beauty that is an excellent foil to the graceful theme which immediately follows it; the rest of the movement is in the usual sonata form. The second movement is that which gives the work its popular name, for the repeated chords of the accompaniment are very suggestive of the slow ticking of a clock. Over this is heard a sedately shaped melody of great charm, typically eighteenth-century music. The whole thing is especially human and understandable. After the usual Minuet, we come to the rapid last movement; here it will be interesting to try to determine the formal scheme used — is it sonata form or rondo?

HAYDN AND MOZART COMPARED

Sacheverell Sitwell in his little book on Mozart, a book that contains some strange inconsistencies, as well as much that is good, has a neat word to say as to the differences between the music of Haydn and that of Mozart — differences which are easier to feel than they are to describe. " If music is loved for its simple and pure qualities," he says, " unmixed with introspection and self-analysis, the best of Haydn's symphonies are as beautiful as anything that the civilization of Europe has given us. Their clean, neat workmanship; the manner in which the simplest things of life are taken up and charged with humor and poetry; the grace and liveliness of his minuets; the speed and brilliance of the finales. Mozart is more delicate, less earthly; his perfection of beauty is to be found in the *andante* (the slow movement). There he has an angelic, a seraphic tranquillity; a peace in which, as it were, you could hear Haydn breathe. In the Minuet and Trio Haydn is always predominant; in the hands of Mozart the Minuet is very often the subject of a courtly and aristocratic sadness; with Haydn it is a true dance which touches the blood. The Trio grows out of it, not merely stands in contrast with it, and it sometimes has the character and force of a Ländler or Viennese waltz; when the Minuet comes back again after the Trio, it is with the grateful comfort of music heard once more that might have gone forever." [2]

Mr. Sitwell thinks, and with good reason, that the physical contrasts of the two men have a great deal to do with these differences: Haydn was a strong, peasant sort of man, robust, straightforward, with an unspoiled childhood back of him and the good chance of a strong maturity before him; Mozart's childhood had been spent playing at all the courts of Europe. His hectic life, the fact that he was always pressed for money, that he must have realized that his earthly course was to be soon run, give a nervousness and a sadness to much of his music, even as they add, of course, an aristocratic distinction and polish to it. The richness, quickness, and facility of his invention are inevitably felt in everything that Mozart wrote; they are the hallmarks of his inimitable style. Haydn went more slowly and for that reason very often goes more deeply and more convincingly into the emotions.

LIST OF SUGGESTED MUSIC [3]

C Major Symphony, No. 34	Mozart
Eine kleine Nachtmusik	Mozart
Symphony in D Major	Mozart
Symphony in G Minor	Mozart
Surprise Symphony	Haydn
Clock Symphony	Haydn

[2] From *Mozart* by Sacheverell Sitwell, quoted here by kind permission of D. Appleton-Century Company, publishers.

[3] The piano scores of the first four works in this list are available in the Breitkopf edition. Orchestral scores (miniature size) are in both the Philharmonia and the Eulenburg editions.

The piano scores of the *Surprise Symphony* and the *Clock Symphony* are in the following editions: Breitkopf, Universal, Schirmer (edited by Daniel Gregory Mason), Ditson (edited by Percy Goetschius) No. 1 (*Surprise* only).

The orchestral miniature scores are in the Kalmus editions: *Surprise*, No. 25; *Clock*, No. 106

TOPICS FOR FURTHER DISCUSSION

Following on the section "Haydn and Mozart Compared," can you add some impressions of your own as to the clear distinctions between (*a*) the aims and (*b*) the styles of these composers? How far were their aims determined by the differing circumstances of their life and work? This point, about the influence of a composer's circumstances upon his work, might be discussed in relation to others, both earlier and later than Haydn and Mozart.

What do you consider one of the strongest formal elements in Haydn's finales — one that is rarer in Mozart's?

By referring to the scores, compare the orchestration of the following: Wagner's *Götterdämmerung*, Beethoven's *Fifth Symphony*, Mozart's *G Minor Symphony*, Haydn's *Surprise Symphony*.

SUGGESTIONS FOR READING

Mozart, Davenport. (New York: Scribner; London: Heinemann)
> The author makes Mozart a living figure, even if the account is somewhat sentimentalized and fictionalized after the modern post-Strachey manner.

Life of Mozart, Holmes. (New York: Dutton)
Music in London, 1890–1894, Shaw. (London: Constable)
> (In three volumes) See Vol. III for index of references to Mozart and Haydn.

Mozart, Sitwell. (New York: Appleton-Century; London: Davies)
The Letters of Mozart & His Family. Translated and edited by Anderson. (New York: Macmillan)
Mozart, Blom. (New York: Dutton; London: Dent)
In Search of Mozart, Gheón. Translated by Dru. (London: Sheed & Ward)

Haydn, a Croatian Composer, Hadow. (London: Seeley). Out of print.
> One of the very few books in English on this composer, it is now incorporated in Hadow's *Collected Essays* (Oxford).

Haydn, Brenet. (New York and London: Oxford)
Haydn, Hadden. (New York: Dutton; London: Dent). New edition, 1934, revised by Blom.

CHAPTER XXXIV

Back to Bach

THE BAROQUE BACH

IN the course of our backward historical survey, we have
marked a number of definite " movements," each of them
climaxing in the works of a single composer. We found, for
instance, that nineteenth-century Romanticism — that mighty
period of achievement — started with the symphonies of Beethoven and came to a close with the works of Wagner. In spite
of the wealth of musical material found in the Wagnerian music
dramas, no one has appeared who has been able to develop them
further. Seemingly Wagner exhausted the possibilities of his
medium, and later developments had to take place in other directions — impressionism, and so on. So it was with Mozart; his
best works mark the end of the period of eighteenth-century
Classicism, and beyond them there was nothing more to be said in
that particular manner. The composer whose works we are now
to study — Johann Sebastian Bach — likewise marks the end of
an epoch, the so-called period of polyphony.

It is not easy to place Bach as a composer, for there are several distinct and widely differing phases of his tremendous creative personality. We can say definitely that he shows at least
a triple personality in his music, and if we are to understand this
music we should be able to recognize these different aspects of
his genius. The German historians like to say that Bach is the
great man of the Baroque era; and they are right, in so far as one
phase of his nature is concerned. Just as Haydn and Mozart were
to an extent the representatives of the German Rococo period in
which they lived, so some of the works of Bach suggest aspects
of the earlier Baroque art out of which the Rococo developed and
of which it was a refinement. The desire for the expression of a
buoyant and rich vitality in art may be said to be the underlying
principle of the Baroque. Stimulated by the richness and the mag-

nificence of the French and earlier Italian architectural creations,
catering to the rather satiated and cynical taste of the time, architects and painters, landscape gardeners, and sculptors evolved
the gorgeous, grandiloquent manner of expression which we
know as the Baroque. In all the great capitals of Europe, especially those of the southern countries, as well as in the large number of small centers throughout Germany, building flourished;
the princely rulers desired to demonstrate their power of domain
through costly and elaborate architectural creation. Nor was this
confined to secular kings and princes; after the religious schism
that divided the church in Germany, the authorities of the older
faith bent every energy to re-secure a hold upon the emotions of
men. They paid a great deal of attention to the erection of
churches and abbeys in the same eloquent and grand style as that
employed by the princes, and devoted large sums of money to
rich decorations and sumptuous fittings, using these as " means
of approaching the spirit of the pious traveler and liberating it
from the trammels of daily life." It was a period of luxuriant
strength, of colorful vitality, of almost overpowering magnificence of creative thought; and this spirit, of course, affected all
phases of artistic activity. From his great predecessors — men
like Reinken and Buxtehude in the north of Germany, and Pachelbel in the south — Bach inherited a certain predilection for
this ponderous grandiloquence of expression, and many of his
great organ works unmistakably show its influence. Certainly
there is a striking similarity of spirit between some of his works
— the great *Toccata and Fugue in D Minor,* or the *Fantasia and
Fugue in G Minor,* for instance — and such architectural creations of his time and country as the Brühl Palace near Cologne,
the Residenz in Würzburg, or the Church of Our Lady of
Dresden.

In comparing these similar forms of different arts, our first
impressions are those of the monumental impressiveness and tremendous sweep of creative power to be found in both. The architects of these impressive structures were men possessed not only
of great imagination but also of superabundant technical powers;
their superb craftsmanship was equal to their vision. If we stop
to examine these Baroque creations carefully, we shall find their
imposing magnificence to be made up of a wealth of meticulously
executed detail; carefully balanced members, gracefully molded

phrases, majestic rhythmic patterns give significance and purpose to the whole. And in them all we find the inevitable leading on of our spirits, a piling up of effects, a magnificent ascent to a final and monumental climax that marks the true spirit of the Baroque. In this phase of his career, Bach was as great a designer of Baroque music as were Neumann, Bähr, or the Brothers Asam of Baroque architecture.

But this was not the only nor the most significant aspect of Bach's transcendent genius. If he had written nothing else than these Baroque organ and choral works, magnificent and impressive as they are, present-day lovers of music would hardly consider him the greatest creative genius of their art. A second phase of his work will perhaps be best understood if we review his career as a musical official in the service of the Protestant Church in Germany. He was born in a family that had maintained a musical tradition for generations, many of his ancestors having been organists and town musicians. In fact, the association of the two terms, Bach and musician, was so close throughout the district of Thuringia that a musician was usually called Bach, no matter what his name happened to be! The members of this great family were as noted for their sturdy piety as for their musical ability, and so it is no wonder that much of Johann Sebastian Bach's greatest and most characteristic work was done during the discharge of his duties as church organist and choir director. In fact, it is not too much of an exaggeration to say that the finest fruits of Bach's genius are to be found in his religious works — the chorale preludes which he wrote for the organ, his two great settings of the incidents connected with the death of Christ, the *Passions according to St. Matthew and St. John*, the tremendous *B Minor Mass*, and some of his cantatas; these works were written for practical performance in church, and in them Bach is far removed from the merely monumental impressiveness of his Baroque compositions. There is in these church works the spirit of an earlier period — the Gothic — a period which strove after loftiness and sublimity in architecture, towards an inward and spiritual beauty in painting and a " yearning for the infinite in the works of sculptors, stone cutters, and brass founders." Nothing greater has been done in music than some of the organ preludes, or such parts of the Mass as the *Incarnatus est*, full of the mystic spirit by which Christ became incarnate in man; the *Cru-*

cifixus, heavy with the pain and sufferings of his death; or the *Credo,* an affirmation of faith as tangible, definite, and as carefully wrought as any Gothic cathedral ever built. In these church compositions we find the simple piety, the naïve, unquestioning faith, the sense of a mystic communion with the Divine One that is characteristic of Gothic art. With Bach there was no question of a conscious attempt to recapture the spirit of a bygone age, however; his music was a natural expression of a belief acquired through generations of God-fearing, simple-living ancestors, sheltered from the devastating ways of the world, and heightened by an unusually fertile imagination and superb technic.

Bach's Chorale Preludes

No better introduction to Bach could possibly be found than the chorale preludes. They were intimately associated with his career as a church composer and could have sprung from no other source. The Protestant Church in Germany had as one of its tenets the popularizing of its services, and so encouraged the participation of the people in the liturgical part of its worship. To this end the chorale or hymn was developed so that large congregations could sing easily in unison and with great effect; the services did not have to depend upon a trained choir as had been the case in the older branch of the Church. The chorale goes back to the very beginnings of the Protestant faith, for Luther was himself a musician and poet of ability and wrote some of the earliest examples of this type of worship music. By Bach's time there had been produced a great number of these fine, sturdy tunes (about five hundred of them in all), and one of his most significant contributions to musical literature was the reharmonizing and rearranging of these chorales so that they would be effective for congregational singing with the accompaniment of the organ. These Bach chorales represent in a shortened form the same technical mastery that is evident in his greater works, as well as an inherent strength of emotional expression that is peculiar to them. They were set largely in harmonic style (in distinction to the contrapuntal style which he employed so largely for his other works) and have today a tremendous appeal for all kinds of listeners, learned as well as ignorant. " Nothing in music is more wonderful, perhaps more surprising, than the power and grip which these chorales have over all classes of musical listeners and over the singers themselves. In all choirs . . . these simple four-part harmonic compositions hold singers and listeners probably more strongly than any other form of art. The Bach chorale has, in fact and in the supremest degree, a religious and mystic effect upon the hearer that cannot be analyzed or explained " (Hannam).[1]

At the end of this chapter will be found a short list of some of the best of these chorales. In case you are not familiar with them, listen to them carefully if you would penetrate to the soul of Bach's music. Even playing them on the piano will give a hint of their spiritual beauty; but really to appreciate their mighty power, one should hear them sung by a large chorus or congregation.

One of the most common forms of composition in Bach's time was the chorale prelude, formed by taking the melody of one of these chorales (very familiar to the congregation, of course) and weaving other parts with it in such a way as to bring out its beauty in the highest degree. These were written for the organ and were meant for practical use in the church services. They are in reality miniature tone poems embodying the spiritual character of the words of the chorale upon which they are based. Some of them are meditations uttered from the loneliness of the composer's soul; others are paeans of praise, outbursts of joy and thankful gratitude for blessings received. They are a world in miniature, containing every possible emotion and manifesting all the powers of expression of which Bach deemed the organ capable. They differ in the richness of their expression from everything else he wrote.

As instructive a way as is possible for realizing the difference between the harmonic and the contrapuntal ways of writing music, as well as of acquiring an acquaintance with the great beauties of Bach's more intimate music, is to select a chorale and then compare it with the chorale prelude which Bach evolved from it. These chorales in the form still used by the German Lutheran congregations will be found in a number of editions: those issued by the Oxford Press (edited by Terry) and those

---

[1] Reprinted from *On Church Cantatas*, by permission of the Oxford University Press.

selected and edited by Boyd and Riemenschneider (published by Schirmer) will be most readily available. A number of the chorale preludes have been recorded in two different versions, in the original organ arrangement and in a transcription for modern orchestra, made from the original organ score; both have certain points of superiority. Here are some of each so that you can judge for yourselves as to which way of playing these lovely little masterworks seems most appealing to you:

For organ:

Das alte Jahr vergangen ist

Christ lag in Todesbanden

Herzlich tut mich verlangen

The first of these short chorale preludes is based on the chorale beginning, " The old year now has passed away." In it Bach broods mournfully upon the " pathos of things that are gone and the sadness of all terminations, of that which is past and irrecoverable."

The second uses an Easter hymn, " Christ Lay in Bonds of Death "; there is a sense of joy and freedom in the music, in contrast to the brooding sadness of so many of these chorale preludes.

The third, based on a tune that was originally secular in character, is full of that deep longing that Bach expressed so often and so well:

> Lord, hear my deepest longing
> To pass to thee in peace,
> From earthly troubles thronging,
> From trials that never cease.

It is available in both organ and orchestral recordings, so that a direct comparison may be made between the two different styles of playing these works.

For orchestra:

Aus der Tiefe ruf' ich

In this chorale prelude Bach makes use of a set of beautifully contrived variations to bring out the suppliant character of the tune. The original tune

Slow

is square-cut and prosaic in comparison with the way in which he presents it to us at the beginning; and each variation — quite free as to form — seems to accentuate the expressiveness of the words: " Out of the deeps have I called upon thee, O Lord; hearken to my crying and let thine ears be attentive to the voice of my supplication." No better proof could be found of the essential spirituality of this sort of music.

Wir glauben all' an einen Gott

" We all believe in one God, the Father Almighty, Maker of all things visible and invisible, and in one Lord . . . substance of the Father; God of God, Light of Light, very God of very God . . . by whom all things were made, both in heaven and in earth."

No wonder that Bach, when he decided to write a chorale prelude upon the tune associated with these words, turned naturally to the fugue as his best means of expression. For no other method of treatment known at that time (or, for that matter, since) seems as adequate for the strong affirmation of these foundational principles of Christian faith — principles which, we must remember, underlay the very roots of Bach's existence. The fugue, as we shall see, is a structural synthesis built upon a single idea; it grows entirely from one element, and nothing else could therefore be so suggestive of the idea of Oneness that pervades the words of this chorale. Hence the choice of the fugue here was a stroke of genius: We all believe in *one* God. We can easily hear that the one short phrase heard at the very beginning, a phrase which Bach took from the opening measures of the chorale, permeates the whole structure; it is heard in various parts and piles up to a tremendous climax, while through the bass stride giantlike progressions suggestive of the composer's faith.

BACH THE MASTER OF MUSICAL CONSTRUCTION

The third great aspect of Bach's manifold musical nature is to be found in his natural preoccupation with, and superb mastery of, the forms of musical construction. Certainly no other composer has equaled him in this; he wrote naturally and freely in the difficult forms current in his day — the invention, the fugue, the partita — but we have no feeling that these gave him any trouble whatever, even if the music which he produced in the process does not always represent him at his greatest. He manipulated the form of the fugue with an ease and fluency that is somewhat disarming, for it is probably the most abstract and difficult of all the forms that have been employed by composers

JOHANN SEBASTIAN BACH AT THIRTY-FIVE
Painted by Jok Jak, Ihle. The original is in the Bach Museum at Eisenach.

The Bavarian Hofkapelle Led by Orlando di Lasso
A sixteenth-century choir singing contrapuntal music.

in the course of music's development. We find over forty fugues in his organ works alone, and there are many others scattered throughout his instrumental and vocal works. This elaborate form of polyphonic composition was evolved during the fifteenth and sixteenth centuries from a simple principle in " imitative " writing. Everyone knows the round, or canon, as it is more formally called — a sequential presentation of one musical phrase by various voices. It is this simple idea that underlies the construction of the fugue; but in this elaborated presentation, things are ordered so as to allow each of the two, three, four, or five voices in which the fugue may be written equal participation in the general effect. Just how this is done may be seen by analyzing a typical Bach fugue and comparing it with the simple canon or round which was its structural ancestor. In a three-part round

gain!

dame's lame, tame crane   Feed and come home a - gain!

the melody as given by one voice is usually imitated tone by tone
by each of the other voices; sometimes one of the voices, in order
to keep the melody within singing range, has the tune transposed
into another key.

Non   no - bis   Do - mi - ne, Non   no - bis   sed no-mi-ne

Non   no - bis Do - mi - ne, non no - bis   sed

Non   no - bis Do - mi - ne, non no

tuo_____   da glo - ri - am.   Sed no - mi - ne

no - mi - ne tuo_____   da glo - ri - am   Sed

bis   Sed   no - mi - ne tuo_____   da glo - ri -

tuo_____   da glo - ri - am   Non no - bis   Do - mi - ne.

no - mi - ne tuo_____   da glo - ri - am   Non   no - bis non.

am   Sed   no - mi - ne, tuo_____   da glo - ri - am   glo - ri - am

This idea was in time developed so that by bringing in the
theme (the Subject, we call it in fugue form) in different keys,

built up into a unified whole by the use of Episodes, a work could
be produced which was compact and meaty, one which could
keep the listener keenly interested in its fashioning, and — if the
composer were a man of strong feeling, as was true of Bach —
by no means devoid of emotion. A short diagram of a typical
fugue from Bach's great collection called *The Well-tempered
Clavichord* (known for short as *The Forty-eight*, because that is
the total of its preludes and fugues — forty-eight of each) will
show the general scheme:

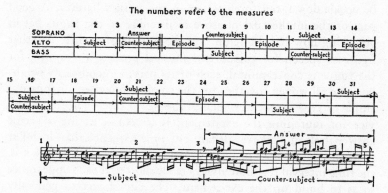

The Subject is generally short and always characteristic,
easily remembered because it is to be followed in various appearances, wholly or in part, throughout the fugue. The Answer is
the name given to the same theme's second appearance, this time
in a dominant key and in another part or " voice." This Answer
is accompanied by the Counter-subject. If there are only two
parts performing in the fugue, we get just the Subject followed
by the Answer with its accompanying Counter-subject. If there
are three parts (as in the example given), one has the Subject, the
second the Answer (the same tune, remember), and the third the
Subject again. If four, the fourth has the Answer again — in
the dominant key, like the former Answer.

It may be taken that this simple setting forth of the one
main theme, with an accompaniment, makes the first section of
the fugue. In the second, which follows without a break, things
begin to happen to both the subject and its accompaniment tune.
The composer begins to build with these materials; he uses (*a*)
subject entries and (*b*) episodes, mostly made out of the same
material. Thus there is high unity in the fugue, and the compos-

er's skill must provide variety and cumulative interest. He is
very widely free; so long as everything he does contributes to the
unified fashioning of the piece, he can do anything he likes —
even introduce fresh ideas, although this is not very common.
If you examine *The Forty-eight*, you will find an amazing diversity of *method*, whilst the amount of *material* used in any one
fugue is quite small. There are far more ways of treating the
Subject and the Counter-subject than one might at first imagine;
they may come in longer or shorter notes than at first; they may
be upside down, tail foremost, or in any guise whatever. A good
part of the intellectual pleasure in listening to the fugue lies in
observing how it is built up into the bundle of its life. Another
figure of speech for this sort of musical process is *weaving*, for
the fugue is contrapuntal, each of its parts as good as its neigh-
bor, and all woven together for the common good — a happy example of true democracy such as the world rarely affords. A device for tautening the excitement is *stretto* — letting a theme
answer itself at a shorter distance of time sequence than it did at
first; this device may be used several times in a fugue, and if it is,
the time interval is almost always made shorter at each appearance
so as to build up the excitement. The closest stretto generally
comes just when we are entering the home stretch — the third
section of the fugue; here, after the adventures of the middle section, the subject generally enters, like a giant refreshed, in the
original key. Thereafter to the end of the fugue the "coda
spirit" prevails and we receive the definite impression that our
flight is about to be ended. Fugue, you must remember, means
"flight" — a flight of fancy, and how wonderfully the fancy of
a genius such as Bach can use the fugue form for the most expressive flights can be readily grasped by anyone who will run
through some of *The Forty-eight*, comparing the splendid diversity of neighboring fugues — as, for instance, the rich dignity
of the fourth in Book I with the *pomposo* fifth; or the lovely
serenity of No. 9 in Book II with the lively marching style
of No. 10.

BACH'S HEALTHY WHOLENESS

Perhaps any attempt such as we have made at a strict classification of a composer's output is rather academically dangerous,

for it presupposes the idea that everything a man such as Bach wrote falls logically into one or another pocket, which can be definitely separated and labeled. This, of course, is not true, for many times the characteristics of one type are found in works which generally belong to another. When we say, for instance, that Bach was largely concerned with the problem of form in one broad type of music which he wrote, this does not necessarily mean that these formal works are devoid of emotional expression; many of the fugues in *The Well-tempered Clavichord* are full of deep feeling, as we have already suggested. Nor should such a classification be construed to mean that the works which fall within the second of our groups are lacking in structural strength — they are carefully and superbly put together.

Nevertheless, some such grouping is a help in understanding the seeming contradictions in Bach's genius. Many a person has been somewhat repelled by what he has called the mathematical aspect of Bach, without knowing anything about the emotionally moving chorale preludes or parts of the cantatas; others have been so fascinated by the supreme perfection of Bach's structural form that they have neglected or perhaps have not understood his essential romantic characteristics; and certainly some of the interpreters who have gloried in the grandiloquent, Baroque aspect of Bach's genius have never paid attention to the still, small voice of his more intimate works. Thus is he really the universal composer.

SOME OUTSTANDING BACH CHORALES

Den Vater dort oben (" God in Heaven Almighty ")
Wachet auf, ruft uns die Stimme (" Sleepers Awake, A Voice Is Calling ")
  These are magnificent examples of an exalted religious expression.
Das alte Jahr vergangen ist (" The Old Year Now Has Passed Away ")
  Here Bach ponders on the inscrutable flight of time and the mystic goodness of God.
Wenn wir in höchsten Nöthen sein (" When in the Hour of Utmost Need ")
Jesu, Jesu, du bist mein (" Jesus, Thou Art Mine ")
  The intensity of expression is almost unbelievable in so short a piece of music.

O Welt, ich muss dich lassen (" O World, I Now Must Leave Thee ")
    This is one of the secular tunes which Bach turned to religious use;
        it is full of tender feeling.
O Haupt voll Blut und Wunden (" O Sacred Head Now Wounded ")
    The most famous of them all, this one is largely used as a Lenten
        hymn.

SOME OF BACH'S OUTSTANDING ORGAN WORKS

Toccata and Fugue in D Minor
Toccata and Fugue in F Major
Fantasia and Fugue in G Minor
Preludes and Fugues in G Major — in A Minor — in C Minor
Fugue in G Minor (" Short ")
Passacaglia and Fugue in C Minor

SOME OF BACH'S OTHER MASTER WORKS

Mass in B Minor (entire work recorded)
The Passion according to St. Matthew (entire work recorded)
Christ lag in Todesbanden (Cantata)
The Well-tempered Clavichord (partly recorded)

TOPICS FOR FURTHER DISCUSSION

Ernest Newman, discussing the tremendous output of composers in
the eighteenth century, says (not excluding Bach and Mozart) that they
" wrote far too much music." " They had," he says, " a set of formulae
which, if they were not at their best that particular day, at all events
allowed them to turn out something which, to the easy-going ear,
sounded as near like the real thing as made no matter." Discuss the
danger of accepting everything a great man wrote as if it were a masterpiece; and the thought that " de-bunking," so popular a sport today,
would rarely be necessary if greater critical discrimination were used
from the start. How is such discrimination to be developed, especially
among the works of great composers?

Writers have sometimes described the fugue as " the strictest of all
musical forms." Others call it the freest. Discuss the two views, with
reference to any fugue you happen to know.

How does a fugue illustrate the artistic principle of " unity in variety "?

Can you explain the modern vogue of Bach?

Discuss the subject of modern adaptations and transcriptions of Bach.

SUGGESTIONS FOR READING

J. S. Bach, Schweitzer. (New York: Macmillan)
> Translated by Newman, this book contains one of the best biographical sketches, together with a very carefully documented description of his music.

The Music of Bach, Terry. (London and New York: Oxford)
> Here is a good discussion without biography.

The Little Chronicle of Magdalena Bach, Meynell. (New York: Doubleday, Doran)
> This is a somewhat romanticized but reasonably faithful account of Bach's life from the standpoint of his second wife.

Johann Sebastian Bach, Parry. (New York: Putnam)

CHAPTER XXXV

Pre-Bach

A Golden Age

AS has already been remarked, this is not a history of music but rather a gleaning from the specially attractive fruits of the historical orchard. And although we have covered in this selective way about two and a half centuries, how much there remains ungleaned! But before closing even such a brief summary as this, it will be necessary that we say something about the period that was pre-Bach — roughly a matter of some nine centuries. The history of music is absurdly short, compared with that of most other arts. We know next to nothing of art music before about 800 A.D.; and for about six of these nine pre-Bach centuries composition can scarcely be said to have existed. But the period from about 1400 to the time of Bach (who was working soon after 1700) covers a wonderful amount of fine music — so much that we call part of it music's " golden age."

The Earliest Art Music

Let us see briefly what music was doing during the troubled ages that we call " medieval." We must remember how filled with disturbances these were, how plagues and famines, crusades and wars, wasted man's substance and confused his will. The chart at the end of this chapter shows only the important events in music's development during this time; the background of these ages of confusion should be grasped through reading some such account as that given in Wells's *Outline of History,* so that we may realize what little chance the arts had. With this fact we must associate another, that of music's youthfulness. Where is the music to compare with the literature and sculpture of ancient Greece? We

336

know practically nothing about it, but it cannot have had anything like the same developed form.

We can deduce that present-day music had two principal origins: that of plainsong and that of folk song — sacred and secular sources. The developments from these followed concurrent paths, but it is much easier to trace those of ecclesiastical music, since its written records are so much more plentiful. In the earliest days of the Christian era church music took its themes from ancient Greek and Hebrew sources that had come down to the early Christians through tradition. These themes the Christian musicians wove into unison melodies having small vocal compass (called plain chant or plainsong), set to the words of the liturgy used in the services of the Church. Each of these melodies was written according to one of the " modes " used by the Greeks. These unisonal chants have come to be known as " Gregorians," from St. Gregory who sorted and ordered them for practical use during the sixth century.

It was a long time before the idea of singing in two parts at once occurred to the church musicians. The first results were primitive enough, being achieved through melodies sung in two pitches at once — in fourths and fifths. This was the practice in A.D. 900, before modern notation was used. " Organum," as this process was called, had its theorists, among whom we chiefly remember the monk Hucbald, one of those remarkable Flemings who later were to blaze the trail for the " golden age." Organum started as parallel movement between the two lines of melody, and developed into the more elaborate oblique and contrary forms — one part at first going always in the same direction as the other; then, after all manner of experiments that must have seemed bold and exciting at the time, going a way of its own. Guido d'Arezzo, some time after 1000 A.D., wrote about it and showed how to write the music down surely and (as far as it went) scientifically. What we now call two-part counterpoint (two independent melodies combined) became the thing in church singing; but it must have been dull, for there was no " time " as we understand it — no variety of rhythm in the parts. Experiments with the rhythm of *words* were fruitful, and there was established the basic triple time that for so long held sway. Various subtleties developed which we cannot go into in such a general treatment as this, and there were rather wild shots at freedom of parts,

as when one part sang a simple bit of melody and another " dis-
canted " above it.

So composition was born with, probably, a great many happy
accidents among the laborious fittings of words and notes. Not
until about 1300 did musicians find how delightful a change it
would be to have two-time. About this period some of the variation experiments and queer combinations became rather scandal-
ous — at least Pope John XII thought so, for in 1322 he ordained
a simpler style of church music. The tune was again copied exactly by the singers, but at the octave and third, as well as the
fifth, above. This made for a richer type of music, in " common
chords " we would say. But it was not enough for composers, who
began to find charm outside the walls of the church. We have
one famous little part song that is a marvel for its time — the
round *Sumer is icumen in,* which belongs to 1240 or thereabouts.
It sings of open-air springtime joys, and there probably was a
great deal of other secular music like it. What a pity that this has
disappeared, leaving us with only an inkling of the freer, more
" human " music which developed outside the church!

MADRIGALS AND CHURCH MUSIC

English-speakers like to hail John of Dunstable as one of the
first really free composers who provided all his own parts, instead
of taking a church theme and working upon it. But though the
English may have started it, the Flemings, energetic, inventive,
exploratory, brought about the first glories of composed music
in the way of madrigals and church music. Dufay, Josquin des
Prés, Di Lasso, and others developed counterpoint into a lovely
art. Listen to one or two works of theirs (many have been recorded and, since the early works of these composers are rather
infrequently sung, these recordings are the best means we have
for becoming acquainted with them); primitive they may sound,
but who shall say that they are short of perfection of their own
kind?

The new delight spread over France, Spain, Italy, and into
England. The last had a magnificent group of composers of this
type of music, from Tallis through the long-lived Byrd and Morley, Weelkes, Wilbye, to Orlando Gibbons. The Flemings carried

their art to Italy, and the composers in residence in that land of
beauty clarified and intensified it; up to the time the Italians
made this music their own there was still a great deal of dusty
scholasticism in it. Perhaps it is not without significance that
democracy was just beginning to work out its destiny, too; the
Church dominated, but life was flourishing outside its command.
Palestrina it was who brought this music to a pinnacle, always under the auspices and guiding hand of the fatherly Church. Palestrina felt with the Church that music's function was not only
to cheer men's minds, " but also to guide and control them." In
that sentence we have the key to the medieval view of music, but
the key must not be thought of as too harshly turning in what
we moderns may regard as the excessively massive lock of that
time. There entered the oil of mysticism to smooth its turning.

MYSTICISM IN MUSIC

This aspect of the age has been admirably treated in Daniel
Gregory Mason's chapter on " Palestrina and the Age of Mysticism " in his book, *Beethoven and His Forerunners*. It will suffice
here to suggest that much of the mysticism of that time, though it
aspired nobly, had not reached that conception of the spirit which
Dean Inge has defined as " the attempt to realize in thought and
feeling the immanence of the temporal in the eternal and the eternal in the temporal." We remember the sixteenth-century revival of intense mysticism in Spain and Italy, and recall the names
of St. Teresa and St. Catherine of Siena. In the midst of much
earthly misery — of war, famine, plague — men turned, passive,
to the Church for comfort, not so much in this life as in that
to come. Man was vile; his appetites must be subdued, morti-
fied. Nowadays we believe that a fuller understanding of psychology shows where this kind of mysticism, though it might
produce much holiness, went wrong, for it tended to mortify the
mind as well; but it had its intense beauties, not the least of them
the music of Palestrina, leading away from human affairs towards
the Infinite. Only if we try to bring ourselves in imagination
into the devout, submissive spirit of the time will we be able to understand something of the meaning of Palestrina's gently flowing,
harmonious, acquiescent music, supreme as it is in this selfless,

exalted kind. We remember, too, the basilicas and cathedrals in which this music was sung — the architecture a soaring counterpart of the aspiring music.

After this mounting, the art of music had to come down to the valley before other peaks could be ascended. Bach, as we shall see, soared, too, but it was on the wings of man's endeavor. In Palestrina the heavenly ones reach down to succor helpless man; in Bach, man, aware of himself and of his task, girds on his sword and aspires to the highest.

SOLO SONG EMERGES

The complexities of this woven choral music were considerable. Other ways of thought, now developing, demanded greater flexibility and humanity in music. Before the end of the sixteenth century, even whilst Palestrina was penning his masterpieces of contemplative devotion, composers were turning to the greater freedom of solo writing; and this led on to the great new form of *opera*. We go into its development, which has as a center date (roughly) 1600, in another chapter.

Turning to Germany, we find a strong influence for the simpler solo type of music in Luther and his ideas as reforming the Church. We have already suggested that these made unison singing popular. Schütz (born in 1585) belongs to the century just before Bach; he composed Passion music which was greatly strengthened by his feeling for drama. Opera and oratorio, then, are the important new forms of music in the seventeenth century.

The chart at the end of the chapter puts into tabular form, in chronological order, the historical developments up to this time.

LIST OF SUGGESTED MUSIC

The only way to obtain an accurate idea of these pre-Bach developments is by hearing good musical illustrations of the various periods. Fortunately this is not so difficult as it might seem, for the recording companies have provided a number of fine records of this early music.

Some of these have been brought together in collections, thus making them readily available for the student. By far the best of these are the magnificent 2000 *Years of Music* edited by Dr. Curt Sachs and issued by Decca, and the *Columbia History of Music* (Vol. I), Percy Scholes. Many of the records listed below have been taken from these sets; other record numbers have been given in order to facilitate the finding of these rather unusual records. Records from the Decca collection are marked * and those from the *Columbia History of Music* #. Other Columbia records are indicated by " Col."

The Traditional Sources of Gregorian Chant:

* *Hymn to Apollo, the Sun-god;* written by Mesomedes in the second century B.C. The scale used in this Greek chant corresponds to

There is a restricted vocal range; the rhythm depends upon the words.

* *Kaddish, Abodah, Selection from the Book of Esther;* Jewish chants. These are very suggestive of the chants in use in the Jewish ritual of the present day. The text of some of them has come down to us from the eighth and ninth centuries B.C. Notice the recitative-like character of the Esther selection.

Gregorian Chant (Plainsong):

* *Misit Dominus* (Fifth Mode)

This example of Gregorian is not so effectively sung as it might be, but it shows in a striking way the manner in which these melodies were set to the text. The words are from the Gradual of the Mass for the second Sunday after Epiphany:

" Misit Dominus verbum suum, et sanavit eos: et eripuit eos de interitu eorum. Confiteantur Domino misericordiae ejus: et mirabilia ejus filiis hominum."

You will hear that the single voice of the chanter is answered by the massed voices of the choir. The scale, one of the eight modes used at this time, corresponds to this (notice in this example that the B is flattened in descending passages; this is, of course, extraneous to the mode proper):

Fortunately it is possible to hear really artistic recordings of Gregorian chant made under the most favorable auspices. Many records have been made by the choir of the Abbey of Solesmes, near Cambrai in France, whose monks have for a century made a study of the proper method of singing this chant. These records are especially recommended to the student.

Victor 7343   Graduals: *Qui sedes* (Seventh Mode) ⎫
                  Dirigatur oratio mea
                          (Seventh Mode) ⎬ Solesmes
                  Christus Factus Est   ⎪ Choir
                          (Fifth Mode) ⎭

The Beginnings of Part Music:

\# Plainsong with organum: *Veni Sancte Spiritus* (about tenth century)

> The vocal lines here run in exact parallel, the tenor holding the Gregorian melody, the bass singing a fourth below it. Soprano and alto duplicate tenor and bass an octave higher, the whole thing thus being a consecutive series of 4ths, 5ths, and octaves.

\# *Mira lege* (eleventh century)

> Here the music is in two parts, the lower carrying the plainsong, and the upper weaving a much freer part than in the preceding example.

* *Congaudeant Catholici* (about twelfth century)

> This illustrates a plainsong melody with discant: the upper part here attains an even greater individuality. It is interesting to follow the words:

" Congaudeant Catholici,   " Clenus pulchris carminibus,
Letentur cives celici   Studeat atque contibus
Die ista.   Die ista.

" Haec est dies laudabilis,   " Ergo caventi terminus
Divina luce nobilis   Benedicamus Domino
Die ista.   Die ista."

\# Secular part song: *Sumer is icumen in* (thirteenth century)

> This is a lilting spring song which is so written as to make a canon for four voices, with two extra bass voices repeating

a phrase which gives support to the whole. The result is a most effective manipulation of simple material and seems to be far ahead of contemporary sacred music. The words, modernized, are:

" Summer is a-coming in,   " Ewe now bleateth after lamb,
Loud now sing cuckoo;   Loweth after calf the cow;
Groweth seed and bloweth mead,   Bullock starteth, buck now verteth,
And spring the woods anew.   Merry sing cuckoo! "

Developments of the Fifteenth Century:

*   *Gloria in excelsis* (about 1450)   G. Dufay

*   *Et incarnatus est* (about 1500)   Josquin des Prés

These are fine examples of the early developed polyphony of the fifteenth century — works which lead naturally into the glorious compositions of the " golden age." The first was written for two voices and two trumpets.

*   *Christ ist erstanden* (about 1500)   H. Finck

A strong example for five voices, this music is set to an Easter text, with a Gregorian melody in the tenor. It shows what the Germans were doing in those days.

The Golden Age:

Hodie Christus natus est (*Christ the Lord Is Born Today*)
                                             Palestrina Col. D
Benedictus   Palestrina 17195

Here is magnificent singing of typical Palestrina excerpts by a fine Dutch choir.

*# *Sanctus* from *Missa Papae Marcelli*   Palestrina

These are the words transfigured by Palestrina's setting: " Sanctus, Sanctus, Sanctus Dominus Deus Sabaoth. Pleni sunt terra et coeli gloria tua. Hosanna in excelsis." (Holy, Holy, Holy, Lord God of Hosts. Heaven and Earth are full of thy glory. Hosanna in the highest.)

* *Miserere*   Orlando di Lasso

>   This is another example of the great school of the vocal con-
>   trapuntal style. Di Lasso is less mystic, more earthly than
>   Palestrina, but he is a magnificent master of his craft and
>   makes his music do his complete bidding.
>   " Miserere mei Deus Secundum misericordiam meam."

* *Resti di darma noia*   Carlo Gesualdo

>   Madrigals — contrapuntal compositions set to secular words
>   — were written concurrently with compositions for the church
>   by the masters of the sixteenth and seventeenth centuries,
>   Flemish, French, Italian, German, Spanish, and English. Of
>   these the Italians were perhaps the greatest, with the English
>   composers a close second. Gesualdo, who lived from about 1560
>   to 1613, wrote madrigals which, because of their peculiar use
>   of chromatic harmonies, sound modern. This is an excellent
>   illustration of his style. The following is a free rendering of
>   the Italian words:

>   > " Still in my heart is grieving
>   > This false and bitter fancy,
>   > I never more can be
>   > That which pleases thee.
>   > Dead is for me all joy,
>   > Hope cannot cheer me
>   > Once again to be joyful."

* *Mein Lieb will mit mir kriegen*   Hassler

>   This shows how the German composers of the period imitated
>   the Italian style. It was written about the beginning of the
>   seventeenth century for two choirs. The words are charac-
>   teristically graceful: — " My Love would do me battle, but I
>   would flee her powers, for a struggle of this kind have I never
>   sought. Alas! I have been wounded by her tender eyes, I've
>   lost much blood and am wounded unto death. Love, I pray that
>   thou give me life, and thy prisoner will I be forever."

\# *As Vesta Was from Latmos Hill Descending*   Weelkes

\# *The Silver Swan*   Gibbons

\# *Fair Phyllis*   Farmer

SUMMARY OF HISTORICAL DEVELOPMENTS [1]

Music of Antiquity	The practice of music in the ancient civilizations — Egyptian, Hebrew, Greek, and Roman.
Early Christian Era to about 800 A.D.	One-part vocal music; a single melody with no accompanying parts.
Medieval Age; 800–1450	Organum: Melodies running in parallel parts. Discant: Gradual substitution of more independent parts and greater freedom of rhythm. Counterpoint: The evolution of involved part writing with much use of imitation between the parts. Polyphony: The perfection of the contrapuntal art in the fugue.
The Renaissance; 1450–1600	New ideas of homophony and instrumental style introduced; study of chords and " vertical " music. Evolution of opera and oratorio.
The Seventeenth Century	Gradual adapting of the older contrapuntal styles to the new medium of instruments and the development of instrumental forms (suite, and so on) climaxing in the works of Bach (1685–1750) and his perfecting of fugal art.
The Classic Period; 1700–1800	The development of the instrumental forms of the sonata, symphony, quartet. Music essentially homophonic in style (one chief melodic line with a harmonic accompaniment). Works of Haydn and Mozart.
The Romantic Period; 1800–1900	Romantic composers: Beethoven through to Wagner. Gradual evolution of program music. Nationalism. Impressionism as the last manifestation. Strauss and the tone poem. Songs.
Modern Era; 1900–	Realism, etc. Polytonalities, polyrhythms, and so on. Smaller intervals than half tones. New instruments.

[1] The dates of the periods are only rough approximations, for there is much overlapping; and they are meant to refer to musical, not historical, developments.

TOPICS FOR FURTHER DISCUSSION

In the music of which modern composers do you find the closest analogue to the medieval spirit of mysticism? Do you think such a spirit is likely to grow in music of the immediate future?

Many people do not find quite satisfying the reasons generally given for the decline of the madrigalian style. Do you? Which of the reasons do you consider most important, and the most suggestive as to the path that music was next to take?

Why do so many modern performances of the music of Palestrina, Di Lasso, and Victoria leave the listener cold? What are the conditions necessary for an adequate interpretation of these works?

SUGGESTIONS FOR READING

Grove's Dictionary of Music and Musicians. (New York: Macmillan)
  Articles on " Motet " and " Madrigal "
Beethoven and His Forerunners, Mason. (New York: Macmillan; London: Gollancz)
  Introductory article
Music in the History of the Western Church, Dickinson. (New York: Scribner)
Palestrina, Pyne. (New York: Dodd)
The Middle Ages, Thompson. (New York: Knopf; London: Routledge)
  Chapter XXIX: Medieval Architecture, Art, and Music
Mont-Saint-Michel and Chartres, Adams. (Boston: Houghton)
  The book contains one of the best descriptions of medieval ideals available in English.
The History of Music, Gray. (New York: Knopf)

A LIST OF COMPOSERS

In order that the reader may have a comprehensive understanding of the various composers and their works we have prepared the following list, giving the names of the principal creative artists in music in chronological order, suggesting the chief characteristics of their music, and occasionally mentioning their most important works.

The Renaissance
                    Josquin des Prés   1450–1521
Josquin, the first composer in the history of the art whose music is interesting to modern ears, wrote a great deal of church music.

Giovanni Pierluigi da Palestrina   1525–1594
The greatest of all Italian Renaissance composers, Palestrina devoted his whole life to the service of church music. There is a mystic
detachment to his Masses and motets that makes them quite individual.

Orlando di Lasso   c. 1530–1594
One of the most cosmopolitan of composers, Di Lasso wrote in
many styles and in different countries. Unfortunately, not much of his
music has been recorded.

Tomás Luis de Victoria   c. 1540–1611
The music of Victoria, the greatest of the Spanish composers, has
a peculiar depth of feeling and wealth of color, in contrast to that of
his Italian contemporary, Palestrina. He confined himself to church
music entirely.

William Byrd   1542–1623
Sometimes called the English Palestrina, Byrd was the outstanding figure in an important English school of the Renaissance. He wrote
in all forms and styles.

Claudio Monteverdi   1567–1643
He excelled as a writer of both contrapuntal madrigals and the
new-style operas. His works in the latter form are the first successful
compositions in this difficult and complicated medium.

Seventeenth and Eighteenth Centuries

Henry Purcell   c. 1658–1695
A writer of outstanding religious as well as secular music, Purcell
is considered one of the greatest of English composers. His misfortune was to have lived at a time when music was no longer cultivated
in England as in the Renaissance. Perhaps his best-known work is the
opera *Dido and Aeneas*.

Arcangelo Corelli   1653–1713
Corelli was one of the earliest writers of violin music.

François Couperin   1668–1733
A French counterpart of Sebastian Bach, Couperin *le Grand* (as he
was called in distinction to the other members of his family) wrote
a great deal of fine instrumental music.

Alessandro Scarlatti   1659–1725
Domenico Scarlatti   1685–1757
Father and son, these two have great names in Italian music. The
first was famous for his operas, the second for his harpsichord music.

Johann Sebastian Bach   1685–1750
One of the most famous of all composers, Sebastian Bach wrote in
practically every form then in use, except opera. He is known chiefly
for his organ and church music.

George Frederic Handel   1685–1759

The possessor of a direct, vigorous style, Handel wrote operas and oratorios in abundance, as well as a great deal of fine chamber music, concertos, suites, and so forth.

Christoph Willibald von Gluck   1714–1787

One of the great reformers of opera, Gluck is the earliest composer whose operas still hold the stage. His lovely *Orphée et Eurydice* is his best-known work.

Franz Josef Haydn   1732–1809

A pioneer in orchestral and chamber music, Haydn said a great deal that is still interesting to modern ears. He wrote in every form; his symphonies and chamber-music works are chiefly heard today.

Wolfgang Amadeus Mozart   1756–1791

Probably the greatest genius among all composers, Mozart, beginning at the age of five, wrote an unbelievable amount of great music during his short lifetime. This includes some of the world's greatest operas and symphonies.

Ludwig van Beethoven   1770–1827

Standing at the crossroads between the eighteenth and nineteenth centuries, Beethoven is probably known to more people than any other single composer. Successful in all forms, except that of opera, he is best known for his magnificent series of nine symphonies.

The Romantic Composers

Carl Maria von Weber   1786–1826

One of the earliest nationalist composers, Weber is known today for his operas, the first successful German works written in that genre.

Franz Schubert   1797–1828

The greatest of the lyricists, Schubert is known today principally for his unequaled songs and a few symphonies. But he wrote a great deal in other forms.

Hector Berlioz   1803–1869

Berlioz was an outstanding French composer and pioneer in the development of the modern orchestra and music written for it. The *Symphonie fantastique* is his best work.

Felix Mendelssohn   1809–1847

He was a talented Romantic composer with strongly Classic leanings.

Frederic Chopin   1810–1849

Unlike most composers, Chopin confined himself to writing music of one type, that for piano. In this particular field he excelled.

Robert Schumann   1810–1856

One of the most characteristic Romantic composers, Schumann excelled in writing music for the piano — he loved to " dream with the pedal down," as someone put it. Some good songs and a few chamber-music works, in addition to his piano compositions, are still played.

Franz Liszt   1811–1886

Although he wished to be known to posterity as a composer, Liszt's reputation rests on his unusual ability as a virtuoso pianist. There is a tinseled element in much of his music that has not contributed to its lasting qualities.

Richard Wagner   1813–1883

Wagner is the greatest of all opera composers. His name is one of the most outstanding in all music. Paderewski called Wagner's opera *The Mastersingers* one of man's greatest creative achievements, and most unprejudiced listeners would agree with this pronouncement.

Giuseppe Verdi   1813–1901

The outstanding composer of Italian operas, Verdi was very prolific, and many of his best works are still popular — a good proof of their quality.

César Franck   1822–1890

A Belgian composer, Franck lived almost all his life in Paris. He is chiefly famous for his symphony and some good chamber music; although he was an organist and a devout churchman, most of his organ and church music is inferior in quality.

Anton Bruckner   1824–1896

Bruckner is an Austrian composer whose complex scores are not too well known outside his native land.

Johannes Brahms   1833–1897

A doughty and valiant Romantic who excelled in his symphonies (of which he wrote four) and orchestral works, Brahms composed in practically all the other forms except that of opera.

Modeste Moussorgsky   1839–1881

He is the most individual of the Russian nationalists. His great opera *Boris Godunov* must always remain the outstanding work of its kind.

Peter Ilich Tchaikovsky   1840–1893

The fervor, passion, and peculiar melancholy of this composer's music will always endear him to large numbers of people. His six symphonies (particularly the last three) and a few other orchestral works are best known, although Tchaikovsky composed in many different forms.

Anton Dvořák   1841–1904

This genial Czech composer wrote a great deal of interesting and colorful music, none of it, perhaps, of prime significance.

Nicholas Rimsky-Korsakoff   1844–1908

Rimsky-Korsakoff was a creator of highly colored, Oriental-hued Russian music.

Edward Elgar   1857–1934

Elgar first succeeded in bringing his native England out of the musical doldrums in which she had drifted since the Renaissance.

Gustav Mahler   1860–1911

Mahler was an extremely talented composer with a sensitive, tortured soul. His music shows Romanticism in decline.

Claude Debussy   1862–1918

The greatest of the impressionists, Debussy wrote music which at its best has not been excelled for delicacy of imagination and utmost refinement of expression. He has had few followers.

Richard Strauss   1864–

The great German follower of Wagner, Strauss is a man who carried the latter's Gargantuan orchestral developments to their ultimate conclusion. Strauss wrote mostly program music, and one great opera.

Frederick Delius   1863–1934

A self-taught, highly imaginative English impressionist, Delius wrote a few things that could have been done by no one else.

Jean Sibelius   1865–

Still a much disputed figure, Sibelius has remained aloof from the rest of the world and has been content to express himself in a most individualistic manner. The results have often been impressive.

Sergei Rachmaninoff   1873–1943

Equally famous as composer, conductor, and pianist, Rachmaninoff has written some interesting, if not very individual, music.

Arnold Schönberg   1874–

Starting his composing career as a lush Romanticist, Schönberg is known today chiefly for his experiments in atonal writing. Some of his pupils have succeeded in this style better than did he.

Maurice Ravel   1875–1937

Ravel was the most sophisticated — and sometimes superficial — of the impressionists. His genius was equally at home in orchestral music, piano music, and opera.

Manuel de Falla   1876–

Falla is an outstanding Spanish impressionist.

Ernest Bloch   1880–

Bloch's music is filled with the fervor and eloquence of the Jewish spirit. He has long been a citizen of the United States.

Igor Stravinsky   1882–

Stravinsky is a sad example of a talented composer who was once a genius. His best work was written before the first World War.

CHAPTER XXXVI

Folk Song

ROOTS OF LIFE AND ART

A S we have already shown, the history of art music may be said to have begun somewhere around 1500. Folk music — the popular music that was evolved by the people themselves because of their desire to express their own feelings and describe their own interests — had probably existed from the earliest historic times. For human beings have always loved to give vent to their fundamental instinct for expression by means of dance and song. The ancient Hebrews and Egyptians, the later Greeks and Romans, the barbaric German tribes of the early Christian era, the common serfs and the brave knights of the Middle Ages, all have had their own songs and ballads. At the very time that the foundational principles of the art of musical composition were being slowly developed under patronage of Church and State, the people of the fifteenth, sixteenth, and seventeenth centuries were composing their own songs of love, of work and play, of religion. Some of these songs were the products of poets and composers entirely forgotten; some the composite result of various collaborators. All of them have been handed down from generation to generation and, since there was no direct way of writing them down, only the best have survived. The result of a long evolutionary process, the folk song thus has a sense of finality and an eternal quality possessed by no other music. These simple products of unknown masters represent in miniature the same results that were achieved later by the more sophisticated composers; for unconsciously the creators of these folk songs constructed them according to principles of design and balance, and gave them depth of feeling and universality of thought. Using materials found at hand, and expressing the ideas of the people who gave them birth, folk songs and dances utter the racial feelings and show the different characters of all the nations.

Throughout the entire history of music, serving as a fructi-fying and stimulating influence for some of its most impressive developments, there is woven this colorful thread of folk music. Naturally a great deal of it has disappeared in the course of the centuries. There must have been, for instance, a great deal of folk music composed by such peoples as the Spaniards and the Irish during the Middle Ages; but this has all been lost, although we have a number of manuscripts of the troubadours and the trou-vères that were written down during the same period. But there have come down to us a great many examples of this art of the people that were composed centuries ago — no one knows in every case just how many. In more recent times these have been written down, collected, and arranged; there are hundreds of these folk songs and dances, most of them strongly characteristic of the different races. We have work songs, play songs, dances for many different occasions, patriotic hymns, lullabies and children's songs, religious songs (which have definitely influenced the more sophisticated church music), drinking songs, funeral songs, nar-rative ballads, epic legends, and, of course, love songs.

THE UNIVERSAL APPEAL OF FOLK SONG

The late Charles V. Stanford, writing for the first volume of *The Musical Quarterly*, has given us a fine panegyric on the uni-versality of folk music.[1] He said in part:

" There is no diet so life-giving and so life-preserving as the natural outpouring of the songs of the soil. They have the sanctity of age coupled with the buoyancy of youth. As far as art work can be, they are in their nature immortal. Their claim to immor-tality is founded on the spontaneity of utterance and their inher-ent simplicity. There is no flummery or sophistication about them. They do not scruple to be coarse and are not ashamed to be refined when the sentiment and the environment demand. How well and truly they represent the spirit and the tendencies of a nation is obvious even to the least tutored ear."

According to Stanford there have been three main streams of European folk songs: Celtic, Slavic, and Germanic. Included in

[1] " Some Thoughts Concerning Folk-Song and Nationality," Charles Villiers Stanford. *The Musical Quarterly*, April, 1915; New York: G. Schirmer.

the Celtic races would be the Highland Scots, the Irish, the Welsh, the Cornish, and the Breton. The Slavs would include such peoples as the Russians (Great Russia, White Russia, and the Ukraine); the Czechs (Bohemians, Moravians, and Slovaks); the Jugoslavs (Serbs, Croats, and the Slovenes); the Poles; the Lithuanians; the Bulgarians; and some of the Rumanians. The Germanic songs include those of Austrian origin and are closely allied to those of England. Then there are lesser strains: the Hungarian, the Scandinavian, the Italian, and the French.

A PRACTICAL METHOD OF BECOMING ACQUAINTED WITH FOLK SONGS

There is no better way of becoming acquainted with the rich literature of the folk song than through the fine examples that have been recorded by the various phonograph companies. It would be impossible to list all these records here, but we are including a few typical examples of each of the above-mentioned " streams," together with an additional list, from which the enthusiast may choose some fascinating items. These folk-song records are especially valuable in that they give authentic renderings of the songs, sung by artists qualified to give them the proper interpretation. By listening to them we may obtain a much truer idea of the real characteristics of the songs of the various nations than would be possible from looking them up in printed collections, or by hearing them sung by those not qualified to understand their real spirit.

It must be remembered that the folk song and the art song have to some extent interfused, some folk tunes, almost always originating in the countryside, having been taken up by the townspeople and popularized through drawing-room and stage performance. On the other hand, some folk tunes, for instance those of the chantey type sung by merchant seamen, have occasionally originated as art music of a lowly kind, such as sailors might hear in taverns and music halls and then adapt to their own uses. Those who wish to go into this fascinating subject of popular song will find it necessary to distinguish broadly between three types: first, the pure folk tune, generally transmitted through the generations without having been written down; second, the nontraditional, amateur, homemade ballad in folk style — the type, for instance, that goes with many of Burns's Scots songs and Moore's Irish verses, and the American cowboy ballads; third, the pure drawing-room or music-hall ditty, such as " The Roast Beef of Old England " or " Drink to Me Only with Thine Eyes," often mistakenly classed among folk songs.

In this particular classification we have thought it wise to give the actual record numbers,[2] since these songs are permanent in the lists of the various recording companies and are rather difficult to find. In some cases we have been able to include English translations of various folk songs in other languages, where such translations will help the reader to understand the spirit of the song.

CELTIC

The outstanding characteristics of the Celtic race have always been their enthusiasm, their lively understanding, and their vivid imagination. According to one of their own writers, they are " always dreaming dreams and seeing visions," leading very largely an inner life. All these characteristics are strongly felt in their songs: these are full of a deep, tender beauty.

Irish

" The Londonderry Air "   V 8734
There are no authentic old words to this magnificent tune; most of those that exist have been supplied by the ballad mongers. Therefore we have included it here in an orchestral version.

Scottish

Lowland Melodies: " Comin' Thro' the Rye "   V 1146
Highland Melodies: *Gradh Geal Mo Chridh* (" Dear Love
of My Heart ")   C 357 M
The Celtic Scot, to use a description by one of their own writers, is an imaginative individual, a dreamer of dreams, tender, of quick perception, living an imaginative life. The Lowlander, on the other hand, is likely to be placid, pastoral, more canny and practical. The music coming from these two regions strongly reflects these differ-

---

[2] The symbols in the list of records may be interpreted as follows:
V   Victor   C   Columbia
H   His Master's Voice   D   Decca
    (English Victor)

ences; for most musicians the imaginative Gallic music far excels the more commonplace Lowland tunes.

Welsh

" Gower Wassail Song "   ⎫
" Young Henry Martin " ⎬   C 372 M
                 ⎭

These songs from the Gower peninsula in Wales show how, in a few isolated places of the world, people have been able to preserve their own folk traditions in face of the encroachments of modern civilization. They are here sung by a seventy-year-old farmer.

SLAVONIC

Some authorities derive the meaning of *Slav* from *slowo* — " word " — thus meaning an articulate race as distinguished from other nations whom the Slavs called *niemetz*, or mutes. This is a happy description of Slavonic folk music, for, in all its many ramifications, it is above everything else fluent and articulate. Here are some typical examples:

Russian

" Song of the Volga Boatmen " (the familiar one)   V 20309
" The Volga Boatmen's Song " (a different and better one) C 4215 M
" The Legend of the Twelve Brigands " (sung by Chaliapin)   V 7717
" The White Whirlwind "   C 4204 M
Asiatic Russian Folk Songs   C P4230–4231
" Stenka Razin "   C P 406 M

Down the Volga in traditional times there came the great Cossack hero, Stenka Razin, and his fair Persian bride. Behind their boat came the disgruntled followers of the great Stenka, jeering and whispering among themselves: " He has forgotten that he once was a warrior; in one night Stenka Razin has become lost to us." As this malediction comes to his ears, the leader stands proudly in the prow of his ship and shouts in tones of pealing thunder:
" Mother Volga, as you flow peacefully 'neath the sun
    You have never received a fit present from a great warrior.
    And so, in order that peace may reign between me and my men,
    Give, O Mother Volga, this girl a grave."
And lifting his bride high in the air, he hurls her into the dark waters of his beloved river.
" Dance, ye fools, and make ye merry;
    Why should ye weep now?
    Now's the time to raise your voices
    In a song to honor the place where beauty lies."

Czech

"Dance Song"   V 20309
    The words of this are mere jingles, composed to fit the infectious
rhythms of the dance.

Slovakian

Tancuj   C 297 M

GERMANIC

German

Zwischen Berg und tiefem Tal ⎫
Seh' ich dich mein Herzensliebchen ⎬   C 4186 M
Erlaube mir, Feinsliebchen ⎫
Mein Mädel hat'nen Rosenmund ⎭   V 7795
    Brahms made some wonderful settings of German folk songs which
must always stand as models of the way in which simple songs
should be arranged. These two are from his collection.

Austrian

Peasant Dances   V 4489–4490

Rumanian

Music for the Pipes of Pan   D 18060–18063
    Shepherd Pipe Solos
Folk Dances (arranged by Bartók)   C 17089 D

HUNGARIAN

    The Hungarian gypsy songs and dances should be carefully differ-
entiated from the genuine Magyar music, uninfluenced by the gypsies.
The Magyar music has been carefully and painstakingly collected by
two enthusiasts — Hungary's greatest composers, Béla Bartók and Zoltán Kodály. Many of their versions of folk songs have been recorded;
the following will serve as examples:

Körtefa ("The Pear Tree") ⎫
Virágos kenderem elázott ("All the Hemp Is Wasted") ⎬   H AM 1675
Meghalok ("Woe Is Me!") ⎭
    "Stand quiet as of old, pear tree of Gyöngyös,
      Once your branches sheltered men weary of fighting,

Hans Larwin: Hungarian Rhapsody

THE SINGERS
by Luca della Robbia (1400?–1482)

'Neath your branches, cool shadow; overhead, warm sunshine.
Well may we laugh together, we who love each other so! "

" The hemp has long been wasted,
So why hurry to your wheel, my beloved — why leave me?
I have lost my distaff, and there's none to help me find it;
No one to comfort me or drive away my sadness."

" Woe is me, for I am dying, though young and strong,
Let me sleep forever in my silent grave.
Vainly I long for thee, yearn for thine embrace,
Sad my nights and days: my death is near! "

Hungarian Gypsy

" Frisky Palko "
" My Fiddle Is Broken "   C 381 M
" The Proud Fort of Krasznahoika "
Hungarian Gypsy Music   D Albums 173, 196

SPANISH

Spain has exceptionally varied and interesting folk music, differing in character in the various regions of the country. Perhaps the most
widely sung are the Andalusian songs, from the mountainous districts
of the south; these are strongly flavored with the influences of the Moorish gypsies who once occupied this section and who are responsible for
much of its man-made picturesqueness. Good recordings are:

Flamenco

Casa Cunan
Juan Palomo
Bajo un Nuevo Sol   V 38628–38629
Ya No Te Quiero
Saetas   ⎤
Alegrias ⎥
Seguidillas ⎬   C 412–413 M
Peteneras ⎦

SCANDINAVIAN

Swedish

Värmeland Du Sköna   V 19923
Rospiggspolska   C 391 M

Norwegian

Fantasia on Norwegian Folk Songs   C 7339 M

ITALIAN

Santa Lucia (Neapolitan Boat Song) ⎫
O sole mio   V 1263
La Vinca (North Italian Folk Dance)   C 297 M

FRENCH

Malbrouk s'en va-t-en guerre ("Duke of Marlborough")   V 20152
Sur le pont d'Avignon   V 22178
La pauvre laboureur ⎫
Le retour du Marin ⎰   C 4124 M
Chants d'Auvergne   C 7238, 7249, 2662 M

These are magnificent examples of what can be done with simple folk songs if they are properly arranged for modern use. They are from a district in western France and were arranged by a contemporary composer, Canteloube.

ENGLISH

" As I Was Going to Banbury " ⎫
" My Johnny Was a Shoemaker " ⎬   C 254 M
" A Bold Young Farmer " ⎭

Folk Dances

" Corn Riggs " ⎫
" Three Around Three " ⎰   C 336 M
" The Long Eight "   C 334 M
" Northern Nancy "   C 335 M

AMERICAN

For folk songs and dances from the Americas, see Chapter XXVIII.

CHAPTER XXXVII

The Art Song; Voices and Their Classification

HISTORY OF THE DEVELOPMENT OF THE ART SONG

WE have already shown how song has been a universal means for the communication of feeling and of ideas, and how large a role the simple folk songs have played in the development of music. Many of the greatest composers have given attention to the song as a medium for expression, and a consideration of the art or consciously composed song is of importance to the student who wishes to obtain a comprehensive idea of the world's music. And some description of the various types of voices — the means by which song is produced — will be of great help in this. Professor Redfield has suggested in his book *Music: a Science and an Art* that in the final analysis all music is but singing, or at least singing and dancing. For instruments are but artificial voices, developed for use when we have no natural voice, or for more power when our natural voices are too weak, or to provide us with voices more to our liking as to compass and tone color. The theories as to the origin of music may be as antithetic as those of Fétis, who defines music as the art of moving the emotions by combinations of sound, and of Herbert Spencer, who considers music as a form of expression arising from the reflex action of the vocal organs under emotional stress. But all authorities agree that song was probably the earliest form of human music. And we know that as soon as music became a conscious art it was associated with speech, and that drama and poetry were early used with music. The movements and rhythms of the dance were used to supplement it, and instruments were developed to provide accompaniments. The universal prevalence of instrumental music at the present time should not lead us to forget that the whole development of the first sixteen centuries of music was along vocal lines. By 1700 the Church had developed a perfection of singing that has ever remained as one of the art's chief glories. We have already sketched the way in which this church music developed. Let us turn aside to see how freely song was used outside the influence of the Church.

EARLY SECULAR SONGS

Church song was for a long time less progressive than secular song. In the ninth and tenth centuries churchmen encouraged minstrels to perform sacred plays, at first in villages and then in church. Latin, used at first, in time gave place to English. (Many of these old " mystery " and " miracle " plays have been revived.)

Music outside the church followed its own path, cherished largely by minstrels, troubadours, trouvères, and minnesingers. History, too, was bound up and propagated in the narrative ballads of the bards. Minstrels were lowborn or highborn; the latter class (trouvères and troubadours, in France) were educated, and most of them were trained musicians. As education in those days centered upon the abbeys, their music showed very strongly the influence of the Church, on the one hand, and of the people among whom their songs became popular, on the other. These songs of the troubadours and trouvères are probably the first composed songs that we have that are of importance; many of them have survived and are worthy of study. The minnesinger was the German counterpart of the French troubadour. Tannhäuser was a minnesinger — you remember his story, and the contest of song, in Wagner's opera. Later came the mastersingers, burgher musicians, and these also Wagner celebrated in an opera. The themes of the French songs of this period deal largely with topics such as love and chivalry; the German writers included a contemplation of nature and her beauties. There are lovely subtleties here which we cannot pursue.

THE INFLUENCE OF THE OPERA

Any discussion of the history of art song must include a word about the use of the voice in early opera, in sixteenth-century Italy, when instrumental music was little cultivated. These early writers of opera learned how to write effectively for the voice, and the arias from the operas of Monteverdi and Carissimi showed the way for later improvements. Unfortunately the cultivation of the solo song, as opposed to the complexities of the madrigal style of the time, led inevitably to one of music's permanent banes — the excessive glorification of the soloist. These singers from the very beginning tried to improve upon the ideas of the composers, decorating them with inventions of their own. Caccini, one of the earliest writers of opera, has deplored the way in way in which his pieces were " torn and altered." The liberties of singers, he said, were such that he considered it necessary to have his music printed in order to show what he had written.

We deal more extensively with opera, the new form that Caccini and his contemporaries were seeking, in the next chapter. Now we must review briefly the other events in the development of song as an art form. The so-called lute airs, songs written for a solo voice with lute accompaniment, were extremely popular on the continent and in England in the Tudor period; Dowland, through these, succeeded in turning the attention of musicians to the possibility of using the song as an individualized form of expression, although it was not until the time of Schubert that the song can be said to have come into its own. Practically all the important composers from Dowland to Schubert wrote songs — men like Scarlatti, Purcell, Bach, Handel, Mozart, and Beethoven; but they incorporated them in their operas, oratorios, and cantatas. Bach wrote only two separate songs aside from those difficult arias contained in his great church works; Mozart wrote a few, and Beethoven still less. But in no case did these men think of the song except as an incidental, unimportant form, chips which might fall from their workbench while they had been engaged in important works. Exceptions to this universal neglect of the song at this period are the beautiful early Italian arias of such composers as Giordani, Pergolesi, Caldara, and Marcello.

LATER DEVELOPMENTS

With Schubert begins a new epoch, for he was above all else a writer of songs. Possessing an instinct for pure melody that

flowed as easily as water gushes from a spring, he wrote song after
song with perfect balance and coherence between the words and
the music. He raised the song from a place of obscurity to one of
the great historic forms of musical expression and laid the secure
foundations upon which his successors — Schumann, Franz,
Brahms, and Wolf — built so well. Carl Loewe wrote some stirring narrative ballads; Schumann incorporated a more elaborate
and poetic piano accompaniment into his songs; Liszt gave us a
few magnificent songs that are not known so well as they should
be; Brahms's songs, according to many critics, represent him at
his best. Robert Franz and Hugo Wolf concentrated their creative activity almost entirely upon songs. The intense German
Romanticism of Franz has caused his songs to become dated; the
greatness of Wolf's songs, however, transcends all periods and
times, and his works stand as the high-water mark in song literature. Extremely difficult to interpret, and requiring an imaginative power possessed by few singers, these songs are not heard so
frequently as they deserve. Grieg's pure lyricism displays itself
beautifully in his songs. Richard Strauss's best songs, the product
of his earlier years, stand among the greatest in the literature.
Writers of French songs — César Franck, Debussy, Fauré, Du-
parc, and Ravel — have produced some works of great beauty,
and the Russian writers — Moussorgsky, Rimsky-Korsakoff,
Gretchaninov, and Rachmaninoff — have contributed a number
of gorgeously colored songs of deep feeling to the repertoire of the
artist. Modern English and American writers have composed some
excellent songs which, if not of the highest rank, deserve the attention of vocalists.

WHAT IS THE VOICE AND HOW DOES IT WORK?

Redfield, in the book already mentioned in this chapter,
shows that the voice differs in no important respect from other
instruments as a device for producing the successive pulsations
in the atmosphere that reach our ears as tone. The piano hammer
starts the string in vibration; as the string vibrates it causes condensations and rarefactions of the air which travel to the listener's
ear as fast as they are produced. This pulsing of the atmosphere
gives us the sound of the piano string. So with the clarinet reed

fluttering back and forth between the air cavity in the player's mouth and that within the clarinet, or the trombone where the air from the player's lungs escapes between his tightly stretched lips, causing them to vibrate and so produce the successive condensations and rarefactions in atmosphere. The human voice resembles most closely such an instrument as the oboe, for it has two membranes (called the vocal cords), the same kind of sound-producing mechanism as the double reed. When the cords are drawn towards each other by means of the muscles that control them, and air is passed across them from the lungs, they vibrate, and the sound reaches our ears through the pulsating particles of the atmosphere. These weak vibrations need reinforcement or resonance, and this is provided by a three-chambered y-shaped resonator, comparable, broadly, to the air column that exists within the body of the clarinet, the French horn, or the trombone. In the case of the voice this resonance is given by the air cavities above the vocal cords; and any practical singer will testify that the quality of the tone he produces depends to a great extent upon the combination of these resonance chambers — (1) larynx to top of throat, (2) the mouth, and (3) the passage continuing from the throat up behind the nose.

The actual mechanism, then, by which the voice is produced is part of the individual who plays the instrument, which fact accounts for the intimate, personal quality that it is possible to inject into vocal music. Truly, a lovely voice is the most appealing of all instruments, but it is impossible always to hear it at the best advantage, for the conditions of the singer's instrument depend not only upon his physical well-being, but upon his mental attitude as well. And there is a further handicap which must be overcome by the singer — the lack of definite and practical instruction in the way his instrument should be used. A clarinet player may take his clarinet to a teacher, and because clarinets are all alike, receive exact information as to how to manipulate it under different conditions of blowing, fingering, and so forth, to produce the tones desired, whereas no two voices are ever exactly alike, since nature never repeats exactly the same conditions as to size of vocal cords, resonating chambers, and so on.

It is likewise manifestly impossible to detach the instrument while it is in the act of producing tone, but two inventions have in turn enabled us to become much surer about what happens when we sing. One was the laryngoscope (invented by Manuel Garcia, 1805–1906), an arrangement of mirrors for examining the action of the vocal cords. The other is the method of applying X rays to singing, first expounded and illustrated in Evetts and Worthington's *The Mechanics of Singing*. Even so, it is difficult to teach singing, when we consider that almost all such tuition must take place in the absence of scientific instruments and that, after all, the instruments show only what happens, not how to manipulate the organs. It is little wonder that there are still so many varied theories of voice training, and such varied results. It is obvious that no side of music teaching lends itself so readily to charlatanism.

The voice mechanisms of men and of women are exactly alike except as to size; the vocal cords of men are larger, and naturally the male resonating cavities are larger than those of the female. Hence there is a difference in pitch between the voice of the sexes, the average difference being about an octave. All sorts of voices have been developed among both men and women singers: women who have short vocal cords are sopranos, those with longer cords sing alto; men whose vocal cords are short are tenors, those with longer cords and larger resonance chambers have bass voices.

THE TYPES OF VOICES

If the physical conditions are suitable, a soprano voice is often able to soar clear and high, and if this natural facility is trained so as to execute all sorts of " bravura " passages — trills, turns, and rapid series of runs — we call the voice a *coloratura*. These acrobatic types of voices are not so popular today as they once were, perhaps because the general musical taste is of a somewhat higher level; but technical skill of any kind is always able to excite admiration, and coloratura sopranos will probably always enjoy a certain amount of popularity. Such operatic numbers as *Una voce poco fa* from *The Barber of Seville* (Rossini) or the Mad Scene from *Lucia* (Donizetti) serve to display this kind of voice. If a light, high soprano is suited to a fluent melody in which deep sentiment can be expressed, we call that voice a *lyric soprano*. " Solvejg's Song " from Grieg's *Peer Gynt* Suite and the

" Song of India " from Rimsky-Korsakoff's opera *Sadko* are good examples of purely lyric songs. A soprano voice that is a little lower than the coloratura and is useful in opera because of its rich quality and wide range of emotional color is called a *dramatic soprano*. Listen to a good soprano in such operas as *Aïda* or *La Vestale*, and you will become familiar with the velvety quality and the dramatic intensity that a good voice of this kind possesses. But you will also notice that the vocal quality is often of much greater interest to the audience than is the music sung!

A voice lying midway between soprano and alto is called a *mezzo-soprano*. The voice that has the lowest range and the deepest quality among women singers is the *contralto* or, as it is usually abbreviated, the *alto*. Like the baritone in men's voices, this is well adapted for lament or other emotional expression; but its greatest handicap is that its repertoire is decidedly limited. Composers seem to have given their most brilliant inspirations to sopranos, since so much of the dramatic and lyric expression has been inspired by the young heroine, whereas the alto voice is characteristic of the older woman and consequently not so popular, although it is capable of a much wider range of human experience. Onegin singing Brahms's *Sapphic Ode,* or Branzell, Schubert's *Death and the Maiden*, or Schumann-Heink *Der Erlkönig* will give you an idea of the glories of the alto voice.

The highest and lightest tenor voice is known as the *lyric tenor*, a voice that is apt to become tiresome because of its overinsistence upon sentimentality. Von Bülow certainly had lyric tenors in mind when he made his famous quip: " A tenor is not a voice — it's a disease." And yet it seems to have been, and still is, a necessary disease. Wagner gave all his principal roles to dramatic tenors (who have a somewhat lower range and a rounder, fuller quality than the lyric tenors), in spite of the fact that the standards of singing in his time were probably no better than they are in ours. The tenor of heroic proportions is called a *tenore robusto;* the Germans use the term *Heldentenor,* heroic tenor. It is hardly necessary to cite examples of lyric tenor songs — they are numerous and very well known; unfortunately many of the sticky Irish ballads and sentimental mother songs have been perpetrated by this type of singer. Fine examples of dramatic tenor songs are the " Prize Song " from Wagner's *Die Meistersinger* (if sung by a good voice — the chances are unfortunately against it) or *In fernem Land* from the same composer's *Lohengrin*. An excellent robust tenor solo is the ever-popular *Céleste Aïda* from Verdi's opera. Italian composers and singers know how to make the most of this style.

Of all voices, male or female, the baritone has the greatest range of possibilities. A *lyric baritone* has much the same range as the *tenore robusto* but possesses more of a bass quality, especially in the lower voice. To appreciate the completely satisfying quality of this kind of voice, listen to a program by such a favorite singer as John Charles Thomas or Schlusnus, representing, as it does, all types and sorts of songs. A *bass baritone* is lower in range than the lyric baritone and has a heavier quality. The *basso profundo* has the lowest voice in range, and the deepest in quality; the Russians seem both by birth and training to have produced the best of these voices. Chaliapin, the great singing actor, is an outstanding example; he can be heard on many fine records, notably in the " Aria of Khan Kontchak " from the opera *Prince Igor* and the " Song of the Viking Guest " from Rimsky-Korsakoff's *Sadko*.

VOCAL COMBINATIONS

Single voices are often used in combination: in duets, trios, quartets, quintets, and so forth. The chorus, a grouping of a large number of voices singing the various parts under the direction of a conductor, corresponds within limits to the effectiveness of the instrumental orchestra. Duets usually comprise contrasting voices — tenor and baritone, soprano and alto, and so on. They are a favorite form of expression with the Italian opera writers; witness the great pact duet from Verdi's *La forza del destino,* or the impressive final duet sung against a choral accompaniment in the last scene from the same composer's *Aïda.* The effect of the latter is gained by fusing voices of similar quality. The trio is somewhat of an unwieldy form in comparison with the duet or the quartet, and consequently has never become very popular. The quartet must always remain the most used of the smaller vocal ensembles, for it contains all the parts necessary for full harmony. The popular American term " harmonizing " means singing in quartet, and we hear constantly all sorts of this combination of voices, good, bad, and indifferent, mostly the last. To sound well together, four

voices must have sympathetic blending qualities, each voice sup-
plementing and complementing the others. The most artistic combination is the mixed quartet — soprano, alto, tenor, and bass;
the most popular, the male quartet — two tenors and two basses
(sometimes with an alto in place of one of the tenors).

A cappella singing — that is, singing after the fashion of a
choir, without accompaniment — is to the minds of many music
lovers the most supremely satisfying form of musical expression.
And there is reason for such an opinion, for the intimate appeal
of the human voice to which we have already referred suffers no
diminution when a large number of singers is heard together.
There is a charm in the blending of the various parts as they inter-
weave one with the other, constantly separating and then flowing
together again, as well as a striking purity and beauty of well-
tuned chording not found in every kind of music. In a cappella
singing we have the possibility of a purity of intonation that gives
the music an appeal something like that of the string quartet and
makes us realize how much of a compromise the tempered scales
of the keyboard instruments are. Hearing a good choir sing dead
in tune (and fortunately there are many such opportunities)
should convince the most skeptical of us that the advantages are
not all on the side of equal temperament (see Glossary), even
though the employment of such a scheme has made possible our
modern instrumental music.

THE LISTENER'S REPERTOIRE OF SONGS

In preparing a repertoire of songs for the listener we are
faced with a peculiar difficulty due to the fact that the form
associates music so closely with words. In writing a song, the composer is first concerned with the words; from them he draws his
inspiration for music, and out of them the musical structure
grows naturally and inevitably. So, in interpreting a song, the
artist must strive above all things to emphasize the meaning of
the words and should make his rendering of the music a means to
that end. Unfortunately for English-speaking peoples, most of
the world's great songs have been written to texts in other languages, and so in listening to them music lovers lose a great deal
of the effect intended by the composer. Two courses are open to

English-speaking audiences: the words of the original can be translated and sung in English by the artist, thus making the meaning of the song clear enough but often doing violence to the composer's association of text and music; or the listener can familiarize himself in advance with a translation of the original text and thus approximate the general meaning of the song as he listens to the artist sing it in the original language. In the latter course the intimate connection between the verbal and musical phrases is lost. In any case, if the hearer is to realize the great beauty of mastersongs, he must by some means familiarize himself with the meanings of their words.

ART-SONG REPERTOIRE [1]

SONGS OF THE TROUBADOURS AND TROUVÈRES

Blondel de Nesle:	*A l'entrant d'esté*	AS 18
Perrin d'Angicourt:	*Quand voi an la fin d'estey*	AS 18
Thibaut of Navarre:	*L'autrier par la matinée*	V 20227
Adam de la Halle:	*Or est Baisrs en la Pasture*	C 70701D

SONGS OF THE MINNESINGERS

Walter von der Vogelweide:	*Palestine Song*	AS 18
Meister Rumelant:	*Ob aller mynne*	AS 18

EARLY OPERA AND CANTATA AIRS

Monteverdi:	*Oblivion soave (L'Incoronazione di Poppea)*	V 17915
	Maledetto, sia l'aspetto	C 17174D
Carissimi:	*Vittoria, Mio Core*	V 4003

[1] The symbols in this list of records may be interpreted as follows:

V Victor
H His Master's Voice (English Victor)
C Columbia
P Parlophone
AS L'Anthologie Sonore
G Gamut
NMQR New Music Quarterly Recordings
D Decca
PD Polydor

Elizabethan Lute Songs

Dowland:	" Come Again, Sweet Love "	C 4166M
	" Come, Heavy Sleep "	V 15166

Other Art Songs

Lully:	Bois épais (Air d'Amadis)	C X117
A. Scarlatti:	Son tutto duolo	V 2062
Purcell:	" Dido's Lament " (Dido and Aeneas)	V 17257
	" I Attempt from Love's Sickness to Fly "	V 4009
J. S. Bach:	Aus Liebe will mein Heiland sterben (St. Matthew Passion)	V 7275
	Bist du bei mir	V 8423
Handel:	" I Know That My Redeemer Liveth " (Messiah)	V 9104
	" Oh Sleep! Why Dost Thou Leave Me " (Semele)	V 15826
	" Where'er You Walk " (Semele)	C 50234D
Mozart:	Das Veilchen	V 1556
	Alleluia	V 1367
Haydn:	" With Verdure Clad " (The Creation)	P
	" Rolling in Foaming Billows " (The Creation)	V 9654
Beethoven:	" Creation's Hymn "	PD 67467
	" Adelaide "	PD 95391
Schubert:	Der Erlkönig	V 9674 and 7177
	Der Wanderer	C L2134
	Die Winterreise (Cycle)	C and V sets
	Der Dopplegänger	C L2135
	Du bist die Ruh'	V 7778
	Am Meer	V 7473
	Der Tod und das Mädchen	C 67431D
Loewe:	Der Erlkönig	C L2303
	Edward	C L9874
	Archibald Douglas	H C2396

Schumann:	*Die beiden Grenadiere*	C G9043M
	Frauenliebe und Leben	
	(Cycle)	C G4070M and ff.
	Du bist wie eine Blume	V 20804
	Mondnacht	C 2202D
Liszt:	*Du bist wie eine Blume*	P E11011
	Die Lorelei	V 7075
Franz:	*Im Herbst*	V 15645
	An die Musik	V 1861
Wolf:	*Verborgenheit*	C 2226D
	Anakreons Grab	V DA1170
	Heimweh	
	Das Ständchen	H Wolf Society
	Auf einer Wanderung	Albums
Grieg:	" Solvejg's Song "	C 9577
	" The Nightingale "	C 9423
Brahms:	*Sapphische Ode*	V 7085
	Immer leiser wird mein	
	Schlummer	V 6755
	Feldeinsamkeit	V 7793
	Von ewiger Liebe	V 6755
	Auf dem Kirchhofe	V 7794
Franck:	*La procession*	H DB1457
	Panis Angelicus	V 6708
Richard Strauss:	*Morgen*	D 20339
	Ständchen	V 7707
	Traum durch die Dämme-	
	rung	V 1980
	Zueignung	V 1853
	All' mein Gedanken	V 7707
Debussy:	*Chansons de Bilitis*	V 1771–1772
	Fêtes galantes No. 1 and	
	2 (6 songs)	V 1768–1769
		V 1771–1772
Fauré:	*Au cimetière*	V 15036
	L'Horizon chimérique	V 15037
	La bonne chanson	V 15033–5
Duparc:	*Chanson triste*	V 1892
	Testament	V 15799
	Soupir	V 1892
Ravel:	*Shéhérazade:*	
	La flûte enchantée	C DB 1301
	L'indifférent	D 20537

Mahler:	*Ich atmet einen Lindenduft*	C DB 1787
	Ich bin der Welt abhanden gekommen	C 4201
Moussorgsky:	" Song of the Flea "	V 6783
	Songs and Dances of Death	G Set 5
Gretchaninov:	" The Mournful Steppe "	D 29049
Rachmaninoff:	" Oh! Do Not Sing Again "	D 29050
Ives:	" Charlie Rutlage "	NMQR 1412
Griffes:	" By a Lonely Forest Pathway "	V 36224
Carpenter:	" When I Bring You Colored Toys "	V 36224
	" Serenade "	V 16780
Barber:	" Dover Beach "	V 8998

ARIAS FROM THE OPERAS

It would obviously be impossible in the case of the prolific composers of opera to give anything like a representative list of their best arias. Even one air from each opera would bulk far too largely. We thought it a pity, however, to omit these composers, and so have treated them briefly, well aware of the many treasures we are leaving unnamed:

Gluck:	*Che farò senza Euridice* (*Orpheus and Eurydice*)	V 6803
Mozart:	*Voi che sapete* (*The Marriage of Figaro*)	V 7076
Rossini:	*Una voce poco fa* (*The Barber of Seville*)	V 6580, 7110
	Largo al factotum (*The Barber of Seville*)	V 7152, 7353
Donizetti:	" Mad Scene " (*Lucia*)	V 6611
	Una furtiva lagrima (*The Elixir of Love*)	V 6570, 7194
Verdi:	*Caro nome* (*Rigoletto*)	V 6580, 7383
	Ah, fors' è lui (*La Traviata*)	V 7438
	Final Duet (*Aïda*)	V 8111
	Céleste Aïda (*Aïda*)	V 6595
	" Willow Song " (*Otello*)	V 7393
Weber:	*Ozean, du Ungeheuer* (*Oberon*)	H D1717
	" Caspar's Drinking Song " (*Der Freischütz*)	H E591

Wagner:	*Am stillen Herd* (*Die Meistersinger*)	V 11162
	Was duftet doch der Flieder (*Die Meistersinger*)	V 7425
	"Walther's Prize Song" (*Die Meistersinger*)	V 7649
	In fernem Land (*Lohengrin*)	V 6904
	Dich, teure Halle (*Tannhäuser*)	V 6831
	Herzeleide (*Parsifal*)	H DB862
	Liebestod (*Tristan und Isolde*)	V 1169, 1363
	O sink' hernieder (*Tristan und Isolde*)	V 7274
	Wotan's Abschied (*Die Walküre*)	H D1225
	Heil dir, Sonne (*Siegfried*)	H DB1710
Bizet:	*Habanera* (*Carmen*)	V 8091
	"Toreador Song" (*Carmen*)	V 8124
Gounod:	*Dio possente* (*Faust*)	V 7086
	"The Jewel Song" (*Faust*)	V 7179
Puccini:	*Addio di Mimi* (*La Bohème*)	V 6561
	Un bel di vedremo (*Madam Butterfly*)	V 6790
	Vissi d'arte (*Tosca*)	V 1346
Richard Strauss:	"Marschallin's Monologue" (*Der Rosenkavalier*)	V 11134
Debussy:	"Duet of the Tryst" (*Pelléas et Mélisande*)	V set M 68
Rimsky-Korsakoff:	"Song of India" (*Sadko*)	V 1570
	"Song of the Viking Guest" (*Sadko*)	V 6867
Borodin:	"Aria of Khan Kontchak" (*Prince Igor*)	V 6867
Weinberger:	*Wie kann ich denn vergessen* (*Schwanda*)	H B4124
Gruenberg:	"Prayer" (*The Emperor Jones*)	V 7959

TOPICS FOR FURTHER DISCUSSION

What is your opinion of the standard of professional singing today, compared, say, with that of orchestra playing?

Discuss the reason for the great diversity of singing "methods." Why do so many charlatans exist — more than in any other department of music teaching?

What is the present status of song writing? Are composers maintaining the quality of their songs?

SUGGESTIONS FOR READING

The Art of the Singer, Henderson. (New York: Scribner)

Some Forerunners of Italian Opera, Henderson. (New York: Holt)

Songs and Song Writers, Finck. (New York: Scribner)
  The book is somewhat prejudiced and incomplete, but interesting.

Grove's Dictionary of Music and Musicians, 1927 Edition. (New York: Macmillan)

Music, a Science and an Art (Article on Song), Redfield. (New York: Knopf)

The Mechanics of Singing, Evetts and Worthington. (New York: Oxford; London: Dent)

CHAPTER XXXVIII

Opera and Its Various Styles

THE BEGINNINGS

THE beginning of the art form that we know as *opera* — a peculiar hybrid born of the union of music and the drama — may be traced to the type of musical declamation used by the Greeks in reciting their poetry and in producing their great dramas. The modern opera as we know it came into being during the exciting days of the Renaissance through the endeavors of a group of Florentine noblemen. These musical amateurs, possessing the characteristic enthusiasm of the period for the culture of the Greeks, tried to write music in imitation of the Greek declamation; the result was a work that may be fairly said to have been the first opera — *Eurydice* by Peri and Caccini, produced in 1600. But long before that the eternal human passion for dressing up and enacting dramas (many of them containing bits of music) began to show the way towards a final union of the two forms. The medieval miracle and mystery plays contained music, and they must have turned the attention of composers toward a possible music-drama union. Italian soil was particularly fruitful, and when the madrigal had reached the great heights of its development and no more could be done in that direction, the influence of songs inserted into stage comedies, and of the *dramma pastorale*, permeated Italian thought about the stage in the sixteenth century. The intricate weavings of the music of the madrigals made their poetry of little account, and people were wanting fresh emotional interest in their music. Drama took hold of the imagination, and the solo voice, always beloved by the Italians, began to seek mastery. The solo song with lute accompaniment was very popular as a form of musical expression during the late sixteenth and early seventeenth centuries: Dowland's " Awake, Sweet Love " is a fine example of this new interest in music for the single voice. Harmony instead of counterpoint (that is, the think-

374

EARLY OPERA IN PARIS

A EUROPEAN COURT THEATER

It was in surroundings such as this, the royal theater in a European castle, that the early developments of opera occurred. The stage is here set for a typical Baroque opera.

ing of music in vertical terms rather than in terms of horizontal weaving) had its chance; and the orchestra crept into being. Instead of thought in the mass, and singing in the mass, there was more and more interest in individual thought and performance. The round date 1600 is an easy one to remember, but the gradual growth of the idea of what we call opera during the whole sixteenth century must be kept in mind. There was no sudden birth.

Nearly all the composers of vocal music up to that time had been singers. Monteverdi, the first extensive prober of the possibilities of the new form, was almost the first composer who was not a singer. Some of his harmonies were wonderfully fresh, and he experimented valiantly with orchestration, using the heterogeneous collection of instruments that came to his hand. The form of the opera was of no importance at first — almost the whole work was written in a sort of *recitative*. Only gradually were the mechanics of this new union of drama and speech worked out. The *recitative* — a sort of tonal declamation in imitation of dramatic speech, with a very spare instrumental accompaniment — was found to be the best means for carrying on the dramatic action, while the *aria* — a set song with richer orchestral accompaniment — was used for displaying reflective emotion. The various solo voices were grouped into different combinations — duets, trios, quartets — while the chorus took a subordinate part. Characteristic themes were employed, and the orchestration devised so as to introduce dramatic effects.

THE EARLY DEVELOPMENTS

The great advances made by Monteverdi over the original ideas of Peri and Caccini may be realized by comparing such an aria as *Funeste piaggie* from the setting which they made of *Eurydice* (" Ye dismal hillsides, how lonely and sad you are without Eurydice ") with Monteverdi's *Ecco purch' a voi ritorno* from his setting of the same story, called *Orfeo*. In this latter, which is sung as Orpheus realizes that his Eurydice will never return to him, we recognize a much greater freedom of melody and sense of dramatic strength. The great era of dramatic music begins with Monteverdi. The vanity of singers, fanned by popular applause, before long carried the vocal floriations which composers

had introduced into their arias to great excesses. The singers were
not content to sing what the composers had given them but had to
enrich and embroider this with all sorts of vocal gymnastics and
ornaments. The composers raged, but in vain; they had to give the
public what it demanded, and the form of the opera became exceedingly popular. Opera houses were opened — at Venice in
1637, in London in 1656, and in Paris in 1669. From a recreation
of the nobility, opera became the joy of the masses. Names we may
remember in this Italian development of the early opera are, besides Peri and Caccini and Monteverdi, Cavalli, Cesti, Caldara,
Stradella. And there were many others who were writing in this
new mode.

EARLY DEVELOPMENTS OUTSIDE ITALY

Lully carried these new ideas to France, and started opera
there under royal patronage. The French loved the ballet, and
that soon played a strong part in their adaptation of the style.
Early French operatic writers were not so brilliant as those of
Italy, and there are fewer really distinctive names to remember,
those of Destouches and Campra being among them.

Germany got the operatic taste from Italy, too, and opera
houses were built in Hamburg and Vienna, with native composers
to provide music for them. England developed her operatic ideas
from the liking for the masque, that aristocratic entertainment
of poetry, dancing, music, and scenic display that was cultivated
before the Civil War. After the Restoration of Charles II (1660)
we note, as an operatic landmark, Purcell's *Dido and Aeneas*.
Handel, a German composer who lived in England and wrote
Italian operas, composed a whole series of works for London, beginning with *Rodrigo* in 1706. He largely swamped English effort, but was not the man to realize the need for reform in the
artificial, singer-dominated form he used.

Gluck was the one who attempted this Herculean task of
making the opera a truer, more dramatic unity. Like Wagner,
Gluck learned as he went along, beginning in the Italian style,
whose artificiality he sought to leaven with finer art. He was in
Vienna in 1746 when he was just over thirty, and for sixteen years
he developed mastery of his medium in such works as *Alcestis*,

Orpheus, Paris and Helen, Iphigenia in Aulis, and *Iphigenia in Tauris.* The overture, from being a movement dramatically unimportant and even unrelated, became something to " prepare the audience for the action of the opera, and serve as a sort of argument to it," as Gluck puts it. But old habits were too strong, and after his death, Gluck's reforms did not endure. No finer example of this composer's success in achieving dramatic feeling in his music could be found than the great aria *Che faro senza Euridice* (" I Have Lost My Eurydice ") from *Orpheus.* It will be interesting to compare this with versions by earlier composers.

THE DEVELOPMENTS OF THE EIGHTEENTH AND NINETEENTH CENTURIES

In Italy, Rossini was the grand figure of the early nineteenth century, with Donizetti and Bellini as popular second and third strings. Another Italian of this period deserves to be remembered: Cimarosa (1749–1801). The perfection of his sense of comedy may be realized in the popular overture to his opera *The Secret Marriage.* He settled at Vienna, where, too, we find the young Mozart. The influences upon the development of this young genius, in so far as his operatic writing was concerned, were almost entirely Italian. Like Handel, Mozart was no reformer, but he had a magnificent dramatic imagination and knew how to make every note tell and every instrument add to the emotional coloring. He loved the voice, so singers and listeners love his vocal writing. Such things as the Page's Song (*Voi che sapete*) from *The Marriage of Figaro* and *Batti, batti, O bel Masetto* from *Don Giovanni* well illustrate Mozart's brilliant style of lyric writing, as well as his essentially Italian treatment of the voice. Beethoven's one opera, *Fidelio,* has a noble theme (something rare in opera), and he made fine drama of it, human and tender. It was not until Weber that pure German opera found its prophet; and he, with his fine feeling for the German hearth and its affections in legendary heroism and romance, led directly on to Wagner. Weber's operas, *Der Freischütz, Euryanthe,* and *Oberon* (even though the last was written to an English text), may be said to be the first great German operas; Agatha's aria from *Der Freischütz, Wie nahte mir der Schlummer,* is a typical Weber aria.

The Italian style of writing culminates in the operas of Verdi, who was born in 1813, the same year as his great contemporary, Richard Wagner. Verdi's works divide naturally into two groups, the earlier, more popular operas such as *Rigoletto, Il Trovatore, La Traviata, La forza del destino,* and the mature *Aïda, Otello,* and *Falstaff.* A close student of Wagner's work, Verdi changed his style in his later works, the last two of which were written after he was seventy-five, employing a richer instrumentation and more dramatic treatment than in the earlier operas with their " salt-box-and-tongs " accompaniment and excessive insistence upon vocal display. Someone has rightly said that Verdi began his career as a composer of operas appealing to the taste of the period and ended it as a writer of works that will live for all time. Even in the mature works, however, it will be noticed that Verdi always keeps the voice supreme, with the orchestra furnishing a subordinate accompaniment — in complete contrast to Wagner's reversing of this process. It is not difficult to hear the Verdi operas; they are popular in every opera house in the world, and most of them have been recorded in full, so that the inquiring student may easily compare the various styles. These selections are characteristic of his mature style:

Credo; Ave Maria; Salce, Salce (" Willow Song ") from *Otello*
Sul fil d'un soffio etesio (" From Secret Caves ") from *Falstaff*

After Verdi the Italian traditions were taken up by Puccini, probably the most popular of all the Italian composers at the present time. His many works — the best known are *Manon Lescaut, La Bohème, Tosca,* and *Madam Butterfly* — abound in technical resource, dramatic invention, and power of emotional expression. They are tremendously effective works when seen upon the stage; whether or not we like them depends upon our taste for the Italian operatic conventions. In *Turandot,* which he left unfinished, he seemed to be moving towards new strength.

THE OPERAS OF RICHARD WAGNER

It is impossible to treat adequately of Wagner's contributions to operatic literature in a few paragraphs; his greatest works, *Tristan und Isolde, Götterdämmerung,* and *Die Meistersinger,* transcend the limiting borders of operatic style and must be classified as among the greatest treasures of all music. Put briefly, Wagner was the great reformer of opera; and his ideal was to do away with those operatic traditions which he considered too artificial for real dramatic expression. In place of these accepted forms, he devised a new one which he called the " music drama " and which in its dramatic elements was founded on the plays of Shakespeare and Schiller, and in its musical elements on the works of Bach and Beethoven. Theoretically the music, the drama, and the staging were of equal importance to his scheme, but in reality the music overshadowed everything else. In order to obviate the overimportance of the voice that was so disturbing an element in the older scheme, Wagner made the orchestra the chief exponent of his dramatic action, weaving its score out of the short and characteristic " leading motives " (*leitmotifs*) definitely associated with various dramatic situations. In fact, these motives in such works as *Götterdämmerung* and *Tristan und Isolde* are woven into such a poignant and expressive musical fabric and form such an eloquent commentary upon the ever-changing dramatic situation as to make the staging and singing almost superfluous.

The actors in these great works of Wagner's use a sort of declamation (*Sprechstimme,* he called it) which has striking dramatic power, but comparatively little musical interest. Consequently most of the operagoers of Wagner's day, as well as some of them today, were at a loss to comprehend the new form, listening, as they did, to the voice for their chief interest. It is the orchestra that tells Wagner's story, and in richness, variety, and impressiveness of effect his scores have never been equaled. He wrote his own librettos, using as subjects various Germanic legends, and these he changed and manipulated to suit his dramatic needs. These librettos may leave something to be desired from the dramatic point of view, for they are full of strange and unnecessary inconsistencies and are often couched in phraseology that is anything but clear. As drama, for instance, the four operas that constitute the cycle of *The Nibelung Ring* (*Das Rheingold, Die Walküre, Siegfried, Götterdämmerung*) are something of monstrosities, built upon motives that are not consistent and which have to be laboriously " explained " at length time and time again. They provide for an excess of dramatic action that sometimes becomes unmanageable, and demand cumbersome spectacular development that is difficult to make convincing. *Tristan und Isolde*, on the other hand, suffers from the absence of varied dramatic motives; it is only in *Die Meistersinger* that Wagner achieved a real balance between dramatic impulse and consequent action. But the more one hears these Wagner operas, the more he realizes that the only function of the libretto is to stimulate musical development, and provide a sustained musico-dramatic element that had never been thought possible before Wagner's time and has never been equaled since.

In Wagner's early works — *Rienzi, The Flying Dutchman, Tannhäuser*, and *Lohengrin* — there may be traced his gradual evolution from a devotee of the grandiose traditions of the German-Italian schools, through various experiments that gave more variety and refinement to his style, to the final achievements of his musical personality. His mature period begins with the first of the Ring cycle, *Das Rheingold*, and continues through the rest of that monumental series, to *Tristan und Isolde, Die Meistersinger*, and *Parsifal*, his last work. In all these, as he himself put it, he tried to get rid of the former mistakes in the form of opera in which the means of expression (the music) was the end, and the end to be expressed (the drama) was made the means. But, in spite of these intentions, the music became so much more important than any of the other elements in the fusion that today we go to the mature operas of Wagner to revel in their music and not because of their dramatic power. As time passes, we see Wagner more and more in correct perspective — as a musical figure of the most colossal proportions. " He is one of those masterminds that belong to no time and no nation, whose work lives as one of the vital forces of civilization."

Since his death no one has arisen to carry on his work; there have been attempts to write in his style, but the results have been mostly unimportant. Humperdinck, in his two charming operas *Hänsel und Gretel* and *Königskinder*, uses the Wagner idiom with taste. Richard Strauss has written a number of works in a style peculiarly his own, achieving powerful effects without directly imitating the Wagnerian technique. The most important of these are *Salome, Elektra*, and *Der Rosenkavalier*, in which Strauss, an avowed admirer of Mozart, achieved a great and world-wide success.

THE OPERA HOUSE AT BAYREUTH

Built by Wagner for the production of his operas.

Cartoon by E. Simms Campbell; © King Features Syndicate, Inc.

"HERE COMES THE PART I LIKE BEST . . . WHERE THEY MUR-
DER THE SOPRANO."

An American cartoonist here depicts what he considers to be the
typical reaction of his countrymen to opera — a social amenity beloved of the ladies, to which men are dragged against their will. As
a matter of fact, however, statistics show that opera was more popular in the United States in the year 1940 than it had ever been before, having been produced in 32 states by 124 organizations.

THE DIFFERENCES OF OPERATIC STYLE

A brief word may well be given as to the essential differences between the several operatic styles, differences which should be taken into account when listening to the various works. We should not expect Wagnerian profundity of thought or greatness of inspiration in the Italian works; nor do we look for Italian simplicity and melodious grace in the German operas. From the very beginnings of the opera, Italians have loved melodic flow and provided opportunities for vocal display and sonority in their works, oftentimes at the sacrifice of dramatic sincerity and musical worth. The Germans, on the other hand, are a much more introspective people dramatically and have demanded above everything else sincerity and musical truth in their operas. Gluck summarized the requirements of opera in this fashion, a summary that has influenced all German writers in this genre — Beethoven, Weber, Wagner, and Strauss: " The true mission of the music is to second the poetry, by strengthening the expression of the sentiments and increasing the interest of the situations, without weakening or interrupting the action by superfluous means for tickling the ear or displaying the agility of fine voices." These requirements have been met in various ways, perhaps most successfully in Wagner's *Die Meistersinger,* an almost perfect equation between dramatic impulse and musical action.

FRENCH OPERA

The French taste in opera was originally borrowed from the Italians; early works stressed the importance of the spectacle and the ballet, but gradually there was evolved a definite national opera style. Lully realized the possibilities of the *recitative* as a dramatic factor, and made it an essential part in the development of the plot and not just a conventional link between arias and choruses. Rameau's works are now considered by the French to be the foundation stones of their operatic style; these contain more feeling and show much more constructive skill than do the operas of Lully. Gluck's reforms were mostly carried out in Paris and were the chief means by which the course of French operatic development was changed and rescued from Italian influences. The writers of opera during the Romantic period in France were men who were important enough in their own day, but most of their works have disappeared from the present operatic repertoire. Meyerbeer, a German Jew possessed of real genius, lived most of his creative life in Paris; he was clever enough to give the people what they liked, paying little attention to anything but his own immediate success. The lighter forms of opera writing chiefly engaged native talent at this time; men like Monsigny, Grétry, Gossec, Méhul, Boieldieu, Auber, Hérold, and Halévy developed the special characteristics of the *opéra comique* — comic, light opera that was not, as time went on, very much different from *grand opera*.

Later important names in the development of French opera are Gounod, whose fame is largely the result of his opera *Faust*, whose languorous love music and sweet, cloying harmonies have made it one of the most popular operas ever written; Bizet, the genius who wrote *Carmen*, to many people an almost perfect opera; Saint-Saëns, who was equally at home in all forms, and whose *Samson et Dalila* has contributed two important arias to the repertoire of the operatic singer; Massenet, who has achieved great popularity both in Europe and in America for his sweetly scented romantic style; Charpentier, composer of the well-known *Louise*, based on a story of life in Bohemian Paris; and, greatest of all, Debussy, whose *Pelléas et Mélisande* is a work that is absolutely *sui generis*, standing alone in its difficult, reserved beauty as the one great modern French opera.

OPERAS OF OTHER COUNTRIES

The Russians have produced some very powerful works written in a most distinctive style: operas like Moussorgsky's *Boris Godunov*, Borodin's *Prince Igor*, or Rimsky-Korsakoff's *Le coq d'or*. Smetana's *Bartered Bride* stands, together with Weinberger's *Schwanda*, as representative of the Czech opera — works that are colorful and rhythmic, without being very important. The other nations, including the English-speaking ones, have never seemed to be fitted for the rather exacting demands of operatic thought and have not as yet produced any outstanding serious works in their various experiments with the form. Ballad opera was once very popular in England (*The Beggars' Opera* is the type), and in this line Vaughan Williams's *Hugh the Drover* is a modern production. But the most popular English operatic style is " Gilbert and Sullivan " — comic opera.

LIST OF SUGGESTED MUSIC

" Hymn to Apollo "   Transcribed by Reinach

Very probably this transcription of one of the few authentic examples of Greek declamation-chant sung in translation does not sound to our ears the way it did to those of the Greeks of the first century B.C. It is impossible to reproduce these historical examples without such reproduction being affected by modern ideas and tastes. Nevertheless this Greek fragment suggests the general character of the means which the Greeks used for the musical projection of their poetry and drama.

Other examples are recorded on Decca 20156.

" Awake, Sweet Love "   John Dowland

This is one of the best of the sixteenth-century solo-songs. Dowland, born probably in Ireland (1563), was a widely traveled cosmopolitan, and his compositions were known all over Europe.

Funeste piaggie from *Eurydice*   Peri

This is an example of recitative from the first opera ever written.

Ecco purch' a voi ritorno from *Orfeo*   Monteverdi

This shows Monteverdi's great improvement over his predecessors.

Al sen ti stringo e parte from *Ariodante* (1734)   Handel

Here is Handel's Italian style at its best.

Che faro senza Euridice from *Orpheus*   Gluck

Overture to *The Secret Marriage*   Cimarosa

Voi che sapete from *The Marriage of Figaro*   Mozart

Una voce poco fa from *The Barber of Seville*   Rossini

Una furtiva lagrima from *The Elixir of Love*	Donizetti
Komm, O Hoffnung from *Fidelio*	Beethoven
Agatha's aria from *Der Freischütz* (*Leise, leise*)	Weber
Caro nome from *Rigoletto*	Verdi
Ah, fors' è lui from *La Traviata*	Verdi
The Final Duet, Act III, *Aïda*	Verdi
" Willow Song " from *Otello*	Verdi
" Credo " from *Otello*	Verdi

These different Verdi selections give an excellent opportunity for comparing the characteristics of his early, middle, and late styles.

Addio di Mimi from *La Bohème*	Puccini
Un bel di vedremo from *Madam Butterfly*	Puccini
Overture to *Rienzi* [1]	Wagner
" Spinning Chorus " and " Senta's Aria " from *The Flying Dutchman*	Wagner
Overture to *Tannhäuser* [1]	Wagner
Dich, teure Halle from *Tannhäuser*	Wagner
Prelude to *Lohengrin* [1]	Wagner
" Elsa's Dream " from *Lohengrin*	Wagner

This group of selections represents the earlier Wagner style.

Prelude to *Tristan und Isolde* [1]	Wagner
Prelude to *Die Meistersinger* [1]	Wagner
Prelude to *Parsifal* [1]	Wagner
Funeral March from *Götterdämmerung* [1]	Wagner

[1] Orchestral selection.

Wotan's Abschied from *Die Walküre*   Wagner

" Walftraute's Narrative " from *Götterdämmerung*   Wagner

Isolde's " Love Death " from *Tristan und Isolde*   Wagner

Was duftet doch der Flieder from *Die Meistersinger*   Wagner

Wahn! Wahn! from *Die Meistersinger*   Wagner

Good Friday Music from *Parsifal*   Wagner

No better means for understanding the method employed in the later Wagner works of building up the score from a multitude of leading motives can be found than in such excerpts as these.

Monologue of the Marschallin and Presentation of
    the Silver Rose from *Der Rosenkavalier*   Strauss

" Salome's Dance " from *Salome* [2]   Strauss

Overture and Pantomime from *Hänsel*
    und Gretel [2]   Humperdinck

Ich bin der Schwanda from
    Schwanda, the Bagpipe Player   Weinberger

Coronation Scene and Death of Boris from
    Boris Godunov   Moussorgsky

" Hymn to the Sun " from *Le coq d'or*   Rimsky-Korsakoff

" Aria of Khan Kontchak " from *Prince Igor*   Borodin

Polovtzian Dances from *Prince Igor* [2]   Borodin

Habanera, Seguidilla, and " Toreador's Song "
    from *Carmen*   Bizet

" Flower Song," " Jewel Song," and " E'en Bravest
    Heart " from *Faust*   Gounod

Il sogno from *Manon*   Massenet

            [2] Orchestral selection.

Il est doux from *Hérodiade*	Massenet
Depuis le jour from *Louise*	Charpentier
" Oh, Caesar, Great Wert Thou! " (*The King's Henchman*)	Taylor

TOPICS FOR FURTHER DISCUSSION

Why has opera been one of the most popular forms of music?

Why was Wagner never able to work out his complete union of drama, staging, and music?

What are the present-day ideas of the possibility of further development in the field of the opera?

Discuss the various reforms of Gluck, Weber, Wagner.

Why was Brahms never tempted to write an opera? What are the essentials of a good opera composer?

Summarize Wagner's contributions to the development of the opera.

SUGGESTIONS FOR READING

Stories of the Great Operas, Newman. (New York: Knopf)
 (Vols. I, II and III)
 The stories and plots of the best-known operas are told by a master.
The Opera, Past and Present, Apthorp. (New York: Scribner)
A History of Opera, Elson. (Boston: Page)
 The book gives the rise and progress of the different schools, with a description of the masterworks in each.
Aspects of Modern Opera, Gilman. (New York: Dodd; London: John Lane)
Book of Operas, Krehbiel. (Garden City: Garden City Publishing Co.)
 Here are given, in good form and for a very reasonable price, the histories, plots, and description of the music of the principal operas.
The Opera; a History of Its Creation and Performance, Brockway and Weinstock. (New York: Simon & Schuster)
The Wagnerian Romances, Hall. (New York: Knopf)
 This is the best treatment of the Wagner stories ever given in English.

CHAPTER XXXIX

Instruments: The Means for Making Music

"Some to the lute, some to the viol went,
And others chose the cornet eloquent." — *Marvell*

E VEN though the skill of the composer enables him to write down his ideas by means of black notes on a white sheet of paper, music does not exist, practically speaking, until it has been " produced " by some sort of physical means. Before they have any value for the average person, these ideas must be brought to life through the medium of some instrument which, be it lute, viol, or " cornet eloquent," is but a machine for producing sound by putting air into vibratory motion. For sound is produced, of course, through but one means, the setting up in various ways of air pulsations which are communicated to our ears through the ability of the air particles to transmit motion. If these pulsations strike upon our sensitive hearing mechanism irregularly, at varying periods of time, we call the sensation they give us " noise "; if they come at regular intervals, we say we hear musical tones. The means for setting the air particles in vibration are many and vary from the simple banging on the stretched skin of a native drum, through the vibrating strings and reeds of the orchestral instruments, to the elaborate electrical vibratory mechanisms of our time. Instruments are the means by which sound impinges upon the consciousness of the average music lover.

THE INTERACTION OF GROWTH: INSTRUMENTS AND EMOTION

Once music outgrew its early savage state, its development has been surprisingly conditioned by the instruments available for its production. Up to the beginning of the seventeenth century it was produced largely by the human voice; as soon as the possibilities of music made by instruments were thoroughly understood, a new art, that of instrumental music, arose, and the most glorious period in the whole development of the art began. The reasons for the choice of a particular instrument for the expression of the thoughts of a composer have always been a source of interesting speculation for the musical amateur; for in listening to great music we must realize that a great deal of its poignance and effect is due to the choice of instrumentation made by the composer. (In this connection it is important to realize that the composer of serious music, in contradistinction to most of the writers of popular music, writes his own orchestration, which is never changed in interpretation.) In writing his immortal *Fifth Symphony*, it is difficult to imagine Beethoven choosing any other instrument than the orchestra for depicting this noble revelation of his soul; a string quartet would have been inadequate and the piano almost ridiculous. On the other hand, many of the best compositions of Haydn and Mozart belong inherently to the string quartet, and would lose their essence if transposed to any other instrument. In this connection, we must remember that the symphony orchestra, although composed of a large group of individual instruments, is really an instrument itself, co-ordinated and played upon by the will of the conductor, and that a trio or a string quartet — combinations of violin, viola, and violoncello, or two violins, viola, and violoncello — are likewise instruments in an individual sense. A great deal of Schumann's and almost all of Chopin's music sprang directly from their love for and understanding of the piano, as we shall see. The majestic dignity and architectural splendor of Bach's organ works are due to his careful cultivation of the resources of that huge instrument and are unthinkable on any other, unless it be the modern orchestra. Furthermore, each age seems to have selected its own particular instrument, one which definitely expressed its own characteristics and which was developed for its needs. The lute suggests the romantic spirit of the sixteenth century; the organ, in spite of many modern improvements which have made it more easily playable, is a quiescent instrument today — its period of great glory extended from the latter part of the seventeenth century to the early eighteenth century.

THE BOSTON SYMPHONY ORCHESTRA

THE ORCHESTRAL STRINGS

THE INFLUENCE OF POLITICS

The eighteenth century was the great period of the string quartet and other " chamber " (or room) music. The nineteenth was the century of the piano — an age of individualism, of star performers demanding a solo instrument capable of complete, single mastery, and suitable for great displays of virtuosity. The choice of these instruments for the varying periods was no haphazard one; political changes and economic conditions had a great deal to do with it. The organ reached its dominance and achieved its importance during the seventeenth century because Germany at the time (immediately following the Thirty Years' War, 1618–1648) was a poverty-stricken country, unable to support the elaborate and costly court music to which France and Italy were accustomed, and looked to the stimulating influence of the strong Protestant Church to satisfy its love for music. Opera had its genesis (the first opera was written in 1600 for the celebration of the marriage of Henry IV and Maria de Medici in Florence) and largely developed during the following years through the demands of the luxurious European courts for amusement. The division of eighteenth-century Europe into various petty courts, each with its own prince and its royal establishment, made possible the system by which chamber-music organizations flourished so widely. The democratic idea in government swept away the petty prince, and with him the string quartet and chamber music organizations maintained for his court concerts. The passing of nineteenth-century Romanticism with its great individualistic figures — Liszt and Chopin — (the last of the giants, Paderewski, died in June, 1941) sounded the death knell of the piano as the deified deliverer of self-conscious soul-strivings.

It is no accident that the great bulk of the music that we have chosen for hearing up to this time has been orchestral music; the symphony orchestra is the instrument of our time, and its music, although almost incredibly complex in many instances, is better understood and more easily appreciated than music written for instruments of another period. Not so many years ago it was thought to be a mark of cultural distinction to be a regular attendant at symphony concerts; now, rather unfortunately in some ways, orchestral enthusiasts are only too common. The orchestra, because of its size, its capacity for varying tone color and all shades of dynamics, appeals to all types of listeners, to the musically trained and the musically ignorant. As someone has well said, it is as modern as present-day industry — one big thing made up of many parts — and it suits our age as the simpler instruments suited handicraft times.

THE GROWTH OF THE ORCHESTRA

Most of us are hardly aware how new an instrument the modern symphony orchestra is. We are so accustomed to the fine orchestras of today, with their almost unbelievable perfection of technic, that it seems as if they must have been in existence for many centuries. As a matter of fact, the first real attempt at developing an orchestra in the present-day sense must be credited to a German prince, Karl Theodore, Elector Palatine in 1743, whose band at Mannheim developed a beauty of tone, a unanimity of playing, and a degree of dynamic shading that had been entirely unknown before; in this sense, as well as in the type of music it played, this orchestra can be said to have been the first " symphony orchestra " according to our modern way of thinking. Most historians credit this band of players with being the experimental laboratory out of which came our present ideas of symphonic music. Charles Burney, the most famous musical traveler of the eighteenth century, gives an interesting account of this orchestra of Karl Theodore: [1]

I found it to be all that its fame had made me expect: power will naturally arise from a great number of hands; but the judicious use of this power, on all occasions, must be the consequence of good discipline; indeed there are more solo players and good composers in this than perhaps in any other orchestra in Europe; it is an army of generals, equally fit to plan a battle, as to fight it. [We cannot help wondering what Burney might have said of the Boston, the Philadelphia, or the London Philharmonic orchestras!]

But it has not been merely at the Elector's great opera that instrumental music has been so much cultivated and refined, but at his concerts, where this extraordinary band has " ample room and verge enough " to display all its powers, and to produce great effects without the impro-

[1] *Present State of Music in Germany, Netherlands, and United Provinces* — Charles Burney (London, 1773).

priety of destroying the grandeur and more delicate beauties peculiar to vocal music; it was here that Stamitz . . . first surpassed the bounds of common opera overtures, which had hitherto only served in the theatre as a kind of court crier, with an " O Yes " in order to awaken attention and bespeak silence at the entrance of the singers. Since the discovery which the genius of Stamitz first made, every effect has been tried which such an aggregate of sound can produce; it was here that *Crescendo* and *Diminuendo* had birth; and the *Piano,* which had before chiefly been used as an echo, with which it was generally synonymous, as well as the *Forte,* were found to be musical colours which had their shades as much as red or blue in painting.

I found, however, an imperfection in this band, common to all others that I have ever yet heard, but which I was in hopes would be removed by men so attentive and so able; the defect I mean is the want of truth in the wind instruments. I know it is natural to those instruments to be out of tune, but some of that art and diligence which these great performers have manifested in vanquishing difficulties of other kinds, would surely be well employed in correcting this leaven which so sours and corrupts all harmony. This was too plainly the case tonight, with the bassoons and hautbois (oboes), which were rather too sharp at the beginning, and continued growing sharper to the end of the opera.

My ears were unable to discover any other imperfection in the orchestra throughout the whole performance; and this imperfection is so common to orchestras in general that the censure will not be very severe upon this, or afford much matter for triumph to the performers of any other orchestra in Europe.

The Elector, who is himself a very good performer upon the German flute, and who can, occasionally, play his part upon the violoncello, has a concert in his palace every evening when there is no public exhibition at the theatre; but when that happens, not only his own subjects, but all foreigners have admission gratis.

The going out from the opera at Schwetzingen, during the summer, into the electoral gardens, which, in the French style, are extremely beautiful, affords one of the gayest and most splendid sights imaginable; the country here is flat and naked, and therefore would be less favorable to the free and open manner of laying out grounds in English horticulture, than to that which has been adopted.

His electoral highness' suite at Schwetzingen during summer amounts to fifteen hundred persons, who are all lodged in this little village at his expense. To a stranger walking through the streets of Schwetzingen during summer, this place must seem inhabited only by a colony of musicians, who are constantly exercising their profession: at one house a fine player on the violin is heard; at another, a German flute; here an excellent hautbois; there a bassoon, a clarinet, a violon-

cello, or a concert of several instruments together. Music seems to be
the chief and the most constant of his electoral highness' amusements;
and the operas and concerts, to which all his subjects have admission,
form the judgment and establish the taste for music throughout the
electorate.

THE ORCHESTRAL FAMILIES

We have already had something to say about the **four great
divisions** of the orchestra: the strings, which produce their tone by
setting into vibration stretched strings, by means of bows; the
wood winds, instruments in which the wind vibrates in a hollow
tube, or in which the vibrations are caused by reeds; the brass
winds, in which the players' lips act as the vibrating medium;
and the percussion — drums, cymbals, gongs, and so on. We may
best remind ourselves of the qualities which these instruments
contribute to the modern orchestra by dividing them into
" families ":

STRING	WOOD WIND	BRASS	PERCUSSION
Violin	Flute (piccolo)	Trumpet	Kettledrums
Viola	Clarinet	French horn	Bass drum
Violoncello	Oboe	Trombone	Side drum
Contrabass	English horn	Tuba	Bells
	Bassoon		Cymbals
	Bass clarinet		Celesta, and so on
	Contrabassoon		

These are combined in various ways and in differing proportions. In an orchestra adapted to playing the symphonies of
Haydn and Mozart (Haydn died in 1809 and Mozart in 1791)
we would have about the following proportion of musical instruments:

8 first violins		2 flutes
8 second violins		2 clarinets (occasionally)
5 violas	to balance	2 oboes (occasionally)
5 cellos		2 bassoons
4 double basses		2 horns
		2 trumpets
		2 kettledrums

(sometimes only four to six wind instruments)

For a Beethoven symphony two extra horns would be added, together with more strings to balance the increased use of brass and wood wind, giving a total of about forty-five strings in an orchestra of sixty. Since the reforms of Berlioz (who died in 1869) and Wagner (who died in 1883), the brass group has mightily increased in importance, both as to numbers and as to quality; naturally this in turn demands more strings for balance, so that properly to interpret modern works with well-balanced forces, an orchestra of approximately a hundred players is necessary. Wagner's last work, *Parsifal*, for instance, calls for the following instrumentation: 3 flutes, 3 oboes, 1 English horn, 3 clarinets, 3 bassoons, 1 contrabassoon, 4 horns, 3 trumpets, 3 trombones, 1 tuba, kettledrums and strings to balance.

One of the legitimate pleasures of concert-going is the ability to recognize the different instruments of the orchestra by both sight and sound. To do this, it is useful to know how an orchestra is seated. Different conductors have different ideas as to the best seating plan for their orchestra, but all give those instruments which have the smaller tone opportunities for being heard to the best advantage. Thus the strings are usually placed in front, with the first violins generally to the conductor's left; the wood winds are directly behind the strings, and the brass and percussion bring up the rear. Because of the necessity for securing a good foundation tone for the whole orchestra, the double basses are placed in the rear or to one side, upon an elevation, so that their voices can penetrate the whole tonal mass.

THE IDEAL CONDUCTOR

The conductor's function is, of course, to keep the whole band together, securing unanimity through his signals; he is likewise responsible for obtaining the effects intended by the composer and marked in the score — interpreting the music, as we say. It is hardly necessary to add that this interpretation is a tremendously important factor in the impressions received by the listener, so important that very often the interpreter gets more credit for the effects produced than does the composer. Music is a unique art in that, as we have already said, a third person must be interpolated between the composer and the listener in order that the latter may receive the impressions desired by the former. This fact has made possible the present-day overemphasis on the conductor as a musical influence, especially as most hearers of orchestral music do not know the real functions of the conductor. Some listeners seem to think that through some occult means, while the performance is in progress, the conductor is presented with brilliant inspirations which he transmits to his men as they play. And the showman-like gyrations of many of our conductors do not help in disillusioning the public!

A good conductor studies his score carefully, decides just what effects are to be desired in various places, the proportions and balance of tonal effects desired, and the shaping of the various musical phrases. Then in long and very often laborious rehearsals, he impresses these ideas upon his men so that they know exactly how they are expected to play each phrase, how their parts are to balance with the others, and so forth. Henderson tells us how he once asked Arthur Nikisch, one of the world's greatest conductors, if he was accustomed to making changes in the reading of an orchestral work during the course of its performance. He replied that if he realized that the music was going rather heavily, he might increase the pace, but otherwise he made no attempt to change details or general outlines. At the concert performance the conductor can work his men into the frenzy of inspired playing, but to do this he has to build upon the solid foundation of careful advance preparation. Today's magnificent orchestral performances are the result of constant and painstaking rehearsals and are in strong contrast to the conditions at the time when Beethoven conducted the first performance of his *Fifth Symphony* in Vienna, which was then (1808) the musical capital of the world. Not one full rehearsal for the program had been held; Beethoven had to stop the orchestra in the middle of a passage when a player lost his cue, and the response of the few auditors in the unheated hall, Beethoven tells us, was anything but enthusiastic, owing to the wretched performance his music received.

With the coming of radio another factor intrudes between conductor and audience — the volume controller, a musician-engineer who can alter the dynamics at will, so that there shall not be inaudibility or "blasting" in the listener's receiving set. He has to legislate for average sets, of course. This is just another of the many reasons why we must not forsake the concert room for the radio set if we want to hear music as nearly as possible as the composer conceived it. In phonograph recording, too, there is " control." No reproducing machine gives the truth, the whole truth, and nothing but the truth.

GETTING ACQUAINTED

How can we listen so that we may obtain the most from the complexities of this wonderful modern instrument, the orchestra? We have already suggested in an earlier chapter (Chapter VII) that the recognition of the *timbre* of the different instruments, played singly as well as in combination, is one of the most obvious pleasures that we can derive from listening. The most practical manner of learning to recognize timbres is through observing what the various classes of tone sound like — what massed string tone is like, or the beauties of the wood-wind ensemble, or the sonorous glories of the brass choir. This may easily be done at orchestral concerts where we may see as well as listen, or rather, see while we listen. Below and on page 396 are shown some seating plans of the orchestra as used by various present-day conductors: study them carefully and you will know where to look for the various choirs.

Recognition of the various orchestral timbres may be aided by a study of the many fine recordings of the orchestra now available. Take such a familiar composition as Wagner's *Tann-*

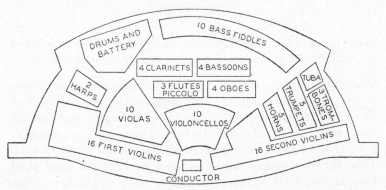

This diagram of the seating plan of the Chicago Symphony Orchestra is one version of traditional arrangement.

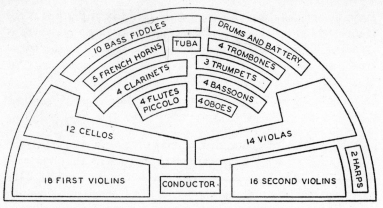

Here is another version of the traditional seating arrangement. The symphony orchestra conducted by Arturo Toscanini keeps its strings forward.

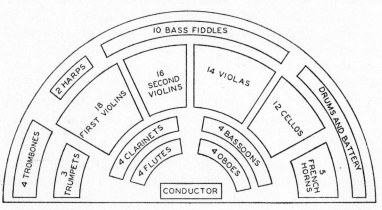

This is Leopold Stokowski's radical rearrangement of the Philadelphia orchestra. Brasses and wood winds are down front, strings back.

häuser Overture, for example; before the music has run the course of fifty measures, the listener has obtained the essential color of the different orchestral choirs. In the first fifteen measures the wood winds are heard alone; the French horn is often counted as a wood-wind instrument because of its peculiarly smooth tone. Then for some twenty measures more we have the wood wind blending with the strings, and finally some of the brass choir sounding the melody of the Pilgrims. The beginning of the Waltz from the *Nutcracker* Suite is also a good tonal illustration of the

wood-wind ensemble. There is a flowing background here supplied by the harp, an instrument that belongs to none of the regular orchestral classifications but is used for occasional effects. Then
there is the beginning of the second movement of Brahms's *Third
Symphony*. Certainly we can hardly find a better illustration of
the richness possible from the wood-wind ensemble; there is an
occasional interpolation of a measure or two from the strings in
order to set off the peculiar wood-wind timbre desired by the
composer. In fact this whole lovely movement is given over almost entirely to a combining of the wood winds and the strings;
only occasionally a trombone enters to help sustain the whole and
tie it together. This is music worthy of many hearings; in trying
to realize just how the composer used these two groups of orchestral instruments, the hearer will incidentally become familiar
with some of the world's noblest music. Another place for recognizing the contrasting colors of strings and wood winds is at the
very beginning of Tchaikovsky's *Symphonie pathétique*. After a
slow introductory melody on the bassoon accompanied by low-
toned strings, the whole string section suddenly bursts into animated action, followed immediately by the wood winds taking up
the same phrase.

GOOD POPULAR MUSIC

Take Dohnányi's *Suite*, Opus 19, as an example of music that
is popular in the best sense; the hearer anxious to familiarize himself with the various colors of modern orchestration cannot do
better than listen to the first movement of this work — a series
of variations on a tune that is played first by the entire wood-
wind ensemble, with the oboe, clarinet, and flute taking the upper
parts of the harmony, and the English horn (in reality an alto
oboe) filling in, and the bassoons furnishing a foundation for the
whole. The peculiarly bitter-sweet, sharply pungent tone of the
wood-wind choir is here heard at its best; note well how it blends
with the string choir a moment later. If you will follow through
all these variations, you will notice that the fifth one gives opportunity for the use of the percussion group (the kettledrums
here), and that the last displays the brass choir to wonderful advantage, in a broad, dignified version of the main tune, above

which float the strings and the wood winds. The whole movement clearly and unmistakably contrasts the essential characteristics of the various groups: the pungent quality of the wood winds, the broad, singing eloquence of the strings, the controlled strength and dignity of the brass, and the pulsating rhythmic impulses of the percussion.

INSTRUMENTAL CHARACTERISTICS

The strings are the foundational group of the orchestra; they take up its main burden and are helped and relieved by the other choirs. Here, as we found to be true in the case of the wood winds, there is a diversity of duties: the violins are divided into two groups, firsts and seconds, and generally take the melody; the violas take an alto part, the cellos a broad flowing tenor or baritone part, and the basses supply the foundation tones for the whole. Listen to the beginning measures of Beethoven's *First Symphony;* the strings have the main say, the violins on top sounding the melody. They are joined occasionally by the wood winds, but the chief color is that of the strings, forming a background for the characteristic qualities of the other groups. What a portentous beginning the deep-toned strings (cello and bass) give to Schubert's *Unfinished Symphony!* There is a lightening of the mood when the violas and the violins are added a few measures later, and the whole section forms a background for the melody sung by the blended oboe and clarinet. In all orchestral compositions the strings are heard much alone: sometimes the composer writes a whole composition for them, as Mozart did in his *Eine kleine Nachtmusik,* composed for some special occasion in Vienna. Here from the four movements of this serenade we can gain a good idea of the varied possibilities of the string choir, ranging from the introspective rendering of sentiment to a light, fleet celerity of which no other instruments in the orchestra are capable.

The brass with its impressive choir of trumpets and trombones can on occasion " roll up the heavens like a scroll." Witness the opening measures of the last movement of Beethoven's *Fifth Symphony,* or the Introduction to the last movement of Brahms's *First Symphony* (measures 30–60), where the effect of the whole

THE ORCHESTRAL BRASS

THE ORCHESTRAL WOOD WINDS

is determined by the golden weight of this important family of instruments. But this brass group can also speak eloquently with a still, small voice; what more suitable opening can possibly be imagined than the beginning measures of Weber's *Oberon* Overture, with its faint " horns of elfland, softly blowing "? Wagner uses the brass choir for tremendous, resounding effects, as well as for some delicate, imaginative ones. The Funeral March from *Götterdämmerung,* for instance, gains its almost overpowering poignancy through the inexorable way in which Wagner uses the brass, here including 4 horns, 3 trumpets, a bass trumpet, 4 trombones, a tenor tuba, 2 bass tubas, and a contrabass tuba. The effect of all these sounding together is unforgettable, cataclysmic, a fit prelude to the destruction of the gods. On the other hand the composer's delicate use of the horns at the beginning of the second act of *Tristan und Isolde* gives exactly the proper mood for the moonlit scene that follows in the lovers' garden.

A fact which the orchestral listener is likely to forget is that, because of difficulties inherent in their construction and mechanism, wind instruments (both brass and wood-wind) have to be kept in tune with one another and with the rest of the orchestra by " main force." Every note on all the wind instruments used in the orchestra must be tempered by the use of the breath and the lips of the player if it is to sound in tune with the rest of the ensemble.[2] And this is true today, even after considerable improvements which the makers (particularly the Belgian C. J. and A. J. Sax and the German Theobald Boehm) have made in the methods used in constructing instruments. No wonder that Bach, Haydn, and Mozart used the oboes, bassoons, flutes, trumpets, and horns of their day so sparingly; or that it was not until Beethoven's scores that the clarinet became a regularly functioning member of the symphony orchestra. The problems — adjustment of valve lengths, proper breath and lip pressure, the correction of deflection from pitch due to temperature changes — connected with the playing of wind instruments are so complicated that they have never been completely solved. And the mechanical imperfections of these instruments are still so great as to make necessary a great deal of lip and breath control on the part of the player. It is this

[2] The slide trombone, however, because of the infinite number of positions possible with the slide, can be played in perfect tune, without the need of tempering by use of lip and breath, with any instrument or combination of instruments.

fact that makes these sections the most temperamental depart-
ments of the orchestra; even in the best of ensembles occasional
out-of-tune playing by these instruments is sometimes noticeable.

The percussion family is probably the oldest of all the orchestral divisions in actual point of time; most of its members contribute to the rhythmic, coloristic, or dynamic qualities of the
ensemble rather than to its harmonic or melodic enrichment. Such
instruments of indefinite pitch as the side or snare drum, the bass
drum, the tambourine, cymbals, and so on, are used entirely for
special dynamic effects. The kettledrum, bells, celesta, glocken-
spiel, and xylophone are instruments capable of producing definite
pitch and are often used by composers for special instrumental
effects; of them all, the kettledrums are the most consistently used
by post-eighteenth-century writers.

Every opportunity should be taken for observing these and
other similar tonal groupings, for it is in this way that the listener
is brought to realize the part that is played by the orchestral
voices in combination. After he has familiarized himself with the
sound of these groups, he will be interested to notice the individual timbres of the various instruments. We all have our favorites,
and learning to recognize their voices gives an added refinement
of pleasure to orchestral listening. Perhaps we are particularly enamored of the horn; Gilman has called it the romantic poet of the
tonal world and said that, like Blake's Evening Star, it can " bid
the west wind sleep on the lake and wash the dark with silver."
Or the cello, eloquent amorist and imposing rhapsodist of the
orchestra; how like the voice of a friend bringing comfort in
trouble is the cello passage at the beginning of the second movement of Beethoven's *Fifth Symphony!* And yet the same instrument, if not treated with respect and given music suited to its
inherent capabilities, may sound like a Hebrew prophet doing
handsprings, as someone has put it. The crystal clearness of the
clarinet melody in the *Oberon* Overture, the pastoral sweetness of
the oboe and the flute in the third section of Liszt's *Les Préludes,*
the nostalgic longing of the English-horn melody in the second
movement of the César Franck *Symphony,* and its prophetic sadness in the shepherd's tune at the beginning of the third act of
Tristan und Isolde, all these are highlights of unforgettable
beauty. The violin is a universal favorite, for it can " dance and
mock and flirt like Columbine, as well as sigh and glow like

National Orchestral Association

THE TYMPANI

National Orchestral Association

THE SCORE

Juliet "; it is an instrument equally capable of light-hearted gaiety, empty-headed brilliance, or soulful discourse on things of mighty import. It can be the means of suggesting playful badinage, as in the first measures of the last movement of Beethoven's *First Symphony,* or of conveying such grave commitments as are entrusted to it by Brahms in the second movement of his *First Symphony.* A detailed consideration of the timbre of the different instruments is of real importance to the listener, and will be our care in the next chapter.

LIST OF SUGGESTED MUSIC

Tannhäuser Overture	Wagner
Funeral March from *Götterdämmerung*	Wagner
Prelude to Act II of *Tristan und Isolde*	Wagner
Shepherd's Tune, beginning of Act III of *Tristan*	Wagner
Waltz from *Nutcracker* Suite	Tchaikovsky
First Movement of *Pathetic Symphony*	Tchaikovsky
Second Movement of *First Symphony*	Brahms
Second Movement of *Third Symphony*	Brahms
First Movement of *Suite, Op. 19*	Dohnányi
First and Last movements of *First Symphony*	Beethoven
Second Movement of *Fifth Symphony*	Beethoven
First Movement of *Unfinished Symphony*	Schubert
Eine kleine Nachtmusik	Mozart
Oberon Overture	Weber
Pastoral section of *Les Préludes*	Liszt

Largo from *New World Symphony*   Dvořák

Instruments of the Orchestra   Decca
   Set 90 Strings
   Set 91 Wood winds
   Set 92 Brass
   Set 93 Percussion

TOPICS FOR FURTHER DISCUSSION

A book has been written claiming that almost all instruments are defective, even the violin. Discuss, according to your knowledge, this general charge.

One able musician has suggested that saxophones may take the place of clarinets in the symphony orchestra. Would that be an advantage?

What factors must we remember when considering even the best phonograph records as representative of the effects produced by the orchestra?

Discuss the instrumentation used by the following composers: Stravinsky, Richard Strauss, Wagner, Berlioz, Beethoven, Haydn, Bach, Monteverdi.

SUGGESTIONS FOR READING

The Orchestra and Orchestral Music, Henderson. (New York: Scribner)
The History of Orchestration, Carse. (New York: Dutton; London: Routledge)
Orchestration, Forsyth. (New York and London: Macmillan)
   This is the standard work of its kind; it is invaluable for the practical student of orchestration.
The Orchestral Instruments and What They Do, Mason. (New York: Gray)
   Here is a concise and valuable treatise for the amateur.
Grove's Dictionary of Music and Musicians. (New York: Macmillan)
   Article on *Orchestra*

CHAPTER XL

Instrumental Timbre

LIVING EXAMPLES — WIND AND PERCUSSION

IN learning to recognize the characteristic tone color of each instrument, the records issued by the various phonograph companies are valuable; these are easily available and give a short excerpt played by each instrument in turn. But the chief thing necessary is to obtain practice in listening to the living examples — places in the great works where the masters have expressed their inspirations through individual instruments. The following examples are suggestive:

FLUTE. *Danse des Mirlitons* ⎱ *Nutcracker* Suite   Tchaikovsky
Danse Chinoise ⎰
    Here the flutes have the top melody against a background of bassoons, clarinets, and strings.

        Scherzo from *A Midsummer Night's Dream*   Mendelssohn
        L'après-midi d'un faune   Debussy

    The flute has remarkable agility, for it " speaks " quickly; its lower tones have rather a hollow, woody sound, its middle tones are full and mellow, and its upper tones brilliant and clear. It is the only wood-wind instrument in which the tone is not produced by means of a vibrating reed; in the flute the air is set in vibration by the player's blowing across a hole near the end of its closed cylindrical tube. Because of a perfected system of manipulation, developed in the nineteenth century by Theobald Boehm, a German maker, it is the most perfectly tuned wind instrument in existence — some of the others leaving a good deal to be desired in this respect. The piccolo is an octave higher in pitch and gives a peculiarly brilliant tone for special effects.

OBOE. Second Movement, *Eroica Symphony*   Beethoven
    In the repetition of the theme heard in the violins the oboe comes in at the very beginning.

403

| First Movement, *Fifth Symphony* | Beethoven |

A short solo passage interrupts the flow of the music just before the restatement.

| Third section, *Les Préludes* | Liszt |
| Second Movement, *Second Symphony* | Brahms |

There are many beautifully tender passages here in contrast with the other wood winds.

| Second Movement, *Fourth Symphony* | Tchaikovsky |

The oboe is an ancient and honorable instrument created originally in the Semitic world; the medieval name for the instrument was *shawm*. The tone is produced by a double reed placed in a mouthpiece at one end of its tube, and its acrid, somewhat nasal quality always has a suggestion of plaintiveness. To the oboe is assigned the task of sounding the tuning note for the other instruments.

ENGLISH HORN. Second Movement, *New World Symphony* — Dvořák
Second Movement, *Symphony in D Minor* — César Franck
Romanza, *Suite*, Op. 19 — Dohnányi

The English horn is an oboe of lower pitch, with a peculiarly melancholy tinge and tender quality in its tone.

CLARINET. Overture to *Oberon* — Weber
First Movement, *Symphonie pathétique* — Tchaikovsky
The English horn comes in at the repetition of the slow theme.
Prelude to *Le coq d'or* — Rimsky-Korsakoff
Siegfried's Rhine Journey, *Götterdämmerung* — Wagner
Here there is a duet between the clarinet and the bass clarinet.

The tone of the clarinet is produced by the vibration of a single reed; it is the most useful of all wood-wind tones because of its beauty and flexibility, its wide range of dynamics, and its wide compass; that is, range of pitch. It can play both louder and softer through its whole range than can any of the wind instruments. Having a range of three and a half octaves, it can be used both as an instrument for accompaniment and for solos. Its tone is a pleasing contrast to the thin, penetrating oboe and has more body than the limpid flute; it is perhaps the favored instrument of the wood winds because of the fact that it blends so well with almost any combination of strings or wind, adding richness but never becoming obtrusive.

BASSOON. Overture and Nocturne, *A Midsummer*
      Night's Dream   Mendelssohn
     In the Hall of the Mountain King, *Peer*
      Gynt Suite, No. 1   Grieg
     First Movement, *Symphonie pathétique*   Tchaikovsky
      A bassoon solo appears at the very
     beginning.
     Through the Looking Glass Suite   Taylor

The bassoon is a wooden, double-reed instrument originating in the sixteenth century, the usual function of which is that of supplying the bass of the wood-wind group. It possesses unusual versatility and compass and is suitable for solo effects as well as for ensemble uses. Its air column, if stretched out, would measure 109 inches, but by doubling back on itself, the height of the instrument is reduced to a little more than four feet. It is a useful instrument but not a perfect one, for no two bassoons seem exactly alike. The intonation of any particular instrument depends to a considerable extent upon the skill of the player and his knowledge of his own instrument's peculiarities. The mouthpiece is curved and fits into the side of the wooden tube so that the instrument is carried sideways.

The double bassoon (contrabassoon) is the weightiest of the wood winds. Beethoven, that great liberator of instruments, was the first who realized its usefulness.

TRUMPET. *Leonora Overture, No. 3*   Beethoven
     Notice the middle section.
     March from Act II, *Tannhäuser*   Wagner
     Sword and Siegfried themes from *Die*
      Walküre   Wagner

There is less chance for confusing the individual instruments of the brass group than those of any other choir, for the types are familiar and the differences easily noticed. The trumpet is the soprano of the choir, and its brilliant tone and ease of handling in its modern form make it useful for adding resplendence and strength to the ensemble. It is rarely used alone.

HORN (FRENCH HORN). Till's Theme from *Till*
        Eulenspiegel's Merry
        Pranks   Strauss
      Nocturne from *A*
        Midsummer Night's
        Dream   Mendelssohn
      Finale, *Fourth Sym-*
        phony   Tchaikovsky

The horn is a brass instrument with a coiled tube that gradually widens until it ends in a large bell. It has been developed from the old hunting horns which, for convenience in carrying, were made with circular turns and carried over the shoulder. About a hundred years ago valves were introduced, allowing the player to play semitones; before that the horns were able to produce only a limited number of notes. The quality of the tone of the horn lies midway between the wood wind and the brass, and it blends equally well with either. While its tone is capable of great power, it can be made unobtrusive in the softest passages. It has a full, mellow tone, adapting it for a supporting instrument, filling in and sustaining the general harmonies; but it can on occasion be a fine solo instrument.

TROMBONE. Overture to *Tannhäuser*   Wagner
      Fourth Movement, *Fifth Symphony* Beethoven

The trombone is an instrument that originated from the trumpet sometime during the fifteenth century; the essential nature of its construction has not changed from that time to the present day. Its pitch is regulated by varying the length of the vibrating air column by means of a telescoping slide. It is capable of full, sonorous, majestic effects as well as of soft ones. There are three sizes, forming the alto, tenor, and bass voices of the brass choir.

TUBA. Siegfried's Funeral March from *Götterdäm-*
    merung   Wagner
    The Dragon Motive from *Siegfried*   Wagner
    Torch Dance   Meyerbeer

The rich, sonorous double-bass of the brass choir, the tuba, is a modern instrument, invented in 1835. Surprisingly agile, considering the depth and weight of its tone, it was used by Wagner with great effectiveness in different pitches.

KETTLEDRUMS. Scherzo, *Ninth Symphony*   Beethoven
        Connecting passage between Third
            and Fourth movements, *Fifth
            Symphony*   Beethoven
        Enigma Variations   Elgar

The most important of the percussion instruments, these drums look like huge copper kettles covered with parchment, and are capable of being tuned to pitch. Usually there are two to four kettledrums in a modern orchestra, tuned to varying notes in order to bring out climaxes. Very often the drums are rolled to add impressiveness.

ACQUIRING ORCHESTRAL EXPERIENCE

Useful as is a knowledge of the various individual orchestral instruments, and pleasurable as the recognition of the different tone colors that go to make up the orchestral ensemble may be, the really important thing to know about the orchestra is its repertoire — the music that has been written for it. A moment's thought will show that it is no accident that a great proportion of the world's finest music has been written for this composite instrument.

Percy Buck in his fine little *History of Music* describes exactly what a musical composition is: " an attempt to express feeling in terms of sound. A man is emotionally moved by some experience, and if he is gifted with creative imagination, his irrepressible desire is to embody his feelings in a permanent form. His power to do this adequately depends upon two things only — that his imagination will suggest an idea and that his mind will know what to do with it. That is the composer's technique: the creation of an idea and the molding of it into form. And every genuine musical composition owes its existence to the fact that a man was moved and had the technique to express himself." If we attempt to make an outline of the characteristics that determine whether or not a piece of music is great, we may well follow Buck's suggestion, and consider two things: first, the material of which the music is composed, and second, the manner in which the composer treated this material.

Now it is not difficult to realize that the better the composer's material, that is, the finer the quality of his ideas (as conditioned by the depth, sincerity, and intensity of his feeling), the greater will be his need for expressing himself through the means of the most adequate technique possible. This will demand the medium of the most effective instrument possible; thus the medium through which the composer expresses his ideas is an inherent part of the value of these ideas to his hearers. There are other determining factors, but we can make the general statement that the greater the feeling of the composer, the more likely will he be to turn to an instrument which he considers the most adequate for its expression. When Beethoven was fired with a desire to write an apotheosis of the heroic in man or to express his understanding of the great books of Fate, " through which sweep the storm winds of our agitated life," he turned to the orchestra as the fittest medium for his expression, and such works as the *Third* and the *Fifth* symphonies were the result. It is impossible to think of Beethoven's heroic expression of triumph over struggle, his *Ninth Symphony,* except in terms of the orchestra; Wagner's herculean epics — such works as *Götterdämmerung* and *Die Meistersinger* — would not have been possible without the developed medium of the modern orchestra. Brahms's sublimity of conception and glow of romantic warmth find their best medium for expressive outlet through the orchestra. In the light of these facts, we may amend Ruskin's famous dictum to read: " He has produced the greatest art who has embodied in the sum of his works the greatest ideas, expressed with the most perfected technic and through the greatest means." The music that the great composers have written for the orchestra is an epitome of the finest creations of the art.

Just what is the extent of this orchestral music? And how much of this repertoire may a music lover become familiar with in a reasonable time? Is it at all possible to suggest a sort of irreducible minimum of orchestral music with which the music lover should have a listening acquaintance? These are questions that are constantly being asked those who attempt the teaching of music appreciation. They are not easily answered. For it must be remembered that the process of familiarizing oneself with all the masterpieces of orchestral music is a lifetime task, or rather a lifetime pleasure. And the making of such a list as this is a difficult process, for it opens the compiler to criticism as to its adequacies. Nevertheless it is worth trying, if for no other reason than that it crystallizes the whole question in our minds and makes us realize what a wealth of music stands ready for our acquaintance.

AN ORCHESTRAL REPERTOIRE FOR THE LISTENER

Including Transcriptions and Concertos

Johann Sebastian Bach   1685–1750
   Suite in B Minor (for flute and strings)
   Air from the *Suite in D Minor* (often called " Air for the G
      String ")
   Concerto for two violins in D minor
Josef Haydn   1732–1809
   Surprise Symphony
   Clock Symphony
   Oxford Symphony
Wolfgang A. Mozart   1756–1791
   Eine kleine Nachtmusik
   G Minor Symphony
   C Major Symphony (*Jupiter*)
Ludwig van Beethoven   1770–1827
   First Symphony in C major
   Third Symphony in E flat major
   Fifth Symphony in C minor
   Seventh Symphony in A major
   Ninth Symphony in D minor
   Piano Concerto No. 5 in E flat major (*Emperor*)
   Violin Concerto in D major
   Leonore Overture No. 3
Carl Maria von Weber   1786–1826
   Overture to *Oberon*
   Overture to *Der Freischütz*
Franz Schubert   1797–1828
   Symphony in B Minor (*Unfinished Symphony*)
   Symphony in C Major
Felix Mendelssohn   1809–1847
   Overture and Scherzo, *A Midsummer Night's Dream*
Robert Schumann   1810–1856
   Piano Concerto in A Minor
Franz Liszt   1811–1886
   Symphonic Poem: *Les Préludes*
   Faust Symphony

Richard Wagner   1813–1883
    Overture to *Rienzi*
    Overture and Bacchanale to *Tannhäuser*
    Prelude to *Lohengrin*
    Wotan's Farewell and Magic Fire Music ⎱ from *Die Walküre*
    Ride of the Valkyries ⎰
    " Siegfried Idyll "
    Siegfried's Funeral March ⎱ from *Götterdämmerung*
    Siegfried's Rhine Journey ⎰
    Prelude to *Die Meistersinger*
    Introduction to the Third Act, *Die Meistersinger*
    Prelude and Isolde's Love Death from *Tristan und Isolde*
    Prelude to *Parsifal*
    Good Friday Music from *Parsifal*

César Franck   1822–1890
    Symphony in D Minor

Johannes Brahms   1833–1897
    First Symphony in C minor
    Second Symphony in D major
    Third Symphony in F major
    Fourth Symphony in E minor
    Piano Concerto No. 1 in D minor
    Piano Concerto No. 2 in B flat major

Anton Dvořák   1841–1904
    Symphony in E Minor (From the New World)

Peter I. Tchaikovsky   1840–1893
    Fifth Symphony in E minor
    Sixth Symphony in B minor
    Piano Concerto in B flat minor

Nicholas Rimsky-Korsakoff   1844–1908
    Symphonic Suite: *Scheherazade*

Vincent d'Indy   1851–1931
    Symphonic Variations: *Istar*

Edward Elgar   1857–1934
    Enigma Variations

Claude Debussy   1862–1918
    Nocturnes 1 and 2 (Nuages, Fêtes)
    L'après-midi d'un faune
    La mer

Richard Strauss   1864–
    Symphonic Poems: *Don Juan*
                 Till Eulenspiegel
                  Don Quixote

Jean Sibelius   1865–
   Second Symphony in D major
   Fourth Symphony in A minor
   Swan of Tuonela
Igor Stravinsky   1882–
   The Firebird
   Petrouchka
   Le sacre du printemps
Maurice Ravel   1875–1937
   Daphnis et Chloé Suites No. 1 and 2
Arnold Schönberg   1874–
   Gurrelieder
   Verklärte Nacht (Transcribed for strings)
Alban Berg   1885–1936
   Concerto for Violin and Orchestra
Paul Hindemith   1895–
   Mathis der Maler
Dmitri Shostakovich   1906–
   Fifth Symphony
   Seventh Symphony

TOPICS FOR FURTHER DISCUSSION

How would you describe to a non-musician the difference (*a*) in appearance, and (*b*) in tone quality, between: oboe and clarinet; oboe and *cor anglais;* cornet and trumpet?

By means of the chart at the end of this book, trace the ancestry of the wood-wind and brass instruments.

CHAPTER XLI

Chamber Music

HISTORICAL BACKGROUND

WE have already suggested (in Chapter XXI) something of the history of the origins and early developments of chamber music; it now remains for us to have a word regarding the place which this type of composition occupies in modern musical life. Although chamber music, because of its very nature, may be said to belong peculiarly to the eighteenth century, all the great composers since that time have made important contributions to musical literature in this style. It was Haydn who, taking advantage of the experiments carried out by other men, started chamber music on the paths that it has followed ever since. Not content with having a miscellaneous grouping of varied instruments held together by a harpsichord, he definitely selected the string quartet as the form, and worked out for it certain principles which have since proved their validity for all other chamber-music combinations. First of all, he developed a form, using in general the same scheme that he had worked out for the symphony: four movements, each of them contrasting in mood and structure. Then he felt that the instruments in a small combination must be of equivalent musical capacity and on equal tonal planes. It would be useless, for instance, to match a slow-speaking, relatively awkward instrument with others more agile and facile — a double bass with a violin. Or it would be poor taste to introduce any instrument, a trumpet, for instance, that would shatter the tonal ensemble of a small group. Furthermore, and this was of great importance for future developments, the individual parts were written for each player, and every note written for the various instruments was intended to be heard as written. There was to be no mere " doubling " of parts, no filling in by an instrument such as the piano, which was liable to smear the general effect while binding it together. In the style of chamber music as initiated by Haydn there is no opportunity for filling in or thick-

412

ening up, as is the case with orchestral writing. And this is one great reason why it is extremely difficult to write good chamber music, as well as why this music is not the easiest to understand or, perhaps, at first to enjoy.

NEWER TRENDS

Later came an alteration in ideals. The conception of society as held in the eighteenth century was that there were two classes — the privileged, governing class, and the servile, governed class. This conception, by the way, had great value for the development of art, since it gave an intelligent support that otherwise would have been lacking. This assorting of society gave way under the personal aspirations of the nineteenth century, when it began to be realized that every man had a soul and a mind of his own, a right to freedom from oppression, and that there was a moral law directly opposed to the law of force. These new ideas led to the tremendous expressions that Beethoven gave us through the means of the string quartet, expressions which no composers of his time, and very few since, have been able to equal. Beethoven regarded the string quartet as the purest of all musical forms, and remained deaf to those who appealed to him to write more oratorios and opera; instead he applied himself with enthusiasm to this most difficult form of pure music.

Other composers have carried on the traditions of chamber music as they were started by Haydn. Schubert wrote some of his finest things as chamber-music works. Schumann, pianist and poet, likewise wrote chamber music with somewhat indifferent success, in spite of the real power of his thought. Johannes Brahms was one of the great composers who seemed to find this kind of music especially congenial, for he wrote twenty-four important works in this form, nearly all of them very fine. There is everywhere in his chamber music a noble elevation of ideals, a virile strength, and a depth of feeling that make it one of the glories of German art. Other writers of chamber-music works deserving mention even in such a cursory survey of the field as this are César Franck, Dvořák, Debussy, Ravel, and Schönberg, the last carrying radical tendencies into this classic field.

What is it that makes chamber music particularly appealing

to some musicians who have had a great deal of practice in listening, and equally baffling to others who have not versed themselves in the niceties of listening? There is no doubt that chamber music has gained a supreme place in the affections of many music lovers; nor is there doubt that the average listener is left cold by the lack of dramatic appeal in this music, and is puzzled by its intricacies.

Sir Henry Hadow [1] has a good word to say on this subject; he is a writer well known for his musicianship as well as for his understanding of the average listener's position:

Among all forms of composition, chamber music is that which to my taste is the most complete and satisfying. Its transparent texture makes it easy to hear and understand; one is never distracted or bewildered by overcharged sound or overemphasized emotion. And this very transparence renders it necessary that the composer's drawing should be perfect and his design sure. With a very wide range of emotion, it is vowed, in the first instance, to the sense of pure beauty — to beauty of melody, of harmonization, of structure, in which every point tells and every phrase is significant. Heine speaks of Goethe's prose as a pellucid ocean through which one can see his golden thoughts: that simile seems to me wholly suitable to the great classics of chamber-music composition.

POSSIBLE COMBINATIONS

Before giving a repertoire of characteristic chamber music, it will be well to see what combinations of instruments have been used by composers who have written in this form. German musicians seem to consider that it takes at least three instruments to constitute a chamber-music group, but the general consensus of opinion admits the duet to this classification. The usual duo combinations are those of violin and piano, or cello and piano; but many duets have been written for the piano and some wind instrument, such as horn or clarinet. Trios for piano, violin, and cello contain some of our loveliest chamber music, probably because this combination offers a fullness of tone that is unusual. Haydn, Mozart, Beethoven, Schubert, and Brahms have all written fine trios. Then there are string trios for violin, viola, and cello — a difficult combination to make effective — trios for piano, violin,

---

[1] Reprinted from Cobbett's *Cyclopedic Survey of Chamber Music*. By permission of the Oxford University Press.

and horn, for piano, clarinet, and cello, both these latter combinations having been tried by Brahms with great success.

In the string quartet for two violins, viola, and cello we have, as has been said, the purest and highest form of chamber music, perhaps of all music. There are, however, other quartets for piano and strings (violin, viola, and cello), but this combination does not rank with the pure string quartet for beauty of tone, since the use of the piano necessarily confines the other players to its tempered intonation. String quintets are very little different from quartets, the extra instrument being either another viola (Mozart has given us the outstanding work for this combination) or a cello. Both Mozart and Brahms have written quintets combining the clarinet with the string quartet; and there are popular piano quintets, notably those of Schubert (the *Forellen Quintet*) and Schumann. Composers have attempted to write for groups of five wind instruments, such as flute, oboe, clarinet, horn, and bassoon. Brahms has given us two great string sextets — for two violins, two violas, and two cellos.

There are many different combinations for other instruments, most of them grouping the strings with one or more wind instruments: Schönberg's beautiful sextet *Verklärte Nacht* and his *Pierrot Lunaire* (for piano, flute [piccolo], clarinet, violin, cello, and voice); Stravinsky's *Trois poésies de la lyrique Japonaise* (voice, piano, flute, clarinet, and string quartet) indicate the trend of modern ideas as to possible chamber-music combinations.

Something of the difficulty of selecting a listening repertoire of chamber music may be realized if we say that Beethoven left about 95 compositions in this medium, Brahms 24, Haydn over 80 quartets, Mozart over 30 quartets. Nevertheless it will be helpful to attempt such a compilation, if for no other reason than to show the riches that are available.

A CHAMBER-MUSIC REPERTOIRE [2]

DUETS

Mozart: *Sonata for Violin and Piano in B Flat Major*
Beethoven: *Sonata for Violin and Piano in A Major* (*Kreutzer*), Op. 47
  Sonata for Violin and Piano in G Major, Op. 96

[2] All the works mentioned have been recorded.

Brahms: *Sonata for Violin and Piano in A Major*, Op. 100

This is one of Brahms's most lyrical works.

Sonata for Violin and Piano in G Major, Op. 78

Op. 78 is quite the opposite of Op. 100 — dramatic, impassioned in utterance.

César Franck: *Sonata for Violin and Piano in A Major*

Here is one of the best-known violin sonatas, full of mystic power.

Grieg: *Sonata for Violin and Piano in A Minor*, Op. 45

Probably the best example of this composer's style, it is lyrical and melancholy — " A monument in the sonata literature of the north."

TRIOS

Schubert: *Trio in B Flat Major*, Op. 99

This is a beautiful introduction to chamber-music literature.

Brahms: *Trio for Piano, Violin, and Horn*, Op. 40

An interesting combination, this shows Brahms's love for dark colors and emotional depths.

Dvořák: *Trio in E Minor*, Op. 90 (*Dumky*)

Really a suite with folk flavor, this trio has alternating bursts of melancholy and gaiety.

Poulenc: *Trio for Oboe, Bassoon, and Piano*

An excellent example of modern tendencies that are based upon solid foundations, this trio is full of pungent discords and interesting color combinations.

QUARTETS

Haydn: *Quartet in F Major*, Op. 3, No. 5 (with Serenade)

Quartet in D Major, Op. 64, No. 5 (*The Lark*)

Quartet in G Major, Op. 77, No. 1

These show Haydn at an early, a mature, and a late period.

Mozart: *Quartet in C Major*

One of the standard works in the repertoire, it has a surprisingly modern introduction.

Beethoven: *Quartet 1, 2, or 4*, Op. 18

Of the set of six in Op. 18, these three are the most representative; they belong to Beethoven's early period.

Quartet in F Major, Op. 59, No. 1

This is the first of the three Rasoumovsky quartets, dedicated to a Russian count and employing Russian folk themes. It contrasts with Op. 18 in reflecting a more mature sense of the tragic quality of life.

Quartet in B Flat Major, Op. 130

One of Beethoven's last works, this quartet is in six movements. There is wild grandeur and restrained emotion; " here the boundary

between life and music is effaced. Experience, not analysis, is demanded "
(Cobbett).

Schubert: *Quartet in D Minor* (*Death and the Maiden*)

The slow movement is based upon one of the composer's songs: the
whole is a brooding on the subject of death.

César Franck: *Quartet in D Major*

This is Franck's only quartet; it is of considerable length and
complexity.

Debussy: *Quartet in G Minor*, Op. 10

Debussy's only attempt at chamber music, this is a fine example
of the use of the absolute forms with impressionistic medium.

Hindemith: *Quartet Number Three*, Op. 22

Here is modern music in a very personal style; it is most interesting.

QUINTETS

Scarlatti: *Quintet for Flute and Strings*

The authorship of this is somewhat doubtful, but it is a charming example of the chamber music of the period of Johann Sebastian
Bach.

Mozart: *Quintet in G Minor*

This is the finest work in Mozart's chamber music.

Schubert: *Quintet in C Major*, Op. 163 (for strings, with two cellos)

" The most romantically conceived work in all chamber music; from
the lyrical and dramatic point of view nothing so ideally perfect has
ever been written for strings as this inexpressibly lovely work " (Cobbett).

Schumann: *Piano Quintet in E Flat Major*, Op. 44

This is the freshest and most spontaneous of this composer's works.

Brahms: *Piano Quintet in F Minor*, Op. 34

     Clarinet Quintet in B Minor, Op. 115

Here are good examples of Brahms's sublimity of thought.

Bloch: *Quintet for Piano and String Quartet*

TOPICS FOR FURTHER DISCUSSION

Discuss the influence of the eighteenth-century European society
upon the development of music as an art, and the possible influence of
the society of today upon composition and performance in the future.

Why did chamber music develop so largely in Germany, and not
in Italy?

Would you give a non-musician his first introduction to the art
through chamber music, or preferably through some other medium?
Why?

SUGGESTIONS FOR READING

See Chapter XXI of this book, and in addition:
The Chamber Music of Brahms, Mason. (New York and London: Macmillan)
Beethoven, The Man Who Freed Music, Schauffler. (New York: Doubleday, Doran)
    (Chapters XLI, XLII, XLIV, XLV, XLVII, XLIX)

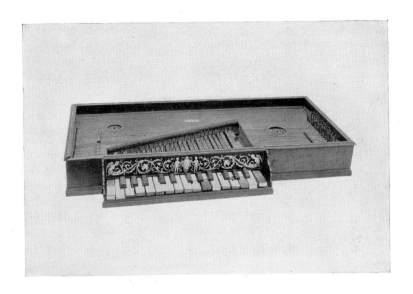

CLAVICHORD, GERMAN, *circa* 1533

A direct descendant of the Monochord. Usually of four octaves, its keys were fitted with blades of brass called " tangents " to strike the string and divide it, producing at the same time tone and pitch. Clavichords had a soft, hesitating tone.

SPINET, ITALIAN, SEVENTEENTH CENTURY

The "Plectra" or quills fitted into the jacks set the strings into vibration by plucking them. With one string to each note, volume was small and instruments of this type were in general incapable of dynamic modification of tone by differences in touch.

CHAPTER XLII

The Piano

THE HISTORY OF THE PIANO FAMILY

KEYBOARD instruments have been popular throughout the development of modern European music, and with good reason. For they have been fairly accessible for players everywhere, and they are comparatively easy to play. The accuracy of ear that is so necessary for the players of instruments like the violin, the cello, and the trombone is not an important factor in the case of the keyboard instruments. Players of the organ, the piano, and the harpsichord find their tones already formed for them, and their ability as players depends upon their powers of coordination and manual dexterity.

Our present-day piano is a logical descendant of two types of earlier keyboard instruments, the clavichord and the harpsichord. These forerunners of the piano were themselves the result of the attempt, somewhere about the fifteenth century, to produce tone from the existing stringed instruments by means of a keyboard or clavier, each key of which would set in vibration one string. In the clavichord type, the tone was produced by means of metal tangents that were fixed to the end of a long lever, on the other end of which was the key. These tangents were forced up against the string when the key was depressed, making a delicate, metallic sort of tone, well suited to a small room but quite lost in a large one. Since the tone could be varied in volume (for the harder one hit the key, the firmer was the tangent forced against the string) and had a sympathetic quality, this instrument was a favorite of musicians for several centuries. The harpsichord (in its smaller forms it was called *spinet* or *virginal*) tone was louder and more definite; but it was incapable of direct control as to volume. It was produced by mechanically plucking the string by means of a plectrum made of quill or leather inserted in the action; this gave a twangy, guitar-like quality of tone that

419

had considerable power, especially when the instrument was of concert size. But the incapability of direct variation in tonal power of this instrument led the makers to seek a new type, one that would give a brilliant tone and yet that would be able to play both softly and loudly. In the early part of the eighteenth century Cristofori, an Italian clavier maker, announced that he had perfected such an instrument, a *gravicembalo col piano e forte* — a harpsichord that could play both soft and loud. But Cristofori's instrument was not a harpsichord, for the tone was produced by means of small hammers which struck the strings; it did what Cristofori claimed, however, and the name stuck. The century following the announcement of this invention was given over to improving the action of the instrument, largely by German and English makers. In the first part of the nineteenth century Broadwood, an English maker, supplied pedals which made possible the sustaining of the tones generated by the strings, as well as softening them. The problems of stringing the piano so as to produce the maximum of richness and depth of tone were among the most important that the later makers had to solve. In the early years of the nineteenth century American manufacturers invented a complete iron frame which was capable of withstanding a tension of thirty tons, and in 1853 steel wire instead of iron wire began to be used, allowing a much greater string tension and thus improving the tone immeasurably. The development of our modern Gargantuan instrument has been a gradual one, but it seems now to have reached the stage where further improvement seems improbable.

THE PIANO — BOON AND BANE

The piano — its full and formal title is the pianoforte — may rightly be called the universal musical instrument. Although, as we have already suggested, it was the typical instrument of the nineteenth century, its popularity has lasted well into our own time and programs of piano music are greeted with great enthusiasm during every modern concert season. There is good reason for this popularity. For not only has the piano one of the richest repertoires of any instrument, but it can on occasion assume that of other instruments, be they voice, violin, orchestra, or organ.

HARPSICHORD, ITALIAN, *circa* 1680

The most important keyed instrument of the eighteenth century, in form and arrangement resembling a grand piano. Usually of four to five octaves with two or three strings to each note. A jack and quill action gave individuality of tone, some power, but lacking in expressive character through touch. Used more in the orchestra than as a solo instrument.

"Piano e Forte," Christofori's, Italian

The Dulcimer was the prototype of the Piano, and Christofori's invention of the hammer action about 1710 gave this instrument more power and a wide dynamic range. The hammer and its escapement provided the foundation for subsequent improvements in France, Germany, and England.

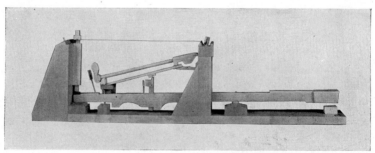

Courtesy of Steinway and Sons, New York

It is one of the few instruments capable of furnishing not only a
solo part but a harmonic accompaniment also, one that is sometimes of great complexity; in this way it functions as an instrument as the violin, clarinet, or trombone never can. It is as well
suited to the demands of the virtuoso as to those of the modest
amateur — both find in it a satisfying medium for the convey-
ance of their ideas and the display of their abilities. It is, as Fox-
Strangways has said, the boon as well as the bane of present-day
music, for with all its ingratiating qualities, the piano lacks a soul
of its own. And this is a fact that with instruments as with people
we realize only gradually and upon long acquaintance. The piano
is like a brilliant friend who seems master of every situation in
which he finds himself, attractive in personality, versatile in con-
versation, brilliant in wit, and yet when we really get to know
him, one who reveals himself as having no personality of his own.
" The piano is a first-rate actor: it can assume any part and make
a good thing of it — sing, dance, prattle, argue, storm, wail, and
do all these things in different voices." But all the time its percussive tone is incapable of being modified or prolonged to any
appreciable extent. Once the piano tone has been produced by the
hammers which set its strings vibrating, there is no way of pro-
longing, shading, or otherwise altering the tone. The only thing
that can be done is to produce another tone having the desired
change. This is a serious handicap, for certainly the long drawn
melody is the soul of music. In order to have that sense of continuity — of going on — that is the very essence of its life, music
must consist of more than short, choppy phrases such as are suggested by the quickly fading tones of the piano. A composer for
the orchestra can make use of its power for sustaining tone, its im-
mense range of different degrees of power, its infinite possibilities
of combining different tone colors. A writer for the piano must
not only recognize the incapacities of his instrument in these respects; he must find means to overcome them and to suggest to the
hearer more than is actually transmitted to the ear by inferring
things of which the instrument is not actually capable. In other
words, the writer of music for the piano has had to evolve a style
of writing which takes advantage of the instrument's peculiar
characteristics — ease and facility of handling, which means that
there must be plenty of fast and brilliant passages in piano writing; the attaining of great elasticity in accent through the ability

of the player directly to emphasize any note or group of notes he plays, which means that piano music must have plenty of rhythmic appeal. But these are not enough in themselves. Music written to exploit these rather crude possibilities alone would make the pianoforte one of the most objectionable instruments ever invented and one of the most potent depravers of human taste imaginable. The piano, Jekyll and Hyde among instruments, can also sing angelically — fit interpreter for a Chopin or for a Franck.

Indeed the attempt to remedy these natural handicaps of piano tone has resulted in the only individual contributions that it has made to the world's great musical literature. For in spite of the fact that since 1850, the date when the modern form of the instrument may well be said to have been perfected, piano music has been one of the most frequent forms of composition, there have been only a few great composers who have made essential contributions to piano literature — who have written music that would be unthinkable on any other instrument. And these few — Schumann, Liszt, Chopin, Debussy, and Ravel — have recognized the shortcomings of the instrument; but they have done more — they have used these shortcomings to the advantage of their own piano style. All the other great composers have, with very few exceptions, written voluminously for the piano; but in so doing they have convinced us that they could express themselves better through other instruments — the orchestra, or perhaps the string quartet.

THE RESOURCES OF THE PIANO

What are these characteristics of music peculiarly indigenous to the piano? A little practical experimenting will help to answer such a question. Go to a good piano and strike a full chord, holding down the keys after the hammers have produced the tone; the notes will sound with gradually diminishing tone until the strings have entirely ceased to vibrate. Now strike the same chord again, at the same time holding down the damper pedal (the one to the right) and remove your fingers from the keys as soon as the hammers have struck. Exactly the same result will follow, for the pedal locks off the strings the dampers belonging to the keys that have been struck, thus allowing them to vibrate until they cease of their own inanition. The natural function of these dampers when they are not acted upon by the pedal is to clamp down on the string as soon as the player removes his finger from the key, and thus stop further vibration and consequent mixing of tones. Now, holding down the damper pedal, play the same chord in varying parts of the keyboard — low, medium, and high; or better still, break it up into an arpeggio. Notice how this sustains the tone, giving it a semblance of the same notes being prolonged; it is this plan of playing scales and arpeggios and ornamental passages so as to give the idea of sustained utterance that is one of the cardinal principles of good writing for the piano. Liszt and his followers developed this idea to such an extent and with such virtuosity of technic, massing chord upon chord in such reckless profusion and producing such climaxes of cascading tone as to make the piano seem almost like a sonant instrument.

Now try another experiment: while sounding the arpeggio of any common chord on the piano with the damper pedal down, introduce a few notes that do not belong to this chord; notice what such a procedure does to the *color* of the result, provided the added notes are not too discordant. There seems to be a new richness of *timbre*; and it is this introduction of a sort of shimmer and iridescence to piano music by the inclusion of just the right notes in his runs and arpeggios that was Chopin's great contribution to piano writing. Listening to his romantic Preludes or Nocturnes, we are almost persuaded that the piano is not a monochromatic instrument. Robert Schumann was the great Romanticist of piano music; he loved to dream " with the pedal down, and came nearer than anyone else ever has to finding a soul in the piano. He seized upon its peculiar capacities and gave it what others would have given to the orchestra, and not entirely unsuccessfully — far more successfully than when he gave to the orchestra what he should have given to the piano." His short pieces *Aufschwung* ("Soaring") and *Warum?* ("Why?"), or the *Romance*, Opus 28, No. 2, will give the hearer an idea of this composer's love of blended chords and poetic thought. The evanescent quality of the piano and its capacity for blending and mixing tone by the use of the damper pedal make it the ideal instrument for playing impressionistic music. And men like Debussy and Ravel were able to wash in their colors with broad sweeps and blur their outlines without making them so indistinct as to lose character. Debussy's *Clair de lune* from the *Suite Bergamasque,* or his *Jardins sous la pluie,* or any of his Preludes, as well as Ravel's *Pavane pour une infante défunte* or *Jeux d'eau,* illustrates the adaptability of the piano for this type of music. There are many who think, indeed, that this kind of writing shows the piano at its best.

WHEN IS A PIANO NOT A PIANO?

The most recent attempt to remedy the inherent weakness of the piano's method of producing tone is the "Neo-Bechstein," an instrument which, once the strings have been set in vibration by the hammers, conveys these impulses by means of electromagnets to a loud speaker, through which the tone is produced. This piano has a swell pedal like that of an organ, which allows a note to be increased or diminished at will, thus doing away with the aforementioned ancient defect of the piano as an instrument. The new device requires more legato fingering, and its tone has some decided differences from that of the normal instrument.

A REPERTOIRE OF PIANO MUSIC

The compiling of a repertoire of piano music for the listener is a difficult task because of the enormous quantity and the very variable quality of the material. Most of the early music now played by pianists was written for other instruments and so loses some of its character when transcribed for our modern concert pianos. Nevertheless some of it is decidedly worth acquaintance, notably Bach's *Chromatic Fantasia and Fugue* [1] and the forty-eight Preludes and Fugues in his *Well-tempered Clavichord*. Someone has well called these latter the Old Testament of the pianist's Bible. The following are good ones to hear first:

Volume I   No. 8 in E flat minor [1]
            No. 21 in B flat major [1]
            No. 22 in B flat minor
Volume II No. 9 in E major

Other selections from this early music are:

"Harmonious Blacksmith" [1]   Handel

[1] Indicates that the music has been recorded.

Leçons:

Soeur Monique [1] and *Les baricades mistérieuses* [1]	Couperin
Sonatas in A major [1] and A minor [1]	Scarlatti

A great deal of Haydn's and Mozart's piano music is dated, probably because of the fact that it was written for a piano that was quite a different instrument from that which we use; but we can become acquainted with the general style of this music through such works as:

Fantasia in C Minor [1]	Mozart
Sonata in A Minor [1]	Mozart
Sonata in A Major [1] (starting with theme and variations)	Mozart
Sonata in E Flat, No. 1 [1]	Haydn

Beethoven's great contribution to piano literature was his set of sonatas, thirty-two in all; these may be called the New Testament of the aforementioned pianist's Bible. They vary considerably in quality; perhaps the following may be said to be the most representative of the different periods in this composer's development:

Sonata in C Minor, Op. 13 (*Pathetic*) [1]
Sonata in A Flat, Op. 26 [1]
Sonata in C Sharp Minor, Op. 27, No. 2 (*Moonlight*) [1]
Sonata in C Major, Op. 53 (*Waldstein*) [1]
Sonata in E Flat, Op. 81a (*Les adieux*) [1]
Sonata in A Flat Major, Op. 110 [1]

Schubert wrote a great deal of piano music, but it has all been overshadowed by the works of other men; his great contributions to musical literature were in the fields of song, chamber music, and symphony. Schumann is one of the pianist's stand-bys. His music can hardly be called great, but it is very idiomatic and comes off well on the instrument. His most played works are:

Carnaval [1]
Études symphoniques [1]
Soaring [1]
Prophet Bird [1]

The same may be said of Liszt's piano music; he was probably the greatest player of the piano that ever lived, and he wrote many things for his favorite instrument that today seem cheap and tawdry, their principal value being that they provide an opportunity for the display of a pianist's virtuosity. But there are some fine things in his tremendous output of piano music; the following may be mentioned:

Sonata in B Minor [1]
Au bord d'une source [1]
La Campanella [1]
Concert Study in D flat [1]
Weinen Klagen [1]

Chopin represents the high-water mark of the development of the instrument, and since his time nothing new has been added to its potentialities other than the impressionist's use of color. Chopin's works represent every possible style and mood, and a great many of them have been recorded. The following are very characteristic and may be said to be representative of the various types of his works:

Sonata No. 2 in B flat minor, Op. 35 [1]
Ballade No. 1 in G minor, Op. 23 [1]
Scherzo No. 3 in C sharp minor, Op. 39 [1]
Fantasie in F minor, Op. 49 [1]
Études, Op. 10:
    In E major, No. 3 [1]
    In C minor, No. 12 [1]
Études, Op. 25:
    In A flat, No. 1 [1]
    In G flat, No. 9 [1]
Preludes, Op. 28:
    In C major, No. 1 [1]
    In F sharp minor, No. 8 [1]
    In B flat minor, No. 16 [1]
    In D minor, No. 24 [1]
Waltzes:
    In A flat major, Op. 34, No. 1 [1]
    In C sharp minor, Op. 64, No. 2 [1]
Mazurka in F sharp minor, Op. 6, No. 1 [1]
Polonaises:
    In E flat minor, Op. 26, No. 2 [1]
    In A major, Op. 40, No. 1 [1]
Nocturnes:
    In F sharp major, Op. 15, No. 2 [1]

In G minor, Op. 37, No. 1 [1]
In G major, Op. 37, No. 2 [1]
Barcarolle in F sharp major, Op. 60 [1]

Although César Franck was all his life an organist, he wrote one or two great things that are essentially pianistic in thought and execution:

Prelude, Chorale, and Fugue [1]
Prelude, Aria, and Finale [1]

Brahms expressed some of his finest thoughts of later life through the medium of the piano. A few representative examples of his style are:

Ballade in D Minor, No. 1 [1]
Ballade in D Major, No. 2 [1]
Ballade in G Minor, Op. 118, No. 3 [1]
A number of shorter piano pieces in Op. 116–119 (some recorded).

We have already mentioned most of the important works of the impressionists Debussy and Ravel for the piano; these additional things by Debussy will be of interest in showing how indigenous to the instrument are these impressionistic compositions:

La cathédrale engloutie [1]
Minstrels [1]

Practically all of the more recent writers have paid homage to the piano: MacDowell, the American, wrote his best works for it; the Spaniards Albeniz and Granados have composed pleasant piano pieces, as have men like Rachmaninoff (who, by the way, *has* written other Preludes than the one in C sharp minor!) and Scriabin. Some typical pieces of Romantic piano music are:

Three Sonatas, Op. 30, 53, 70 [1]	Scriabin
Two Sonatas: *Norse* and *Tragic*	MacDowell
Sea Pieces	MacDowell
Ballade, Op. 24 [1]	Grieg
Piano Sonata, Op. 7	Grieg
Moy Mell (two pianos) [1]	Bax
Sonata (two pianos) [1]	Bax
Suite: *Iberia* (some items recorded)	Albeniz
Goyescas	Granados

Contemporary piano music we leave entirely alone, as providing material that is too controversial for our present purpose.

TOPICS FOR FURTHER DISCUSSION

What are the chief differences in action between the clavichord and the harpsichord? Do you think there might be any future for the former (in view of its very gentle tone) in a world of thin-walled apartments?

Can you imagine any further developments of the keyboard instruments in the line suggested by the Neo-Bechstein piano?

Discuss the history of piano making in this country.

Owing to the present vogue for radios, the manufacture of pianos has been greatly curtailed. Do you think the piano will " come back "?

SUGGESTIONS FOR READING

Chopin's Musical Style, Abraham. (New York and London: Oxford)

Chopin, the Man and His Music, Huneker. (New York: Scribner)

The Romantic Composers, Mason. (New York and London: Macmillan)

The History of Pianoforte Music, Westerby. (New York: Dutton; London: Routledge)

The Pianoforte and Its Music, Krehbiel. (New York: Scribner)

History of the Pianoforte and Pianoforte Players, Bie. (New York: Dutton; London: Dent)

CHAPTER XLIII

The Organ[1]

THE KING OF INSTRUMENTS

A RECENT writer on musical subjects laments the fact that a modern performer on the organ is not regarded by critics and concert-goers as in the same artistic class as a Cortot, a Casals, or a Kreisler. " Lists of virtuosi in various branches of music invariably omit mention of the organist with the same regularity as the critic demurs from listening to his playing or treating his instrument with serious regard." Anyone familiar with the musical situation will readily confirm the truth of this statement and at the same time wonder why such things be. For the organ, one of the most ancient of instruments, has always been held in a certain esteem by music lovers: grand, sublime, impressive, inspiring — these are the adjectives which have been used from time immemorial in characterizing the tone of this King of Instruments. As an ancient writer puts it: " When its tones swell forth, there is no denying it, it is like the fiat of the Omnipotent." And a modern lover of the organ thus apostrophizes it:

> Temple of Tone art thou! The shrine supreme
> Of sound's mysterious powers and richest gifts,
> God-given thought alone could have inspired
> The human mind to frame so grand a work!
> Great Organ — Monarch of all Instruments.
>
> George Ashdowne Audsley [2]

Why then the musical public's lack of interest? The writer quoted above suggests that the low standard of playing in vogue among organists until recently has been largely responsible; but there are other and remediable causes for the lack of general interest in the organ and its music.

[1] Partly reprinted from *Disques* by permission of the publishers, H. Royer Smith Company.

[2] By permission of J. Fischer & Bro.

429

The impressive, soul-satisfying dignity of the organ's tone is a result of the manner in which it is produced, not by means of beating reed or vibrating string, but by metal and wooden pipes blown, as Emperor Julian described it in the fourth century, " by a blast that rushes up from a leathern cavern beneath their roots, while a mortal running with swift fingers over the keys that are their concordant rulers makes them give forth melodious sounds." In principle the organ is nothing more than a mechanical means for playing a Pan's Pipe or syrinx — one of the earliest of all instruments, consisting of tubes of varying lengths bound together in such a way that they could be blown upon by the player's breath. In the organ the air is supplied mechanically and its admittance to the pipes controlled by means of keys, one of them for each pitch produced. In order to produce varied qualities of tone, the pipes are made in different ways and whole sets of them, one for each note on the keyboard, used for certain qualities of tone desired. In order to build up a suitable ensemble these various sets of pipes are used together, so that oftentimes when a single key is depressed in a large organ it gives breath to as many as fifty or sixty pipes of different sorts all sounding the same note, or its octaves or other ratio notes.

A VARIED HISTORY

The broadly elevated character inherent in organ tone was early recognized by the Christians as being ideal for providing music in their services, and this in spite of its unfortunate associations in so far as they were concerned; for it had been used by the Romans for theatrical and gladiatorial spectacles. Ever since the fourth century, however, its most natural and fitting place has been in the church, especially since the magnificent interiors supplied by the early church builders were ideal places for the proper hearing of organ tone. As ecclesiastical architecture grew more and more magnificent and the church interiors vaster and vaster, those responsible for providing organs for these buildings experimented with various means for flooding these great churches with tone, and the organ's mechanism became more and more elaborate in order to provide adequate tonal resources. It was not until the seventeenth and early eighteenth centuries that the development of the mechanics of organ building allowed the builders to attain their ideal in providing an ensemble completely suitable for their purpose. The organs of these years, in spite of crudities of mechanical control when compared to our modern instruments, were able to provide a rich, satisfying, thrilling tone which sounded to wonderful advantage in the resonant interiors available. And, as has always been the case in similar circumstances, composers were inspired to provide suitable music, once the instrument became capable of playing it. The organ of those days was an important, living, vital instrument in the sense that it hardly is today. Johann Sebastian Bach, one of the supremely great, was providing it with a repertoire which in extent and quality has never been equaled. It had arrived at a point of perfection in its tonal development that has not been greatly improved upon in the years since, and had the advantage of adequate and proper surroundings into which to project its glorious voice.

Since then the organ has fallen on rather evil days, especially as far as most instruments in America are concerned. Although most European builders have followed more or less closely the ideals of the eighteenth century in developing their instruments and have had the incalculable advantage of proper auditoriums for their organs, those following what has come to be known as the " modern trend " have forsaken the sunny fields of adequate, dignified tone and wandered astray into ear-tickling and sensation-mongering paths. This has been partly due to the small, stuffy, " parlor " churches which so many societies have seen fit to provide in order to secure homey, social surroundings for their services. Organ tone, because of its peculiar quality, demands a certain amount of reverberation — echo, to use an everyday term — to make it completely effective. And because this enlivening influence has been impossible in churches of wood and plaster, it was natural that the organ builders and players should turn their attention to effects that could come off in these unresonant surroundings. Soft, enervated tones, effects borrowed from the orchestra, string, wood-wind, and brass imitations, percussive, harp, and chime tones, all of them justifiable in themselves but only as subsidiary to essential organ tone, became the rule. Many of our present-day instruments are built up of a rather miscellaneous collection of these pleasing effects, and the glorious richness and dignified strength which should be provided above all things is likely to be forgotten. And, as was again inevitable, a school of organ composition suitable to these conditions has arisen, and we have the rather pitiable spectacle of the King of Instruments being called upon to discourse sobbing accompaniments or else to produce orchestra-like imitation unsuited to its natural dignity.

THE AUDITORIUM AN IMPORTANT FACTOR

The importance of the character of the auditorium into which an organ sounds cannot be overestimated. Technically speaking, the auditorium is an acoustical device of great importance to any instrument, orchestra, piano, voice, as well as organ. Its chief purpose in so far as music is concerned is to enable persons assembled to hear what occurs in it to best advantage. And the very fact that so many architects have been ignorant or perhaps negligent regarding the action of sound phenomena within confined spaces has given us so many very bad auditoriums. If these are not properly constructed, a resultant echo caused by the reflection of the sound pulsations from the various wall surfaces will so confuse the music being produced as to make it an unpleasant jangle of discordant elements, and thereby destroy its beauty. On the other hand, if every bit of reverberation is removed (as used to be done in a broadcasting studio) the music will sound lifeless and dead to the auditors who are somewhat removed from its source. This period of reverberation is more important for organ tone than for that of any other instrument; and a certain amount of echo, even an amount that would somewhat confuse other types of musical tone, is necessary if we are to get the power and thrill of the full organ as well as the beautiful floating quality possible from some of the softer tones. Those who have heard a properly designed organ speaking into a fine, large, resonant interior, playing the type of music really suited to the character of the instrument, know what organ tone should sound like. Unfortunately the coincidence of these necessary factors in the production of good tone is rare; and so many of us, critics as well as laymen, have never heard great organ music as it may sound, although we are surrounded on every side by instruments that are supposed to produce it. Practically every church in the country possesses one, they are being placed in many auditoriums in all the large cities, and the wailing tones of a certain species of them greet our ears almost continuously on the radio.

Fortunately architects, organ builders, and players are all seeing the light, and in recent years we have had some interiors that are almost ideal for sound; and there is a gradual but certain swing away from the rather theatrical ideals of tonal appointments that have prevailed in recent years back to those of the classic period. Young players are coming to the fore, equipped with splendid technic and possessing high musical ideals, ready to take advantage of the changes which impend. Perhaps we are on the verge of a renaissance in organ music.

Rhythm and Repertoire

There are two factors, however, that mitigate against the organ's becoming a popular instrument in the sense that the piano or the orchestra is one. The first of these is its essentially unrhythmic character. Organ tone by nature is broad, thick, rather unsuitable for any change in pulse; and there is an added difficulty for the organist who strives to maintain a good rhythmic flow in his playing — the mechanical obstacles he must overcome in obtaining accent, the chief means by which rhythm is attained. When a pianist wishes to accentuate a particular note, he does so by extra pressure on the key; the violinist obtains the same effect by a stronger pressure on his bow. But no such direct means are available to the organist. He has to resort to subterfuge, for the only way he can produce accent is by suddenly increasing his tone by the addition of extra stops (an awkward mechanical feat), or by opening the shutters which enclose a group of pipes in a " swell box," thus swelling the tone at the particular place desired, or by breaking the flow of the music so as to give at least a suggestion of pulse. The continuously flowing, largely unaccented tone of the organ, lacking definite percussive quality, becomes confusing to those who are more familiar with orchestral or chamber music.

The other serious handicap of the organ is its lack of repertoire. Whereas instruments such as the piano, the string quartet, and the orchestra have had compositions written for them by such masters as Beethoven, Haydn, Brahms, Chopin, Schubert, Schumann, and so on — and in prodigious amounts — the organ has to fall back upon the works of two writers for its really *great* music: Johann Sebastian Bach and César Franck. And even in the case of these two men, the amount of music available is limited. Practically all the other great masters through a combination of circumstances left the organ severely alone. To be sure, Handel has left us some organ music, but like so much of his other work, it is outmoded today; Brahms wrote a few lovely things; Mendelssohn and Rheinberger (neither of whom by any stretch of the imagination could be called great) wrote their best music for the organ. The more recent Germans include Max Reger, who left behind a plethora of involved works interesting largely from the viewpoint of construction, and Karg-Elert, who has given us some well-written program music. And there are the rather pretentious works of the modern French writers, men like Widor, Vierne, and Tournemire, who surround a few interesting pages with stretches of rather disappointing wastes. This limits the repertoire of the organist, unless he falls back upon transcriptions of music originally written for other instruments. A serious handicap, of course, and one which probably precludes the organ from becoming a concert instrument in the full sense of the term unless we come into an unexpected period of fecundity on the part of writers of organ music. Most of the great things that have been written for the organ are suggestive of its religious associations, and its place for many years will probably be in the church, where it sounds at its best.

MECHANICAL PROBLEMS

The problems involved in the development of our modern organ have been three: (1) securing a satisfactory composite tone from a large number of pipes sounding together; (2) obtaining a satisfactory means of controlling the admittance of the air to the pipes by the mechanism of the keys; and (3) perfecting a satisfactory wind supply. All these problems were present in the organ of the Alexandrian, Ctesibius, which was built about 250 B.C. and had rows of bronze pipes controlled by slides connected to iron keys by ropes. They are still in process of development today, for our tonal ideas, as has been suggested, are in a state of flux, and the elaborate electrical mechanisms which

From an etching

THE ORGAN

In its most effective location, placed high in a large, resonant stone church.

have been devised for connecting key and valve controlling the admittance of air to the pipe are not satisfactory in every respect. The early organs in the cathedrals had large keys which were connected by means of ropes and shafts to slides or valves under the pipes; these slides or valves had metal springs to pull them shut when the pressure was removed from the key. Such a crude mechanism was in essence that of our modern organs, but was very difficult to manipulate because it had to work against the wind pressure ready to enter the pipes, and the only way the keys could be depressed was by striking them. And so organ players came to be known as organ beaters, a name they have not entirely lived down today. When more than one note at a time was to be played, a second beater was brought into action, and as can be readily imagined, harmony as we consider it today was quite impossible on these instruments. The providing of wind for these crude instruments was a formidable task; a Winchester chronicler thus describes the organ — an instrument of some four hundred pipes — in his cathedral: there were " ten each to one of forty slides, for which the wind supply came from twenty-six bellows in two rows at which seventy strong men did labor with their arms and covered with the effects of their efforts, yet did each incite his fellows to drive up the wind with all their might." Playing, blowing, and listening to the organ must have been equally strenuous in those days!

In these medieval instruments, there was no way to prevent all the pipes grouped on the slide and controlled by a single key from sounding when that key was depressed; one had to have all or nothing. But in the sixteenth century a Dutch builder invented the " stop," a mechanism which controls the air supply to each set of pipes. If the player pulls out the little lever placed at the side or above the keyboard, the particular set of pipes governed by that lever will sound; if the lever is pushed in, the air supply to that set of pipes is shut off and they remain silent. The same mechanism, called by the same name, is in use today.

There came to be various divisions in the big cathedral organs, developed according to the demands made upon them; each of these divisions was played by means of its own keyboard. Hence we have the two, three, four, or five keyboards or " manuals " in the present-day instrument. We still call one manual the *great*, meaning that the loud stops representing the old medieval organ are largely grouped on this manual. The *swell* division derives its name from the device already mentioned, invented in the early eighteenth century, by means of which the pipes are placed in a box fitted with shutters which can be opened or closed by a pedal, thus giving the organist a means for swelling or diminishing the tone. The *choir* organ is suggestive of the days when this group of pipes was placed at the back of the player (the Germans still call this division the *rückpositiv*) and used to accompany the choir; it consists of the softer stops and provides a pleasant contrast to the tone of the other manuals. The stops which are used *a solo,* that is, by having some particular quality of tone standing out from a softer accompaniment, are grouped on a fourth manual called the *solo* organ. The *pedal* was probably first developed in the fifteenth century and provides a sustained bass to the whole ensemble; this device was later supplemented by the development of an independent pedal organ with pipes of its own, most of them of large size and providing the deep bass which we always associate with organ tone.

The mechanism of this complex instrument for centuries consisted of delicately adjusted levers between the keys and the pipe valves, once the crude early slides and ropes were done away with. Later, because it required too much physical strength from the player's fingers to actuate this mechanism, engineers devised means of doing the actual work of pulling down the pipe valves by small pneumatic bellows. And at the present time the whole mechanism is controlled electrically, so that the organist's touch upon the keys actually completes an electric circuit which in turn actuates a small pneumatic motor regulating the wind supply to the pipe. All this has been so perfected that the response is practically instantaneous once the key is depressed. The problem of wind supply which once was such a troublesome one has likewise been satisfactorily solved; the modern organ is blown by large rotary fans actuated by electric motors, thus giving an absolutely steady and dependable supply of air.

THE ORGAN'S TRUE GLORY

The quality of tone emitted by the pipes depends upon the way they are constructed, their size, the proportion of length to diameter, the materials used, and so forth. This is where art enters the organ industry, for the designing and constructing of the various sets of pipes condition the tonal result of the whole instrument. Music lovers are apt to think of the organ builder as a sort of glorified mechanic; in reality he should be a consummate artist as well as a thorough craftsman. The tendency of modern builders until recently has been so to concentrate their attention upon the mechanical and electrical side of the organ's development as to neglect its tonal improvement. In other words, they became so fascinated with the means that they almost forgot the end for which all the mechanism exists — the production of a glorious blend of tone, brilliant without being harsh, thrilling without being overpowering, masterful and compelling, soothing and appealing in turn, the sort of tone which rightfully belongs to the organ and which cannot be obtained from any other instrument; the sort of tone which not only causes the thrills up and down the spine, but which as well leads closer to the Infinite. Rolland describes such an effect upon Jean Christophe when he hears his first organ music. He is in church with his grandfather; suddenly there is a deluge of sound from the organ. He does not understand or know the meaning of it; it is dazzling, bewildering, and he can hear nothing clearly. But it is good. It is as though he were suspended in mid-aid like a bird; and when the flood of sound rushes from one end of the church to the other, filling the arches, reverberating from wall to wall, he is carried with it, flying and skimming hither and thither with nothing to do but abandon himself to it. This is the real glory of the organ, a glory that is *sui generis* but obtainable only through the necessary coincidence of instrument, auditorium, and player.

In spite of the fact that the days of its greatest glory have apparently departed, the organ has a definite place in the present scheme of the musical universe if we give it an opportunity for being treated as it should be treated. That is, if we place it where it sounds at its best, if we design it so that its full beauty becomes apparent and do not make it merely a collection of pretty-sounding devices, and if we play music on it that suits its real character. Then, in spite of its evident weaknesses and its limited repertoire, the organ will still maintain its place as an instrument worthy of the serious consideration of critics and music lovers.

THE BAROQUE ORGAN OF THE TWENTIETH CENTURY

There has been a recent revival of interest in the type of organ used at the time of Bach, the instrument for which he wrote his grandiose organ works. Organ builders have devoted a great deal of time and energy to studying the instruments in Europe that still survive from the seventeenth and eighteenth centuries, with a view to imitating their tonal qualities in modern organs. The results have been most interesting and, in some cases, very effective. The distinctive feature of these new-old organs (they are called Baroque because they imitate the instruments of that period) is not the massive, diffuse, romantic tone to which most present-day listeners are accustomed, but a brilliant, sparkling, light clarity hitherto unassociated with the organ. The music of Bach and his predecessors takes on a new quality when played on these instruments; it seems more alive, if less impressive; more rhythmic and lyric, if less colorful. These Baroque organs lend themselves well to recording, and a number of good Bach and pre-Bach recordings have recently been made by the different companies; the large sale of these records proves that the public can learn to like this type of organ tone.

A REPRESENTATIVE LIST OF ORGAN MUSIC AVAILABLE ON RECORDS [3]

Here is a fairly representative list of organ music that is readily available on records:

Francesco Landino (*c.* 1325–1397):
  Bench' ora piova   MC
Paul Hofhaimer (1459–1537):
  Fantasia on *On freudt verzer*   MC
Giovanni Gabrieli (1557–1612):
  Ricercare in the Twelfth Tone   AS 4

[3] The symbols in this list of records may be interpreted as follows:
    MC Musicraft
    AS L'Anthologie Sonore
    Pat Pathé
    D Decca
    V Victor
    C Columbia
    AeS Aeolian Skinner Organ Co., Boston, Mass.

Girolamo Frescobaldi (1583–1643):
   Toccata — AS 4
   Chorale Prelude — Pat
Dietrich Buxtehude (1637–1707):
   Prelude, Fugue, and Chaconne — D
   Chorale Preludes — MC
William Byrd (1542–1623):
   Miserere — MC
Johann Jakob Froberger (*c.* 1605–1667):
   Canzona in D Minor — MC
Johann Pachelbel (1653–1706):
   Chorale Prelude: *Vater Unser* — AS 10
                Wie schön leuchtet — MC
Samuel Scheidt (1587–1654):
   Chorale Paraphrase — AS 10
Jan Sweelinck (1562–1621):
   Fantasia in Echo Style — MC
Johann Sebastian Bach (1685–1750). See Chapter XXXIV and, in addition, the Chorale Preludes from *Das Orgelbüchlein* complete. — V M 652, 679, 711
George Frederic Handel (1685–1759):
   Concertos for Organ and Orchestra:
      In B flat major, Op. 4, No. 2 — V
      In D minor, Op. 7, No. 4 — V
      In G minor, Op. 7, No. 5 — V
      In F major (Cuckoo and Nightingale) — V
César Franck (1822–1890):
   Pièce héroïque — V
   Chorale No. 1 in E major — C
   Chorale No. 3 in A minor — V
Studies in Organ Tone — AeS

This is a set of disks which gives an explanation of the manner in which the tonal elements of the organ unite to produce the complex sound which we know as organ tone. The records are interesting for students and lovers of this instrument.

GLOSSARY

THIS glossary is not meant to be a detailed dictionary, but a list of terms that music lovers are likely to come across. A good cheap pocket-sized book giving additional information is Baker's *Pronouncing Pocket-Manual of Musical Terms* (New York: Schirmer; London: Chester).

Absolute music. Music which is sufficient in itself, and does not depend on literary or other outside associations. (See Chapter XII.)

A cappella (It., " in church style "). Music written for unaccompanied singing, or without independent accompaniment.

Accelerando (It.). Accelerating, getting gradually quicker. Its opposite is *ritardando, q.v.*

Accidental. A chromatic sign not found in the signature but introduced in the course of the piece.

Accompaniment. A part added to the leading melody or part in order to support and enrich it.

Acoustics. That branch of physics which treats of the phenomena and laws of sound; the sound-affecting qualities of an auditorium.

Adagio (It., " slow, leisurely "). A slow rate of movement. See scale of speeds at end of Glossary.

Ad libitum (L., " at will "). The performer may employ a tempo or an expression that suits his pleasure. Sometimes used to signify that a passage may be omitted if desired.

Air. (*a*) A melody of sufficient interest to stand alone without accompaniment.

(*b*) A self-contained solo movement from a larger work.

Alla breve (It.). A composition in 4/4 (common) time executed by counting two beats to the measure, hence doubly fast.

Allargando (It.). Gradually growing slower and broadening the time.

Allegretto (It.). Moderately fast; diminution of *allegro*. See scale of speeds at end of Glossary.

Allegro (It., " merry, quick "). A brisk rate of movement sometimes qualified by *non troppo* (" not too much "), or increased by the terms *assai* (" very ") or *molto* (" much "). See scale of speeds at end of Glossary.

Andante (It., " going, moving "). A moderately slow rate of movement which has the implication of moving along or flowing. Some-

440

times qualified by such terms as *sostenuto* (" sustained ") or *con moto* (" faster "). Commonly applied to the slow movement of a sonata or a symphony. See scale of speeds at end of Glossary, page 453.

Animato (It.). Spirited, with animation.

Anthem. A sacred choral composition of moderate length; usually based upon Biblical text.

Antiphonal. Music in which groups of performers answer each other. Most often applied to choral music.

Appoggiatura (It.). A musical ornament consisting of a single note introduced as a suspension before any note of a melody.

Arco (L., " bow "). A direction for bowed instruments to resume bowing after a *pizzicato* (plucked) passage.

Aria (It., " air "). A composition for solo and instrumental accompaniment, taken from a work such as an opera or an oratorio.

Arpa (It.). Harp.

Arpeggio (It.). A chord in which the notes are played one after the other instead of all together.

A tempo (It., " in time "). At the original rate of speed; used after a change of pace.

Atonal. Having no fixed key.

Ballet. A dance performed as an artistic unit, usually employing a dramatic thread or story.

Bar. A vertical line dividing measures on the staff and indicating that the strong beat falls on the note immediately following. The proper emphasis on this strong beat is what creates the rhythmic pulse or flow in music. To the English the term means " measure."

Baroque (Fr., " irregular or bizarre "). A term generally used in art history to signify the style of art prevailing during the late sixteenth, the seventeenth, and part of the eighteenth century and characterized by the use of grandiose and contorted forms. By association it is often applied to music of the same time, especially to that of Bach's general period.

Bass. The lowest register in voices or instruments. The lowest part of a composition.

Batterie (Fr.). The group of percussion instruments in the orchestra.

Beat. In acoustics, the sudden reinforcement of sound, occurring at regular intervals and produced by the interference of sound waves of slightly different periods of vibration. In music, the regularly recurring and periodically accented pulse which constitutes a unit of measurement in music; in practical use, the term is made to refer to the time value of the basic unit within a measure (such as the quarter note in 4/4 time) or the motion of the hand, baton, and so on, used in marking such units.

Ben, bene (It.). Well. *Ben marcato*, well marked.

Berceuse. A cradle song or lullaby.

Binary. A two-part form, A–B; see Chapter XVI. Sometimes confusingly applied to the form A–B–A, as having only two separate subjects.

Bourrée. A dance of French or Spanish origin, in rapid tempo, 2/4 or 4/4 time, frequently employed as a movement of the classical suite.

Cacophony. The dissonant effect produced by sounds which are so combined as to be displeasing to the ear.

Cadence. The series of notes or chords through which a melody or harmony is brought to a temporary or final close. Various types of cadences used have different degrees of finality, the greatest being the *authentic cadence*, that progression of the chord on the dominant to the chord on the tonic (V–I).

Cadenza (It.). An ornamental passage in a concerted work in which a soloist displays his virtuosity. Occasionally it contains fine craftsmanship, but in general, especially when expanded into a lengthy fantasia designed for technical display, it is the curse of the concerto.

Canon. A form in which a melody begins in one part and is exactly copied by one or more parts at a given distance. A good example is the opening of the Finale of Franck's violin and piano *Sonata*.

Cantabile (It.). Singable; in a singing or vocal style.

Cantata. Originally a sung work, as opposed to a played one (" sonata "). Now means a secular or sacred work for soloist(s) and chorus, usually with orchestral accompaniment.

Cantilena (It., " a little song "). A tuneful, songlike flowing passage on an instrument or for a voice.

Cantus firmus (L., " fixed chant "). A given melody or plainsong tune to which other parts are to be set according to rule.

Caprice. Whim or fancy, hence a composition (instrumental) in free form, distinguished by originality in harmony and rhythm.

Cembalo. A name given to many keyboard instruments in musical history.

Chaconne. An instrumental piece consisting of a series of variations over a ground bass. Differs from the traditional *passacaglia* in that the bass theme may occur in an upper voice.

Chamber music. Compositions written for a small concert room, to be played by a small musical organization. See Chapters XXI and XLI.

Chant. A liturgical vocal melody. See also *Gregorian*.

Chorale [sometimes spelled *choral* (Ger.)]. A hymn tune of the Lutheran church, slow and dignified.

Chord. A simultaneously sounding group of two or more notes of different pitch. Chords can be built upon any note of the scale, their character depending upon their constituent notes.

Chorus. A body of singers, or a composition for them.

Chromatic (" colored "). Largely including, or moving by, half tones. Opposed to *diatonic*, *q.v.* Also used to mean containing notes foreign to a given key.

Classicism. The style of composition in which the strongest emphasis is laid upon formal beauty coupled with feeling (as distinguished from *Romanticism*, *q.v.*).

Clavichord. A precursor of the piano; a keyboard instrument in which the strings are struck by small brass tangents operated by the keys.

Clavier (" keyboard "). A word used colloquially for whatever keyboard instrument was fashionable; at one period it meant the harpsichord, later the pianoforte. To the Germans it meant the clavichord.

Clef. A sign (formerly a letter) put at the start of a line of music, to fix the name and pitch of one note, from which all others are reckoned.

Coda (" tail "). A concluding phrase or section rounding off a piece.

Concert overture. A separate orchestral piece, usually in sonata form, and not infrequently programmatic.

Concerto. A work for one or more soloists and orchestra.

Concord; consonance. Sounds which by themselves give a sense of completion.

Counterpoint (" note against note "). Used to refer to a type of composition made up of various simultaneously sounding musical lines. Also known as *polyphony*.

Countersubject. In a fugue, the counterpoint stated in continuation of the *subject*, while the answer is being given in another voice.

Courante. Early French dance in triple measure and lively tempo. Frequently found in the classic Suite, as the second of its four cornerstone movements.

Crescendo. See *dynamics*.

Cyclic form. A scheme of construction in which certain ideas reappear in various movements. Franck and D'Indy were fond of it.

Czardas (*csardas*). A Hungarian popular dance consisting of the contrasting " Lassu " (slow and impassioned) and " Friss " (lively).

Da capo [*D.C.*] (It., " from the head "). Repeat from the begir.ning. *Da capo al fine*. Repeat from the beginning to end (*i.e.*, " fine "). *Da capo al segno*. Repeat to the sign (:S:).

Decrescendo. See *dynamics*.

Development. The building up of the thematic material in a work afteĸ it has been expounded. See *Sonata form*.

Diatonic. Pertaining to, or designating, the standard major and minor
scales made up of tones and semitones, as distinguished from *chromatic,* made up entirely of semitones.

Diminuendo. See *dynamics.*

Discant (descant). The first attempts at polyphony with contrary motion in the parts, as opposed to *organum,* in which parallel motion
was the rule. Now used to mean a free part added to a principal
melody.

Dissonance. Sounds which require progress into others in order to give
a sense of completion.

Dominant. The fifth tone of the major or minor scale. *Dominant chord.*
A chord having the dominant note as its root (dominant triad,
dominant seventh, dominant ninth).

Duet; duo. Composition for two performers.

Dynamics. Of, or pertaining to, the scheme of tonal power used in interpreting music. The following abbreviations are in common use
for designating various volumes of tone:

fff	*fortissimo assai*	As loud as possible
ff	*fortissimo*	Very loud
f	*forte*	Loud
mf	*mezzoforte*	Moderately loud
mp	*mezzopiano*	Moderately soft
p	*piano*	Soft
pp	*pianissimo*	Very soft
ppp	*pianissimo assai*	As soft as possible
fp }	*forte piano* or	A quick transition from loud to
pf }	*piano forte*	soft, or soft to loud
sfz	*sforzando*	A sudden increase of tone, applied to single notes
rfz }	*rinforzando*	A sudden increase of tone, applied to musical phrases
rf }		
cresc	*crescendo*	A gradual increase of tone
dim	*diminuendo*	} A gradual decrease of tone
decresc	*decrescendo*	

Enharmonic chords. Chords differing in notation but alike in sound.

Ensemble ("together"). A term applied to any group of executants,
and to the art or effect of their playing together.

Entr'acte. Interval between acts; hence a light instrumental composition or short ballet, for performance between acts of a theatrical
performance.

Episode. In general, a term applied to those portions of a musical work
which connect portions of greater significance. In the fugue, it
represents a digression from the principal theme, interpolated between the developments of the latter. In such large works as sym-

phonies and quartets, episodes may be said to be synonymous with *bridge passage; i.e.*, they perform the function of furnishing musical continuity between main theme sections.

Étude (Fr., " study "). Frequently designed for particular technical difficulties; many are intended for concert performance, *e.g.* Schumann's *Études symphoniques.*

Euphony. The acoustic effect produced by sounds so combined as to please the ear.

Exposition. The first section of a movement in sonata form, in which the themes are " exposed " or set forth. See *Sonata form.*

Fantasia. A composition free in form and feeling.

Figure. An easily recognizable pattern of notes.

Finale. The last movement of an extended work. Sometimes given as the title to a separate piece, suitable to conclude a concert.

Flat. The character (♭) which lowers by a semitone the pitch of a note before which it is placed.

Folk music. Music which comes from the folk and becomes traditional with them.

Form. The element in music that is concerned with its scheme of architecture or design. Without some formal scheme music would result in meaningless incoherency.

Fugue (" flight "). A contrapuntal composition in which one part starts and the other parts follow at certain distances. See Chapter XXXIII.

Fuoco (It.). *Con fuoco:* with fire; *i.e.*, forcefully and fast.

Gavotte. An early French dance in strongly marked quadruple time, beginning on the third beat. Frequently employed as a movement of the classical suite.

Gigue. An early dance in rapid tempo and in triple or compound time. In the classic suite it is usually the last movement.

Glee. An English invention of the eighteenth century: an unaccompanied vocal piece for (usually) four males.

Glissando (It., " slide "). In piano music, playing with the nail of one or more fingers, producing a very brilliant scale; *glissando* on bowed instruments demands a flowing, unaccented execution of a passage.

Grace note. A nonessential note as an embellishment, generally designated in small notation.

Grave (It.). Slowly and solemnly.

Gregorian. The form of liturgical chanting ordained by Pope Gregory the Great (Pope, 590–604), and ever since widely used. See Chapter XXXV.

Harmonics (Harmonic overtones). Additional notes produced when a fundamental sound is generated. They give to a sound its individual character. Also flutelike tones produced on stringed instruments by touching the string lightly with the finger.

Harmonization. The arrangement of tones so as to create chordal harmony.

Harmony. The science of manipulating chords. Also used of the music produced by such manipulation.

Harpsichord. See Chapter XLII.

Homophony. Music in which one part stands out and the others accompany, mainly in chord effects. The music is thus formed vertically, as opposed to *polyphony,* where the parts move horizontally.

Imitation. The contrapuntal device of employing a melodic or rhythmic figure in one voice which had been stated in another.

Incidental music. Music played during the incidents and intervals, but not the whole course, of a dramatic work.

Instrumentation. The choice of instruments for a composition. ("What is the instrumentation of Haydn's *Surprise Symphony?*" "Strings, with two each of flutes, oboes, bassoons, trumpets, horns, and drums.")

Intermezzo. A short piece intended, or suitable, for an interlude.

Interval. The pitch distance between two notes.

Intonation. Quality of tone; also, truth of pitch; also, the beginning of chanting in *plainsong.*

> *Just intonation* is tuning by exact mathematical ratios; the opposite procedure is called tuning by *temperament* — tempering the wind, as it were, to various shorn lambs of intervals, so as to make them work tolerably well in all keys. *Equal temperament* is the modern method of tuning.

Introduction. A preliminary section.

Kapellmeister (G., "chapel master"). Generally applied to the director of music in eighteenth-century choirs, often in princely houses. Now used in Germany to mean a conductor at the theater or concert hall.

Key. The particular system of tones and semitones built upon a selected tone (the *tonic*) as a basis. The keynote or tonic thus becomes the first note of the scale and provides the name of the key, such as D major or C minor. The term *key* is also used for the black and white digitals of the keyboard.

Larghetto (It.). Slightly faster than *largo.* See scale of speeds at end of Glossary.

Largo (It.). Slowly and with dignity. See scale of speeds at end of Glossary.

Ledger line. A short line used for scoring notes above or below the staff.

Legato (It., "bound"). Smooth.

Leitmotiv (Ger., "leading theme"). In dramatic music, an identifying theme associated with a particular character, mood, or situation, and usually accompanying its reappearances.

Lento (It.). Slow. See scale of speeds at end of Glossary.

Libretto. The "book" of words of an extended choral composition, such as an opera, a cantata, or an oratorio.

Lied (Ger., "song"). Strictly used of the great number of art songs by German composers; they are most fittingly sung only with the original German text.

Madrigal. A secular, contrapuntal vocal work, usually in linked sections, originally sung by a few voices to each part. See Chapter XXXV.

Major. As applied to scales, a pattern of seven steps (eight sounds), consisting of tones and semitones, the latter occurring between the third and fourth and seventh and eighth steps. A major interval is one semitone greater than a minor. Major chords and keys are those in which major intervals predominate.

Marcato (It.). Marked, *i.e.*, each note played with emphasis.

Mastersinger. German bourgeois member of a medieval musical guild; successor to the *Minnesinger, q.v.*

Mazurka. A Polish national dance in triple time and moderate tempo, with variable accents on the third beat.

Measure (*bar*). A rhythmical unit of two or more beats.

Melody. Any agreeable and familiar series of notes. See Chapter IX.

Meter (*Metre*). Any specific scheme of rhythm, determined by the number and length of the notes it contains.

Mezzoforte (It.). Moderately loud. See *Dynamics*.

Mezzopiano (It.). Moderately soft. See *Dynamics*.

Minnesinger (Ger., "love singer"). The German counterpart of the *troubadour, q.v.*

Minor. As applied to scales, the pattern of seven steps consisting of tones and semitones, the latter either between the second and third, fifth and sixth, and seventh and eighth steps (harmonic form); or between the second and third and seventh and eighth steps ascending, and the second and third and fifth and sixth steps descending (melodic form).

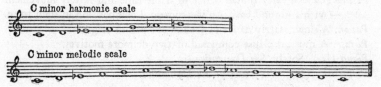

Minuet. An old French dance in dignified 3/4 rhythm. It is conventionally found as the third movement of the classic symphony. As an art form it is usually a double minuet with contrasted sections, the first section repeated after the second (trio).

Mode. Strictly, any mode or manner of arranging tones and semitones to form a scale. Generally, the term refers to the ancient scales used for both religious and folk music.

Modulation. The process of going from one key to another.

Motet. A religious counterpart of the *madrigal, q.v.*

Motive. A brief theme or figure, either an integral part of a larger theme or the generating idea out of which the theme develops.

Movement. A piece complete in itself, forming part of an extended work.

Music drama. Wagner's name for his operas.

Mute. A means of mechanically damping resonance of tones.

Natural. The character (♮) which contradicts a sharp or a flat.

Nocturne (" night piece "). Usually a piece of subdued, poetic feeling.

Note. The written or printed symbol for a tone.

Nuance. A shade of difference in tone color, tempo, or degree of force.

Obbligato (It., " indispensable "). An accessory part written for a particular instrument: as a violin part, additional to the piano accompaniment of a song.

Octave. A series of eight consecutive diatonic tones; also the interval between the first and eighth of such a series.

Opera. A play set to music that is nowadays usually, though it was not invariably, continuous.

Opus (" work "). A conventional word used by composers in numbering their works, as an *opus number.*

Oratorio. The sacred counterpart of opera, but invariably without stage appurtenances.

Orchestration. See *Instrumentation.*

Organ point (pedal point). A tone sustained in one part (usually the bass) while harmonies are executed in other parts.

Organum. The earliest attempts at harmonic or polyphonic music in which two or more parts progressed in parallel motion (fifths, fourths, and octaves).

Overtones. See *Harmonics.*

Overture. An instrumental prelude to a choral work. See also *Concert overture.*

Passacaglia. An early Italian dance in triple time and stately movement — with a ground bass. An instrumental composition in such form.

Pavan. A slow, stately dance of Italian or Spanish origin.

Phrase. A musical clause composed of two or more motives.

Piano (It.). Softly. See *Dynamics.*

Pianissimo (It.). Very softly. See *Dynamics.*

Pizzicato (It.). Plucked (of strings).

Plainsong (*plain chant*). The music of the early Christian centuries; based on modal scales. Rhythm and tempo were governed by word accent; sung in unison.

Polka. A lively round dance in 2/4 time originating in the early part of the nineteenth century as a peasant dance in Bohemia.

Polonaise. A dance of Polish origin in 3/4 time and moderate but animated tempo.

Polyphony. See *Counterpoint.*

Portamento. A smooth gliding from one tone to another, more deliberate than *legato,* actually (though rapidly) sounding intermediate tones. Banal except when artistically employed.

Prelude. An introductory section or movement. A *chorale prelude* is a polyphonic instrumental treatment of a chorale. See Chapter XXXIII. The prelude to an opera is usually called the *Overture.*

Presto (It.). Very fast. See scale of speeds at end of Glossary.

Program music. Music based on some scheme of literary or associative values, evoked by means of sound. See Chapter XII.

Quartet. Group of four executants. Also, the music they perform.

Quintet. Group of five executants. Also, the music they perform.

Recapitulation (*restatement*). The third section of a movement in sonata form, in which the themes are presented as at first.

Register. Section of an instrument's compass, characterized by a distinctive quality of tone.

Requiem. Mass or service for the dead. Also used of a memorial choral work.

Resolution. The process of discords progressing to concordance.

Rhapsody (" a stitching together "). A title borrowed from literature, originally meaning an epic poem. In music, a declamatory type of piece, in free form.

Rhythm. Generally speaking, the regular recurrence of like features in an artistic composition. The placing together of music's elements so as to ensure progression and shape. Recurrent pulses or patterns.

Ritard., ritardando (It.). Gradual slowing of tempo.

Rococo (Fr.). A florid and ornamental style characteristic of the eighteenth century. Often applied to music of that time. See Chapter XXXII.

Romanticism. A style of composition in which the strongest emphasis is upon the personal expression of poetic sentiment, as distinguished from *Classicism, q.v.*

Round. A vocal *canon* (*q.v.*) at the unison or octave.

Rubato (It., " robbed "). Practically, the opposite of robbery, since time borrowed in one part of a phrase is replaced in another part of it; or a whole phrase might be slightly hurried, and the next slightly slowed. A characteristic element in the performance of most romantic music: to be sparingly used in older works.

Saraband. A stately dance of Spanish or Oriental origin in slow tempo and triple time. Its place in the *Suite*, as the slowest movement, is before the *gigue*.

Scale. A succession of tones in some arranged order, used as the basic material for writing a piece. The modern scales developed out of the *modes, q.v.*

Scherzo (" a jest "). A type of third-movement form, a development of the *minuet*, introduced into the symphony by Beethoven.

School. A group of musicians animated by ideas held in common or using common principles of structure.

Score. The parts of the various voices or instruments laid out beneath one another. *Short score* puts more than one part on each stave; *open score* gives each part its own stave. A *vocal score* gives all the voice parts of, say, an opera or an oratorio, together with, as a rule, a two-stave accompaniment, compressed from the orchestral score. A *piano score* of such a work would be on two staves only but would often show where the voices come in.

Semitone. A half tone.

Sequence. The repetition in succession of a melodic figure at different pitch intervals.

Serenade (" evening song "). Applied to suites of light music suitable to be played in the open air.

Sextet. A composition for six executants. Also, the music they perform.

Sharp. The character (♯) which raises by a semitone the pitch of a note before which it is set.

Siciliano. A dance of the Sicilian peasants, a kind of pastoral in moderately slow tempo and 6/8 or 12/8 time, frequently in a minor key.

Signature. The signs set at the head of the staff at the beginning of a piece of music. *Key signature:* The chromatic sign or signs (sharps or flats). *Time signature:* The figure or fractional sign indicating the measure.

Signs. Certain symbols are commonly used by composers for conveying performing directions. The ones most frequently used are:

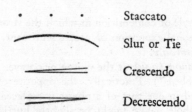

Staccato

Slur or Tie

Crescendo

Decrescendo

tr   Trill

⌢   Hold

▬▬▬▐▐▬▐▬▬▬   Repeat

Sonata form. A misleading term for which *first-movement form* is perhaps better substituted. A *sonata* is the whole work for one or more soloists, in several movements, each having its own form. The form of the first movement is that in three sections, of which the first (Exposition or Statement) sets forth the thematic material, usually in two chief "subjects" or tune groups, in contrasted keys; the second (Development) works out and builds up this material; and the last (Recapitulation, or Restatement) brings back the tune material (in the *tonic key*) — in the earlier sonatas, pretty much as at first, but in later practice (Beethoven's, *e.g.*) often with some further treatment towards the end.

Song form. A term derived from the classic procedure of alternating two or more contrasted sections; probably originating in the simple contrasts of ideas in the song. Many slow movements of sonatas and symphonies are in song form.

Sostenuto (It.). Sustained.

Staccato. Detached or separated; a style of performance in which the notes or chords are more or less abruptly disconnected, as opposed to *legato, q.v.*

Staff. The five parallel lines used in modern notation.

Statement. See *Exposition.*

String quartet. Two violins, viola, and violoncello. Also, applied to the music played by these executants.

Style. A characteristic manner of expressing ideas.

Subject. A tune or theme.

Suite. A set of pieces either centering upon some general subject (*e.g.,* Grieg's *Peer Gynt* Suite), or made up of contrasting but associated rhythmical styles (*e.g.,* Bach's suites based upon old dances).

Symphony. A *sonata* for orchestra.

Syncopation. A temporary displacement or shifting of the normal beat or accent of a piece of music. Sometimes applied to music which contains this device.

Technic; technique. All that relates to the purely mechanical part of musical performance. Mechanical training, skill, dexterity.

Temperament. System of tuning instruments so as to allow modulation without the use of a large number of pitch distinctions. See *Well-tempered.* Certain adjustments are made so as to get rid of physical inaccuracies in the intervals between certain notes.

Tempo. Time. Mostly used to mean " pace."

Ternary. Having three sections. Used of A–B–A form.

Tessitura (It.). The " lie " of a passage — its position in the compass of the instrument or voice.

Theme. A tune or subject.

Timbre (Fr.). Tone color or characteristic.

Timpani. Kettledrums.

Toccata. " Touch piece " — one designed to display brilliance of execution.

Tone color. A term borrowed from painting to denote the varied qualities of tone.

Tonic. The keynote of a scale. *Tonic chord.* A chord having the tonic note as its root.

Transition. Used of passages which lead from one principal idea or key to another.

Transpose. To put into a different key or position on the staff.

Tremolo. Quivering or fluttering; in singing, a tremulous, unsteady tone, caused by improper breath or muscular control; on bowed instruments, an effect produced by the very rapid alternation of down bow and up bow; on the piano the rapid alternation of the tones of a chord.

Triad. A three-note chord: root, third, fifth.

Trill. The even and rapid alternation of two tones a major or a minor second apart; the lower tone is the principal note, the higher the auxiliary.

Trio. Three performers, or the music they perform. Also, the middle, contrasting section of a *minuet* or a *scherzo.*

Troubadour. High-born minstrel in medieval France (Provence, *c.* 1100–1300). See Chapter XXXVII.

Trouvère. The Northern French counterpart of the *troubadour;* also included minstrels not highly born.

Unison. A tone of the same pitch as a given tone; also, a higher or a lower octave of the given tone.

Variation. A new presentation of a musical idea. The *theme and variations* is one of the oldest of musical forms; it is a " dinner of one sort of fish served up in many courses," each having a little different cooking and sauce.

Vibrato (It.). A foul form of ululation fantastically imagined by most of its users to add beauty to singing or playing. Subtly used by an artist, it is a legitimate means of heightening emotion.

Virtuoso. A superlatively equipped executant.

Vivace (It.). Vivaciously.

Well-tempered. Equally tuned. Applied to keyboard instruments tuned so that music in all keys can be played upon them.

Whole-tone scale. A scale moving by full tones: from C it comprises C, D, E, F sharp, G sharp, A sharp (or B flat), C.

Wood wind. The group of wood-wind instruments in the orchestra, as opposed to the brasses.

A SCALE OF SPEEDS

Largo⎱ ⎰Lento ⎱
Grave⎰ – ⎱Adagio ⎰ –Andante–Allegretto–Moderato–Allegro⎱ –Presto–Prestissimo
                                      Vivace⎰

Slow   Fast

BIOGRAPHICAL LIST OF COMPOSERS

PRONUNCIATION

MARKINGS: ā in lāte, å in chåotic, â in câre, ă in făt, ä in fär, à in làst, ȧ in sofȧ; ē in mē, ê in rêturn, ĕ in mĕt, ĕ in quiĕt, ē in uppēr; g in get; ī in fīne, ĭ in tĭn; ᴋ = ch in German *ach*; ṇ = ng, ɴ = ng in its effect (nasal) on the preceding vowel, but is not itself sounded; ō in nōte, ô in ôbey, ô in fôr (same sound as aw in saw), ŏ in nŏt, ŏ in sŏft, ö (set lips as if to say oh, but then say ĕ as in met, keeping the lips fixed in the first position); ōō in schōōl, ŏŏ in wŏŏl; ŧħ in ŧħine; ū in tūne, ŭ in nŭt, û in bûrn, ŭ in sŭbmit, ü (set lips as if to say oo as in boot, but then say ee as in beet, keeping the lips in the first position); (′) indicates the heavily accented syllable, (′) indicates the syllable with secondary accent.

Adam de la Halle (ă·däɴ′ dü lä äl), b. Arras, 1238?; d. 1288. A prominent trouvère; master of the chanson.

Albeniz (äl′bȧ·nēth′), Issac, b. Camprodon, Spain, 1860; d. 1909. Spanish composer of note who reproduced the rhythms and other characteristics of Spanish popular music.

Arensky (ȧ·rĕn′skĕ), Anton, b. Novgorod, Russia, 1861; d. 1906. A prominent Russian composer-pianist of the Tchaikovskyan rather than the extreme nationalist school.

Bach (bäᴋ), Carl Philip Emanuel, b. Weimar, Germany, 1714; d. 1788. Son of J. S. Bach; a pioneer of the sonata form and symphonic orchestration.

Bach, Johann Sebastian, b. Eisenach, Germany, 1685; d. 1750. The greatest composer of the polyphonic period, and one of the greatest of all time.

Balakirev (bä′lä·kē′rĕf), Mily, b. Novgorod, Russia, 1836; d. 1910. A pianist and composer; one of the Russian " Five."

Bartók (bär′tŏk), Béla, b. Transylvania, 1881. Modern Hungarian nationalistic composer and pianist.

Bax (băks), Arnold, b. London, 1883. English neo-romantic composer with Celtic sympathies.

Beethoven (bā′tō·vĕn), Ludwig van, b. Bonn, Germany, 1770; d. 1827. One of the greatest of all composers, especially in the realm of symphonic and chamber music. Historically he welded together the " Classical " and self-conscious " Romantic " periods.

Bellini (běl·lē'nē), Vincenzo, b. Catania, Sicily, 1801; d. 1835. Prominent Italian opera composer.

Berg (bârg), Alban, b. Vienna, 1885; d. 1936. Modern atonal theorist and composer; pupil and follower of Schönberg.

Berlioz (běr'lē·ôs'), Hector, b. Côte Saint André, France, 1803; d. 1869. A pioneer of program music.

Bizet (bē'zě'), Georges, b. Paris, 1838; d. 1875. Well-known French opera composer.

Bloch (blŏk), Ernest, b. Geneva, Switzerland, 1880. Modern Jewish composer of distinction, whose music epitomizes the history and aspirations of his race.

Boccherini (bôk'kà·rē'nē), Luigi, b. Lucca, Italy, 1743; d. 1805. Prolific Italian composer, especially of chamber music.

Borodin (bŏr'ŏ·dǐn'), Alexander, b. St. Petersburg, 1834; d. 1887. One of the Russian " Five "; he utilized folk music in his scores.

Brahms (brämz), Johannes, b. Hamburg, Germany, 1833; d. 1897. One of the greatest composers of all time; combined romantic expression with classic form.

Bruch (brōōκ), Max, b. Cologne, Germany, 1838; d. 1920. A talented German composer, excelled in choral music.

Bruckner (brōōk'nēr), Anton, b. Ausfelden, Upper Austria, 1824; d. 1896. Symphonic composer of great facility.

Busoni (bōō·zō'nē), Ferruccio, b. Empoli, Italy, 1866; d. 1924. Pianist and composer of great influence on modern music. Transcribed and arranged many of Bach's organ works for the piano.

Buxtehude (bōōks'tě·hōō'dě), Dietrich, b. Helsingborg, Sweden, 1637; d. 1707. Eminent organist and composer who influenced Bach's early career.

Byrd (bûrd), William, b. London, 1542; d. 1623. One of the greatest of Elizabethan madrigal composers.

Caccini (kă·chē'nē), Giulio, b. Rome, 1558; d. 1615. One of the pioneer opera composers. Collaborated with Peri in writing *Dafne*, the first opera ever produced.

Carpenter (kär'pěn·těr), John Alden, b. Park Ridge, Ill., 1876. Successful American composer in many forms.

Casella (kä·sěl'lä), Alfredo, b. Turin, Italy, 1883. Prominent modern Italian composer.

Chadwick (chăd'wǐk), George Whitefield, b. Lowell, Mass., 1854; d. 1931. American composer in the classic style.

Chaminade (shà'mē'nàd'), Cécile, b. Paris, 1861. French composer in the lighter forms.

Charpentier (shàr'päΝ'tyä'), Gustave, b. Dieuze, Lorraine, 1860. French composer famous for one opera — *Louise*.

Chausson (shô'sôn'), Ernest, b. Paris, 1855; d. 1899. Pupil of César
   Franck and composer of distinguished individuality.
Cherubini (kā'rōō·bē'nĕ), Maria Luigi, b. Florence, Italy, 1760; d. 1842.
   A composer of the contrapuntal period, successful in both operatic
   and sacred forms.
Chopin (shô'păn'), Frederic, b. Warsaw, Poland, 1810; d. 1849. The
   most individual and popular composer for the piano. Confined his
   work almost entirely to this instrument.
Coleridge-Taylor (kōl'rĭj-tā'lĕr), Samuel, b. London, 1875; d. 1912.
   English Negro composer.
Corelli (kō·rĕl'lĕ), Arcangelo, b. Imola, Italy, 1653; d. 1713. Violinist
   and composer; founder of violin style and technic.
Couperin (kōō'pē·răn'), François (surnamed le Grand), b. Paris, 1668;
   d. 1733. Most eminent of a famous family of composers. His music
   is full of Baroque grace and charm.
Cui (kü·ē'), César, b. Vilna, Russia, 1835; d. 1918. One of the Russian
   " Five "; wrote in many forms, but his vocal works are his best
   compositions.
Czerny (chĕr'nĕ), Karl, b. Vienna, 1791; d. 1857. A pupil of Beethoven; eminent pianist and pedagogue.
Debussy (dē·bü'sē'), Claude Achille, b. Paris, 1862; d. 1918. Founder
   of the school of impressionism in music, and one of the most individual composers.
Delibes (dē·lēb'), Léo, b. St. Germain-du-Val, France, 1836; d. 1891.
   Popular ballet composer.
Delius (dē'lĭ·ŭs), Frederick, b. Bradford, England, 1863; d. 1934. An
   important English composer.
Diaghilev (dyä·gē'lĕf), Sergei Pavlovich, b. Novgorod, Russia, 1872;
   d. 1929. Founder of the famous Russian ballet which bore his name;
   commissioned the writing of many modern ballets, including the
   best works of Stravinsky.
Dohnányi (dō'nän·yĕ), Ernst von, b. Pressburg, Hungary, 1877. Hungarian pianist, conductor, and composer. His compositions are conservative and individual in style, carrying on the romantic traditions of the nineteenth century, not the least attractive element
   being a tincture of Brahms's spirit.
Donizetti (dō'nē·dzĕt'tĕ), Gaetano, b. Bergamo, Italy, 1797; d. 1848.
   Popular opera composer.
Dukas (dü'käh'), Paul, b. Paris, 1865; d. 1935. French composer of
   considerable attainment, especially successful in the larger symphonic forms.
Dvořák (dvôr'zhäk), Anton, b. Mühlhausen, Bohemia, 1841; d. 1904.
   Leading Bohemian composer; lived several years in America.

Elgar (ĕl'gĕr), Edward, b. Worcester, England, 1857; d. 1934. The leading composer of modern England.

Falla (fäl'yä), Manuel de, b. Cadiz, 1876. Spanish composer of opera and ballet, showing folk and nationalistic influences.

Foster (fos'tĕr), Stephen Collins, b. Pittsburgh, Pa., 1826; d. 1864. Creator of the American Negro folk song.

Franck (frängk), César, b. Liége, Belgium, 1822; d. 1890. France's most important composer.

Franz (fränts), Robert, b. Halle, Prussia, 1815; d. 1892. Master of German lied.

Gibbons (gĭb'ŭnz), Orlando, b. Cambridge, England, 1583; d. 1625. A leading English madrigal composer.

Glazunov (glä'zōō·nôf'), Alexander, b. St. Petersburg, 1865; d. 1936. Popular Russian composer.

Glinka (glĭng'kä), Michael, b. Smolensk, Russia, 1803; d. 1857. Pioneer Russian nationalistic composer.

Gluck (glōōk), Christoph Willibald von, b. Weidenwang, Upper Palatinate, 1714; d. 1787. An operatic reformer of importance.

Goldmark (gŏlt'märk'), Karl, b. Keszthely, Hungary, 1830; d. 1915. Popular composer in many forms.

Gounod (gōō'nō'), Charles, b. Paris, 1818; d. 1893. Popular opera composer.

Grétry (grä'trē'), André Ernest, b. Liége, 1741; d. 1813. Important French opera composer.

Grieg (grēg), Edvard, b. Bergen, Norway, 1843; d. 1907. Outstanding Scandinavian composer.

Handel (hăn'd'l), George Frederic, b. Halle, Prussia, 1685; d. 1759. Well known for his classic forms and styles, especially his oratorios.

Harris (hăr'ĭs), Roy, b. Oklahoma, 1898. Important American composer.

Haydn (hī'd'n), Franz-Josef, b. Rohrau, Austria, 1732; d. 1809. Innovator of classic form; father of the symphony and sonata form.

Hindemith (hĭn'dĕ·mĭt), Paul, b. Hanau, Germany, 1895. Facile composer in modern style.

Holst (hōlst), Gustav, b. Cheltenham, England, 1874; d. 1934. Modern British composer.

Honegger (hŏn'ĕg'ĕr), Arthur, b. Havre, 1892, of Swiss parentage. Lively exponent of advanced, piquant tastes. Enjoys using counterpoint.

Humperdinck (hōōm'pĕr·dĭngk), Engelbert, b. Bonn, Germany, 1854; d. 1921. A talented composer and follower of Wagner; famous for his opera *Hänsel und Gretel*.

Indy (ăN'dē'), Vincent d', b. Paris, 1851; d. 1931. Most famous pupil and follower of César Franck, and one of France's leading composers.

Josquin des Prés (zhŏs·kăn' dē·prä'), b. Burgundy, 1450?; d. 1521. A pioneer in vocal polyphonic music.

Kodály (kō·dä'ē), Zoltán, b. Kecskemét, Hungary, 1882. Modern Hungarian composer and arranger of folk music.

Lasso (läs'sŏ), Orlando di, b. Mons, Belgium, 1530?; d. 1594. Great master of sacred as well as secular polyphony.

Leoncavallo (lā'ŏn·kä·väl'lŏ), Ruggiero, b. Naples, 1858; d. 1919. Popular Italian opera composer.

Liszt (lĭst), Franz, b. Raiding, Hungary, 1811; d. 1886. World's greatest piano virtuoso and successful composer in many forms, especially the symphonic poem.

Loeffler (lĕf'lĕr), Charles Martin, b. Mühlhausen, Alsace, 1861; d. 1935. Alsatian-American composer in the modern style.

Lully (lü'lē'), Jean-Baptiste, b. Florence, 1632; d. 1687. Important pioneer in opera; developed the overture and introduced the brass into the orchestra.

MacDowell (măk·dou'ĕl), Edward A., b. New York, 1861; d. 1908. Well-known American composer.

Mahler (mä'lĕr), Gustav, b. Bohemia, 1860; d. 1911. Conductor and composer of symphonies, many of which are fantastic in conception.

Malipiero (mäl·ê·p'yä'rŏ), Francesco, b. Venice, 1882. Distinguished modern Italian composer.

Mascagni (mäs·kän'yĕ), Pietro, b. Leghorn, Italy, 1863. Popular composer of Italian opera.

Mason (mä's'n), Daniel Gregory, b. Brookline, Mass., 1873. Grandson of Lowell Mason and distinguished teacher and composer.

Mason, Lowell, b. Medfield, Mass., 1792; d. 1872. Pioneer American teacher and composer.

Massenet (mä's'nĕ'), Jules, b. Montaud, France, 1842; d. 1912. Popular composer of French opera.

Mendelssohn (mĕn'dĕl·sōn), Felix, b. Hamburg, 1809; d. 1847. Talented composer in many forms.

Meyerbeer (mī'ĕr·bär), Giacomo, b. Berlin, 1791; d. 1864. Creator of spectacular and popular operas.

Milhaud (mē'yō'), Darius, b. Aix-en-Provence, France, 1892. One of the modern French group known as the " Six."

Monteverdi (mŏn'tâ·vâr'dĭ), Claudio, b. Cremona, 1567; d. 1643. Pioneer of modern harmony and homophonic style.

Morley (môr'lĭ), Thomas, b. England, 1557; d. 1603? Well-known Elizabethan madrigalist.

Moussorgsky (mōō·sôrg'skê), Modeste, b. Karev, Russia, 1839; d. 1881. Extremely nationalistic Russian composer.

Mozart (mō'tsärt), Wolfgang Amadeus, b. Salzburg, 1756; d. 1791. Perhaps the greatest natural genius music has ever known, and a prolific composer throughout his short life.

Nicolai (nē'kô·lī), Karl Otto, b. Königsberg, Germany, 1810; d. 1849. Gifted operatic composer.

Offenbach (ôf'ĕn·bäк), Jacques, b. Cologne, 1819; d. 1880. Popular composer of light operas.

Paderewski (pà'dĕ·rĕf'skê), Ignace Jan, b. Podolia, Poland, 1860; d. 1941. Renowned Polish pianist and composer.

Paganini (pä'gä·nē'nê), Niccolo, b. Genoa, Italy, 1782; d. 1840. One of the greatest violinists in history; composer of many melodies which were later transcribed by others.

Palestrina (pä'lâs·trē'nä), Giovanni Pierluigi da, b. Palestrina near Rome, 1525; d. 1594. The greatest and most important composer of the vocal polyphonic period.

Peri (pā'rê), Jacopo, b. Florence, 1561; d. 1633. The composer of *Dafne*, the first opera, in collaboration with Caccini.

Prokofiev (prō·kō'fē·ĕf), Serge, b. Russia, 1891. Prominent Russian modernistic composer.

Puccini (pōōt·chē'nê), Giacomo, b. Lucca, Italy, 1858; d. 1924. Popular Italian operatic composer.

Purcell (pûr'sĕl), Henry, b. London, 1658?; d. 1695. One of England's greatest composers.

Rachmaninoff (räк·mä'nê·nôf), Sergei, b. Onega, Russia, 1873. Outstanding composer-pianist.

Rameau (rà'mō'), Jean Philippe, b. Dijon, France, 1683; d. 1764. One of the important men in the development of French opera; wrote more than twenty operas.

Ravel (rà'vĕl'), Maurice, b. Ciboure, France, 1875; d. 1937. Modern composer of many works in the manner of Debussy.

Respighi (rĕs·pē'gê), Ottorino, b. Bologna, Italy, 1879; d. 1936. Accomplished modern Italian composer.

Rheinberger (rīn'bĕrg'ĕr), Josef, b. Liechtenstein, Germany, 1839; d. 1901. Eminent organist, teacher, and composer.

Rimsky-Korsakoff (rĭm'skê-kôr'sà·kôf), Nicholas, b. Novgorod, Russia, 1844; d. 1908. A leading Russian composer with a distinct feeling for the Oriental style.

Rossini (rôs·sē'nê), Gioacchino, b. Pesaro, Italy, 1792; d. 1868. Popular Italian opera composer.

Rubinstein (rōō'bĭn·stīn), Anton, b. Bessarabia, 1830; d. 1894. Brilliant pianist and popular composer.

Saint-Saëns (săn'säns'), Charles Camille, b. Paris, 1835; d. 1921. Distinguished French composer.

Sarasate (sä'rä·sä'tà), Pablo de, b. Pamplona, Spain, 1844; d. 1908. Great violinist and minor composer.

Scarlatti (skär·lät'tĕ), Alessandro, b. Trapani, Sicily, 1659; d. 1725. Pioneer in opera; advanced monodic composition.

Scarlatti, Domenico, b. Naples, 1685; d. 1757. Son of Alessandro; developed harpsichord style and technic.

Schmitt (shmĭt), Florent, b. Blamont, France, 1870. Modern and original French composer, trained in the impressionistic school.

Schönberg (shûn'bĕrĸ), Arnold, b. Vienna, 1874. One of the outstanding representatives of extreme modernism in music; founder and leading exponent of atonalism.

Schubert (shōō'bĕrt), Franz, b. Vienna, 1797; d. 1828. One of the great natural geniuses of music; had a prodigious output throughout his tragically short life.

Schumann (shōō'män), Robert, b. Zwickau, Saxony, 1810; d. 1856. Important early romanticist; possessed novel ideas as creator, interpreter, and critic of music.

Scriabin (skryà·bĭn'), Alexander, b. Moscow, 1872; d. 1915. Important Russian composer with unusual and often fantastic ideas.

Shostakovich (shŏs·tă·kō'vĭch), Dmitri, b. 1906. Russian composer, neo-romantic, original. One of the Leningrad group, developing from Rimsky-Korsakoff. Has written both symphonies and operas.

Sibelius (sĭ·bā'lĭ·ŏŏs), Jean, b. Tavastehus, Finland, 1865. Well-known and extremely talented nationalistic Finnish composer.

Sinding (sĭn'dĭng), Christian, b. Kongsberg, Norway, 1856. Well-known Scandinavian composer.

Smetana (smĕ'tä·nä), Bedřich, b. Leitomischl, Bohemia, 1824; d. 1884. Distinguished Bohemian composer.

Spohr (shpōr), Louis, b. Brunswick, Germany, 1784; d. 1859. Violinist, teacher, composer.

Strauss (shtrous), Johann, Jr., b. Vienna, 1825; d. 1899. The " waltz king "; wrote over 400 waltzes.

Strauss, Richard, b. Munich, 1864. Distinguished composer in many forms, especially eminent as a song and symphonic composer.

Stravinsky (strà·vĭn'skĕ), Igor, b. near Petrograd, 1882. One of the leading modernists, especially significant as a composer of ballets and symphonic works.

Taylor (tā'lĕr), Deems, b. New York, 1885. Distinguished American composer of operas and symphonic works.

Tchaikovsky (chī·kôf'skĕ), Peter Ilich, b. Votkinsk, Russia, 1840; d. 1893. Eminent romantic Russian composer.

Thomas (tò'mä'), Ambroise, b. Metz, 1811; d. 1896. Successful composer of popular French operas.

Vaughan Williams (vôn wĭl'yămz), Ralph, b. Wiltshire, England, 1872. Individual and talented modern British composer.

Verdi (vâr'dĕ), Giuseppe, b. LeRoncole, Parma, 1813; d. 1901. Greatest Italian opera composer, master of vocal melodic writing.

Vivaldi (vē·väl'dĕ), Antonio, b. Venice, 1676?; d. 1743? Violinist and composer of distinction.

Wagner (väg'nēr), Richard, b. Leipzig, 1813; d. 1883. The greatest dramatic composer of all time, replacing the old-fashioned opera with music drama.

Weber (vā'bēr), Carl Maria von, b. Oldenburg, Germany, 1786; d. 1826. Important German composer, especially in the field of opera; influenced Wagner's early career.

Weinberger (vĭn'bĕrK·ēr), Jaromir, b. Prague, 1896. Writer of picturesque operas, the most famous of which is *Schwanda*. Now a resident of the United States.

Widor (vē'dôr'), Charles Marie, b. Lyons, France, 1845; d. 1937. Distinguished French organist, teacher, and composer.

Wieniawski (vyĕ'nyäf·skĕ), Henri, b. Lubin, Poland, 1835; d. 1880. Brilliant violinist and composer for the violin.

Wolf (vôlf), Hugo, b. Styria, 1860; d. 1903. One of the immortal masters of German lieder.

Wolf-Ferrari (vôlf'-fĕr·rä'rĕ), Ermanno, b. Venice, 1876. Popular opera and song composer.

INDEX